BASICS OF
COMPUTER SCIENCE AND DIGITAL ELECTRONICS

Exploring the Core Concepts from
Computer Basics to Advanced Technologies

BASICS OF COMPUTER SCIENCE AND DIGITAL ELECTRONICS

Exploring the Core Concepts from
Computer Basics to Advanced Technologies

Yash Paul

an imprint of Highlyy Publishing LLP

ISBN: 978-93-6009-368-6
First Published : 2024
Copyright ©Author

Publisher's Note:

All Rights reserved under International Copyright Conventions. No part of this publication may be reproduced, stored in a retrieval system, or transmitted in any form or by any means, electronic, mechanical, photocopying, recording or otherwise without the prior written consent of the publisher and the copyright owner.

The content of this book is the sole expression and opinion of its author(s), and not of the publisher. The publisher in no manner is liable for any opinion or views expressed by the author(s). While best efforts have been made in preparing the book, the publisher makes no representations or warranties of any kind and assumes no liabilities of any kind with respect to the accuracy or completeness of the content and specifically disclaims any implied warranties of merchantability or fitness of use of a particular purpose.

The publisher believes that the contents of this book do not violate any existing copyright/intellectual property of others in any manner whatsoever. However, in case any source has not been duly attributed; the publisher may be notified in writing for necessary action.

> Cataloging in Publication Data--DK
>   Courtesy: D.K. Agencies (P) Ltd. <docinfo@dkagencies.com>
>   Paul, Yash, 1981- author.
> Basics of computer science and digital electronics / Yash Paul.
>   pages cm
>   Includes bibliographical references and index.
>   ISBN 9789360093518 (paperback)
>   ISBN 9789360093686 (hardback)
>   1. Information technology. 2. Computer science. 3. Digital electronics.   I. Title. II. Title: Computer science and digital electronics.
> LCC T58.5.P38 2024 | DDC 004   23

Published by :

an imprint of Highlyy Publishing LLP

Correspondence
Address :

4/30 A II Floor, Double Storey Buildings
Vijay Nagar, Delhi-110009
Editorial: +91 9811026449
Sales : +91 9999953412
Email: info@howacademics.com
Website: www.howacademics.com

Contents

Foreword — xi
Preface — xiii
Acknowledgement — xv
About the Author — xvii

1. Introduction — 1
   i. Computer and its Characteristics — 1
   ii. Computer History/Evolution/ Computer Generations — 4
   iii. Basic Computer Organisation — 8
   iv. The Von Neumann Machine — 9
   v. Information Technology and its Applications — 11
   vi. History of Information Technology — 14

2. Input and Output — 17
   i. Input Devices — 17
- Keyboard Devices — 17
- Point and Draw Devices — 18
- Data Scanning Devices — 23
- Digitizer — 25
- Electronic card-based devices — 26
- Speech recognition devices — 28
- Vision based devices — 29

   ii. Output Devices — 30
- Monitors — 30
- Printers — 33
- Plotters — 39
- Projector — 40
- Voice Response Systems — 41

3. Storage Devices — 43
   i. Magnetic Disk — 45
   ii. Optical Disk — 48
   iii. Memory Storage Devices — 49
- Flash Drive: (Pen Drive) — 49
- Memory Card (MMC/SD) — 51

4. Operating System — 55
   i. Operating System and its Logical Structure — 55
   ii. Objectives of OS — 56

	i.	Functions/Modules of an OS	56
	ii.	Types of Operating Systems	59
		⇒ Manual Loading System	60
		⇒ Batch Processing System	60
		⇒ Multiprogramming Systems	61
		⇒ Multitasking	63
		⇒ Multithreading	63
		⇒ Multiprocessing	64
		⇒ Time Sharing System	65
		⇒ Distributed Operating Systems	66
		⇒ Real-Time Operating System	66
	iii.	Disk Operating System: (Internal/External) Commands	67

5. E-Governance — 81

	i.	E (Electronic)- Governance	81
	ii.	E-Governance in India	83
	iii.	Types of E-Governance	85
		⇒ Government-2-Citizen (G2C)	85
		⇒ Government-2-Business (G2B)	85
		⇒ Government-2-Representative (G2E)	85
		⇒ Government-2-Government (G2G)	86
	iv.	Advantages and Disadvantages	86
	v.	E-Governance Models	87
		⇒ Broadcasting Model	87
		⇒ The Critical flow Model	88
		⇒ Comparative Analysis Model	89
		⇒ E-Advocacy Model	89
		⇒ The Interactive Service Model	90
	vi.	MOOCs	91
		⇒ 1. Definition and Overview	91
		⇒ 2. History and Evolution	92
		⇒ 3. Challenges	93
		⇒ 4. Pedagogical Approaches	94
		⇒ 5. Integration with Traditional Education	95
		⇒ 6. Practical Applications	97
		⇒ 7. Ethical and Social Implications	99
		⇒ 8. Future Trends and Innovations	101
	vii.	SWAYAM	103
		⇒ Overview of Swayam Platform	103
		⇒ Structure and Organization of Courses	103
		⇒ Pedagogical Approach and Learning Experience	104
		⇒ Accessibility and Inclusivity	104
		⇒ Future Directions and Impact	105
		⇒ Conclusion	105

	i.	Difference between SWAYAM and MOOCs	105
6.	**E-Commerce**		**109**
	i.	E-Commerce and its Types	109
		➲ Business-to-Business	109
		➲ B2C Business-to-Consumer	110
		➲ C2B Consumer-to-Business	110
		➲ C2C Consumer-to-Consumer	110
		➲ M-Commerce	111
	ii.	Types of E-Commerce Business Models	111
		➲ Drop Shipping	112
		➲ Wholesaling and Warehousing	112
		➲ Private Labelling and Manufacturing	112
		➲ White Labelling	113
		➲ Subscription Ecommerce	113
	iii.	Advantages of E-Commerce	114
	iv.	Architecture	115
		➲ Two Tier Client -Server Architecture	115
		➲ Three Tier Architecture	116
7.	**Computer Viruses**		**119**
	i.	Basic Classifications of Viruses	119
		➲ Worm Viruses	119
		➲ Boot Viruses	119
		➲ Macro Viruses	119
		➲ Trojan Viruses	119
		➲ E-Mail Viruses	120
		➲ FAT viruses	120
	ii.	Steps on How to Minimise Your Exposure to Viruses	120
	iii.	Stages in the Life of a Virus	121
	iv.	Virus Generations	121
8.	**Computer Networks and Data Communication**		**123**
	i.	What is a Computer Network?	123
	ii.	Network Topologies	123
		➲ Mesh Topology	123
		➲ Bus Topology	124
		➲ Star Network Topology	126
		➲ Ring Network Topology	126
		➲ Hybrid Topology	127
	iii.	Types of Computer Network	128
		➲ LAN (Local Area Network)	128

		⮞ WAN (Wide Area Network)	129
		⮞ MAN (Metropolitan-Area Network)	129
	i.	Internetwork or Internet	130
	ii.	Internet Services	131
		⮞ Electronic Mail	131
		⮞ File Transfer Protocol (FTP)	132
		⮞ Telnet	133
		⮞ Usenet News	134
	iii.	World Wide Web (WWW)	134
	iv.	Data Communication	136
	v.	Data Communication IoT and Cloud Computing Modes/Data Flow/ Transmission Modes	137
		⮞ Simplex Mode	138
		⮞ Half-Duplex	138
		⮞ Full-Duplex	138
	vi.	What is IoT	139
	vii.	What is Cloud Computing?	141

9. GIS (Geographic Information System) — **143**

	i.	What is GIS?	143
	ii.	History of GIS Development	144
	iii.	GIS Model	146
	iv.	Components of GIS	147
	v.	Applications of GIS	149
	vi.	What is GIS Mapping Software?	152
	vii.	Properties of GIS Software	152

10. Artificial Intelligence — **155**

	i.	Introduction	155
		⮞ What is Artificial Intelligence (AI)?	155
		⮞ Philosophy of AI	155
		⮞ Goals of AI	155
		⮞ What Contributes to AI?	156
	ii.	What is AI Technique?	156
	iii.	Applications of AI	157
	iv.	History of AI	158
	v.	Types of Intelligence	159
	vi.	Task Classification of AI	163
	vii.	Information Technology and IT Acts	164

11.	**Microsoft Word**		**171**
	i.	Exploring the Word 2016 Environment	171
	ii.	Formatting Text	198
	iii.	Printing a Word Document	216
	iv.	Format Painter	249
	v.	Templates (Supplemental)	255
	vi.	Raffle Tickets	257
	vii.	Navigating the Document	277
	viii.	Cleaning up our Document	278
	ix.	Mail Merge	279
12.	**Microsoft Excel**		**289**
	i.	Section 1: Entering Text and Numbers	290
	ii.	Section 2: Entering Excel Formulas and Formatting Data	299
	iii.	Section 3: Creating Excel Functions, Filling Cells, and Printing	310
	iv.	Section 4: Creating Charts	321
	v.	Section 5: More on Entering Excel Formulas	327
13.	**Number System and Codes**		**337**
	i.	Introduction	337
	ii.	Radix or Base	337
	iii.	Binary Arithmetic Operation	345
	iv.	Gray Code	353
14.	**Logic Gates**		**355**
	i.	Logic Gates	355
	ii.	Different Types of Logic Gates	355
	iii.	Introduction	363
15.	**Boolean Algebra**		**369**
	i.	Introduction	369
	ii.	Axioms and Laws of Boolean Algebra	369
16.	**Sequential Logic Circuit**		**389**
	i.	Sequential Circuit	389
	ii.	Racing Condition	393
	iii.	Triggering Methods	395

	i.	JK FLIP-FLOP	396
	ii.	T Flip-Flop	397
	iii.	Characteristic Table	398
	iv.	Flip-Flop Conversions	401
17.	**Combinational Logic Circuit**	**407**
	i.	Binary Adder–Subtractor	407
18.	**Logic Families**	**427**
	i.	Some Operational Properties of Logic Family	428
	ii.	CMOS Logic Levels	429
	iii.	Transistor-Transistor Logic	430
	iv.	ECL: Emitter-Coupled Logic	135
	v.	Basic ECL Circuit	435
19.	**Counter**	**437**
	i.	Synchronous Counter	437
	ii.	Asynchronous Counter	439
	iii.	Binary Counter	441
	iv.	Decade Counter	441
	v.	Up/Down Counter	443
	vi.	Johnson Counter	444
	vii.	Ring Counters	445
20.	**Registers**	**449**
	i.	Introduction	449
	ii.	Buffer Register	449
	iii.	Serial in, Parallel out Shift Register	452
	iv.	Applications of Shift Registers	457
	v.	Quantization Error	461
	vi.	Stair Step A/D Converter / Ramp A/D Converter	462
	vii.	Dual Slope A/D Converter	464
	viii.	Successive Approximation A/D Converter	465
	ix.	Performance Characteristics of A/D Converters	466
	Bibliography		467
	Index		471

Foreword

It is with great pleasure that I introduce this comprehensive textbook authored by Dr. Yash Paul, an esteemed scholar in the field of computer science and information technology. Dr. Paul's extensive experience and expertise shine through in the meticulous coverage of a wide array of topics, ranging from the foundational concepts of computing to the latest advancements in artificial intelligence and data communication. This book serves as a valuable resource for students, educators, and professionals alike, offering clear explanations, illustrative examples, and references for further exploration. Dr. Paul's thorough understanding of the subject matter is evident in the detailed discussions on computer architecture, operating systems, e-governance, e-commerce, computer viruses, and much more.

As a single-author endeavor, this textbook is a testament to Dr. Paul's dedication and scholarship. His commitment to excellence is reflected in the depth and breadth of the content presented within these pages. Whether you are a novice seeking to gain foundational knowledge or an expert looking to expand your understanding of advanced topics, this book provides the necessary tools and insights to navigate the dynamic landscape of computer science and information technology

I commend Dr. Yash Paul for his outstanding contribution to the field and am confident that this textbook will serve as a valuable resource for students, educators, and professionals for years to come.

Sincerely,
Dr. Godfrey Winster S
Associate Professor
SRM, University, Chennai

Preface

IT gives me an immense pleasure to introduce my humble work on "Basics of Computer Science and Digital Electronics" (2024 Regulation), intended for the different Universities curriculum across the country, for B.E., BCA, MBA, MCA, PGDCA, etc. Different institutions of the country introduce "IT Skill" course under skill Enhancement Course (SEC) and multidisciplinary course (MDC) as per NEP 2020. Thus, this book covers all the basic IT Skills necessary for the beginners or for the students from different faculties who opted IT skill course under SEC. This book is also suitable and easy to understand for the students who have non-IT background and it contains clear description of computer and digital electronics concepts step by step. I have kept its scope narrow in the interest of speed and size. I have covered the entire scope of the subject and it will be very useful not only for students but also to the subject handlers. I thank all who have helped us in the preparation of this book. As usual, the publishing process was made easier by the professionals at HOW Academics who have given immense support to get this book in time with quality printing. I do hope that the contents and concepts of book will be highly useful and helpful to the readers. Suggestions and comments for further improvement of this book will be acknowledged and well appreciated.

Author

Dr. Yash Paul

Acknowledgement

I cannot express my gratitude in words to my parents, who are truly an inspiration in my life. A sincere thanks to Hon'ble Vice Chancellor Professor Ravinder Nath, and Professor Sahid Rasool, Dean of Academic Affairs, Central University of Kashmir for their valuable guidance and support at the University. A sincere thanks to my PhD Supervisor Professor Sandor Fridli, Professor and Chair Eotvos Lorand University, Hungary, who guided me on how to write the scientific contents. Thanks to my two little flowers, Divam and Mishthi for your love and strength to complete this project. Without the support of my family members and friends it was not possible to achieve this milestone. I thank my all teachers and mentors throughout my career who shaped my life and made me in a position to complete this book.

I thank the State Council for Technical Education & Vocational Training Govt of Odisha for helping me by giving valuable information about number system and digital logic topics are covered in this book.

A special thanks to Professor Aloy Onyeka, CEO/Proprietor, OWERRI CBT HI-TECH, Owerri, Nigeria for guiding and providing material related to MS Word and Excell.

Thanks to MC-NPL Computer Lab, USA for helping in preparing material related to MS Word.

Last but not the least, a special thanks to each and every faculty of Central University of Kashmir, for supporting us in improving the quality of this book.

About the Author

Dr. Yash Paul is currently serving as an Assistant Professor in the Department of Information Technology at the Central University of Kashmir, under the Ministry of Education, Government of India. With over 14 years of experience in both teaching and research, he has made significant contributions, nationally and internationally.

Dr. Paul holds a Bachelor's degree in Computer Science and Engineering from Govt. College of Engineering and Technology, Jammu, and a Master's degree in Computer Science and Engineering from Anna University, Chennai. He embarked on his teaching career in 2009 at IIET, Tamil Nadu, where he was recognized with the Best Teacher Appreciation Award. Subsequently, in 2010, he assumed the role of Assistant Professor on a permanent basis at BGSB State University of Jammu and Kashmir. Since 2012, he has been a valued member of the faculty at the Central University of Kashmir.

In 2016, Dr. Paul was honored with an Indo-Hungarian fellowship to pursue his Ph.D. in Computer Science and Engineering from the esteemed Eotvos Lorand University in Budapest, Hungary. He successfully completed his doctoral studies, further enriching his expertise in the field.

Dr. Yash Paul's achievements extend beyond academia. In 2019, he was bestowed with the Best Scientific Paper Award at the International Conference ICRIC-2019. Furthermore, in 2023, he was recognized with the Research Excellence Award by InSc for his outstanding contributions to research.

His research interests encompass a wide range of topics including Machine Learning, Data Science, Mathematical Modelling, Data Mining, Data Structures, Artificial Intelligence, and Biomedical Signal Processing. Dr. Paul has made notable contributions to these fields, with over 15 research papers published in reputed international journals and conferences. Additionally, he holds utility and design patents, underscoring his innovative contributions to the field.

Chapter 1
Introduction

Computer and its Characteristics

The computer is an electronic device that operates on data. After processing the data, the computer generates the result known as information or processed data. The term computer is associated with the word "compute" which means "to calculate". Therefore, the computer can be defined as a calculating machine that can carry out arithmetic operations (ADD., MUL., DIV., SUB.) at very high speed. But this definition of a *computer as a calculating machine* is not appropriate because in reality, less than 20% of the work done by the computer is mathematical in nature (arithmetic and logic operations) and more than 80% of the work done is nonmathematical or non-numerical (collection of data, merging of data, sorting of data, printing of data etc) in nature. Thus, defining a computer as a calculating device means we are ignoring 80% of its functions. From the above discussion, we can conclude that the more appropriate term for the computer is data *processor* because modern computers not only *compute* but also perform other functions with data that flows *to and from* them. The term *data processing* may be defined as, capturing the data, manipulating the data, and finally managing the output results. But recently the term data processing has been replaced with a more appropriate term called *Information Technology*.

Characteristics of a Computer

These are the following important characteristics of a computer:

1. **Automatic:** Computers are automatic machines which means they work by themselves without any kind of human intervention until they finish the assigned job. The computer will perform a specific task by feeding some set of instructions for it. Here human intervention is very minimal and requires just to start a computer and assign the problem.

2. **Speed:** As compared to the human brain the processing speed of the computer is very high i.e. a computer can do in a few seconds what would

take a person his entire lifetime. The speed of the computer can be defined in terms of milliseconds (10^{-3}), microseconds (10^{-6}), nanoseconds (10^{-9}), and picoseconds (10^{-12}). This means that a powerful computer can perform 10^{12} operations per second.

3. **Accuracy:** The accuracy of a computer to produce the desired results is much higher than human when the calculations involved are complex, and the degree of its accuracy depends upon its design. Errors can be in computers but these errors are due to humans because of imprecise or poor thinking.

4. **Diligence:** The computer is free from monotony, tiredness, and lack of concentration but this is not the case with human beings. For example, if a computer has given 100 million calculations to perform, it performs the last calculation with the same accuracy and speed as the first one.

5. **Versatility:** Versatility means the capacity to perform completely different types of tasks. At one point in time the computer prepares payroll slips and Next moment it may perform inventory management or prepare electric bills.

6. **Power of Remembering:** The computer has the power to store any amount of information or data. Any information can be stored and recalled as long as you require it, for any number of years. It depends entirely upon you how much data you want to store on a computer and when to lose or retrieve this data.

7. **No IQ:** The computer cannot perform any task without instructions from the user. It executes the instructions at tremendous speed and with accuracy. So, a computer cannot make its own decisions as we can. Therefore, it is the user who tells the computer what to do, when to do it, what not to do, and in what order to do it.

8. **No Feeling:** It does not have feelings or emotions, taste, knowledge, or experience. Thus, it does not get tired even after long hours of work. It does not distinguish between users.

9. **Storage:** Like human beings, The computer has an in-built memory where it can store a large amount of data. Today's computers can store large volumes of data. A piece of information once recorded (or stored) in the computer, can never be forgotten and can be retrieved almost instantaneously. Usually, it has two types of memory, one is primary (RAM) and the other is secondary (Hard Disk, floppies, Pen Drives etc.) memory and are discussed in the next chapter.

Table 1.1: The storage capacities

Bit	Byte	Kilo-byte	Mega-byte	Giga-byte	Tera-byte	Peta-byte	Exo- Byte	Zeta-byte	Yotta-byte	Bronto-byte	Geo-byte
8	1	-	-	-	-	-	-	-	-	-	-
8192	1024	1	-	-	-	-	-	-	-	-	-
8388608	1048576	1024	1	-	-	-	-	-	-	-	-
8589934592	1073741824	1048576	1024	1	-	-	-	-	-	-	-
6871947673 6	8589934592	107374124	1048576	1024	1	-	-	-	-	-	-
549755813888	68719476736	8589934592	107374124	1048576	1024	1	-	-	-	-	-
4398046511104	549755813888	68719476736	8589934592	107374124	1048576	1024	1	-	-	-	-
35184372088832	4398046511104	549755813888	68719476736	8589934592	107374124	1048576	1024	1	-	-	-
281474976106 56	35184372088832	4398046511104	549755813888	68719476736	8589934592	107374124	1048576	1024	1	-	-
22517998136852 48	281474976106 56	35184372088832	4398046511104	549755813888	68719476736	8589934592	107374124	1048576	1024	1	-
1.801439850948198 e+16	22517998136852 48	281474976106 56	35184372088832	43980465111 04	5497755813 88	68719476 7 36	8589934592	107374124	1048576	1024	1

10. **Reliability:** Computer output is generally very reliable, subject to the condition that the input data entering the computer should be correct and the program of instructions should be reliable and correct. Incorrect input data and unreliable programs give us computer errors and wrong results. Hence, the phrase GARBAGE IN-GARBAGE OUT (GIGO).
11. **Scientific Approach:** To solve the complex problems, the computer uses a highly scientific approach, with some objective and sequentially carried out, leaving no room for emotional and subjective evaluations made by man, which are sources of potential errors and unjustified results.
12. **Reduced Cost: The cost of** computer equipment has dropped drastically over the years. Hardware costs have been decreasing at an estimated annual rate of 25%. Thus, there was a time when companies were not in a position to acquire their own computer system. But now it is not only feasible to acquire a system, But cost-effective as well.

Note: *The storing capacity of a computer is measured in terms of bytes, kilobytes, and gigabytes... is shown in Table 1.1.*

Computer History/Evolution/ Computer Generations

The term "generation" in computer terminology is a step-in technology. There are Five generations known till date. The overview of the major developments and technologies during the five generations of computers is given below.

First Generation (1942-1955): First-generation computers were based on Vacuum tubes. e.g. ENIAC, EDVAC EDSAS UNIVAC I, etc. were first-generation computers. A vacuum tube was a fragile glass device, which used filament as a source of electrons and could control and amplify electronic signals. The vacuum tube computers can perform operations in milliseconds and are called first-generation computers.

Characteristics of first-generation computers are:

a. The memory of these computers used electromagnetic relays.
b. Punch cards were used to feed the data into the system.
c. Programs were written in machine and assembly languages.
d. They were bulky and large in size.
e. They used thousands of vacuum tubes, which emitted large amounts of heat and had to be properly air-conditioned.
f. Vacuum tubes consumed more power.
g. These computers required constant maintenance.

h. Thousands of components were assembled manually into electronic circuits; hence their commercial production is difficult and costly.
i. Used only for scientific computations.

Second Generation (1955-1964): Second-generation computers were developed by using transistors instead of vacuum tubes. Transistors were developed by Johan Bardeen, William Shockley, and Walter Brattain at Bell Laboratories in 1947 and are better electronic switching devices than Vacuum tubes. Examples of such systems are Honeywell 400, IBM 7030, UNIVAC LARC, etc.

Characteristics of Second-generation computers are:

a. Transistors are easier to handle than Vacuum tubes because they are made up of Germanium semiconductor materials rather than glass.
b. They are more robust and reliable than Vacuum tubes because there is no filament.
c. They could switch faster than tubes (almost 10 times).
d. The consumption of power is less (one-tenth of the tube).
e. These systems are less expensive and smaller in size.
f. Produce less heat compared to tubes.
g. They used magnetic cores for main memory and magnetic disks and tape for secondary storage.
h. They had faster and larger memory than vacuum tube systems.
i. Punch cards were still used to feed the data into the system.
j. High-level languages like FORTRAN, COBOL SNOBOL, etc. were used for programming.
k. The concept of a batch operating system was supported.
l. Thousands of transistors were assembled manually by hand into electronic circuits; hence their commercial production is difficult and costly.
m. These computers were increasingly used in business and industry for commercial data processing applications like payroll, inventory control marketing, etc.

Third Generation (1964-1975): The third-generation computers were developed by using Integrated circuits (ICs). IC is a less than 5mm square of silicon consisting of several electronic components like transistors, resistors and capacitors grown on it, eliminating wired interconnection between components. Examples of such systems are IBM 360/370. PDP-8, PDP11 etc. IC technology is also known as microelectronics technology and was invented by Jack St. Clair Kilby and Robert Nyce in 1958. There are two types of IC technology:

a. **Small-scale integration (SSI):** Here IC contains 10-20 components on a single chip.
b. **Medium Scale Integration (MSI):** here it is possible to integrate up to about a hundred components on a single chip.
c. **Large Scale Integration (LSI):** Here it is possible to integrate up to 30,000 components on a single chip and this technology is used in fourth-generation computers.
d. **Very-large-scale Integration (VLSI):** Where one million components are integrated on a single chip and are used in fourth-generation computers.
e. **Ultra large-scale Integration (ULSI):** Ten million components are integrated on a single chip and are used in fifth-generation computers.

Characteristics of Third Generation computers are:

a. Because if ICs were being used these systems would be more powerful, more reliable and less expensive.
b. These systems were cooler to operate than transistor-based systems and were also very fast.
c. Large and fast memory i.e., less than 5 megabytes of main memory and 10s of megabytes of secondary storage, than second-generation computers.
d. The standardized version of high-level languages like ANSI FORTRAN, ANSI COBOL and some other languages like PL/1 PASCAL, and BASIC were used for programming purposes which provides portability.
e. Instead of batch operating systems, time-sharing operating systems (discussed later) were used.
f. Development and introduction of minicomputers also took place in the third generation.
g. They were more reliable and less prone to hardware failures than second-generation systems.
h. Mini computers of the third generation made computers affordable even for smaller companies.
i. Don't require manual assembly of individual components, hence reducing labor and cost involved at the assembly stage.

Note: *Computers built until the early 1960s were mainframe systems that were affordable to big companies only and were based on the concept of batch processing. Development and introduction of minicomputers also took place in the third generation and were based on the concept of time sharing processing where a number of users could access it simultaneously from different locations in the building.*

Fourth Generation (1975-1989): The fourth-generation computers are com-plete computers with a microprocessor (ALU+CU+Core activities), a few additional primary storage chips, and other support circuitry. These systems support both LSI and VLSI technology. Thus, personal computers (PCs) are the invention of the fourth generation and are inexpensive to design and suddenly it has become possible for everyone to buy and own a new computer. Examples of such systems are IBM PC, APPLE II, TRS-80, VAX 9000 CRAY-I, etc. In fourth-generation computers semiconductor memories instead of magnetic cores were used in resulting large random-access memories with very fast access time. On the other hand, hard disks became cheaper, smaller and larger in capacity. Floppy disk as a portable memory is also a part of this generation.

Characteristics of Fourth Generation computers are:

a. PCs were smaller and cheaper than mainframes or minicomputers of the third generation.
b. NO air conditioning was required for the PC.
c. LAN and WAN are also supported in this generation.
d. In addition to unbundled software, these systems also used add-on hardware features that allowed users to invest only in the hardware configuration and software of their need and value.
e. We can use the system personally at home.
f. MS-DOS, MS-Windows, and Apple's proprietary OS were developed which made the use of computer systems easy.
g. High-speed, robust, and inexpensive system.
h. The Unix Operating system and C language was also discovered in this generation.

Fifth Generation (1989-Till Date): In the fifth Generation, the VLSI technology became ULSI technology resulting in the production of microprocessor chips having ten million electronic components. Due to this advancement in computer technology, we have more compact and more powerful computers being introduced almost every year at more or less the same price or even cheaper. Powerful and Portable notebooks, workstations, powerful servers, and very powerful supercomputers are gifted in the fifth generation of computers. Examples of such systems are IBM notebooks, Pentium PCs, SUN Workstations, IBM SP/2, etc.

Some important points about Fourth Generation computers are:

a. Fifth-generation desktop PCs and workstations are several times more powerful than 4th generation PCs.

b. Although fifth generation mainframes computers required proper air conditioning, whereas no air conditioning is required for notebook computers, PCs and workstations.
c. Less power is required as compared to previous generations.
d. They have faster and larger memory as compared to the previous memory.
e. They are general purpose computers.
f. They are more reliable and less prone to hardware failure as compared to previous generations.
g. Use of standard high level programming languages allows programs written for one computer to be portable.
h. E-mail, www E-Commerce, virtual libraries, virtual class rooms, smart class rooms, multimedia applications etc are types of services available in 5th generation computers.
i. These systems involved the concept of unbundled software, and also used add-on hardware features that allowed users to invest only in the hardware configuration and software of their need and value.
j. During 5th generation optical disks emerged as a popular portable mass storage media such as CD-R0M (Compact Disk-ROM).

Basic Computer Organisation

The internal architecture of computers differs from one system model to another but the basic computer organisation remains the same Which is shown in Figure 1.1.

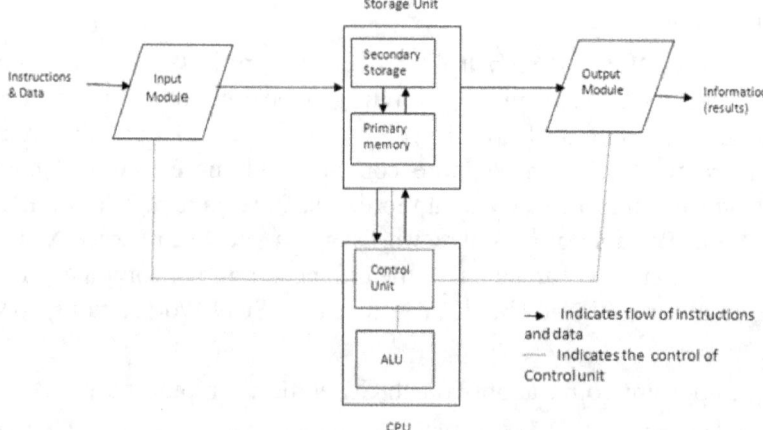

Figure 1.1: *Basic organisation of a computer*

From the above diagram we can say that the basic logical structure (based on the stored program concept) as proposed by Von Neumann, has not changed even though the size, shape, performance cost etc have changed over the time. From the above given diagram we can say that a computer consists of five modules as given below:

1. **Input Module:** The main responsibility of this module is to enter data and instructions into a computer system. It accepts data from the outside world and converts it into a form which is acceptable by the system. It supplies the converted instructions and data to a computer system for further processing. Examples of such input devices like keyboard (text data), mouse (graphical user interface), touch screen, scanner, digitizer etc.

2. **Output Module:** The main responsibility of this module is to accept the results (Coded form) produced by the Central Processing Unit (CPU), convert these coded results into a form which is understandable by the human and supply the converted results to the outside world. Examples of such output devices are like Monitors, printers, plotters etc.

3. **Storage Module:** The main responsibility of this module is to store data and instructions, intermediate results and results for output. There are two types of storage:

    a. **Primary Memory:** Primary memory is also called as main memory of the computer, which holds instructions and data, intermediate results of processing, and recently produced results. Processor used this memory to perform any kind of processing. The data is represented electronically on the main memory chip's circuitry and the CPU can access it directly at a very high speed. This memory is volatile in nature i.e. as soon as the computer system switches off or resets, the information stored in main memory is erased. It is expensive, has limited storage, is very fast and is made up of semiconductor material. RAM is an example of primary memory.

    b. **Secondary Memory:** This type of memory is called auxiliary memory and it overcomes the problems of primary memory i.e. limited storage capacity and volatile nature of the primary memory. This memory is cheap and stores information even if the computer system switches off or resets i.e. its nature is non-volatile. Magnetic disk, magnetic tape, pen drive, floppy drive are the examples of secondary storage.

The Von Neumann Machine

In 1945, after World War II, British mathematician and Hungarian-American mathematician, physicist, computer scientist, and polymath John Von Neumann proposed a flexible computer architecture. Alan Turing was working breaking on the Enigma code in Bletchley Park utilizing the 'Colossus' computer and John Von Neumann was working on the Manhattan Project to make the first atomic bomb which needed an immense amount of manual calculations.

During war-time, if we wanted to do another assignment from the same computer, we were required to reprogram the computer by reconstructing the whole machine. For instance, the early PC called ENIAC took three weeks to re-wire to perform alternate tasks. The new thought was that not exclusively should the data be in the memory, but that the program processing that data must also be put away in a similar memory which leads to less demanding to reprogram. This **'stored-program'** architecture is now commonly known as the **'Von Neumann' architecture** as shown in Figure 1.2..

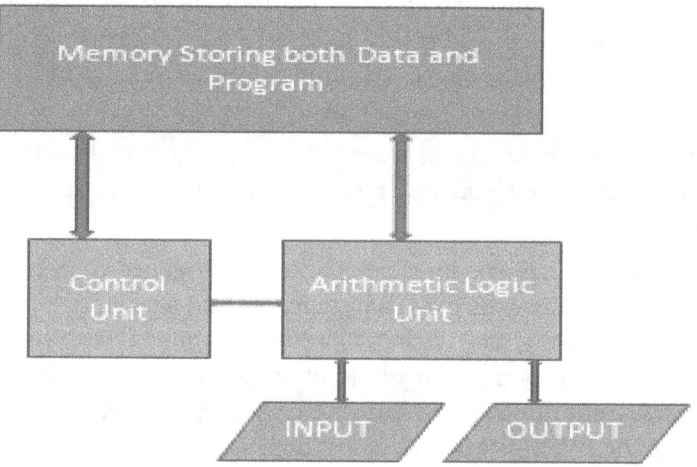

Figure 1.2: *Neumann's/Stored program architecture*

The von Neumann design, also called the Von Neumann Model and Princeton Architecture, and this design is based on the architecture that was portrayed in 1945 by the mathematician and physicist John von Neumann and others in the First Draft of a Report on the EDVAC. This architecture for an electronic PC consists of a processing unit containing an ALU unit and processor registers, a control unit containing instruction registers, program counter (PC), a memory to store the two data and instructions, outer storage, input and output mechanisms. The meaning has evolved to be any stored-program computer in which an instruction fetch and a data operation cannot occur at the same time because they share a common bus. This is referred to as the von Neumann bottleneck and often limits the performance of the system.

The design of a von Neumann machine is easier than that of a Harvard machine, which is also a stored program framework but has a set of data and address buses is utilized for reading and writing the data into the memory and another set is applied for fetching the instructions.

In stored-program design program instructions and its data, is kept in write-read (WR), random-access memory (RAM). Basically, stored-program designs are an enhancement of the program-controlled computers famous in the 1940s, like Colossus and the ENIAC. In Most of current PCs, a same memory is utilized for the two, data and program instruction, Von Neumann and Harvard architectures are distinct in terms of cache organisation and not by main memory.

A set of data and address buses is utilized for reading and writing the data into the memory and another set is applied for fetching the instructions.

Features of a Von Neumann Architecture

- RAM can store both data and the program instructions.
- The control unit will manage the process data, execution of the program, move in and move out the program from memory. Uses registers like 'accumulator' to store intermediate results.
- It follows 'one-at-a-time' phenomenon i.e. The Von Neumann machine is a **sequential processing machine**.
- Flow of information to different parts of the PC is carried out by a 'bus' called data bus and locations in memory are identified by a bus called an 'address bus'.
- Arithmetic and logic operations like Add, Multiply, Divide and Subtract, 'Greater Than', 'Less Than', 'Equal To' etc. are done through ALU.

Conclusion: The Von Neumann architecture is the basic architecture for most of the modern computers, but there are issues like shared memory, memory leaks, speed of data bus and fetch rate problem, where data and instructions may share the same data bus but the rate at which they need to fetch the data may be different.

Information Technology and its Applications

The term *"information"* has distinctive significance in various context, in general speaking *information* is related with knowledge got from study, understanding, or experiences. On the other hand, *technology* is the utilization of information/knowledge practically in human life to change and control human life for their betterment. Technology incorporates the utilization of materials, devices, procedures and tools etc, to make life easy, comfortable work productive. Technology started to impact human efforts when individuals started utilizing tools. The fundamental idea of Information Technology was seen in the World War II where the military and industries worked together towards the development of electronics, computers, and information theory and after the 1940s, the military organisation was the main source of research and development in the field of IT for promoting automation.

Since the 1950s, four different computer generations have advanced where Each generation came with reduced sized computers with more capabilities.

The term Information Technology (IT) was coined by Renowned scientist Jim Domsic nov. 1981 replaced the outdated term "*data processing*" by Information technology. When we are talking about Information Technology as a whole, most likely we use the terms *computers* and *information* both. Information Technology Association of America (ITAA), defines the term "IT" as "the study, design, development, implementation, support or management of computer-based information systems, especially software applications and computer hardware." Therefore, information technology utilizes computers and related software to alter, accumulate, secure, repair, process, broadcast and to retrieve information electronically. In short, IT consists of computers, computer networks, satellite communications, robotics, artificial intelligence video, audio, text, cable television, e-mail, e-games, and automated equipment etc.

Information and Communications Technology (ICT): Especially in the fields of Education and E-Governance instead of using the term IT experts prefer to use the term ICT. In common usage, it is often assumed that ICT is synonymous with IT in like manner use, usually that ICT is considered synonymous with IT but in reality, ICT incorporates any medium to record data, technology for broadcasting data and technology to handle voice and additionally, pictures. It incorporates a wide spectrum of processing equipments, like PCs, servers, centralized servers, cell phones, individual gadgets, MP3 players, application programming etc. In this way, ICT express more advancements by incorporating communicating and remote portable broadcast communications.

Applications of Information Technology: Today's life of people across the globe is directly or indirectly connected with computers and other electronic gadgets. Day by day for the fundamental needs of life humans are getting more and more dependent on IT-enabled devices. Information Technology has applications in almost all aspects of our life and some of the important ones are briefed below:

Science and Engineering: Advanced fields like biotechnology are most reliant on the utilization of PCs and other microprocessor-controlled gadgets. Utilizing supercomputers, meteorologists anticipate future climate by utilizing the stored data from numerous sources, predicting the conduct of behaviour of the atmosphere, and geographic information. Computer Aided Design and Computer Aided Manufacturing devices help the architect to improve their designs etc.

Business & Commerce and Banking: this one of the biggest applications of IT where computers are used to keep and manage and business and financial records. Most substantial organizations keep the business records of every one of their employees and customers in extensive databases that are managed by PC programs. Other software and databases are utilized as a part of business capacities for like billing, tracing payments, and tracking delivered goods.

Nowadays on a smaller scale, numerous organizations have replaced money/cash registers with point-of-sale (POS) terminals. These POS terminals not just print a business receipt for the client yet additionally send data to a PC database when everything is sold to keep up a stock of things on hand and items to be ordered. There is a competition in the banking industry for tremendous profits and reputation in the world or country, therefore it encouraged computerization in the banking industry. The need to modernize and computerized has emerged from operational reasons, for instance the complex Interbank Foreign Exchange Market methods, which require great correspondence every day among central offices and branch offices. Practically in today's life all the information organisations need to do business together and it is possible only if they involve the utilization of PCs and Information Technology efficiently. Almost all money related transactions on the planet are made electronically. More up to date technologies like m-commerce have empowered almost everyone to do financial transactions on the move. E-Commerce, E-Governance are achieved by using IT and are explained in details in coming chapters Management Information System and Chief Information Officer (CIO) are new terms to enterprise management.

Education: In today's world in many cases education is complete only if he/she is computer literate. For the majority of jobs basic literacy in computers is mandatory therefore now computer education across the country and world made mandatory at least up to the primary level. Digital information is increasing day by day and the highly speed internet is making it accessible to everyone across the world. Students have access to world class education where through the internet they can listen and read lectures from reputed professionals of the world. There are many such online platforms for self-learning like "Massive Open Online Course" (MOOCs), SWAYAM, National Programme on Technology Enhanced Learning (NPTEL) which is an initiative by seven Indian Institutes of Technology IIT Bombay, Delhi, Guwahati, Kanpur, Kharagpur, Madras and Roorkee.

Governance: *Electronic government* (or *E-government*) where the governments use ICTs and other web-based telecommunication technologies to improve or enhance on the efficiency and effectiveness of services in the public sector, improves broad stakeholders' contribution to national and community development, as well as deepen the governance process. Computerization of Government offices and exercises makes it less demanding to supervise and review, and makes the government more receptive and active to the requirements of society. It connects the gap between the Government and the general population. Computerization of Government offices and exercises makes it less demanding to supervise and review, and makes the government more receptive and active to the requirements of society. It connects the gap between the Government and the general population (details are available in coming chapter).

Medicine: IT plays a vital role in the medical field. For instance, a scanner takes photos of the body by Computerized Axial Tomography (CAT) or by attractive reverberation imaging (MRI) for the diagnosis. PCs are an incredible means for storage of patient related information and usually important to keep up definite records of the restorative history of patients. Specialists regularly require the data about a patient's family history, physical illnesses, as of now analysed illnesses and recommended pharmaceuticals. This data can be adequately put away in a PC database. They can be utilized to store the data about the medicine recommended to a patient and in addition those, which can't be endorsed to him/her. Restorative diaries, research and analysis papers, critical medicinal reports and reference books can be stored in computers. X-ray machines and a few such medicinal apparatuses depend on computer logic. Computers are utilized for determination of diseases and also utilized for the examination of organs inside the body. 2-D and 3-D digital images inside and outside of the body can be taken for better treatment. CT scan MRI, Endoscopy, surgery etc are computerized.

Entertainment: Information technology has changed the way of living the life of many people. There are various ways for entertainment like games, video and video, digital TV, satellite radio, which are accessible by smart cell phones, PDAs (Personal Digital Assistant), laptops or on TV using cable connection or wirelessly through WIFI (Wireless Fidelity), CDMA (Code Division Multiple Access) or GPRS technologies.

History of Information Technology

Indian IT Industry: The Indian Information Technology industry has played an important role putting India on top of world map. Because of the achievement of the IT industry, India is emerging as a soft power in the world. As per the National Association of Software and Service Companies (NASSCOM), a top software body in India. More than 1.2% of Indian GDP (Gross Domestic Product) is contributed by the IT industry for the financial year 1997-98 which increased to 3.9 for the financial year 2007-2008 and 7.7 for FY-2017. According to National Association of Software and Service Companies, in 2017, this sector generated revenues of US$160 billion, with export revenue of US$99 billion and domestic revenue of US$48 billion which growing at the rate of over 13% as compared to previous years. Direct employment in Indian IT-BPO (Business Process Outsourcing) crossed the

2 million with an expansion of around 389,000 experts over FY-2007.; Indirect job creation is assessed at 8-9 million and IT-BPO trades crossed USD 40.9 billion in FY-2008 as against USD 31.8 billion in FY-2007, a development of 28%. India has the second biggest English-talking technical experts on the planet, second just to the U.S. India is the second-biggest exporter of IT. Exports of the Indian IT industry constitute around 77% of the industry's total income. IT Industry's export contribution in income in total Indian exports was under 4% in FY-1998 which goes to 25% in FY-2012. Some interesting statistics about contribution if IT industry to their GDP are shown below.

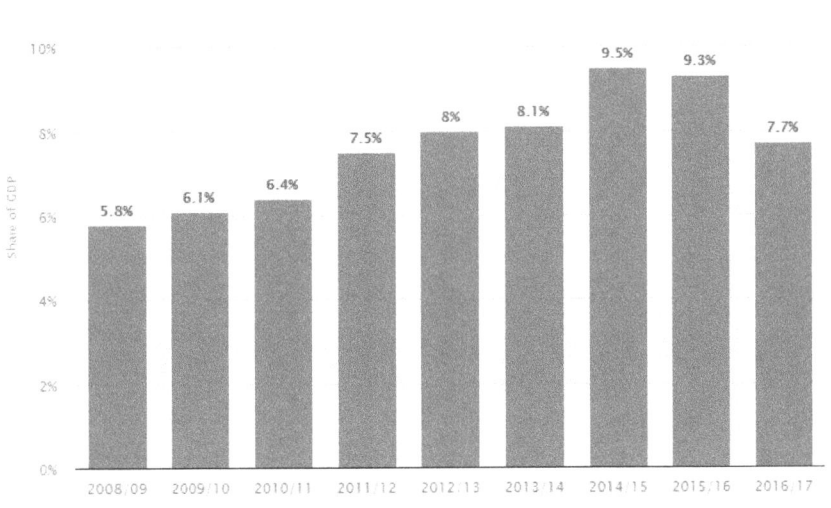

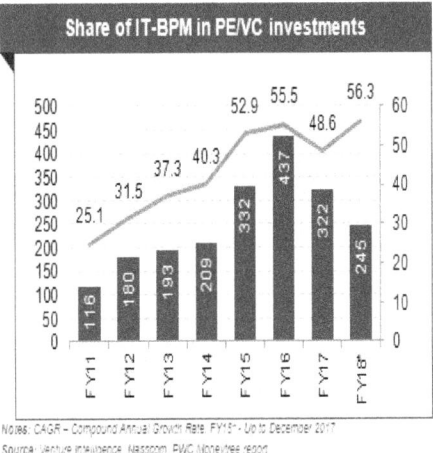

Figure 1.3: *Information technology/business process management (IT-BPM) sector in India as a share of India's gross domestic product (GDP) from 2009 to 2017 [Statista 2018]*

The extraordinary development of the Indian IT Software and Services, IT Enabled Services (ITES) and Business Process Outsourcing (BPO) part has had a distinguishable multiplier impact on the Indian economy in general.

Latest update: June, 2018

- The global digital transformation market size is expected to rise at a CAGR of 18.56 per cent from US$ 1.2 trillion in 2017 to US$ 2 trillion in 2020.
- India's IT industry is increasingly focusing on digital opportunities as digital is poised to be a major segment in the next few years. It is also currently the fastest growing segment, growing over 30 per cent annually.
- Export revenue from digital segment already forms about 20 per cent of the industry's total export revenue as exports have grown at a CAGR of 50.76 per cent to an estimated US$ 25 billion in FY18.
- Revenue from digital is expected to comprise 38 per cent of the forecasted US$ 350 billion industry revenue by 2025.^

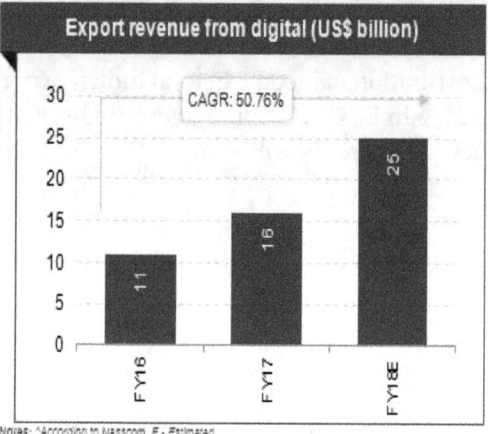

Export revenue from digital (US$ billion)

CAGR: 50.76%

FY16: 11
FY17: 16
FY18E: 25

Notes: ^According to Nasscom, E - Estimated
Source: Nasscom, IDC, Media Sources

Chapter 2
Input and Output

The input and output devices (I/O devices) provide the capabilities to a computer system, to communicate with the external world(user). I/O devices are also called peripheral devices, entering data from the user into primary storage. This data will be processed in primary memory by the CPU and produce the results. Output devices transfer these results (processed data) from primary memory to user or external world. The position of I/O devices in computer organisation is shown in Figure 1.1 of Chapter 1.

Input Devices

An input device is an electromechanical device that accepts data from the outside world, converts it into a form which is understandable by the computer. The input devices are classified into following categories:

a. Keyboard devices
b. Point and draw devices
c. Data scanning devices
d. Digitizer
e. Electronic cards-based devices
f. Speech Reorganisation devices
g. Vision based devices

Keyboard Devices

Keyboard devices are the input devices which are used to insert the data, by pressing a set of keys mounted on a keyboard, into the computer system and these devices are connected to a computer system. Nowadays the popular keyboard used is QWERTY keyboard having 106 keys are mounted on it.

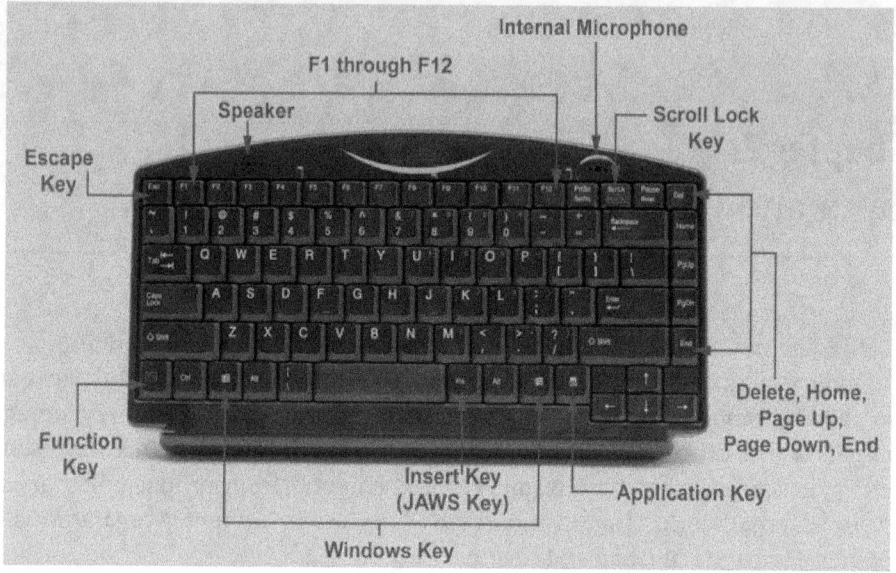

Figure 2.1: *QWERTY keyboard with possible set of keys.*

Usually, the keyboard is used to interact with the computer in text mode i.e. by typing the text, which is awkward and time consuming. Thus, a new type of user interface, called Graphical User Interface (GUI) is devised to interact with the computer system. Graphical user interface provides a screen with a given set of graphic icons. These icons are used to instruct the computer by clicking on these icons. Thus, for efficient utilization of GUI we require the devices called point and draw devices. We can also handle a graphical user interface with a keyboard but it is unsuitable and inconvenient.

Point and Draw Devices

The various point and draw devices are:
      a.   Mouse
      b.   Joystick
      c.   Track ball
      d.   Light pen
      e.   Touch screen

a. Mouse

Mouse is the hand held, point and draw device which supports GUI as the primary user interface. Mouse is the *"must have" device* on modern personal computers and workstations because nowadays all computer applications are based on GUI. When a mouse which is connected to a user terminal is rolled on a flat surface, a graphics cursor moves on the terminal screen in the direction of mouse's movement. To open an icon, place the cursor on the icon and do a click on it. The Figure 2.2 shows a mouse with two buttons on the top.

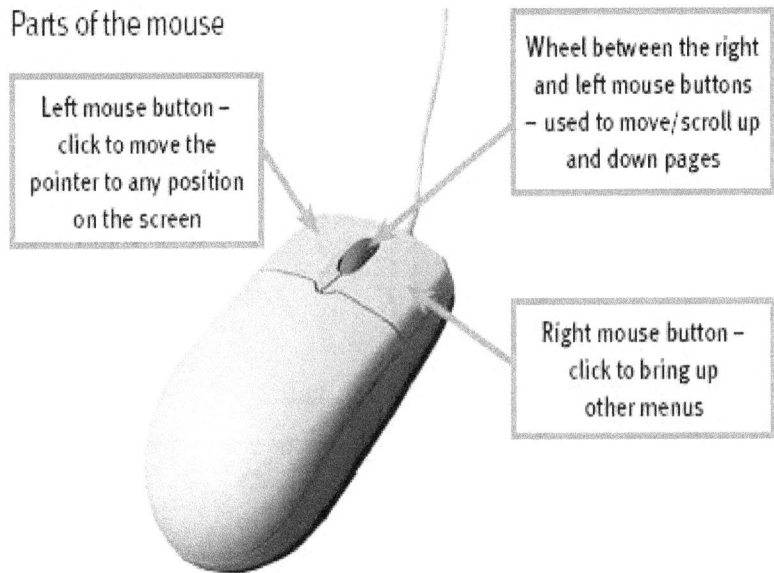

Figure 2.2: *A mouse*

b. Joystick

A joystick is an input device commonly used to control gaming applications and sometimes graphics applications. First published in the United States by C.B. Mirick. It was invented and patented in 1926 by the Naval Research Laboratory. Joysticks are commonly used to control machines or characters within computer programs. Comes with a base and a cane that can be moved left and right. It can also be rotated to different angles to control cursor movement within the computing device. Use the joystick lever to control the pointer or cursor movement. These consist of additional buttons for additional functions and look similar to arcade game controllers. The following Figure 2.3 is an example of a joystick.

Compared to keyboard keys, flexible movement provides better control. Joysticks are also useful as input devices for people with disabilities. Most joysticks have at least one trigger button on the front of the stick and one more button on the top of the stick. There are some joysticks with additional buttons on the base. These buttons can also be operated without a stick. Joysticks typically come with software that allows the user to assign functions to each button. The joystick can also be connected to a computer via a serial port or a simple USB connection. Joysticks mimic the controls of airplanes and other aircraft, making them suitable for flight simulators and flight action games.

However, some players also use joysticks in other types of video games, such as first-person shooters and fighting games. Additionally, some users prefer to use their familiar mouse and keyboard.

Additionally, joysticks are especially needed when specific functions are required or when direct directional control is required.

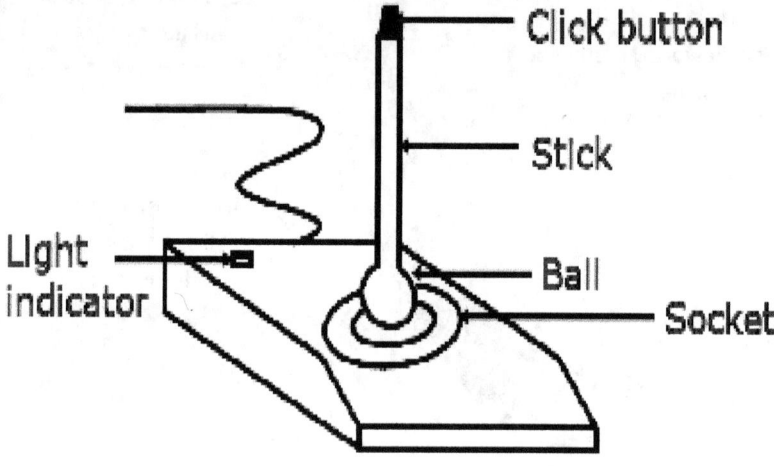

Figure 2.3: *A Joystick*

There are Different Types of Joysticks: Manual isometric joystick, finger-operated joystick, displacement joystick, thumb/fingertip-operated joystick, manual joystick, etc.

c. Trackball

A trackball is a computer cursor control device used on many laptop keyboards and older versions of computer mice. This device consists of a ball held in a socket, which contains sensors that detect the rotation of the ball about two axes. It's like an upside-down mouse with a ball inside. The trackball was invented in 1952 by Tom Cranston and Fred Longstaff. Early trackballs were mechanically complex and cumbersome, but since the 1980s trackballs have been largely replaced by optical mice. The user moves the cursor by rolling the ball with the thumb, fingers, or palm of the hand without moving the arm. Some trackballs have a textured rubber or metal surface to improve grip. Some have removable covers.

Users can use buttons on the top, bottom, front, or back of the device to perform various commands, such as selecting objects or moving objects using drag and drop.

Input and Output

Figure 2.4: *A Trackball*

Advantages

1. One of the advantages of a trackball over a regular mouse is that it can be placed further away from the user's body on the desktop and requires less space to operate.
2. Trackballs also require no moving parts on the surface they are used on.
3. This means there is no friction between the ball and the surface, which is important for accurate movement.

Disadvantages

1. One of the downsides to trackballs is that they take some time to get used to.
2. Another potential problem is that the ball can become dirty or sticky over time, which can affect performance.
3. Some trackballs have limited compatibility with certain types of software or gaming applications.

d. Light Pen

A light pen is a pointing device used to draw objects with a single interface or to scan objects using a CRT (Cathode Red Tube) scanner. The structure of the light pen consists of a tube with a digital photocell and optics. The photocell pointer element detects objects on the screen and sends digital signals to other Monitors. The accuracy of light pen operation depends on the camera calibration angle, probe calibration, and control points. The body of a light pen typically consists of eight infrared LED (Light Emitting Diode) light points and a removable ball probe. A light pen is used in the form of a scanner within the CPU to detect and deliver control systems that affect the measurement of scanner accuracy.

The light pen uses a sensor to scan across pixels in one step, creating a diagram or image of the scanned object.

The Types of Light Pens

- **Wired Photosensitive Device:** An old light pen used for scanning, with a cable attached to the pen to capture pixels from the system.
- **Battery Light Pen:** The Battery Light Pen is a modern device that can be used to manipulate entire elements within a pixel even in the absence of light.
- **Designer Light Pen:** The Designer Light Pen is used by photographers for computer-assisted drawing of designs.
- **LED Light Pen:** This device provides bright illumination to your subject as it scans at the resolution your system requires.

Figure 2.5: *A Light Pen*

Advantages and Disadvantages of Light Pens:

- **Pros:** A light pen can be easily used with any Monitor, including CRT Monitors and LED Monitors. The light pen allows for the precise design of high-resolution pixels that are scanned by the CPU. The light pen ensures the efficiency of measurements depending on probe calibration. The Light Pen helps you scan every pixel at once in your 3D printing projects.

- **Cons:** The light pen does not work when using an LCD (Liquid Crystal Display) Monitor as an interface.

d. Touch Screen

A touchscreen is both a computer's display device and an input device.

Touchscreens are sensitive to touch pressure, so users interact with the screen by touching elements on the screen directly with a finger or stylus, instead of using a mouse or keyboard.

There are four types of touch screens in the market: resistive, surface acoustic wave, infrared, and capacitive.

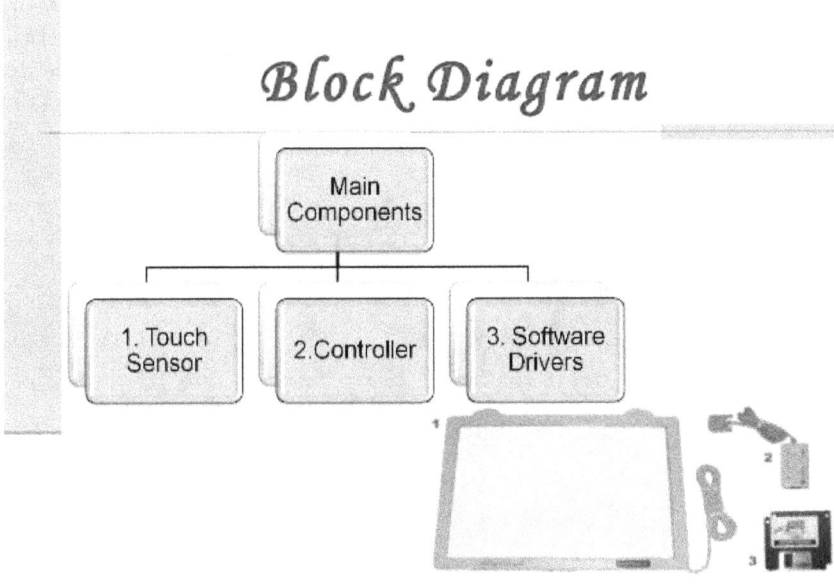

Figure 2.6: *A block diagram of touch screen*

Data Scanning Devices

Data scanning devices are input devices used for direct data entry into a computer system from source documents.

Some important points about data scanning devices are:

a. Now no need to enter the data manually to a system by the user.
b. Automatic data entry reduces errors, increasing timeliness and accuracy of the data.
c. The quality of input documents should be high because poorly typed, strikeovers are normally rejected.

Types of Scanners

Image Scanner: An image scanner is an input device that scans the source document, translates it into an electronic format and finally stores it in a computer. Thus, the stored copy of the document in the computer will never get worse in quality or become yellow or dark with age and can be displayed or printed whenever desired. The stored images can be altered only if the computer has *image -processing software*. Two common types of image scanner are:

1. **Flatbed Scanner:** The flatbed scanner looks like a copier machine. It has a glass plate on its top and a lid that covers the glass. A document to be scanned is placed on the glass plate. A source of light just below the glass plate, moves horizontally from one end to another when activated. After scanning one line, the light beam moves up a little and scans the next line and the process is repeated for all the lines. It takes about 20 seconds to scan a document of size *21 cm 28 cm*. A flatbed scanner is shown in Figure 2.7.

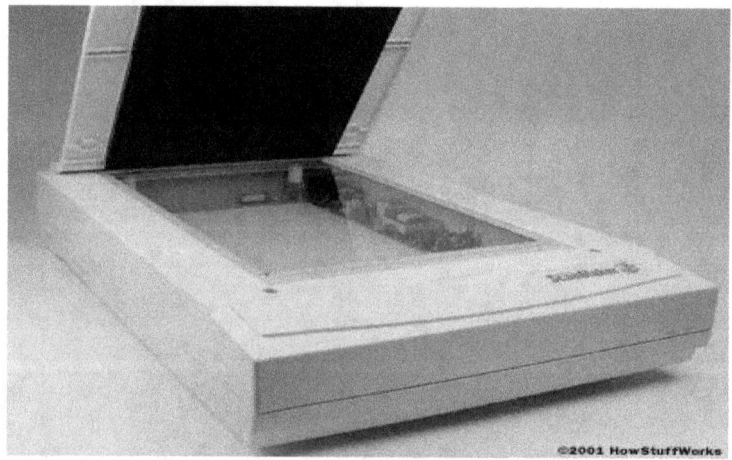

Figure 2.7: *A flatbed scanner*

2. **Hand- Held Scanner:** A hand held scanner has a set of light emitting diodes enclosed in a small box that can be held in hand comfortably. To scan a document, the scanner is dragged slowly over it from its one end to the other end with its light on. These scanners are used only in cases where high accuracy is not needed and the volume of the data to be scanned is low. A hand held Scanner is shown in Figure 2.8.

Input and Output

Figure 2.8: *A hand held scanner*

Optical Character Recognition (OCR): Scanner scans the document and store it as an image. The stored document cannot be modified without any image processing software. If we are succeeding to save an image as a text, it would be quite simple to do any kind of modification in an image. To represent an image in bit-map representation, it requires nearly 15 times more space, because we required at least four bytes to store a colour pixel i.e. three bytes for standard colours red, blue, and green (RGB), and one byte is required to store some information related the pixel. But if it is in text form, then only one byte is required to save a character in the memory. Thus, OCR is a software that converts the bitmap images of characters into ASCII codes or text. These software are designed to recognized texts written OCR fonts i.e. OCR-A (American Standard) and OCR-B (European Standard). OCR-B font is shown in Figure 2.9.

```
ABCDEFGHIJKLMNOP
QRSTUVWXYZÀÄÉÎÕØ
abcdefghijklmnop
qrstuvwxyzàäé&12
34567890($£.,!?)
```

Figure 2.9: *OCR-B Font of Scanner*

Digitizer

A digitizer, also known as a digitizing tablet or graphics tablet, is a computer input device that allows users to draw or write directly onto the surface of the tablet using a stylus or a special pen-like device. The tablet then captures the movement and pressure of the stylus and translates it into digital data that can be processed by a computer.

Here's a detailed breakdown of how a digitizer works:

1. **Physical Structure**: A digitizer typically consists of a flat surface, often with a grid pattern, that serves as the drawing area. This surface is sensitive to pressure and can detect the position of the stylus or pen.

2. **Stylus or Pen**: The stylus or pen is the tool used to interact with the digitizer. It usually has a tip that simulates the feel of writing or drawing on paper, and sometimes buttons that can be programmed for various functions.

3. **Pressure Sensitivity**: One of the key features of digitizers is their ability to detect pressure sensitivity. This means that they can sense how hard the stylus is being pressed against the surface of the tablet. This allows for more nuanced control over drawing and writing, as different levels of pressure can produce varying line thicknesses or shades.

4. **Electromagnetic or Resistive Technology**: Digitizers employ different technologies to detect the position and pressure of the stylus. Electromagnetic digitizers use a grid of wires embedded in the tablet surface and a special pen that emits a signal. When the pen is brought close to the tablet, the grid detects the signal and determines the pen's position. Resistive digitizers use layers of conductive material that create a change in electrical resistance when pressure is applied, allowing the tablet to detect the position and pressure of the stylus.

5. **Connection to Computer**: Digitizers are typically connected to a computer either via USB or wirelessly using Bluetooth or similar technology. The digitizer sends the data captured from the stylus movements to the computer, where it can be processed by software applications such as drawing programs, graphic design software, or handwriting recognition programs.

6. **Applications**: Digitizers are widely used by artists, designers, engineers, and anyone else who needs precise input for digital drawing, writing, or annotation tasks. They are commonly used for tasks such as graphic design, digital art creation, CAD (Computer-Aided Design), handwriting recognition, and electronic signature capture.

Electronic card-based devices

Electronic card-based input devices, also known as card readers or card scanners, are used to input data from physical cards into a computer system. These devices can read various types of cards, including credit cards, debit cards, identification cards, and smart cards. Here's a breakdown of the types of electronic card-based input devices:

1. **Magnetic Stripe Readers**: These devices read data encoded on the magnetic stripe of cards. Magnetic stripe cards are commonly used for credit and debit cards. The reader contains a magnetic head that reads the magnetic fields on the card, translating the encoded data into a format that can be processed by the computer.

2. **Chip Card Readers**: Also known as smart card readers or EMV (Europay, Mastercard, Visa) readers, these devices read data stored on integrated circuit chips embedded in the cards. Chip cards offer enhanced security compared to magnetic stripe cards because they generate dynamic authentication codes for each transaction. Chip card readers typically have slots or contact points where the card is inserted or tapped to establish communication with the chip.

3. **Barcode Readers**: Barcode readers, also called barcode scanners, can read data encoded in the form of a barcode printed on cards. The reader emits light onto the barcode, which reflects back to the reader's sensor. The sensor interprets the pattern of light and dark bars to decode the information encoded in the barcode. Barcodes are commonly used on identification cards, membership cards, and loyalty cards.

4. **RFID Readers**: RFID (Radio-Frequency Identification) readers can wirelessly read data stored on RFID tags embedded in cards. RFID technology uses radio waves to communicate between the reader and the tag. When a card with an RFID tag is brought into proximity with the reader, the reader emits radio waves that power the tag and read its data. RFID technology is used in various applications, including access control systems, public transportation cards, and inventory tracking.

5. **OCR (Optical Character Recognition) Readers**: OCR readers are capable of reading text printed on cards using optical character recognition technology. These devices capture an image of the text on the card and then analyze it to extract the alphanumeric characters. OCR readers are commonly used for reading information from identification cards, passports, and driver's licenses.

Each type of electronic card-based input device has its own advantages and applications, depending on the specific requirements of the task at hand. They play a crucial role in facilitating secure and efficient data input in various industries, including finance, healthcare, transportation, and retail.

Speech recognition devices

Speech recognition input devices, also known as speech-to-text or voice recognition systems, allow users to input data into a computer or device by speaking instead of typing or using other manual input methods. These systems use sophisticated algorithms and technologies to analyze spoken language and convert it into text that can be processed by a computer. Here's an overview of speech recognition input devices:

1. **Microphones**: The primary hardware component of speech recognition input devices is the microphone. Microphones capture the user's spoken words and convert them into electrical signals that can be processed by the speech recognition software.

2. **Speech Recognition Software**: The software component of speech recognition input devices processes the audio input from the microphone and converts it into text. This software utilizes complex algorithms, machine learning models, and linguistic databases to recognize and interpret spoken language accurately.

3. **Training and Adaptation**: Many speech recognition systems allow users to train the software to recognize their voice more accurately over time. This may involve reading aloud a set of predefined phrases or passages to help the system learn the user's speech patterns and nuances. Additionally, some systems adapt to the user's voice and speech patterns automatically as they use the system more frequently.

4. **Natural Language Processing (NLP)**: Speech recognition input devices often incorporate NLP techniques to understand not only the words spoken but also the context and meaning behind them. This enables more accurate transcription and allows the system to interpret commands, questions, and other linguistic nuances.

5. **Real-Time Feedback**: Some speech recognition input devices provide real-time feedback to the user as they speak, such as displaying the recognized text on a screen or providing auditory feedback through synthesized speech. This can help users correct any misunderstandings or errors in real-time.

6. **Integration with Applications**: Speech recognition input devices are commonly integrated with various software applications and operating systems, allowing users to dictate text directly into word processors, email clients, text messaging apps, and other productivity tools. They are also used in virtual assistants and smart speakers to perform tasks, answer questions, and control connected devices using voice commands.

7. **Accessibility**: Speech recognition input devices play a crucial role in accessibility by providing an alternative input method for individuals with physical disabilities or conditions that make typing difficult or impossible. They allow users to interact with computers and devices using only their voice, improving accessibility and inclusivity.

Overall, speech recognition input devices offer a convenient, hands-free way to input data and interact with computers and devices, and they continue to improve in accuracy and functionality thanks to advances in technology and machine learning.

Vision based devices

Vision-based input devices utilize cameras and image processing algorithms to interpret visual information and enable interaction with computers or devices. These devices can detect and track objects, gestures, facial expressions, and other visual cues, allowing users to control software applications, navigate interfaces, and interact with virtual environments. Here are some examples of vision-based input devices:

1. **Webcams and RGB Cameras**: Webcams and RGB (Red, Green, Blue) cameras capture images or video of the user and their surroundings. These cameras can be used for various vision-based applications, including video conferencing, facial recognition, and augmented reality.

2. **Depth Cameras**: Depth cameras, such as Microsoft's Kinect or Intel's RealSense cameras, capture not only color images but also depth information. This allows them to create 3D representations of the scene and detect the distance of objects from the camera. Depth cameras are commonly used for motion tracking, gesture recognition, and virtual reality applications.

3. **Gesture Recognition Systems**: Gesture recognition systems use cameras to detect and interpret hand and body movements made by the user. These systems can recognize specific gestures or movements and translate them into commands or actions in software applications. Gesture recognition technology is used in gaming consoles, interactive kiosks, and virtual reality systems.

4. **Eye-Tracking Systems**: Eye-tracking systems use cameras to Monitor the movement and gaze of the user's eyes. By tracking the direction of the user's gaze, these systems can determine what the user is looking at on the screen and infer their level of attention or interest. Eye-tracking technology is used in research, usability testing, and assistive technology for individuals with disabilities.

5. **Facial Recognition Systems**: Facial recognition systems analyze images or video footage of human faces to identify individuals based on their unique facial features. These systems can be used for security applications, access control, and personalized user experiences in devices such as smartphones and tablets.
6. **Object Detection and Tracking Systems**: Object detection and tracking systems use computer vision algorithms to identify and track specific objects or patterns within a scene. These systems can be used for various applications, including surveillance, robotics, and augmented reality.
7. **Machine Vision Systems**: Machine vision systems employ cameras and image processing algorithms to automate visual inspection and quality control processes in manufacturing and industrial environments. These systems can detect defects, measure dimensions, and perform other tasks that require visual analysis.

Vision-based input devices offer a wide range of capabilities for interacting with computers and devices, from simple gesture control to sophisticated facial recognition and machine vision applications. As computer vision technology continues to advance, these devices are becoming increasingly prevalent in consumer electronics, healthcare, automotive, and other industries.

Output Devices

Output devices are electromechanical devices that accept data from a computer and translate them into a form which is understandable by the outside word or user. The various output devices are given below:

1. Monitor
2. Printers
3. Plotters
4. Projector
5. Voice response system

Monitors

Monitors are output devices which produce soft -copy output. They generate output on a TV like screen. The keyboard and the Monitor together form a Video Display Terminal (VDT)and serve as a input and output device. The word terminal means the end of the communication path. The various types of the Monitors are:

a. Computers are now used in almost every office. There are mainly two types of computer Monitors: Liquid Crystal Display (LCD) Monitors and Cathode Ray Tube (CRT) Monitors.

Input and Output

Figure 2.10: *A LCD Monitor*

Figure 2.11: *A CRT Monitor*

b. Which type of Monitors do you think will consume less energy? LCD Monitors consume less energy than CRT Monitors. Typically, an LCD Monitor uses only about one third of the power of an equivalent size CRT Monitor.

c. CRT Monitors produce images using the same technology as an ordinary television. A CRT Monitor consists of an electron gun which emits a beam of electrons to the screen (Figure. 2.12). When the electron beam strikes the coating of phosphor dots on the screen, the energy of the electrons is transferred to the phosphor and a dot of red, green or blue light is produced. There are devices in a CRT Monitor to change the strength of the electron beam, and to control the electron beam to sweep across the whole area of the screen very rapidly. By changing the strength of the electron beam striking at different positions on the screen, dots of different colours and brightness are produced on the screen, and these dots combine to form the colour image seen on a CRT Monitor.

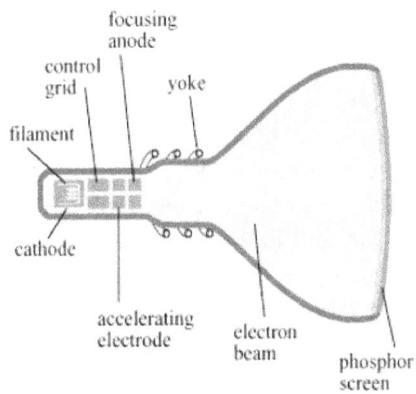

Figure 2.12: *The internal structure of a CRT monitor*

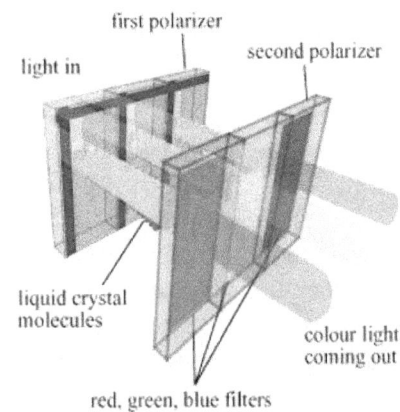

Figure 2.13: *The display unit of an LCD monitor*

d. LCD Monitors work in a very different way. An LCD Monitor uses a kind of material known as liquid crystal. By applying an electrical voltage on a liquid crystal and using special devices known as polarizers, one can control the amount of light that passes through the liquid crystal. An LCD Monitor actually consists of many display units formed by sandwiching liquid crystal between two polarizers (Figure 2.13). These units are illuminated by a light source from behind. Electrical signals are applied to each display unit to control its degree of transparency to the light and thus the brightness of the display unit. The red, green and blue filters placed on the display units give colour to the light coming out. By combining a large number of display units of different brightness and colours, an image is created on the screen.

LCD Monitors use much less energy than CRT Monitors as LCD Monitors do not have to produce an electron beam. Most of the energy supplied to an LCD Monitor is used by fluorescent tubes which form the light source of the LCD display units. Energy efficient use of lighting. There are two main ways to save energy used for lighting. One is to use more energy efficient lighting. The other is to reduce the operating time of the lighting.

Figure 2.14: *The different appearance of T12 (top), T8 and T5 (bottom) fluorescent lamps. Note that the T5 lamp is shorter and thinner (Image courtesy of EMSD)*

Fluorescent lamps are so far the most popular type of lamp used in offices. The most common type of fluorescent lamp is tubular and linear in shape. There are three generations of linear tubular fluorescent lamps: the 1st generation T12 lamps with a diameter of 38 mm, the 2nd generation T8 lamps with a diameter of 26 mm and the 3rd generation T5 lamps with a diameter of 16 mm. T5 lamps are more energy efficient than T8 or T12 lamps. The energy used in lighting systems can also be reduced by using automatic controls. For example, infrared or ultrasonic motion sensors are used to detect the presence of people and automatically turn lights on or off accordingly.

Indirect ways of Saving Energy

The various ways mentioned above can directly save energy in offices. There are also many indirect ways of saving energy. In an office environment, the consumption of paper and stationery can be high. Since the production of paper and stationery requires energy and natural resources, reducing their use can save energy and natural resources simultaneously. For example, we can reduce the use of paper by using both sides of a piece of paper, using emails instead of memos and faxes, and recycling used paper.

    a.   LCD (Liquid Crystal Diode) Monitors

    b.   TFT Monitors

    c.   LED (Light Emitting Diode) Monitors

    d.   Plasama

Printers

Printers are output devices which produce hard copy output. The various types of the printers are given below:

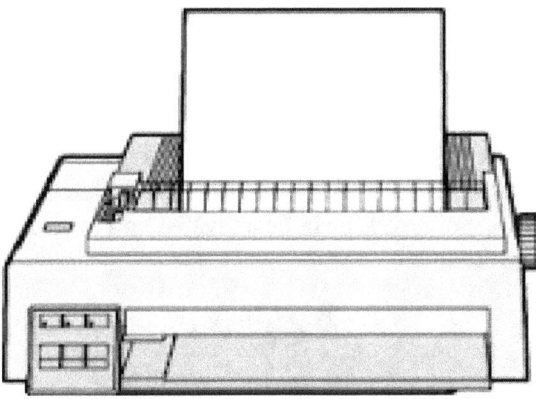

Figure 2.15: *A dot matrix printer*

    Dot Matrix Printers: Dot matrix printers are character printers. i.e. they print one character at a time. They can print graphs, images and characters as a pattern of dot. The printing head (moves left to right and vice versa) of the dot matrix printer contains a set of pins that can be activated independently and strike against an inked ribbon to form patterns of dots on the papers. Suppose if we want to display a character A, a set of pins will be activated in the form of A and they strike against an inked ribbon, resulting in a pattern of dots in the form of A printed on the paper.

To increase the speed of printing, the printing head can move from right to left and left to right. This type of printing is called bidirectional *printing*. Figure 2.15 shows a dot matrix printer.

Advantages

1. They can print a character of any shape and size.
2. They have the ability to print images and graphs.
3. They are impact printers i.e. they print by hammering the pins on the inked ribbon to leave ink impressions on a paper.
4. Because of their impact nature, they produce multiple copies by using carbon paper.
5. They are cheap in terms of initial cost and cost of operation.

Disadvantages

1. They are noisy as compared to non- impact printers.
2. Dot matrix printers are slow with printing speed 30 to 600 characters per second.
3. Printing Quality is also not so good.

Inkjet Printer: Inkjet printers are also character printers and they print characters and images by spraying small drops of ink on a paper. The printing head contains nearly 64 independent nozzles of height 7mm, that can be heated up selectively in a few microseconds by an integrated circuit resistor. When the resistor heats up, the ink near the resistor vaporizes and is ejected through the nozzle making a pattern on the paper placed in front of the print head. Therefore, to print a character a set of nozzles will be activated and heated up by the circuit as the head moves horizontally.

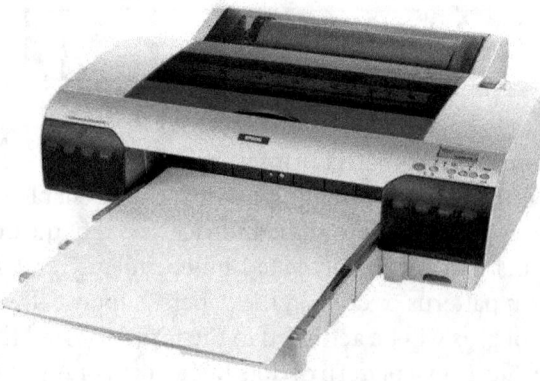

Figure 2.16: *Shows a Inkjet printer*

Advantages

1. It has high quality output as compared to the dot matrix printer.
2. High resolution (around 360 dots per inch) as compared to the dot matrix printer.
3. They can print characters, images and graphics of any shape and sizes like a dot matrix printer.
4. Noise free printers because of its non-impact nature.

Disadvantages

1. Cannot produce multiple copies like dot matrix printers because they are non-impact in nature.
2. They are slower than dot matrix printers and have printing speeds 40 to 300 characters per seconds.

Note: *A colour inkjet printer usually comes with two ink cartridges- black and tri colour (red, blue, yellow). To get any desired colours, an appropriate amount of colours (red, blue, yellow) is mixed with the black colour.*

Drum Printer: Drum printers are line printers. they print the entire line at a time. Drum printer consists of a solid cylindrical drum with a set of characters are printed on its surface in the form of bands. The drum printer is shown in Figure 2.17. The number of bands is equal to the total number of characters in a line.

Drum printer has a set of hammers, one opposite each band. The total number of hammers is equal to the total number of bands on the drum which is equal to the total number of printing positions. Ink ribbon and the paper is placed between the hammer and the drum. To print a line, the drum rotates at high speed towards the printing hammers and a character is printed at a desired printing position by activating the appropriate hammer when the character printed on the band at the print position passes below it. Here first character of a line is printed by the first hammer, second character is printed by Second hammer and so on.

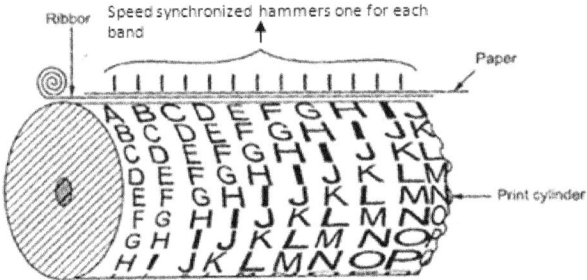

Figure 2.17: *Mechanism of drum printer*

Figure 2.18: *A drum printer*

Advantages

1. Are impact printers and produce multiple copies by using carbon copies.
2. Fast printers as compared with dot and inkjet printers, with printing speeds approximately 300 to 2000 lines per minute.

Disadvantages

1. Drum printers are expensive.
2. They make less noise as compared to dot matrix printers.
3. Don't have the ability to print characters, images and graphs of different shapes and sizes.
4. It is difficult to remove the drum in case of any damage.

Note: *Not all the characters in a line are printed at same time, but the time required to print an entire line is so fast that it appears as if one line is printed at a time.*

Chain/ Belt /Band Printer: Chain printers are line printers like drum printers. It consists of a metallic chain/ band on which a set of possible supported characters is printed or imposed. In order to increase the printing speed the set of characters is printed on a chain many times so that the frequency of each character is increased.

The printer has a set of hammers positioned in front of the chain in a manner that an inked ribbon and paper can be placed between the hammers and chain/band. Thus total number of hammers is equal to the total number of printing positions i.e. number of characters in a line as shown n Figure 2.19.

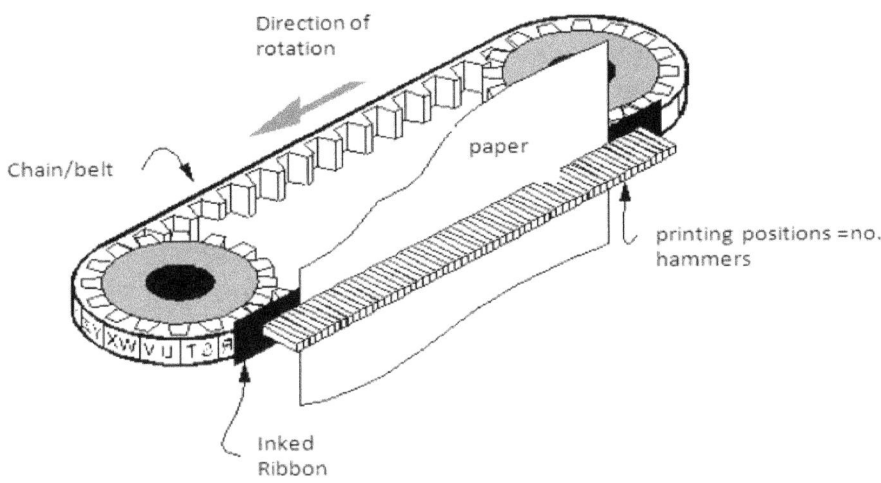

Figure 2.19: *Printing mechanism for band printer*

To print a character the belt rotates at a high speed towards the printing head. A character is printed at a desired print position by activating the appropriate hammer when the character printed on the chain passes below it. Unlike the drum printer, it is not necessary to wait for the chain to make a complete revolution to print the character positioned last on the drum because the characters are repeated several times.

Advantages

1. It is fast as compared to drum printers.
2. Chain can be replaced easily in case of any damaged.
3. Printing speeds of the chain are 400- 3000 lines per minute.
4. They make less noise as compared to drum printers.
5. Can produce multiple copies by using carbon paper.

Disadvantages

1. They are Noisy as compared to the laser printer.
2. Slow as compared to the laser printer.
3. Don't have the ability to print characters, images and graphs of different shapes and sizes.

Laser Printer

From the name itself we can say that this printer is working a laser principle and it is a page printer i.e. it prints one page at a time. This printer has four components:

a. A source of laser beam
b. Multi Sided mirror
c. photoconductive drum
d. Tonner (ink particles)

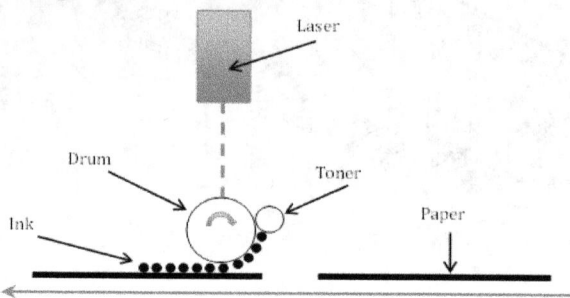

Figure 2.20: *Mechanism of laser printer.*

Figure 2.21: *A laser printer*

To print a page, the laser beam is focused on a photoconductive drum through a spinning multi sided mirror to create a pattern of a printed page, image a graph on drum's surface. Since the drum is photoconductive, a difference in electric charge is created on those parts of the drum surface that are exposed to the laser beam. As a result, the tonner, having oppositely charged ink particles, sticks to the drum in the places where the laser beam has charged the drum's surface. The toner is then fused permanently on the paper with heat and pressure to generate the printed output. Printing mechanism of the laser printer is shown in Figure 2.20.

Advantages

1. Output quality of a laser printer is very high.
2. Their resolution is more than 2000 *dpi*.

3. Can print characters, images and graphs of any shapes and sizes.
4. Printing speeds are more than 20 pages per minute.

Disadvantages
1. Laser printers are more expensive as compared to other printers.
2. Cannot produce multiple copies because they are non- impact printers.

Plotters

Plotters are the output devices which are used in applications like, design the architectural plan of a building, design the mechanical components of an air crafts or car etc Such applications require high quality output on large sheets. Therefore, the printers till now discussed above cannot be used in such types of applications. In short, we can say that plotters are the output devices for architects, engineer's city planners etc. to generate high quality hard-output of different sizes. There are two types of plotters

a. Drum plotter
b. Flatbed Plotter

Drum Plotter: In this type of plotter, a paper on which design is to be made is placed over the drum and there is a penholder mounted perpendicular to the drum's surface. Drum can move in vertical motion and pens can move in horizontal motion. Both drum and pens are program controllable and print characters, images and graphs of different shapes and sizes. Drum plotters are shown in Figure 2.22.

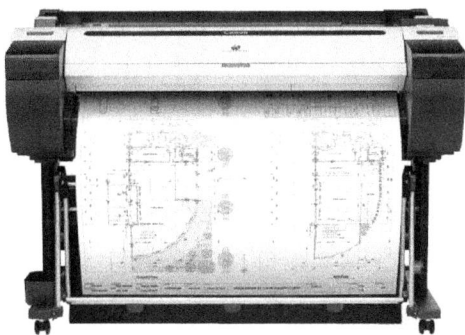

Figure 2.22: *A drum plotter.*

Flatbed Plotter: In this type of plotter, a paper on which design is to be made, is placed on a rectangular flatbed table. Here flatbed table is fixed and all kinds of motions i.e. horizontal and vertical will be done by pens only. Pens having ink of different colours, are program controllable and print characters, images and graphs of different shapes and sizes. The size of the output of these plotters is depend upon the size of drum and flatbed table which can be 2050 ft. Flatbed plotters are shown in Figure 2.23.

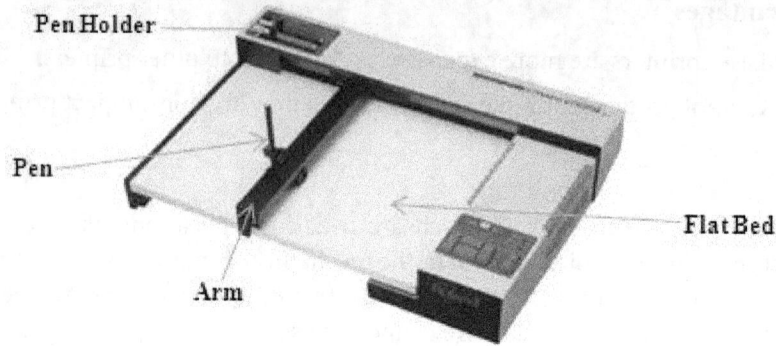

Figure 2.23: *A flatbed Scanner*

Projector

Projector is an output device which is used to project soft information from a computer on a screen so that multiple people can view simultaneously. There are two ways to project the information:

a. Overhead Projector (OHP)

b. Screen Image Projector

Overhead Projector: In earlier, the information which is to be projected, is first written on a special type of transparent sheet called Overhead Printer Sheets (OHP Sheets) be it a special type of pen called OHP pen or print the information on the OHP sheet first. Place the Printed or written OHP sheet over the transparent screen of the overhead projector and the same information can be seen on the wall or screen by a number of people simultaneously. The Overhead Projector and its components are shown in Figure 2.24.

Figure 2.24: *Overhead Projector along with its components*

Image Screen Projector: Overhead Projector does not provide the facility to project the soft information directly from computer on a screen. Therefore, such a shortcoming is overcome by a projector called image screen projector where soft information stored in a computer can be projected directly on a screen. Image Screen projectors are less in weight and are easy to carry from one place to another. They can be used with a notebook, laptop, PC etc. The Image Screen Projector is shown in Figure 2.25.

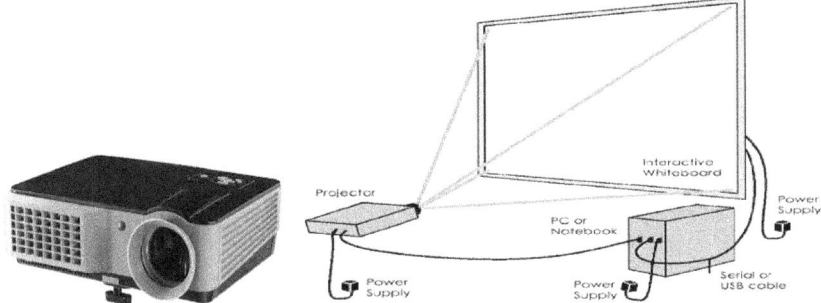

Figure 2.25: *The Image Screen Projector*

Voice Response Systems

Voice response system allows a computer to talk to a user, which is apposite of speech recognition system, where a user is allowed to talk to a computer. There are two types of voice response system:

a. Voice Reproduction System

b. Speech Synthesizer

Voice Reproduction System: A voice reproduction system produces audio output by selecting an appropriate output from pre-recorded responses. These pre-recorded responses are the voices of human beings or some other type of sound. These responses are analog in nature, converted into digital form and stored in memory permanently. When an audio response is to generate, the pre-recoded responses are selected from memory, convert it from digital to analog signal back and route it to a speaker to produce the audio output. Voice reproduction system is shown in Figure 2.26.

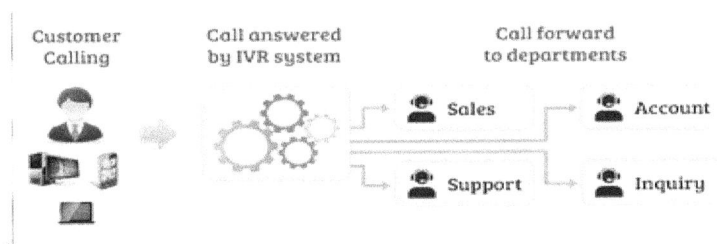

Figure 2.26: *IVR (Voice Response System) voice reproduction system*

Some important points about voice reproduction system are:

a. Guiding the user how to operate the computer system. For example, Banks used Voice reproduction systems in ATMs to guide the customers while withdrawing the cash.
b. Used in video games and talking alarm clocks.
c. Used in telecom companies as an IVR (Voice Response System).

Speech Synthesizer: This device converts the text information into spoken sentences. Words and sentences can be produced by combining the basic units of sounds called *phonemes*. The speech synthesizer system is shown in Figure 2.27.

Figure 2.27: *Speech synthesizer system*

Some important points about speech Synthesizer are:

a. They can be used to alert a blind person about the latest information published in newspapers or books. Books or newspapers are scanned, translated to text by an OCR and finally, feed the text to speech synthesizer.
b. They are helpful to those who are not able to speak by typing the text, finally, the Speech synthesizer converts it into spoken voice.

Chapter 3
Storage Devices

What is secondary storage memory? Why do we require such memory in a computer?

Secondary storage memory or Auxiliary memory is a memory which is non-(cheap) volatile in nature, low cost per bit stored, slower as compared to RAM (Random Access Memory), and used as a backup memory for large amount of data. Apart from RAM in a computer, we required secondary memory for the following reasons:

Limited Capacity of RAM: As we know the size of the primary memory is limited, and the size of the data is increasing almost double after every two years. Thus we required a memory which can store trillions of records in a computer for future reference.

Volatile nature of RAM: Because of the volatile nature of the RAM, the data stored in RAM get lost when power goes off, but a computer system needs to store the data permanently for many months or even years.

The various secondary storage devices are discussed as follows:

Before studying different secondary devices one by one, we must know the various mechanisms of accessing the information from the secondary storage devices. There are two mechanisms which are used to access the information from the secondary storage devices:

a. Sequential access or serial access
b. Random access or direct access

Sequential Access: A sequential access device is one, on which the desired information can be retrieved in the same order in which it is stored **i.e.** if there are 12 records (songs) stored in a device, and we want to listen to the 5th record. This 5th record will be available to the listener only after processing all the records come before 5th record. Such types of devices are used in the applications such as preparation of monthly pay slips, electricity bills etc.

Note: Such type of devices doesn't use any addressing mechanism to store and retrieve the data from the device.

Random Access or Direct Access: A random access device is one on which the desired information can be retrieved or access in a more direct or immediate manner i.e. if there are 12 records (songs) stored in a device, and we want to listen 5th record. There is no need to process all the records before this record which can create frustration to the listener. The desired can be accessed directly without long delay. Such devices are used in banking, railways reservation systems. etc Many books explain there is no difference between a random access and direct access, but few authors have different opinion about these terms, and the define these terms as follows:

Direct Access: Where the access time to access a particular information on a disk depends upon the physical location of the information on the disk i.e. there is no constant access time to different information (records) on the disk. This type of mechanism is found in disk *Random access,* Where the access time to access a particular information on a disk do not depends upon the physical location of the information on the disk i.e. there is a constant access time to different information (records) on the disk such type of mechanism is found in RAM or primary memory.

Note: Such type of devices uses addressing mechanisms to store and retrieve the data from the device.

Magnetic Tape

In the early days of computer technology, magnetic tape was one of the few ways to store data. Magnetic tape consists of a thin plastic strip with a magnetic coating that can store data. Early systems from the 1950s to the 1970s used 10.5-inch magnetic tape, while home computers of the early 1980s used audio cassette tapes to store programs and data. Today, magnetic tape is still widely used for backing up data on network servers and individual computers.

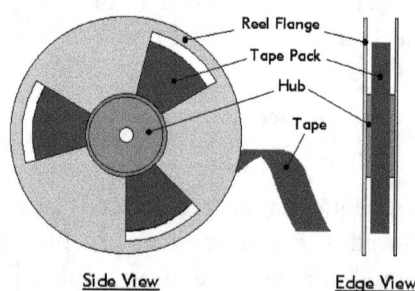

Figure 3.1: *A magnetic tape with different views*

Magnetic tape is a relatively inexpensive form of removable storage, especially suitable for backing up data. For data that needs to be accessed frequently, it is less useful as it is a sequential access medium. You must move the tape back and forth to find the data you need. In other words, to go from file 1 to file 20, you have to go through files 2 through 19. This is in contrast to direct-access media, such as floppy disks, where you can move the head directly to the location of the data you want to access without passing through all the other files in sequence. The structure of the magnetci tape is shown in Figure 3.1.

Magnetic Disk

Magnetic disk is a direct access secondary storage device which is made up of metal or plastic circular plate/platter. This circular plate is coated on both sides with a recording material such as iron oxide which can be magnetized. To store data "1", the coated surfaces of the disk is magnetized and results in an invisible spot on the disk's surface. The binary "0" can be recorded as a non-magnetized spot. The standard binary code used for data recording is EBCDIC (Extended Binary Coded Decimal Interchange Code which supports 28 (256) different characters. Magnetic disks can be erased and reused.

Storage Organisation

The disk surface is divided into concentric circles called *tracks*. These tracks are numbered from outermost to innermost i.e. the number zero is assigned to the outermost track and number *n* is assigned to the innermost track. Further each track is divided into pie-shaped segments, and each of these segments of a track is called *sector*. Sectors can be combined to make clusters as shown in Figure 3.2.

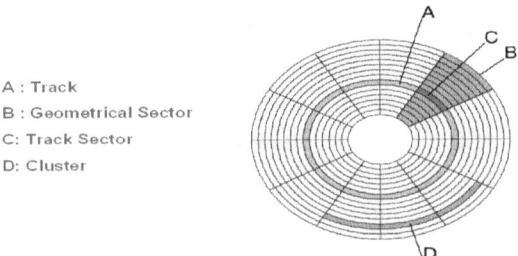

A : Track
B : Geometrical Sector
C: Track Sector
D: Cluster

Figure 3.2: *Sector and cluster Architecture of hard disk*

A sector is the smallest unit with which any disk drive works and its capacity is 512 bytes (number not fixed). It means disk drives are designed to read and write a complete sector at a time i.e. if we want to change only one byte out of 512 bytes in a given sector, it rewrites the entire sector. To *read* a record on a disk, the record's disk address (physical location) must be given, which consists of sector number, track number and surface number (if data is recorded on both sides of a disk).

Disk Pack In this case, a set of magnetic disks is fixed to a spindle, one below the other and forms the disk pack as shown in Figure 3.3.

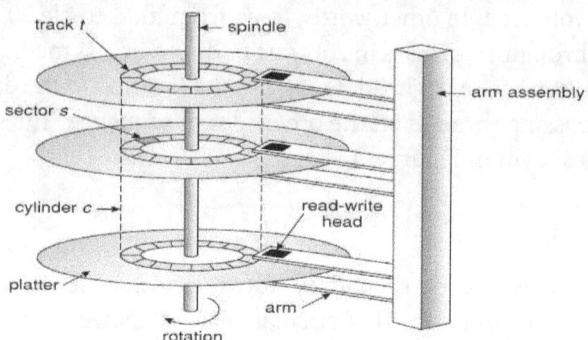

Figure 3.3: *Pack of magnetic disks*

From the above Figure we can conclude that the upper surface of top most disk and lower surface of the last/bottommost disk is not used, because these surfaces may get scratched easily. If we want to read the data from 4th track of disk 2nd, the arm access assembly moves from right to left, and all the read/write heads will be positioned on 4th track of all the disks of the pack, but data will be read out from disk 2nd only.

For faster access of data, a concept called *cylinder* is used for data organisation on disk packs. A *cylinder* is a set of corresponding tracks on all the recording surfaces of a disk pack together form a cylinder. If there are 70 tracks on each disk of a pack, there can be a maximum of 70 cylinders in a disk pack. The addressing scheme used here is called *CHS (Cylinder Head Sector) or Disk Geometry* addressing.

Storage Capacity of a disk = no. of recording surfaces no. of tracks per surface no. of sectors per track no. of bytes per sector.

In fact, the earliest hard disks did have their heads in contact with the media, and this design was changed due to the wear that contact caused. Modern drive heads float over the surface of the disk and do all of their work without ever physically touching the platters they are magnetizing. The amount of space between the heads and the platters is called the *floating height* or *flying height*. It is also sometimes called the *head gap*, and some hard disk manufacturers refer to the heads as riding on an "air bearing" and the whole process is shown in figure 3.4.

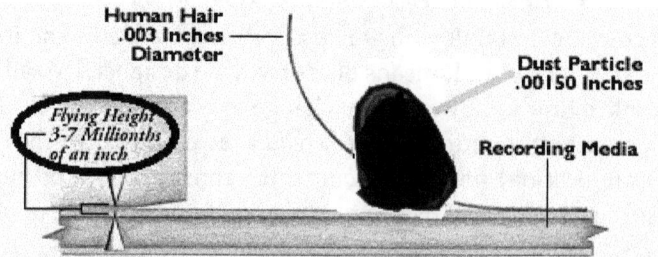

Figure 3.4: *Flying heights significantly lower than 3-7 millionths of an inch*

The distance from the platters to the heads is a specific design parameter that is tightly controlled by the engineers that create the drive. If the height is too great, the heads can't properly read and write the platter. If it is too small, there is an increased chance of a head crash. Thus, a *head crash*, in which the head touches the disk, destroys the data stored in the area of the crash and can destroy a read/write head as well. A modern hard disk has a floating height of an amazing 0.5 microinches. A human hair has a thickness of over 2,000 microinches.

Access Time

Access time is the total time it takes the computer to process a data request from the processor and then retrieve the required data from a storage device. Disk access time depends on three parameters:

a. Seek Time
b. Latency
c. Transfer rate

Seek Time: Seek Time is defined as the amount of time taken by a hard drive's read/write head to find the physical location (desired track) of a piece of data on the disk.

Latency: This is also called rotational waiting time i.e. the time required to spin the desired sector under the head is called latency. It is easily calculated from the spindle speed, being the time for half a rotation. A drive's average access time is the interval between the time a request for data is made by the system and the time the data is available from the drive. Access time includes the actual seek time, rotational latency, and command processing overhead time.

Transfer Rate: The disk transfer rate or called media rate is the speed at which data is transferred to and from the disk media i.e. disk platter and is a function of the recording frequency. It is generally described in megabytes per second (Mbps). Modern hard disks have an increasing range of disk transfer rates from the inner diameter to the outer diameter of the disk. This is called a zoned recording technique. The key media recording parameters relating to density per platter are Tracks Per Inch (TPI) and Bits Per Inch (BPI). A track is a circular ring around the disk. TPI is the number of these tracks that can fit in a given area (inch). BPI defines how many bits can be written onto one inch of a track on a disk surface.

By late 2001 the fastest high-performance drives were capable of an average latency of less than 3ms, an average seek time of between 4 and 7ms and maximum data transfer rates in the region of 50 and 60MBps for EIDE and SCSI-based drives respectively. Note the degree to which these maximum DTRs are below the bandwidths of the current versions of the drive's interfaces – Ultra ATA/100 and Ultra SCSI 160 – which are rated at 100MBps and 160MBps respectively.

Note: If a disk has 100 tracks and 10 sectors per tracks, then it has 1000 (100*10) sectors and 10 Geometric sectors.

Optical Disk

Optical Disk is also a secondary storage device with high storage capacity but slow random access as compared to magnetic tape and disk in a limited space. The random access is slow because the sectors are not at the same distance in a given track from the centre of the disk, as in the case of magnetic disk. An optical disk is a rotating disk, similar to the magnetic disk and its surface is coated with a high reflective material like pure aluminium and gold. To store and delete the data it uses laser beams and hence called laser disk or optical disk.

Storage Organisation

Instead of several concentric circles (tracks), an optical disk has one long track as shown in Figure 3.5 starting at the outer edge and spiralling inward to the centre and is ideal for reading large blocks of sequential data like video and audio.

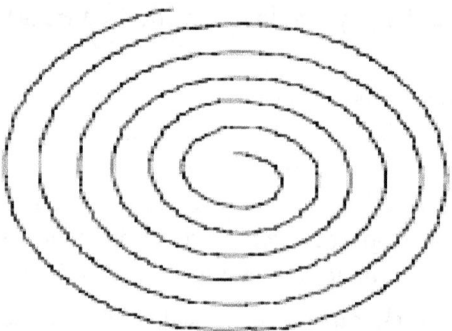

Figure 3.5: *Tack pattern on optical disk*

Difference between Magnetic disk and Optical Disk

Magnetic Disk	Optical Disk
Track pattern is concentric circles It has equal-length sectors regardless of the position of a sector from the centre.	Track pattern is spiral It has sectors of varying length, at the centre sectors are smaller than those that are away from the centre.
Density of the data is not uniform on the magnetic disk i.e. data is dense at the centre.	Density of the data is uniform on the magnetic disk.
Drive mechanism is simple because the rotation speed of the disk is constant while reading/writing the data from centre to outward. Storage capacity is less.	It has a complex driving mechanism because the rotation speed of the disk must vary inversely with the radius. More storage capacity.
It is fast.	It is slow.
Examples: Hard disk, floppy disk, disk pack etc.	CD-ROM, DVD, WORM etc.

Storage Capacity=No. of sectors no. of bytes per sector.

Access Mechanism

As we know optical disk uses laser technology to store the data on the disk. It uses two laser beams, one (high intensity) for recording the data another (lesser intensity) for reading the data. The access mechanism is shown in Figure 3.6.

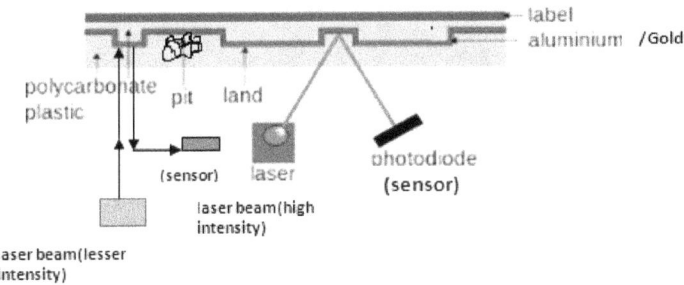

Figure 3.6: *The access mechanism*

To write data, a laser beam is turned ON and OFF at a varying rate due to which tiny pits are burnt into the metal coating of the disk surface along its tracks. To read data, the less powerful laser beam is focused on the disk surface and this beam is strongly reflected by the coated surface called land and weakly reflected by the burnt surface called pit, producing patterns of ON and OFF reflections that are converted into electronic signals of binary 1s and 0s by a sensor.

Memory Storage Devices

Flash Drive: (Pen Drive)

Pen drive is a compact device of the size of pen with some added features such in-build camera, MP3/WMA/FM Radio etc for music. It makes it easy to transport data from one device to another. It plugs into a USB (Universal Serial Bus) port of a laptop, TV or computer and after detecting it, we can read ,write, delete, copy and move the data from one device to another. The biggest advantage of the pen drive is that it does not require any battery, cable and software, and is compatible with most PCs desktop and laptop computers with USB2.0 port. Because of movable parts of the hard disk, it makes sounds while reading or writing the data from the disk, but pen drive is Transistor based semiconductor memory, which operates electronically without any kind of noise. A flash memory is non-volatile, EEPROM (Electrically Erased Programmable Read Only Memory) chip and its life is more than a decade. Their available storage capacities are 1 GB, 2 GB, 4 GB, 8 GB, 16 GB, 32 GB, 64 GB.

How it Stores the Data: There are two types of flash memory:

a. *NAND Flash:* This type of memory is made up of NAND gates and these gates are arranged in serial fashion with each other. They are cheaper than NOR gate but less flexible as compared to NOR gate and now a day's majority of our flash drives use NAND gates to store the data.

b. *NOR Flash:* This type of memory is made up of NOR gates and these gates are arranged in parallel fashion with each other. They are more flexible and higher in cost.

- **Floating Gate:** Floating gate is the place where all our data is recorded and it floats above the "p-type silicon substrate". The floating gate is isolated from the substrate by a thin oxide layer of about 10 nm thick. This layer is needed to enable the floating gate layer to store charge or data.
- **Control Gate:** It controls the flow of charges between the "source" and the "Drain".

Save and Delete the Data

To save the data, a voltage is applied to the control gate which then sends electrons from source to drain. While flowing, the electrons gain energy to penetrate the oxide layer and gets stored in the floating gate, forms the negative charge on the floating gate. Due to this protective layer of oxide this charge will not come out and be stored permanently on the floating gate even if the power goes off, hence data is stored.

The transistors in flash memory are like MOSFETs (Metal Oxide Seminconductor Field Effect Transistor) only they have two gates on top instead of one.

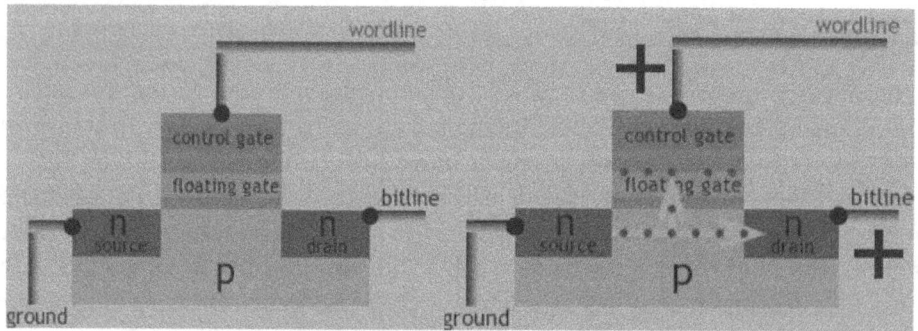

Figure 3.7: *Storing of charge on floating gate*

Both the source and the drain regions are rich in electrons (because they're made of n-type silicon), but electrons cannot flow from source to drain because of the electron deficient, p-type material between them. But if we apply a positive

Storage Devices

voltage to the transistor's two contacts, called the bitline and the wordline, electrons get pulled in a rush from source to drain. A few also manage to wriggle through the oxide layer by a process called tunnelling and get stuck on the floating gate. The electrons will stay there indefinitely, even when the positive voltages are removed and whether there is power supplied to the circuit or not. The electrons can be flushed out by putting a negative voltage on the wordline—which repels the electrons back the way they came, clearing the floating gate and making the transistor store a zero again. Another way of Deleting the data on the pen drive is achieved by removing the charge from the floating gate by applying high(positive) voltage to the source. The positive charge on the source makes the negatively charged electrons move from the negative charged floating gate to the source. Thus, the floating gate loses its charge and our data is released.

Advantages

1. Huge amount of data can be stored on the floating gate.
2. Data is non-volatile and can last for years.
3. NAND flash can be erased and rewritten up to 1,000,000 cycles.

Memory Card (MMC /SD)

Multimedia Card (MMC) is a flash memory card standard. Typically, an MMC is used as storage media for a portable device, in a form that can easily be removed for access by a PC. Secure Digital (SD) is a flash (non-volatile) memory card format and is used for storage. MMC and SD cards differ in their physical size, capacity and their usage. Both come in different memory sizes as well. While MMCs can be used in a standard SD card slot, the latter cannot be used in a MMC slot.

	MMC	SD
Capacity	Up to 128 GB, MiCard - theoretical maximum size of 2048 GB (2 TB).	Up to 2GB.
Compatibility	Compatible with MMC as well as SD card slots.	Compatible only with SD host devices.
Types	Reduced-Size Multimedia Card (RS-MMC), dual voltage MMC card (DV-MMC), MMC plus, MMC mobile, MMC micro and MMC secure.	Standard SD, mini SD and micro SD.
What is it?	The Multi Media Card (MMC) is a flash memory card standard.	It is a flash memory card format.
File system	FAT16.	FAT16.
Stands for	Multi Media Card.	Secure Digital card
Developed	It was developed by Siemens AG and SanDisk, and introduced in 1997.	It was developed by Matsushita, SanDisk and Toshiba in 1999.

Use	They are normally used as storage media for portable devices, such as digital cameras, cellular phones, digital audio players and PDAs.	SD card is used as a storage media in the following: Sony PS 3, Wii, GP2X GNU/Linux based portable games console, DAB radios, Global Positioning System receivers, Camcorders, cellular phones, digital audio players, PDAs etc.
Size	MMC, MMC Plus, SecureMMC -24 mm x 32 mm x 1.4 mm, RS-MMC - 24 mm x 18 mm x 1.4 mm, MMCmicro 14 mm × 12 mm × 1.1 mm.	24 mm × 32 mm × 2.1 mm.

SD (Secure Digital) Cards: An **SD card** is a storage device that has many useful features:

- We can add an SD card to a small device, like a mobile phone, to extend the storage space.
- The SD card in our camera fills up with photos and videos, can swap it out for an empty SD card without deleting any files.
- Can save files to an SD card to transfer them between devices or give them to someone else.
- First iteration of secure digital memory cards.
- Released in 1999.
- Provides up to 2GB of storage.

SD cards conform to standards developed and maintained by the Secure Digital Association. Panasonic, SanDisk and Toshiba formed the SD Association in January 2000 for developing and promoting standards for flash-memory storage. SanDisk's technology, already a global leader in flash memory products.

SDHC Memory Card

- Second iteration of secure digital memory cards - HC meaning high capacity.
- Released in 2006.
- Provides up to 64GB of storage.
- Offers increased speeds.

SDXC Memory Card

SDXC Card.

- Third iteration of secure digital memory cards - XC meaning eXtended capacity.
- Released in 2009.
- Provides up to 2TB of storage.
- Offers increased speeds- up to 300MB/s.

Micro SD

MicroSD Card.

- First iteration of the micro format.
- Released in 2005.
- Provides up to 2GB of storage.
- 80% smaller than regular SD memory cards.

Micro SDHC
MicroSDHC Card.

- Second iteration of the micro format.
- Released in 2007.
- Provides up to 32GB of storage.
- 80% smaller than regular SD memory cards.
- Offers increased speeds over microSD.

Eye-Fi
Eye-Fi Memory Card

Eye-Fi cards are a unique type of SD card with Wi-Fi built right into the SD memory card. Eye-Fi allows your photos and videos to be immediately uploaded over the wifi network instantly clearing up space on the memory card for limitless shooting. You can upload not only to your computer but if you're on the road they can be uploaded to your favorite online service, including Flickr, Facebook, snapfish, YouTube, Picasa, etc. Eye-Fi provides a free hotspot access service internationally for eye-fi owners and also permits you to easily add Wi-Fi networks you have access to. Finally, some Eye-Fi cards can utilize the wireless signals to do geolocation allowing it to geotag your photos similar to a GPS (although less accurate but available indoors where GPS is not).

 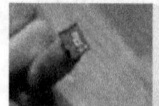   

Micro and mini SD *Micro and SD* *SD and ADHC*

Chapter 4
Operating System

Operating System and its Logical Structure

Operating System also referred as OS is a system software that controls the resources of the computer system to minimize the CPU idle time. The resources of the computer system are: CPU, memory, I/O devices etc. An operating system is also defined as an interface or virtual machine between the user and the computer hardware. The logical structure of a computer system is shown in Figure 4.1.

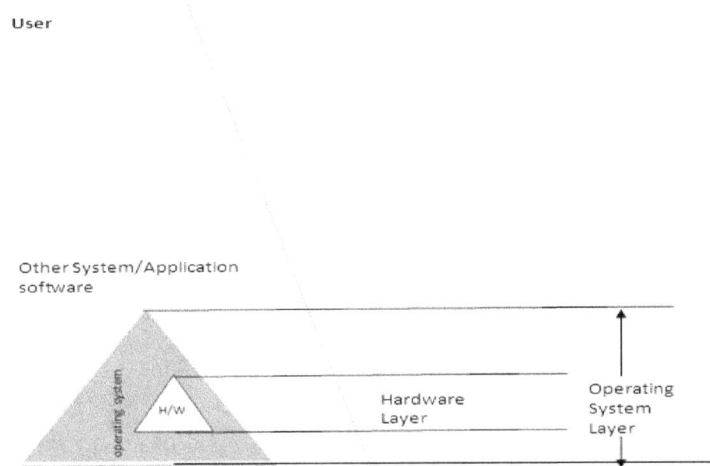

Figure 4.1: *The logical structure of a computer system*

In this Diagram the whole computer system (hardware and software) is divided into four layers:
- a. Hardware Layer
- b. Operating System Layer
- c. Application/Other System Software
- d. User Layer

Hardware Layer: This is the core layer of the computer system which includes the physical components of the system like CPU, memory, I/O unit.

Operating System Layer: This is the first software layer in the computer system. This is first system software layer which is used to control the resources of the system, application software and other system software stored in computer system.

Application/Other System Software Layer: At this layer, all the application software like MS Office package, Adobe Reader, etc. are stored. Apart from application software some other system software like translators, communication software, Utility programs, compilers etc. are stored.

User Layer: This layer is also called outside world layer, where end users view the computer system in the terms of the user interfaces of the application programs.

Objectives of OS

There are two primary objectives of an operating system which are given below:

Makes the computer system easy to handle. By acting as an interface or virtual machine between the user and the computer hardware, it hides the hardware complexity from the user. One of the important characteristics of this virtual machine is that it takes the data of any format from the user, translates it into a form which is understandable by the computer and vice versa.

Controls the resources of the system. Another important objective of the computer system is that it controls the resources of the system. It performs the tasks like, keeping in mind who is using which resource, who is going to release the resource, how many resources are allocated, which one is free etc., and finally controls the sharing of resources among different processes.

Functions/Modules of an OS

The main five different modules and their functions of an operating system are given below:

a. Process Management Module
b. Memory Management Module
c. File Management Module
d. Security Management Module
e. Command Interpretation Management Module

What is a Process?

A program in the execution is called a Process. The process is not the same as a program. A process is more than a program code. A process is an 'active' entity as opposed to a program which is considered to be a 'passive' entity. Attributes held by process include hardware state, memory, CPU etc.

Process State

Processes can be any of the following states:

a. **New:** The process is in the stage of being created.
b. **Ready:** The process has all the resources available that it needs to run, but the CPU is not currently working on this process's instructions.
c. **Running:** The CPU is working on this process's instructions.
d. **Waiting:** The process cannot run at the moment, because it is waiting for some resource to become available or for some event to occur.

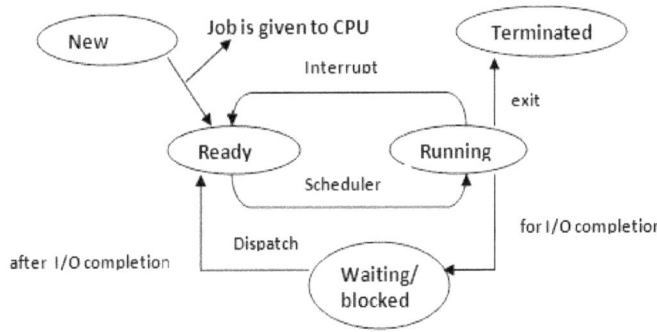

Figure 4.2: *Process states transitions diagram*

Here *scheduler* and the *Dispatcher* are the programs that are used to schedule the programs from *ready* and waiting *queues (Temporary memory)* respectively.

Process Management Module: The various functions of this module are given below:

a. The process management module is responsible for creation and deletion of processes.
b. It performs the scheduling of various resources to different processes requesting them.
c. It is responsible for inter- process communication.
d. It helps in achieving synchronization among processes.

e. Minimize the CPU idle time.

f. It works on the mechanisms like, Uni-programming, Multiprogramming, Time sharing etc.

Memory Management Module: The Various Functions of this Module Are:

a. It allocates the memory to a job before it starts its execution.

b. When a job completes its execution it deallocates the allocated memory space in step a.

c. If memory blocks are distributed at different places in memory, it combines the distributed blocks of memory at one place and are easy to use.

d. It implements the concept of *virtual memory,* in which Programmer feels unlimited memory is available for the execution of a program whose size is huge.

e. It supports Uniprogramming and Multiprogramming memory models.

File Management Module: A *file* is a collection of related information. A file can store bits, byte records (collection of attributes) etc. and this data of a file is called the contents of a file. The various functions of a file are given below:

a. It is responsible for various file operations like deleting a file, creating a file, opening and closing of a file, reading and writing a file etc.

b. It retrieves and stores a file on the disk.

c. It controls the sequential and direct access files.

d. Responsible for file naming.

Security Management Module: The security management module protects the various resources, data and information of a computer system against destruction and unauthorized access. It includes two types of securities i.e. *internal security* and *external security.*

a. ***External Security Module:*** It deals with external threats like flood, earthquake, fire leaking of information by internal personnel etc. The external security issue can be dealt with, by creating the backup copy of the original data, Unauthorized person should not allow it to a computer centre etc.

b. ***Internal Security Module:*** It deals with user *authentication* (access to the internal data is allowed only after user authentication mechanism like checking the password, ATM card number and fingerprints etc.), *Access control* (Where user is restricted to use only the authorized resources), and *cryptography* (Where the actual data is transformed with help of a *key* into a form, which is not understandable by any intruder or hacker, even though he is getting the unauthorized access to the system. Because he or she can understand the meaning of data only if it is decrypted by the same key, which is actually not known by him or her.

Command Interpretation. Command interpretation module stores some set of predefined commands called system calls. If a user wants to give some instructions to a computer to perform some specific tasks, he can instruct the computer only with the help of these commands (system calls). If there is any mistake while typing the command, after interpreting the command, this module display a message that you have entered the wrong command.

There are two types of interfaces which are supported by this module and are given below:

a. **Command Line Interface:** It is a textual interface, where users give commands to the system in the form of text e.g. *"rm source.txt "*. This command in UNIX is used to delete a file having name source.txt from the directory. The problem with this type of interface is that if a job requires more instructions to complete its execution, then the user needs to type all the necessary commands to give instructions which is time consuming and hectic. This problem is overcome by the Job control language (JCL) in which the required instructions are written in JCL, and can be submitted along with the job for execution. The details about JCL are not a part of this book.

b. **GUI (Graphical User Interface):** This type of interface is commonly used nowadays in all types of phones and computers, because they make the system easier to use. Instead of writing the commands in text form, here commands are graphical in nature. Here the screen of the system is full of *icons or images*. If we want to give any kind of instructions to the system, point and draw devices(mouse) are used to select and click the icons so that the system should be instructed. Therefore, this interface is very fast and easy to use as compared to the command line interface.

Types of Operating Systems

In this section we will study various types of operating systems based on the mechanism being used inside the operating system to minimize the CPU idle time. The main mechanisms used are given below:

Following are some of the most widely used types of Operating system.

1. Simple Batch System
2. Multiprogramming Batch System

3. Multiprocessor System
4. Distributed Operating System
5. Real-time Operating System

Manual Loading System

Before batch processing the operating systems were *manual in* nature and are called *manual loading systems*. In this type of operating system, a programmer first writes a program or *job* on a piece of paper and hands it to a computer operator or data entry operator. The data entry operator then writes the data on the tape or card. The data from the card is read out by using a card reader and loaded into the system. The operator executes the job by pressing the appropriate buttons available in the system. After the completion of a job the operator collects the output, and gives it back to the programmer and the same process will be repeated for the next job. Therefore, we can say that these systems are manual loading systems where there is no direct interaction between a user or programmer and the computer. The problem with this mechanism is that the job-to-job transition is not automatic and this increases the CPU idle time.

Batch Processing System

In batch processing system instead of submitting a single job at a time, a batch (group) of jobs is submitted for execution. There is automatic job-to-job transition, which reduces the CPU idle time as compared to manual loading system. Jobs in the batch are controlled by Job Control Language (JCL).

Jobs are executed in following manners:

a. The programmer writes his jobs on cards or tape and submits to the computer operator.
b. Then the computer operator collects the jobs periodically and batch (group) them together and load them together at one time into the input unit.
c. Jobs are batched together by type of languages and requirements.
d. The operator would then give a command to the system to start the execution of the grouped job.
e. Then all jobs are loaded automatically by one -by-one from input unit to memory, and are executed by the system one-by-one without any operator intervention (automatically).
f. A special program, *called Monitor*, manages the execution of each program in the batch.
g. The Monitor is always in the main memory and available for execution.

Disadvantages of this type of system

a.   No (zero) interaction between user and computer.
b.   There is no mechanism to prioritize processes.

Memory model for Batch and manual loading system.

Both batch and manual loading systems support uni-programming memory models where, one program at a time is loaded into the memory, and whole resources of the system are available to the loaded program as shown in Figure 4.3.

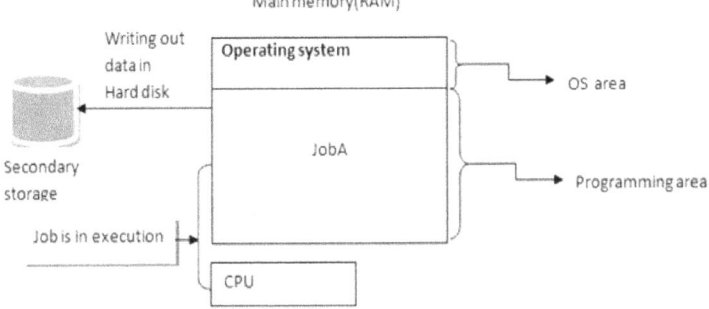

Figure 4.3: *Uni-programming memory model*

Multi-Programming

The interleaved execution of two or more different and independent programs by a computer is called multi-programming. In this scenario the two or more user programs reside simultaneously in the main memory and carry out their interleaved execution. When a program is executing (using CPU), it goes to perform I/O operations, then the CPU is allocated to another job in main memory that is *ready* to use CPU, instead of allowing CPU to remain idle. Thus, in multiprogramming, the CPU switches from one job to another *almost* simultaneously where, jobs share CPU time to keep it busy. The multiprogramming scenario is shown in Figure 4.4.

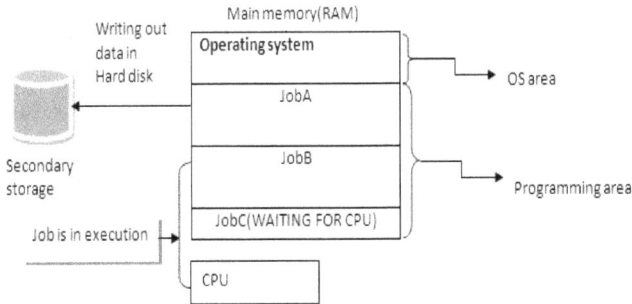

Figure 4.4: *A memory model in multiprogramming scenario*

In case of multiprogramming, all jobs reside in main memory and are one of the following states:

a. New State
b. Ready State
c. Running State
d. Waiting/Blocked State
e. Terminated State

The state transition diagram for multiprogramming scenario is shown is in Figure 4.5.

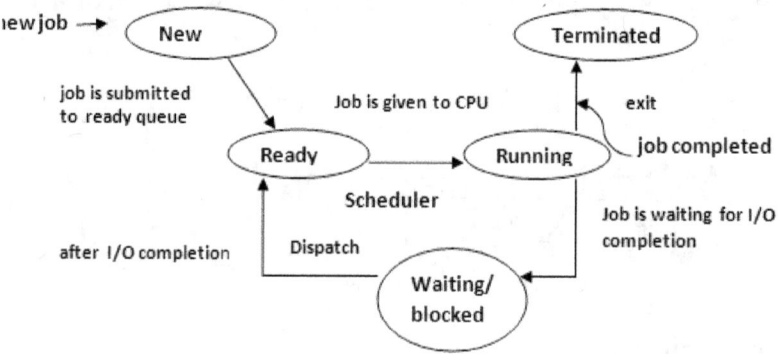

Figure 4.5: *Different states of jobs in main memory in multiprogramming scenario*

Some main points about multiprogramming system are:

a. Here the operating system picks and begins to execute one job from memory.
b. Once this job requires an I/O operation operating system switch to another job, thus, CPU and OS are always busy.
c. Jobs in the memory are always less than the number of jobs on disk(Job Pool).
d. If several jobs are ready to run at the same time, then system chooses jobs by CPU Scheduling.
e. In Non-multiprogram med systems, there are moments when the CPU sits idle and does not do any work.
f. In a Multiprogramming system, the CPU will never be idle and busy on processing.

Advantages

1. These systems have better throughput than multiprogramming.
2. CPU idle time is reduced drastically.
3. Several users can run their programs almost simultaneously.

Multitasking

Technically, there is no difference between multiprogramming and multitasking, but different authors have different perspectives for multitasking and multiprogramming.

Some authors use the term multitasking for single user system (systems that are used by single use at a time like PC) Whereas, some authors use the term multiprogramming for multi user system (the systems that are used by many users simultaneously like server systems) Thus bases on authors perspectives we can differentiate multiprogramming and multitasking systems as follows:

Multiprogramming is the interleaved execution of jobs of different users in a multi user system, while *multitasking* is the interleaved execution of jobs of the same user in a single user system.

Note: The systems which support multitasking and multiprocessing are uni-processing systems (systems having only one processor).

Multithreading

As we know the basic unit of CPU utilization is a process where each process has its own program counter (used to store the address of next instruction), registers, stack (Last In First Out) and memory etc. In case of *threading* the basic unit of CPU utilization is thread. The process is the combination of these parameters and some thread (s) (mini-process) of control. Like a process each thread has its own set Program counter, stack, and registers etc. Single threaded and multithreaded processes are shown in Figure 4.6.

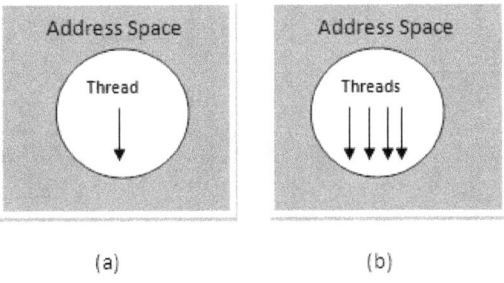

Figure 4.6: *(a) Single threaded (Traditional OS) (b) multithreaded processes*

Some Important Points Regarding Threading are Given Below

a. Improve the performance of the application.
b. All threads of a process share the same memory address.
c. They can also share the global variables.
d. Protection among different processes is required because they belong to different users.
e. There is no protection among the threads of a process because they belong to a single user.
f. Threads can also be called mini processes because they have their own set of registers, stack and program counter etc like a process has.
g. In traditional system, a process has a single thread and is called a heavyweight process.
h. Multiple threads in a process are called lightweight processes.
i. Creating a new process requires more overhead than a creating a new thread within the process.
j. Resource sharing can be achieved more efficiently among threads as compared to among processes, because all threads of a process share the same address space.

Multiprocessing

Multiprocessing systems are those systems having multiple processors (CPUs) and can execute multiple processes or jobs concurrently. In a multiprocessor system all processors operate under a single operating system. A typical architecture is shown in Figure 4.7.

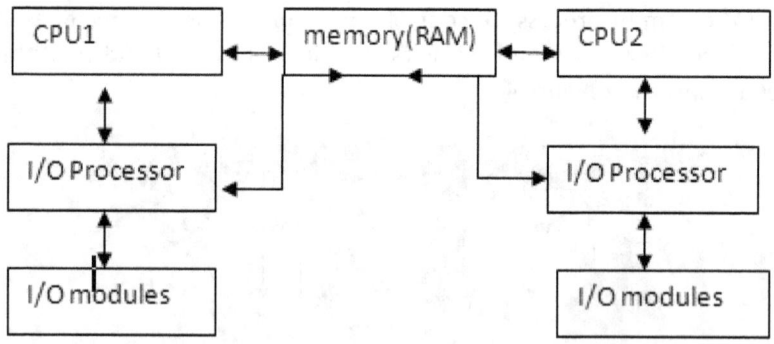

Figure 4.7: *A multiprocessor system*

Here the idea of using I/O processors is to improve the performance of the system and are used to carry out I/ operations concurrently.

Types of Multiprocessing system

There are two types of multiprocessing systems:
a. **Tightly coupled**: Where a single primary memory is shared among all processors.
b. **Loosely coupled**: Processors don't share primary memory and each processor has its own memory.

Advantages

1. Good performance (parallel processing)
2. High throughput (more jobs will be executed in a given time)
3. High reliability (if one processor is failed other will be available)
4. If required, system divides task into many subtasks and then these subtasks can be executed in parallel in different processors. Thereby speeding up the execution of single tasks.

Time Sharing System

Time sharing mechanism provides simultaneous access/use of a computer system by many users, where each and every user feels he is the only user of the system. Time-Sharing Systems are very similar to Multiprogramming systems. Time sharing systems are an extension of multiprogramming systems. Figure 4.8 shows the process state diagram of the time sharing system.

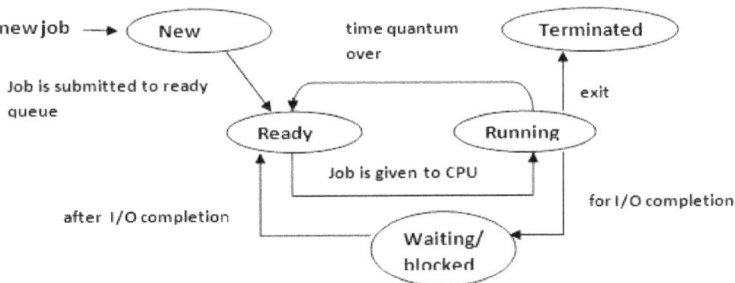

Figure 4.8: *Process state diagram of the time-sharing system.*

In this scenario, a single system is connected to a number of terminals simultaneously, and by using these terminals the multiple users can work on the system simultaneously. Each user process is given a small time (in milliseconds) called time *slice* or *quantum* during which a process gets to use CPU. The processes from memory are selected by a special scheduling algorithm called round robin algorithm and processes use the CPU until the allotted time slice expires or it needs to perform some I/O operation, or it completes its execution during this period.

Some important points about time sharing systems are:

a. It requires large memory to support multiprogramming.
b. It requires a special algorithm that allocates CPU for a short time one by one to each user in a circular fashion (Round Robin)
c. It requires an alarm clock to send an interrupt signal to CPU after every time slice.
d. In time sharing systems the prime focus is on minimizing the response time.
e. While in multiprogramming the prime focus is to maximize the CPU usage.

Advantages

1. It reduces CPU waiting time.
2. Quick response time.
3. Good computing facility.

Distributed Operating Systems

The motivation behind developing distributed operating systems is the availability of powerful and inexpensive microprocessors and advances in communication technology. These advancements in technology have made it possible to design and develop distributed systems consisting of many computers that are interconnected by communication networks. The main benefit of distributed systems is its low price/performance ratio.

Following are some advantages of this type of system:

a. As there are multiple systems involved, users at one site can utilize the resources of systems at other sites for resource-intensive tasks.
b. Fast processing.
c. Less load on the Host Machine.

Real-Time Operating System

It is defined as an operating system known to give maximum time for each of the critical operations that it performs, like OS calls and interrupt handling. The Real-

Time Operating system which guarantees the maximum time for critical operations and completes them on time are referred to as *Hard Real-Time Operating Systems.*

While the real-time operating systems can only guarantee a maximum of the time, i.e. the critical task will get priority over other tasks, but no guarantee of completing it in a defined time. These systems are referred to as *Soft Real-Time Operating Systems.*

Disk Operating System: (Internal/External) Commands

When a computer is switched on, the *POST* (Power on Self-Test) operation will be performed. This operation checks the integrity and functionality of all components (CPU, Memory, I/O devices) of the system. If a component is found faulty or not working properly, an error message will be displayed. In the second step, Once the POST has successfully completed, the software loaded in ROM (sometimes called the BIOS or **firmware**) will begin to activate the computer's disk drives. BIOS (Basic Input Output Services) information is a pre-written program which is permanently stored on a ROM chip. DOS commands are generally classified in two types, *internal commands and external commands.*

The *internal commands* are those commands which reside in COMMAND. COM, loads into memory when the computer system is started and these commands do not reside on disk. Their extension is *.com* and are also called resident commands.

The *external commands* are those commands that do reside on disk and require a separate file to operate having an extension of .COM, .EXE, or .BAT. Both internal and external commands are executed from the MS-DOS prompt.

Now, we can understand this concept of internal and external with an *example given below:*

Example: If we are using the fdisk ("**fixed disk or format disk**" is an most commonly used command-line based disk manipulation utility, With the help of fdisk command you can view, create, resize, delete, change, copy and move partitions on a hard drive using its own user friendly text based menu driven interface.) command to instruct a computer and it does not have the fdisk.exe file, Then we will receive an error message on our screen "Bad command or file name" error message. Here fdisk is an external command that only works if fdisk.exe, or fdisk. com (in some cases), is present.

Note: *As long as MS-DOS is running on your computer internal commands will always be available and does not require other files to run.*

CMD. EXE, in Microsoft Windows, CMD.EXE is the executable of the command line shell. It is more compatible and portable between different hardware platforms when compared to the original COMMAND.COM, which has been used as the command interpreter with DOS for several years. COMMAND.COM is included for backwards compatibility and is recommended that it be used when old MS-DOS programs may not be able to be run in Windows NT, 2000, XP, and later releases of Windows, the command prompt is shown.

What versions of Windows have support for the CMD command?

Microsoft Windows NT, Windows 2000, Windows XP, Windows Vista, Windows 7, Windows 8, and Windows 10 have support for the CMD command.

Advantages of using CMD instead of COMMAND

Using CMD to access MS-DOS is the ability to use long file names. When a user is using COMMAND the short 8.3 name format must be used. For example, if you wanted to access "My Documents" in COMMAND type **cd mydocu~1**. However, to enter the same directory through CMD type **cd "my documents"** or **cd my documents**.

Various External and Internal Command

Internal Commands

Directory Structure of DOS (Disk Operating System): One thing is to be kept in mind is that a directory can have as many child (sub) directories, but the child directory can have only one parent directory.

DIR: This command is used to see all files and sub-directory in the current directory. DIR Command lists file information in five columns; (first) column gives primary name of the file (second) column gives extension of the file (third) column gives the file size - number of bytes used; (fourth) column gives the last updated date; (fifth) column gives the last updated time.

Syntax: c:\users\cuk> dir

Output

Dir/p: It gives the page by page display of file name and directory names

Syntax: c:\users\cuk> dir ⏎

Output

Dir/w: It gives width-wise display.

Syntax: c:\users\cuk> dir/w

Output

```
C:\Users\cuk>dir/w
 Volume in drive C is Windows
 Volume Serial Number is D6B3-5401

 Directory of C:\Users\cuk

[.]              [..]              [.android]      [.RapidMiner5]
[Contacts]       daemonprocess.txt [Desktop]       [Documents]
[Downloads]      [Favorites]       ggg.txt         [Links]
[mobogenieP2sp]  [Music]           [Pictures]      [Roaming]
[Saved Games]    [Searches]        [SkyDrive]      [SupTab]
[Tracing]        [Videos]
               2 File(s)          627 bytes
              20 Dir(s)  888,148,516,864 bytes free

C:\Users\cuk>_
```

Dir/s: displays all sub directory and files in the sub-directory of current directory

Syntax: c:\users\cuk> dir

Output

Currently we are in the CUK *directory, it shows all the subdirectories of CUK and files associated with each subdirectory.*

Dir/a: Display all files and directories including hidden one.

CLS: This command is used to clear the screen.

Syntax: c:\users\cuk> cls

Output

Copy con: This command creates a new file, whatever we are typing(the contents) on the screen will be copied to the file. The file can be closed by giving the command A2 or F6 key OR CTRL+Z

Syntax: c:\users\cuk>copy con yash.txt(file name)

Output

From this output we can see that a file yash.txt is created in directory CUK having 41 characters.

Type: It displays the content of the saved file.

Syntax: c:\users\cuk>type yash.txt(filename)

Output

```
C:\Users\cuk>type yash.txt
hi this is professor yash. how are u guys
C:\Users\cuk>
```

Del: This command is used to delete the file from the directory

Syntax: c:\users\cuk>del yash.txt(filename)

Output

```
C:\Users\cuk>del yash.txt
C:\Users\cuk>dir
 Volume in drive C is Windows
 Volume Serial Number is D6B3-5401

 Directory of C:\Users\cuk

28-06-2016  00:48    <DIR>          .
28-06-2016  00:48    <DIR>          ..
02-06-2014  10:47    <DIR>          .android
28-04-2015  11:39    <DIR>          .RapidMiner5
20-10-2015  10:29    <DIR>          Contacts
02-06-2014  10:47                 0 daemonprocess.txt
27-06-2016  23:19    <DIR>          Desktop
23-06-2016  21:48    <DIR>          Documents
22-06-2016  15:42    <DIR>          Downloads
20-10-2015  10:29    <DIR>          Favorites
14-10-2014  20:57               627 ggg.txt
20-10-2015  10:29    <DIR>          Links
14-11-2014  12:45    <DIR>          mobogenieP2sp
21-06-2016  08:14    <DIR>          Music
20-10-2015  10:29    <DIR>          Pictures
08-01-2014  06:23    <DIR>          Roaming
20-10-2015  10:29    <DIR>          Saved Games
20-10-2015  10:29    <DIR>          Searches
05-05-2014  21:35    <DIR>          SkyDrive
10-08-2015  10:41    <DIR>          SupTab
28-08-2015  03:25    <DIR>          Tracing
20-10-2015  10:29    <DIR>          Videos
               2 File(s)            627 bytes
              20 Dir(s)  888,136,704,000 bytes free

C:\Users\cuk>
```

The file *yash.txt* is deleted from directory *CUK*

Copy: This command is used to copy the content of one file(source) to other file(destination). Let us first create a file yash.txt by using *copy con* in the CUK directory, after creating it, copy it to another file *yash1. txt*, and finally check whether both of these files are available in CUK by **dir** command.

Syntax: c:\users\cuk>del yash.txt(filename)

Output

```
C:\Users\cuk>copy con yash.txt
hi how r u. this is cuka^Z
        1 file(s) copied.

C:\Users\cuk>copy yash.txt yash1.txt
        1 file(s) copied.

C:\Users\cuk>dir
 Volume in drive C is Windows
 Volume Serial Number is D6B3-5401

 Directory of C:\Users\cuk

28-06-2016  01:03    <DIR>          .
28-06-2016  01:03    <DIR>          ..
02-06-2014  10:47    <DIR>          .android
28-04-2015  11:39    <DIR>          .RapidMiner5
20-10-2015  10:29    <DIR>          Contacts
02-06-2014  10:47                 0 daemonprocess.txt
27-06-2016  23:19    <DIR>          Desktop
23-06-2016  21:48    <DIR>          Documents
22-06-2016  15:42    <DIR>          Downloads
20-10-2015  10:29    <DIR>          Favorites
14-10-2014  20:57               627 ggg.txt
20-10-2015  10:29    <DIR>          Links
14-11-2014  12:45    <DIR>          mobogenieP2sp
21-06-2016  08:14    <DIR>          Music
20-10-2015  10:29    <DIR>          Pictures
08-01-2014  06:23    <DIR>          Roaming
20-10-2015  10:29    <DIR>          Saved Games
20-10-2015  10:29    <DIR>          Searches
05-05-2014  21:35    <DIR>          SkyDrive
10-08-2015  10:41    <DIR>          SupTab
28-08-2015  03:25    <DIR>          Tracing
20-10-2015  10:29    <DIR>          Videos
28-06-2016  01:02                24 yash.txt
28-06-2016  01:02                24 yash1.txt
              4 File(s)          675 bytes
             20 Dir(s)  888,137,854,976 bytes free

C:\Users\cuk>_
```

Date: It displays system's date and allows the user to change it if required. it is displayed in the format of **mm - dd - yy.**

Syntax: c:\users\cuk>Date

Output

```
C:\Users\cuk>type yash.txt
hi this is professor yash. how are u guys
C:\Users\cuk>date
The current date is: 28-06-2016
Enter the new date: (dd-mm-yy)
```

Time: It displays the system's time and allows the user to change it.

Syntax: c:\users\cuk>time

Output

```
C:\Users\cuk>type yash.txt
hi this is professor yash. how are u guys
C:\Users\cuk>date
The current date is: 28-06-2016
Enter the new date: (dd-mm-yy)

C:\Users\cuk>time
The current time is:   0:24:25.49
Enter the new time: _
```

md(mkdir): it creates a new directory (folder)or sub directory in the current directory.

Syntax: c:\users\cuk>md Itskills.txt(New directory name)

Output

```
C:\Users\cuk>md itskills.txt

C:\Users\cuk>dir
 Volume in drive C is Windows
 Volume Serial Number is D6B3-5401

 Directory of C:\Users\cuk

28-06-2016  00:34    <DIR>          .
28-06-2016  00:34    <DIR>          ..
02-06-2014  10:47    <DIR>          .android
28-04-2015  11:39    <DIR>          .RapidMiner5
20-10-2015  10:29    <DIR>          Contacts
02-06-2014  10:47                 0 daemonprocess.txt
27-06-2016  23:19    <DIR>          Desktop
23-06-2016  21:48    <DIR>          Documents
22-06-2016  15:42    <DIR>          Downloads
20-10-2015  10:29    <DIR>          Favorites
14-10-2014  20:57               627 ggg.txt
28-06-2016  00:34    <DIR>          itskills.txt
20-10-2015  10:29    <DIR>          Links
14-11-2014  12:45    <DIR>          mobogenieP2sp
21-06-2016  08:14    <DIR>          Music
20-10-2015  10:29    <DIR>          Pictures
08-01-2014  06:23    <DIR>          Roaming
20-10-2015  10:29    <DIR>          Saved Games
20-10-2015  10:29    <DIR>          Searches
05-05-2014  21:35    <DIR>          SkyDrive
10-08-2015  10:41    <DIR>          SupTab
28-08-2015  03:25    <DIR>          Tracing
20-10-2015  10:29    <DIR>          Videos
28-06-2016  00:11                41 yash.txt
               3 File(s)            668 bytes
              21 Dir(s)  888,140,701,696 bytes free

C:\Users\cuk>_
```

After creating the directory *itskills.txt*, we can check it by **dir** command as shown in above output.

rd(rmdir) This command is used to remove a directory from the disk.

Note: *It can't remove a directory which contains sub directory or files, i.e., the child should be removed from the parent.*

Syntax: c:\users\cuk>rd Itskills.txt(directory name)

Output

```
C:\Users\cuk>rd itskills.txt

C:\Users\cuk>dir
 Volume in drive C is Windows
 Volume Serial Number is D6B3-5401

 Directory of C:\Users\cuk

28-06-2016  00:42    <DIR>          .
28-06-2016  00:42    <DIR>          ..
02-06-2014  10:47    <DIR>          .android
28-04-2015  11:39    <DIR>          .RapidMiner5
20-10-2015  10:29    <DIR>          Contacts
02-06-2014  10:47                 0 daemonprocess.txt
27-06-2016  23:19    <DIR>          Desktop
23-06-2016  21:48    <DIR>          Documents
22-06-2016  15:42    <DIR>          Downloads
20-10-2015  10:29    <DIR>          Favorites
14-10-2014  20:57               627 ggg.txt
20-10-2015  10:29    <DIR>          Links
14-11-2014  12:45    <DIR>          mobogenieP2sp
21-06-2016  08:14    <DIR>          Music
20-10-2015  10:29    <DIR>          Pictures
08-01-2014  06:23    <DIR>          Roaming
20-10-2015  10:29    <DIR>          Saved Games
20-10-2015  10:29    <DIR>          Searches
05-05-2014  21:35    <DIR>          SkyDrive
10-08-2015  10:41    <DIR>          SupTab
28-08-2015  03:25    <DIR>          Tracing
20-10-2015  10:29    <DIR>          Videos
28-06-2016  00:11                41 yash.txt
               3 File(s)            668 bytes
              20 Dir(s)  888,138,448,896 bytes free

C:\Users\cuk>
```

From the above output we see that the directory *itskills.txt* is deleted

Ren: This command changes the name of an existing file or directory.

Syntax: c:\users\cuk>ren yash.txt (old file name) **yash2.txt** (new file name)

Output

```
C:\Users\cuk>ren yash.txt yash2.txt

C:\Users\cuk>dir
 Volume in drive C is Windows
 Volume Serial Number is D6B3-5401

 Directory of C:\Users\cuk

28-06-2016  01:12    <DIR>          .
28-06-2016  01:12    <DIR>          ..
02-06-2014  10:47    <DIR>          .android
28-04-2015  11:39    <DIR>          .RapidMiner5
20-10-2015  10:29    <DIR>          Contacts
02-06-2014  10:47                 0 daemonprocess.txt
27-06-2016  23:19    <DIR>          Desktop
23-06-2016  21:48    <DIR>          Documents
22-06-2016  15:42    <DIR>          Downloads
20-10-2015  10:29    <DIR>          Favorites
14-10-2014  20:57               627 ggg.txt
20-10-2015  10:29    <DIR>          Links
14-11-2014  12:45    <DIR>          mobogenieP2sp
21-06-2016  08:14    <DIR>          Music
20-10-2015  10:29    <DIR>          Pictures
08-01-2014  06:23    <DIR>          Roaming
20-10-2015  10:29    <DIR>          Saved Games
20-10-2015  10:29    <DIR>          Searches
05-05-2014  21:35    <DIR>          SkyDrive
10-08-2015  10:41    <DIR>          SupTab
28-08-2015  03:25    <DIR>          Tracing
20-10-2015  10:29    <DIR>          Videos
28-06-2016  01:02                24 yash1.txt
28-06-2016  01:02                24 yash2.txt
               4 File(s)            675 bytes
              20 Dir(s)  888,136,433,664 bytes free

C:\Users\cuk>
```

Ver it displays the version of DOS currently being used in the system.

Syntax: c:\users\cuk>ver

Output

```
C:\Users\cuk>ver

Microsoft Windows [Version 6.2.9200]

C:\Users\cuk>
```

vol: Gives the volume and serial number of volume

```
C:\Users\cuk>vol
 Volume in drive C is Windows
 Volume Serial Number is D6B3-5401

C:\Users\cuk>
```

CD: This is used to change or come out of the directory.

Operating System

Syntax: c:\users\cuk>cd (name of the directory)

Output

```
C:\Users\cuk>cd desktop
C:\Users\cuk\Desktop>
```

First we were working in the CUK directory, but now we are working in the Desktop directory. If we want to come out of the desktop directory write *cd.*

```
C:\Users\cuk\Desktop>cd../..
C:\Users>cd..
C:\>d:
D:\>
```

13. **Prompt** allows the user to set a new DOS prompt instead of usual.

Syntax: D:\> *prompt abc* (name of the prompt)

Output

```
D:\> prompt abc

abc date
The current date is: 28-06-2016
Enter the new date: (dd-mm-yy)

abc time
The current time is: 1:36:06.29
Enter the new time: _
```

External Command

1. **Attrib,** this command is used for protecting the files from accidental changes or modification. It can also be used for making a hidden file, archive files, read only files; Syntax: Attrib +R/-R/+H/-H/+A/-A <file name> +FR protects the file by making it read only, -R removes the read only protection; eg: Attrib + r <file name >

2. **Scandisk/ Chkdisk** this command checks the status of the disk; it shows a graphical display, information about the user file.

3. **Tree** this command graphically displays the path of each directory and sub directory in given drive; Syntax: C:\> tree<
4. **More** it displays one screen of data at a time and is used with another command when one screen is full; if you press any key on the next screen is displayed: Syntax C:\> type abc.doc| more.
5. **Edit** the command loads the MS DOS editor, where we can edit files, create new files, open existing files; Syntax: C:\> edit < file name>
6. **Label** a label is a name given to a disk which refers to collection of filers and directories on disk; Syntax: C:\>label A.
7. **Sort** this command is used for sorting data and displaying the result on the screen: Syntax:C:\>dir/sort/r (reverse order)
8. **Format;** this command prepares a disk by arranging random magnetic impulses in to a series of track and sectors so that it is addressable by a DOS version; Syntax : C:\> format A:/s
9. **Sys** this command transfers MS DOS System files to specified areas to make the disk bootable; Syntax: C:\>Sys A:<

    10 **Pipes** (|) it connects two files ie the standard output of one filter command becomes standard input of another filter; eg Dir/Sort/ more ||
10. **Batch files** all batch files on DOS must have the file extn on bat to execute the batch file, the user has just type the file name and press enter key, in addition to usual DOS command.
11. **Echo** this command can be used to display a message on the screen.
12. **Pause** when this command is obeyed, the system waits for the user to press a key by displaying a line "strike a key when ready".
13. **Rem** a command or remark can be used on a batch file by the rem command; to symbol @ can be put in a REM command to prevent DOS from displaying the command during the execution of batch files.

Config. The purpose of this file is to tell DOS how to configure the computer; it contains configurable parameters of DOS, such as number of drives, files, buffers that can be opened at a time.

break - ON/OFF it can be used to change the frequency to check the break character (Ctrl+c, ctrl+break); it break + OFF, then the frequency of checking is less, otherwise it is ON, then it makes DOS extensively check the break character.

Buffer = 20/10 it tells DOS how many disk buffers are maintained; the default value is 2 each buffer of 528 bytes (512 + 16); this feature is needed for file manipulation because the performance increases with the addition of buffers.

Device: Ansi.Sys/V Disk.Sys/Tapeover it tells DOS how to include a particular device driver that controls and configures a device such as a Floppy disk or Tape Unit.

Files = 10/20/30 it tells DOS how many files to be opened at one time, its default value is 8; a max of 99 files can be opened at a time

Stacks = 15, 128it tells DOS the number of stacks to be used by the H/W interrupts; the default value is 9 with 128 bytes.

Shell = Command.com tells DOS to install the command processor from a particular path such as Shell = C:\DOS\ Command.com.

Chapter 5
E-Governance

E (Electronic)- Governance

To understand the term e-commerce better, first we need to understand the terms E-Government, Governance, E-Governance and Government because these terms are the base for E-Governance as shown in Figure 5.1.

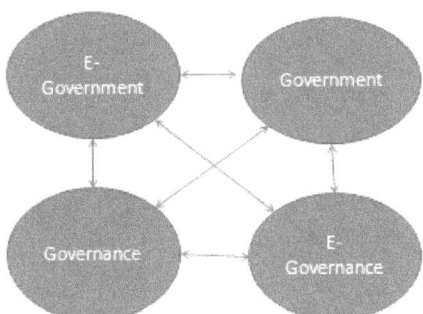

Figure 5.1: *Important fields of E-Governance*

Government: Government is a elected or unelected group of individuals who control or run the administration of a nation and Government may be a majority rules system (democracy) or autocracy.

Governance: is the act of overseeing or running. It is the arrangement of guidelines and laws confined by the administration or government that are to be actualized through the delegates of the state.

According to Löffler and Kim et al., (2005) stated that in modern connected world, public governance can take many forms which may or may not involve the government itself. Governance might come from within the community or be provided by the market. The understanding of governance as the act of governing has been replaced with a model of government as an actor in the process of governance. Therefore, government is a subset or a component of governance within a given polity and has implications for the impact of technology.

Electronic government (or *e-government*) where the governments use ICTs and other web-based telecommunication technologies to improve or enhance the efficiency and effectiveness of services in the public sector, improves broad stakeholders' contribution to national and community development, as well as deepen the governance process.

The process of giving good governance by the governments all over the world to their citizens by using Information communication technologies (ICT) is called E-Governance and sometimes this phenomenon is also known as digital government. Dawes (2008, p. S36) defines: "E-governance comprises the use of information and communication technologies (ICTs) to support public services, government administration, democratic processes, and relationships among citizens, civil society, the private sector, and the state." For two decades it has been a common practice to use the word 'e' in front of governance, government, democracy, commerce, business politics etc. which suggests the use and influence of ICTs to change or improve the field in some fundamental way. Some important definitions of governance by reputed institutions of the world are mentioned below.

> "The exercise of political authority and the use of institutional resources to manage society's problems and affairs." (The World Bank, 1991);

> "The system and manner of providing authority and control" (Integrated Justice Information Systems Glossary, 2009);

> "The traditions and institutions by which authority in a country is exercised" (The World Bank, 20 07) Governance is the exercise of economic, political and administrative authority to man-age a country's affairs at all levels. It comprises the mechanisms, processes and institutions through which citizens and groups articulate their interests, exercise their legal rights, meet their obligations and mediate their differences" (UNPAN, 2011);

> "The ways in which desired forms of behaviour are motivated and incentivized" (Peppard 2009);

"The processes by which governments are chosen, monitored, and changed." (Asian Development Bank Institute, 2011); There are two types of governance

- **Structural governance**
- **Normative governance**

Structural governance explained about 'how' of any government such as processes, structures, lines of authority, laws, regulations, partners, forms of correspondence and responsibilities, the mechanisms by which power is exercised, decisions made, policy is created or changed. Normative governance is the set of value-related features of structural governance including transparency, accountability, integrity, honesty, impartiality, efficiency and so on that governance is desired to enable, to possess or to deliver. Structural governance may be designed to support or achieve normative aims.

Note: *Governance is what a government does and Governance is the physical exercise of the polity while the government is the body through which this is done.*

E-Governance in India

The union government of India sincerely promoting the use of ICT to ensure good governance in various fields by its organisation called National Information Centre (NIC) which is established in 1976 managing its internal processes through its organization NIC, which was set up in 1976. Up to beginning of 1980s government used computers for limited purposes like census, elections, tax administration, surveys in defence, planning, research etc. In 1987 when the Planning Commission (Nitiayaog) started its National Informatics Centre (NIC) through its Information and Communication Technology (ICT) Network - NICNET programme. Under which various programme, the district and state governments and central ministries were connected to share information. In 1998 more intensive steps have been taken towards e-governance by constituting of a National Task Force which later directed all the government department to spend 2–3 % of their allocated budget for promoting digitization in the department. In 2000, under the chairmanship of Cabinet Secretary all ministries, departments of the central government asked to appoint a senior officer as IT Manager to promote IT. The Department of Administrative Reforms and Public Grievances (DARPG) prepared a 12 point 'Minimum Agenda of E-governance comprises of to be implemented by all government ICT infrastructure, training of employees etc. Every Ministry/Departments are directed to prepare a 5-year 'IT plan' and annual 'Action Plans'.

Some of these initiatives of the central govt. are adopted by state governments like Andhra Pradesh, Tamil Nadu and Chandigarh, in May 2006 govt establish National e-Governance Plan (NeGP) with the Department of Information Technology called as the nodal coordinating organization. Initially it was composed of 27 Mission Mode Projects (MMPs) and 8 support components to be implemented at the central, state and local government levels. These projects provide services on road transport, land records, commercial taxes, employment exchanges, agriculture, civil supplies, treasuries, land registration, policy and education, insurance, excise, banking, income-tax, passport, etc. Later on 29 July 2011 they added projects like

Education, Health, Public Distribution System and Posts. For more details about MMPs projects visit http://mit.gov.in. There is an introduction of IT Act 2000, Right to Information Act 2005 and setting up of the second Administrative Reforms Commission in the year 2005. Right to Information Act 2005 allow the citizens of India to access to information under the control of public authorities to promote transparency Other e-governance initiatives include formation of Unique Identification Authority of India (UIDAI) and e-Panchayat Project (village connectivity) of the Ministry of Panchayati Raj under Bharat Nirman II Programme. The UAIDI is responsible for unique identification to residents of India. The unique identification is known as AADHAR which is expected as a good assertive tool to deliver government programmes and schemes to the people especially the poor effectively.

In 2015, India launched the **Digital India programme (DIP)** (http://www.digitalindia.gov.in/di-initiatives) In order to transform the entire ecosystem of public services through the use of information technology, with the vision to transform India into a digitally empowered society and knowledge economy.

The programs are started under the DIP are:

e-Kranti, ACCESSIBLE INDIA CAMPAIGN MOBILE APP, AGRIMARKET APP, BETI BACHAO BETI PADHAO, BHIM (Bharat Interface for Money), CRIME AND CRIMINAL TRACKING NETWORK & SYSTEMS (CCTNS), CROP INSURANCE MOBILE APP, DIGITAL AIIMS, e-GRANTHALAYA, E-PANCHAYAT, Ebiz, ECI EVM TRACKING, eDISTRICT, eGREETINGS, e-HOSPITAL, eMSIPS, eNAM, eOFFICE, ePATHSHALA, EPFO WEB PORTAL & MOBILE APP, ePRISON, ePROCUREMENT PORTAL (CPP), eSAMPARK, eTAAL, eVISA, FARMER PORTAL, FERTILISER MonitorING SYSTEM (FMS), GEOGRAPHIC INFORMATION SYSTEM (GIS), GEOLOGICAL SURVEY OF INDIA (GSI), GOODS AND SERVICE TAX NETWORK (GSTN), HIMMAT APP, ICDS SYSTEMS STRENGTHENING AND NUTRITION IMPROVEMENT PROJECT (ISSNIP), KHOYA PAYA, KISAN SUVIDHA, KNOWLEDGE MANAGEMENT SYSTEM (KMS), LEARNING MANAGEMENT SYSTEM (LMS), MADAD APP, mASSET, MCA21, mCESSATION, mKAVACH, MOTHER & CHILD TRACKING SYSTEM (MCTS), mRAKTKOSH, NATIONAL CAREER SERVICE PORTAL, NATIONAL KNOWLEDGE NETWORK, NATIONAL SCHOLARSHIP PORTAL (NSP), NATIONAL UJALA DASHBOARD, NATIONAL VOTERS SERVICE PORTAL (NVSP), NIKSHAY, NIRBHAYA APP, ONLINE LABS (OLABS), PARIVAHAN, PORTAL, PASSPORT SEVA PROJECT (PSP), PROJECT MANAGEMENT SYSTEM (PMIS), PROJECT MonitorING WEBSITE FOR ECOURTS, PUBLIC FINANCIAL MANAGEMENT SYSTEM (PFMS), PUSA KRISHI, SARANSH, SHAALA DARPAN, Shala Siddhi, SMS-BASED MID-DAY MEAL MonitorING SCHEME SOIL HEALTH CARD, STARTUP INDIA PORTAL AND MOBILE APP, SUGAMAYA PUSTAKALYA, SWATCH BHAARAT app, SWAYAM, UDAAN, UMANG ,UN-RESERVED TICKET THROUGH MOBILE APPLICATION (UTS APP).

Types of E-Governance

The E-Governance model consists of three main components such as citizens, government and businesses that describe the concept of e-governance, citizens and businesses. Based on the communication between the components E-governance mainly classified as G2G (Government to Government) and G2C (Government to Citizen) and G2B (Government to Business) like in e-commerce concepts.

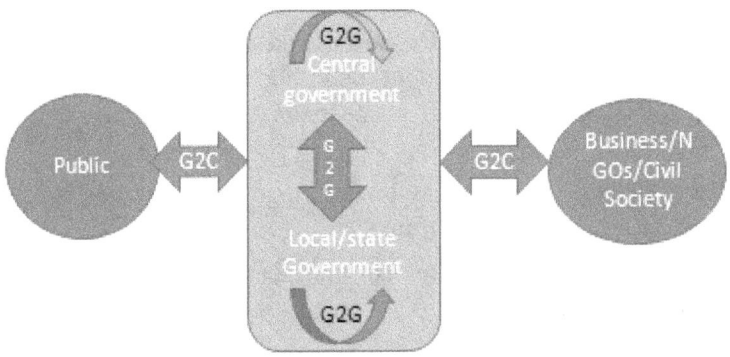

Figure 5.2: *An E- Governance model*

Government-2-Citizen (G2C)

It is the online non- commercial cooperation between local and central government with the people. Citizens can get services such as license/permit, death/birth/marriage endorsements etc. by the government.

Government-2-Business (G2B)

It incorporates the spread of approaches/policies, memos, and protocols of the government.

Government-2-Representative (G2E)

It is the online non-business cooperation between government associations and government workers. It incorporates the arrangement of human resource preparations and advancement.

Government-2-Government (G2G)

It is the online non-business connection between government associations, divisions and experts and other government associations, offices and authorities. This service can be utilized as an instrument of global relations and diplomacy.

Advantages and Disadvantages

Advantages

- ***Transparency and Accountability:*** because citizens will be informed what the government is working on and about their policies they are going to implement resulting in less corruption, better transparency, more convenience, revenue growth etc.
- ***Increases Efficiency:*** It increases the efficiency of the current paper-based system which saves money and time.
- ***Effective Communication:*** Better communication and fast communication between public and govt.
- ***Increase Throughput:*** It increases the throughput of any business
- ***Democratization:*** One objective of e-government will be more prominent national support. Through the web, individuals from everywhere throughout the nation can associate with government officials or politicians and make their voices heard. Blogging and intelligent reviews will enable government officials or politicians to see the perspectives of the general population they speak to on any given issue. A government could hypothetically move more towards a genuine democracy.

Disadvantages

- **Lack of Equality:** The people who are rich and living in urban areas have more access to the computers and internet as compared to the people who are poor and living in rural areas.
- **Hyper-Surveillance:** When the government starts to develop and become more advanced, the citizens will be compelled to interact with the government. electronically e.g.
- This could give rise to a lack of privacy for civilians as their government acquires more and more data from the citizens.

- **Cost:** Although huge measure of cash is spent on the improvement and usage of e-government and the results and impacts are still unacceptable.
- **Inaccessibility:** An e-government website that gives electronic access and support regularly does not offer the possibility to access the individuals who live in the remote regions, have low education levels and exist on poverty line earnings.

E-Governance Models

Prof Dr. Arie Halachimi proposed five different standard models to guide government's initiatives to towards e-governance and are summarized below:
- Broadcasting model
- Critical flow model
- Interactive model
- E-Advocacy model
- Comparative model

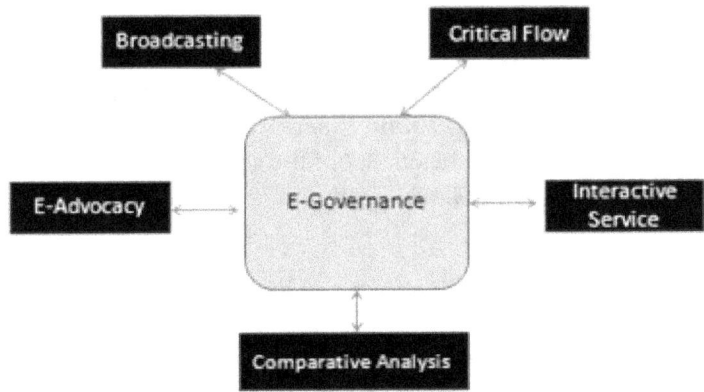

Figure 5.3: *E-Governance Models*

Broadcasting Model

In this model information is communicated to a more extensive scale through utilization of ICT and convergent media. This model emphasizes on spreading information about schemes of govt. to more extensive mass through which the individuals have the capacity to judge the working of existing government systems. It empowers the citizens and govt both where they are ready to take wise decisions.

Main Tasks
- It Shows administrative/ governmental laws and legislation on the web.
- It makes local/territorial/national government authorities details accessible on the web.
- It makes public i.e. on the web the information of the government like, legislative plans, spending plans, and performance reports etc.
- It Makes key legal decisions public which are of great importance to the general public.

The Critical flow Model

This data of basic esteem (which by its extreme nature won't be unveiled by those included with awful administration) is channelized to the focused segment into general society space through utilization of ICT. Directed gatherings incorporate media, influenced parties, opposition parties, judiciary, autonomous bodies or the overall population. This model is more engaged as far as its data content and proposed clients. Because of basic data this model uncovered weakest parts of administration and basic leadership processes illuminate individuals about disappointment in particular cases and awful administration and develop energy for coordinated activity. In the meantime, it builds the pressure on concerned government associations/establishments and people to take into comprehension and cognizance the opinions, suggestions, experiences and interest of masses in the decision making process so that the quality of the services may be increased. Such types of bodies are: Wikileaks, Global Transparency International, India Central Vigilance Committee etc.

The Use of Critical Flow Model Requires a Foresight of

Understanding the "critical and use value" of a particular information set.How or from where this information could be obtained. How could the information be used strategically? Who is the best target group for such information? The users for whom the availability of this information will make a huge difference.

Main Tasks
- It Exposes corruption related information about a specific Ministry/Division/Officials online to its citizens or to the concerned administrative body.
- To Make Human Rights Violations cases freely accessible to Judiciary, NGOs and concerned natives.

- To Make Human Rights Violations cases openly accessible to Judiciary, NGOs and concerned natives.
- Making accessible data that is normally stifled or suppressed.

Comparative Analysis Model

This model ceaselessly joins best practices in the field of governance and utilizes them as benchmarks to assess other governance practices. It utilizes the outcome to advocate positive changes or impact citizen's opinion on these governance practices.

The model uses large capacity of information communication technologies and social media platforms to investigate given information sets with comparable information available in the public or private domain e.g. Human Development Indicators.

Main tasks:

It gains from past approaches and activities and based on the past experiences makes future decisions.

- It assesses the assertiveness of the present strategies and recognize them as positive and negative policies.
- Viably builds up conditions of priority, particularly on account of Judicial or any legal decision making and utilizes it to impact/advocate future decision making.
- Informs/educate decision making at all levels by improving the background knowledge.
- Evaluates the performance and track-record of a specific decision-maker/ decision-making body.

E-Advocacy Model

E-Advocacy/Mobilization and Lobbying Model E-Advocacy/Mobilization and Lobbying Model is a stand out among all models of e-governance and has regular aid from the global civil society to impact on global decision-making processes.

The model depends on setting-up an arranged, guided flow of information to assemble solid virtual partners to supplement activities in reality. Virtual networks of people are created which share similar values and concerns, and these virtual networks of people link up with or support real-life groups/ activities for concerted action. The model forms the momentum of real-world processes by including the sentiments/opinion and concerns communicated by virtual networked people.

The quality of this model is its diversity of the virtual networks, thoughts, aptitude/expertise. The model is able to organize and control human resources and information beyond geographical, institutional and bureaucratic barriers, and is utilized for strong action e.g. PRS legislative, Green Peace, etc.

Main tasks

- Promoting public debates confrontations on worldwide issues, specifically on the topics of upcoming meetings, treaties and so forth.
- Creation of pressure groups on key issues to compel chief decision makers to take their worried opinion into consideration.
- Making accessible suggestions of suppressed groups who are not associated directly with the decision-making process.
- Catalysing more extensive participation in decision making.
- Building up worldwide skill on a specific subject without a confined data to help basic leadership.
- Amplifying the voices of marginalized who are customarily underestimated from decision making.

The Interactive Service Model

In this model the government opens the door for country individuals for direct cooperation and participation in the decision making process by utilizing ICTs. The biggest advantage of this model is that it brings high objectivity and transparency in the decision making process of the government. Resulting in good governance. Govt. initiatives and services are straightforwardly accessible to it's native in an intuitive way and is achieved by opening Government to shopper to government (G2C2G) channels physically or online in different part of the country in different aspects of the governance e.g. Grievance Redressal sites, online booking of tickets, online passport service etc.

Main tasks:

- Making an intuitive communication channel with key policy makers and individuals from Planning Commissions.
- Conducting electronic polls for election of government authorities and other office bearers.
- Open discussions/debates and surveys on issues of concern before making of policies and laws.

- Filing of grievances, criticism and reports by individuals with the concerned legislative body.
- To set up decentralized types of administration.
- Online services like revenue collection, procurement, tendering etc.

MOOCs

Introduction to MOOCs:

1. Definition and Overview

MOOCs, or Massive Open Online Courses, are online courses that are designed to accommodate a large number of participants, typically numbering in the thousands or even hundreds of thousands. These courses are offered over the internet and are accessible to anyone with an internet connection, regardless of geographical location or educational background. MOOCs provide a platform for delivering educational content, including lectures, readings, assignments, quizzes, and discussions, in a flexible and interactive format.

The key features of MOOCs include:

- **Massive Enrollment**: MOOCs attract a large and diverse audience of learners from around the world, creating a global learning community.

- **Open Access**: MOOCs are open to anyone who wishes to enroll, with no prerequisites or admission requirements. Learners can access course materials and participate in activities freely.

- **Online Delivery**: MOOCs are delivered entirely online through web-based platforms, allowing learners to access course content from any internet-enabled device.

- **Scalability**: MOOCs leverage technology to scale educational content to a large audience efficiently, with pre-recorded lectures, automated assessments, and asynchronous learning activities.

- **Diverse Course Offerings**: MOOC platforms offer a wide range of courses covering various subjects, disciplines, and skill levels, allowing learners to explore their interests and pursue their learning goals.

- **Interactive Learning Experience**: MOOCs incorporate interactive elements such as quizzes, assignments, discussion forums, and peer assessments to engage learners actively and promote collaborative learning.

- **Flexibility**: MOOCs offer flexibility in terms of scheduling and pacing, allowing learners to study at their own pace and on their own schedule.

Overall, MOOCs have emerged as a transformative force in education, democratizing access to high-quality educational content, expanding opportunities for lifelong learning, and fostering global collaboration and knowledge sharing.

2. History and Evolution

- **Early Experiments (2000s)**: The concept of MOOCs traces back to the early 2000s with initiatives like MIT OpenCourseWare (OCW), which aimed to make course materials from MIT available online for free. Another notable precursor was the Connectivism and Connective Knowledge (CCK) course offered by Stephen Downes and George Siemens in 2008.

- **Emergence of MOOC Platforms (2010s)**: The term "MOOC" gained prominence in 2012 when Stanford University professors Sebastian Thrun and Peter Norvig launched an online course on artificial intelligence that attracted over 160,000 students. This event led to the creation of dedicated MOOC platforms such as Coursera, Udacity, and edX, which offered courses from prestigious universities and institutions worldwide.

- **Expansion and Diversification (Mid-2010s)**: MOOC platforms expanded rapidly, offering a diverse range of courses across various disciplines, including computer science, humanities, business, and more. The number of participating universities and institutions grew, and partnerships with corporations, governments, and nonprofit organizations increased.

- **Shift Towards Accreditation and Credentialing (Late 2010s)**: As MOOCs gained popularity, there was a growing emphasis on providing learners with tangible credentials and certifications. MOOC platforms began offering options for verified certificates, micro-credentials, and even fully accredited online degrees in collaboration with partner institutions.

- **Integration with Traditional Education (Present)**: MOOCs are increasingly being integrated into traditional educational settings, with universities incorporating online courses into their curricula through blended learning models. MOOC platforms also collaborate with employers to offer courses and programs tailored to workforce development and continuing education.

3. Challenges

- **Low Completion Rates**: One of the major challenges facing MOOCs is low completion rates. Many learners enroll in courses but fail to complete them due to factors such as lack of motivation, time constraints, or difficulty understanding the material. Addressing this challenge requires designing courses that engage learners effectively and providing support mechanisms to help them stay motivated and on track.

- **Quality Control:** Maintaining quality standards in MOOCs can be challenging due to the diverse backgrounds and motivations of learners, as well as the large-scale nature of these courses. Ensuring that course materials are accurate, up-to-date, and engaging requires careful design, ongoing evaluation, and feedback mechanisms to identify and address areas for improvement.

- **Lack of Accreditation:** While some MOOCs offer certificates of completion or micro-credentials, these credentials may not always be recognized by employers or educational institutions. The lack of accreditation can limit the value of MOOCs as a form of formal education or professional certification, particularly in fields where credentials are highly valued.

- **Digital Divide:** Access to MOOCs is limited by factors such as internet connectivity, device availability, and digital literacy skills. The digital divide disproportionately affects individuals from low-income or marginalized communities, exacerbating existing inequalities in access to education and opportunities for socioeconomic advancement.

- **Retention of Knowledge:** Another challenge is the retention of knowledge gained through MOOCs. Without regular reinforcement and practice, learners may forget the material shortly after completing the course. Strategies such as spaced repetition, active learning techniques, and opportunities for real-world application can help improve knowledge retention and transferability.

Overall, while MOOCs offer numerous benefits in terms of accessibility, flexibility, and diversity of course offerings, they also face challenges related to completion rates, quality control, accreditation, digital divide, and knowledge retention. Addressing these challenges requires ongoing innovation, collaboration, and research to ensure that MOOCs continue to evolve as effective tools for education and lifelong learning.

4. Pedagogical Approaches

- **Connectivist Approach:** The connectivist approach to learning emphasizes the importance of networks, connections, and collective intelligence in the learning process.

  In MOOCs, this approach often involves creating learning networks or communities where participants share resources, collaborate on projects, and engage in discussions.

  Connectivist MOOCs (cMOOCs) focus on learner-driven exploration, decentralized content creation, and the formation of personal learning networks.

- **Instructivist Approach:** The instructivist approach to learning is instructor-centered and emphasizes the transmission of knowledge from teacher to learner.

  In MOOCs, this approach is often characterized by pre-recorded lectures, readings, and structured assignments that guide learners through the course content.

  Instructivist MOOCs (xMOOCs) typically feature a more linear and structured format, with clear learning objectives, assessments, and milestones.

- **Constructivist Approach:** The constructivist approach to learning emphasizes active engagement, inquiry-based learning, and the construction of meaning through hands-on experiences.

  In MOOCs, this approach may involve interactive activities, problem-solving tasks, and opportunities for reflection and discussion.

  Constructivist MOOCs aim to create authentic learning experiences that promote critical thinking, creativity, and self-directed learning.

- **Social Learning Theory:** Social learning theory emphasizes the role of social interactions and observational learning in the learning process.

  In MOOCs, social learning is facilitated through online discussion forums, peer feedback mechanisms, and collaborative projects.

  Social learning theory suggests that learners can benefit from observing and interacting with their peers, sharing ideas, and receiving constructive feedback.

- **Experiential Learning:** Experiential learning focuses on learning through direct experience, reflection, and experimentation.

  In MOOCs, experiential learning may be facilitated through simulations, case studies, virtual labs, and real-world projects.

  Experiential learning encourages learners to apply theoretical concepts to practical problems, engage in authentic tasks, and reflect on their learning experiences.

- **Personalization and Adaptive Learning:** Personalization and adaptive learning technologies tailor the learning experience to the individual needs, preferences, and abilities of each learner.

  In MOOCs, adaptive learning platforms may use algorithms and data analytics to adapt the content, pacing, and support mechanisms to match the learner's progress and learning style.

  Personalized learning enhances engagement, motivation, and learning outcomes by providing learners with customized pathways and targeted interventions.

  By incorporating these pedagogical approaches into MOOC design and delivery, instructors can create engaging, effective, and learner-centered learning experiences that cater to the diverse needs and preferences of participants.

Quality Assurance and Evaluation:

- **Course Design:** Discuss the principles of effective course design in MOOCs, including clarity of learning objectives, organization of content, and alignment of assessments with learning outcomes.

- **Assessment Methods:** Explore different assessment methods used in MOOCs, such as quizzes, assignments, peer reviews, and exams, and discuss their strengths and limitations.

- **Evaluation Strategies:** Introduce strategies for evaluating the quality and effectiveness of MOOCs, such as learner feedback surveys, analysis of engagement metrics, and comparative studies with traditional courses.

5. Integration with Traditional Education

Here's how MOOCs can be integrated with traditional education:

- **Blended Learning Models:** Blended learning combines online and face-to-face instruction to create a hybrid learning environment. MOOCs can be integrated into traditional classroom settings as part of a blended learning model.

  In a blended learning approach, students may engage in online activities, such as watching lectures or completing assignments, outside of class time, while face-to-face sessions are used for discussion, group work, and hands-on activities.

  Blended learning allows instructors to leverage the strengths of both online and offline instruction, providing students with flexibility, personalized learning experiences, and opportunities for interaction and collaboration.

- **Flipped Classroom:** The flipped classroom model flips the traditional classroom structure by delivering instructional content online outside of class time and using class time for active learning and application.

  MOOCs can be used to deliver pre-recorded lectures, readings, and other course materials, which students can access before coming to class.

  In the flipped classroom, class time is then used for discussion, problem-solving, group work, and other interactive activities that engage students in active learning and reinforce concepts covered in the online materials.

- **Supplementary Resources:** MOOCs can serve as supplementary resources to support traditional classroom instruction. Instructors can recommend relevant MOOCs to students as additional learning opportunities or enrichment activities.

  Students can use MOOCs to explore topics in more depth, review difficult concepts, or gain practical skills related to their coursework.

  MOOCs can provide students with access to diverse perspectives, expert insights, and up-to-date information that may not be available through traditional textbooks or lectures.

- **Professional Development for Educators:** MOOCs can be used to provide professional development approaches, and stay current with developments in their field.

  Universities and educational institutions can offer MOOCs specifically designed for teachers and faculty members, covering topics such as educational technology, curriculum design, assessment strategies, and classroom management.

- **Continuing Education and Lifelong Learning:** MOOCs can support lifelong learning initiatives by providing opportunities for individuals to pursue education and skills development throughout their lives.

  Universities and colleges can offer MOOCs as part of continuing education programs, allowing alumni, working professionals, and community members to access high-quality educational content and stay connected with the institution.

  MOOCs can also be used to provide workforce development training, helping individuals acquire new skills and stay competitive in the job market.

  Overall, integrating MOOCs with traditional education offers numerous benefits, including increased flexibility, personalized learning experiences, enhanced engagement, and expanded access to educational opportunities. By incorporating MOOCs into their teaching practices, educators can create dynamic and innovative learning environments that meet the diverse needs of today's students.

6. Practical Applications

Here are some key practical applications of MOOCs:

- **Skill Development:** MOOCs are commonly used for skill development in both academic and professional contexts. Learners can enroll in courses covering specific skills such as programming languages, data analysis, project management, language proficiency, and more.

  Practical assignments, hands-on projects, and interactive exercises in MOOCs provide learners with opportunities to apply theoretical knowledge and develop practical skills relevant to their field of study or career goals.

- **Professional Certification:** Many MOOC platforms offer certificates of completion or micro-credentials for learners who successfully complete course requirements. These certificates can be valuable for professional development, career advancement, and demonstrating competency in specific subject areas.

  MOOC-based certifications are recognized by employers, industry organizations, and educational institutions as evidence of skills and knowledge acquired through online learning.

- **Continuing Education:** MOOCs provide opportunities for continuing education and lifelong learning across various disciplines and fields of study. Professionals, working adults, and lifelong learners can enroll in MOOCs to stay current with developments in their industry, explore new interests, or pursue personal enrichment.

  Continuing education programs offered through MOOCs allow individuals to update their skills, expand their knowledge, and remain competitive in the job market.

- **Supplementary Learning Resources:** MOOCs can serve as supplementary learning resources to complement traditional educational programs. Instructors can recommend MOOCs to students as additional study materials, enrichment activities, or opportunities for independent learning.

  Students can use MOOCs to explore topics in more depth, review challenging concepts, or gain alternative perspectives that may not be covered in traditional classroom settings.

- **Professional Development for Educators:** MOOCs offer professional development opportunities for educators to enhance their teaching skills, explore new pedagogical approaches, and stay updated with advancements in education technology.

  Teachers and faculty members can enroll in MOOCs focused on topics such as instructional design, classroom management, assessment strategies, educational technology integration, and teaching methodologies.

- **Workforce Training:** MOOCs are increasingly used for workforce training and corporate learning initiatives. Employers can provide employees with access to MOOCs covering job-related skills, industry-specific knowledge, and professional development.

  Corporate training programs delivered through MOOCs help organizations upskill and reskill their workforce, address skill gaps, and adapt to changing industry trends and technologies.

- **Global Collaboration and Knowledge Sharing:** MOOCs facilitate global collaboration and knowledge sharing among learners from diverse backgrounds and geographic locations. Participants can engage in online discussions, collaborate on projects, and share insights and experiences with peers from around the world.

MOOC-based learning communities provide opportunities for networking, professional connections, and cross-cultural exchange, fostering a collaborative and inclusive learning environment.

Overall, the practical applications of MOOCs encompass a broad spectrum of educational and professional development needs, ranging from skill development and certification to continuing education, professional development, and workforce training. By leveraging MOOCs as versatile learning tools, individuals and organizations can access high-quality educational content, enhance their skills, and achieve their learning goals.

7. Ethical and Social Implications

Here are some key ethical and social implications of MOOCs:

- **Access and Equity:** Ethical Implication: MOOCs have the potential to democratize education by providing access to high-quality educational content to learners worldwide. However, ensuring equitable access to MOOCs requires addressing barriers such as internet connectivity, digital literacy, language barriers, and socio-economic disparities.

- **Social Implication:** MOOCs can help bridge the digital divide and expand educational opportunities for underserved populations, including individuals from low-income communities, rural areas, and developing countries.

Data Privacy and Security:

- **Ethical Implication:** MOOC platforms collect vast amounts of data on learner interactions, engagement patterns, and performance metrics. Protecting learner privacy and ensuring the security of personal data is essential to uphold ethical standards and maintain trust in MOOCs.

- **Social Implication:** Safeguarding learner data helps prevent unauthorized access, data breaches, and misuse of personal information. Transparent data privacy policies and robust security measures are necessary to protect learner confidentiality and maintain the integrity of MOOC platforms.

Intellectual Property Rights:

- **Ethical Implication:** MOOCs often involve the creation and dissemination of educational content, including lectures, readings, assignments, and assessments. Respecting intellectual property rights and acknowledging the contributions of content creators is essential to uphold ethical standards in MOOC development and delivery.

- **Social Implication:** Protecting intellectual property rights fosters a culture of innovation, creativity, and academic integrity. Clear guidelines on copyright, fair use, and licensing agreements help ensure that content creators receive proper recognition and compensation for their work.

Quality Assurance and Accountability:

- **Ethical Implication:** MOOC providers have a responsibility to ensure the quality and integrity of course content, instructional materials, and assessment methods. Maintaining transparency, accountability, and academic rigor is essential to uphold ethical standards and promote trust in MOOCs.

- **Social Implication:** High-quality MOOCs enhance the credibility and reputation of online education, benefiting learners, employers, and educational institutions. Rigorous quality assurance processes help identify and address issues related to course design, instructional effectiveness, and assessment validity.

Digital Divide and Inclusion:

- **Ethical Implication:** MOOCs should strive to address inequalities in access to technology, internet connectivity, and digital literacy skills. Promoting inclusivity and addressing the needs of diverse learners, including those with disabilities or special educational requirements, is essential to uphold ethical principles of equity and social justice.

- **Social Implication:** Bridging the digital divide and promoting digital inclusion are critical for ensuring that all individuals have equal opportunities to participate in online education. Accessible design, inclusive pedagogical approaches, and support services for marginalized groups help promote equal access and participation in MOOCs.

Social Impact and Community Engagement:

- **Ethical Implication:** MOOCs have the potential to foster global collaboration, knowledge sharing, and community engagement among learners from diverse backgrounds. Building inclusive learning communities, promoting cultural sensitivity, and respecting diverse perspectives are essential to uphold ethical principles of respect, dignity, and mutual understanding.

- **Social Implication:** MOOC-based learning communities can promote social cohesion, cross-cultural exchange, and collaborative problem-solving. Encouraging active participation, dialogue, and empathy among learners contribute to positive social outcomes and promote a culture of lifelong learning and global citizenship.

Addressing these ethical and social implications requires collaboration among MOOC providers, educators, policymakers, and stakeholders to develop policies, guidelines, and best practices that uphold ethical standards, promote social equity, and maximize the potential of MOOCs to benefit learners and society as a whole.

8. Future Trends and Innovations

Here are some potential future trends and innovations in MOOCs:

- **Personalized Learning Pathways:** Future MOOCs may incorporate personalized learning algorithms and adaptive technologies to tailor the learning experience to the individual needs, preferences, and abilities of each learner.

  Adaptive learning platforms can dynamically adjust course content, pacing, and support mechanisms based on learner performance, engagement levels, and learning style preferences.

- **Micro-Credentials and Stackable Certifications:** MOOC platforms may offer micro-credentials, badges, and stackable certifications that allow learners to demonstrate mastery of specific skills or competencies.

  Micro-credentials provide learners with flexible pathways for skills development, career advancement, and lifelong learning, allowing them to earn recognition for completing shorter, targeted courses or modules.

- **Blockchain-Based Credentialing:** Future MOOCs may leverage blockchain technology to provide secure, transparent, and verifiable credentials and certifications.

  Blockchain-based credentialing systems offer benefits such as enhanced security, tamper-proof records, and portability of credentials across platforms and institutions.

- **Augmented Reality (AR) and Virtual Reality (VR) Integration:** MOOCs may integrate AR and VR technologies to create immersive learning experiences that simulate real-world environments, scenarios, and simulations.

AR and VR can enhance engagement, retention, and experiential learning by allowing learners to interact with digital content in 3D environments and visualize complex concepts in a more tangible way.

- **Collaborative and Social Learning Features:** Future MOOCs may incorporate more advanced collaborative and social learning features, such as real-time collaboration tools, group projects, and peer-to-peer mentoring.

Social learning platforms can foster community engagement, knowledge sharing, and collaborative problem-solving among learners from diverse backgrounds and geographic locations.

- **AI-Powered Learning Assistants:** MOOCs may utilize artificial intelligence (AI) technologies to provide personalized learning recommendations, feedback, and support to learners.

AI-powered learning assistants can analyze learner data, identify learning patterns, and provide targeted interventions to support learners in achieving their learning goals more effectively.

- **Continued Integration with Traditional Education:** MOOCs will continue to be integrated with traditional education settings, such as universities, colleges, and corporate training programs.

Blended learning models, flipped classrooms, and hybrid educational formats will become more common as institutions leverage MOOCs to complement face-to-face instruction and expand access to educational opportunities.

- **Open Educational Resources (OER) and Open Access Initiatives:** MOOCs may contribute to the growth of open educational resources (OER) and open access initiatives by providing free or low-cost educational content to learners worldwide.

Open access MOOCs can help reduce barriers to education, promote knowledge sharing, and support collaborative efforts to advance open education principles and practices.

Overall, future trends and innovations in MOOCs will continue to shape the landscape of online learning, offering new opportunities for personalized learning, credentialing, immersive experiences, and collaborative engagement. By embracing these trends and leveraging emerging technologies, MOOCs can continue to evolve as effective tools for education, skills development, and lifelong learning in the digital age.

By covering these points in-depth, educators can provide college students with a comprehensive understanding of MOOCs and their implications for education, technology, and society. Through critical analysis, hands-on activities, and thoughtful discussions, students can develop the knowledge and skills necessary to navigate the evolving landscape of online learning.

SWAYAM

1. Overview of Swayam Platform

- **Definition:** Swayam, short for Study Webs of Active Learning for Young Aspiring Minds, is an initiative by the Government of India aimed at providing free and quality education to all, leveraging the power of technology.

- **Mission:** The mission of Swayam is to democratize education by making high-quality educational resources accessible to learners across India, regardless of their geographical location, economic background, or educational qualifications.

- **Features:** Swayam offers a wide range of courses across various disciplines, including arts, science, engineering, humanities, social sciences, and more. These courses are developed and delivered by faculty members from renowned institutions and universities across India.

- **Key Components:** The Swayam platform consists of online courses, study materials, video lectures, interactive quizzes, assignments, discussion forums, and assessment tools. Learners can access course materials and participate in activities at their own pace and convenience.

2. Structure and Organization of Courses

- **Course Structure:** Swayam courses are organized into modules or units, each covering specific topics or themes related to the course subject. Courses may include video lectures, readings, quizzes, assignments, and interactive activities to engage learners in active learning.

- **Course Duration:** The duration of Swayam courses varies depending on the subject and level of complexity. Courses may range from a few weeks to several months, with learners expected to dedicate a certain number of hours per week to study and coursework.

- **Course Levels:** Swayam offers courses at different levels, including undergraduate, postgraduate, and certificate programs. Courses are designed to cater to learners with varying levels of prior knowledge and experience in the subject matter.

- **Course Credits:** Some Swayam courses offer credits that can be transferred to formal degree programs offered by participating institutions. Learners who successfully complete these courses and pass the assessment criteria may receive certificates or academic credits recognized by universities and colleges.

3. Pedagogical Approach and Learning Experience

- **Interactive Learning:** Swayam courses emphasize interactive learning experiences that engage learners actively in the learning process. Courses may include quizzes, assignments, group projects, and discussion forums to promote active participation and knowledge sharing among learners.

- **Self-Paced Learning:** Swayam courses are designed to accommodate learners with diverse learning styles and preferences. Learners can study at their own pace and on their own schedule, accessing course materials and completing assignments at their convenience.

- **Support Mechanisms:** Swayam provides support mechanisms to help learners succeed in their studies. This may include access to online tutors, mentors, academic advisors, and support staff who can provide guidance, assistance, and feedback throughout the course.

4. Accessibility and Inclusivity

- **Open Access:** Swayam courses are open to anyone who wishes to enroll, with no admission criteria or prerequisites. Learners can access course materials and participate in activities free of charge, making education accessible to all.

- **Digital Inclusion:** Swayam aims to promote digital inclusion by providing access to online educational resources to learners from diverse backgrounds and geographical locations. The platform is accessible via the internet, allowing learners to study from anywhere using their computer or mobile device.

- **Language Support:** Swayam offers courses in multiple languages, including English and various regional languages spoken across India. This helps cater to the linguistic diversity of learners and promotes access to education for speakers of different languages.

5. Future Directions and Impact

- **Expansion and Growth:** Swayam continues to grow and expand its course offerings, reaching more learners across India and beyond. The platform aims to collaborate with additional institutions and organizations to develop new courses and enhance the quality and diversity of educational resources available to learners.

- **Impact on Education:** Swayam has the potential to revolutionize education in India by democratizing access to high-quality educational content and promoting lifelong learning. By leveraging technology and innovation, Swayam empowers learners to acquire new knowledge and skills, pursue their educational aspirations, and contribute to the socio-economic development of the nation.

6. Conclusion

In conclusion, Swayam is a groundbreaking initiative that aims to democratize education and promote lifelong learning through online courses and educational resources. With its wide range of courses, flexible learning options, and commitment to accessibility and inclusivity, Swayam has the potential to transform the educational landscape in India and empower learners to achieve their full potential. As Swayam continues to evolve and grow, it will play an increasingly important role in shaping the future of education and fostering a culture of learning and innovation in India.

Difference between SWAYAM and MOOCs

Swayam and MOOCs (Massive Open Online Courses) share similarities in their goals of providing accessible, high-quality education through online platforms. However, there are several key differences between Swayam and MOOCs in terms of their origins, governance, scope, and target audience:

Origin and Governance:

- **Swayam:** Swayam is an initiative launched by the Government of India, specifically by the Ministry of Human Resource Development (MHRD). It is a national platform aimed at providing free and quality education to learners across India.

- **MOOCs**: MOOCs are a global phenomenon that originated in the early 2000s with the launch of platforms like Coursera, edX, and Udacity. These platforms are typically operated by private companies or consortiums of universities and institutions.

Scope and Course Offerings:

- **Swayam:** Swayam offers a wide range of courses across various disciplines, including arts, science, engineering, humanities, social sciences, and more. These courses are developed and delivered by faculty members from Indian universities and institutions.

- **MOOCs:** MOOC platforms offer courses from universities and institutions worldwide, covering diverse subjects and disciplines. While some MOOCs may focus on specific areas or industries, the scope of MOOC offerings is generally broader compared to Swayam.

Target Audience:

- **Swayam:** Swayam primarily targets learners in India, including students, professionals, and lifelong learners seeking to enhance their skills and knowledge. The platform aims to address the educational needs of individuals across different age groups and socio-economic backgrounds.

- **MOOCs:** MOOCs cater to a global audience of learners from diverse geographical locations and cultural backgrounds. While MOOCs are accessible to learners worldwide, the content and instructional materials may be tailored to suit the preferences and needs of a global audience.

Certification and Accreditation:

- **Swayam:** Swayam offers certificates to learners who successfully complete course requirements and pass the assessment criteria. These certificates may be recognized by universities and institutions in India and may carry academic credits that can be transferred to formal degree programs.

- **MOOCs:** MOOC platforms offer certificates of completion or micro-credentials for learners who successfully complete courses. While some MOOC certificates may carry academic credit or be recognized by employers, the recognition and accreditation of MOOC certificates vary depending on the institution and industry.

Funding and Support:

- **Swayam:** Swayam is funded and supported by the Government of India through the Ministry of Human Resource Development. It receives funding from government budgets and may also collaborate with educational institutions and organizations to develop and deliver courses.

- **MOOCs:** MOOC platforms are typically funded through a combination of venture capital, grants, tuition fees for premium features, and revenue-sharing agreements with partner institutions. They operate as independent entities or consortia and may collaborate with universities, corporations, and non-profit organizations.

In summary, while Swayam and MOOCs share common objectives of expanding access to education through online platforms, they differ in terms of their governance, scope, target audience, certification, and funding models. Swayam focuses on providing free and quality education to learners in India, while MOOCs offer a broader range of courses from institutions worldwide to a global audience of learners.

Chapter 6
E-Commerce

E-Commerce and its Types

Electronic commerce also known as E-commerce, alludes to the commercial exercises like on-line shopping and payments carried out by utilizing computers and the Internet and a customer who shops online is called a *cyber consumer*. E-Commerce is not only restricted to online shopping, but also includes preparation of online estimates, interaction with users, maintaining an electronic catalog, real-time management of stock, online payment; tracing of delivered products, after-sales service, online registration of complaints related to products etc.

Types
1. The different types of E-commerce are:
2. Business-Business (B2B)
3. Business-Consumer (B2C)
4. Consumer-to-Consumer (C2C)
5. Consumer-Business (C2B)
6. Mobile Commerce (M-Commerce)

Business-to-Business

A commerce activity that exists between businesses or that happens between a corporations and companies to transfer of services and merchandise. It incorporates web-based wholesaling in which organizations offer materials, items and administrations to different organizations on the websites. B2B model has turned out to be crucial to the worldwide economy. According to the latest forecasts, by 2020, all B2B web-based business income will be around 6.7 trillion USD. The site must represent the business well, easy to understand, and enable forthcoming purchasers to get the data they are hunting down. This brings up an issue about the correct decision of business-to-business web based software.

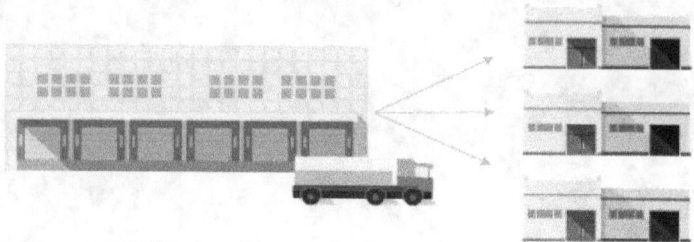

B2C Business-to-Consumer

A commerce activity that exists between business and customers (end users) and so it create an electronic store fronts that offer information, goods, and services between business and shopper online.

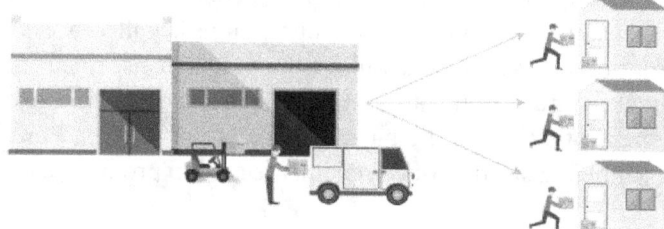

C2B Consumer-to-Business

Is the transfer of services, goods or information from persons to business or it is a business model where end users create products and services that are used by business and institutions.

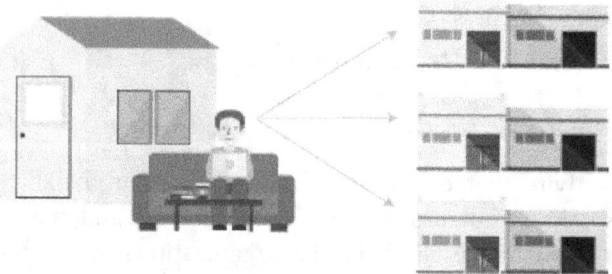

C2C Consumer-to-Consumer

Here transactions are among users this business model supports business between two or more consumers directly. Websites enable clients to exchange, purchase, and offer things in return for a little commission paid to the site. Opening a C2C site takes cautious arranging.

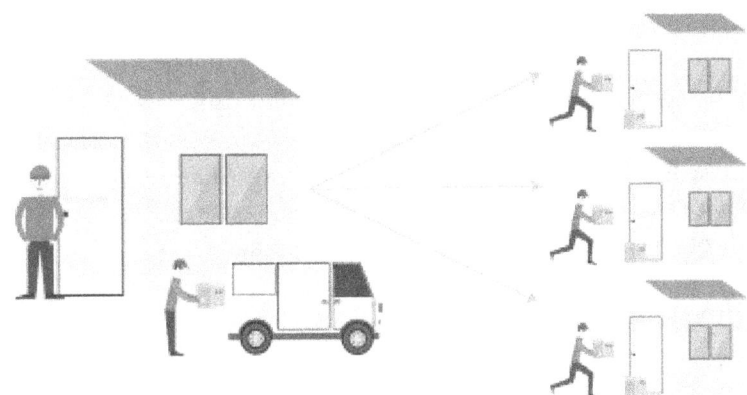

Regardless of the undeniable achievement of stages like eBay and Craigslist, various other sale and arranged locales (the fundamental fields for C2C) have opened and immediately shut because of unsustainable models.

M-Commerce

The term of Mobile Commerce found in 1997 where, purchasing and offering of merchandise, data and information is done by means of remote handheld gadgets with wireless support. For example, cell phones, personal computers. and laptop etc. It is portable trade which permits clients to access the Internet and shopping without any kind of physical connection.

Types of E-Commerce Business Models

The next most important thing to think about is how you want to handle inventory management and sourcing products. Some people like the idea of making their own products and others hate the idea of their garage full of boxes.

Drop Shipping

Consumer places order on online store. — Online store passes order to drop shipper. — Supplier ships order directly to consumer.

The simplest form of ecommerce, drop shipping lets you set up a storefront and take the customers' money. The rest is up to your supplier. This frees you from managing inventory, warehousing stock, or dealing with packaging, but there's a major caveat.

If your sellers are slow, product quality is lower than expected, or there are problems with the order, it's on your head (and in your reviews). Wacky Hippo is an example of an ecommerce site using drop shipping.

Wholesaling and Warehousing

Wholesaling and warehousing ecommerce businesses require a lot of investment at the start – you need to manage inventory and stock, keep track of customer orders and shipping information, and invest in the warehouse space itself.

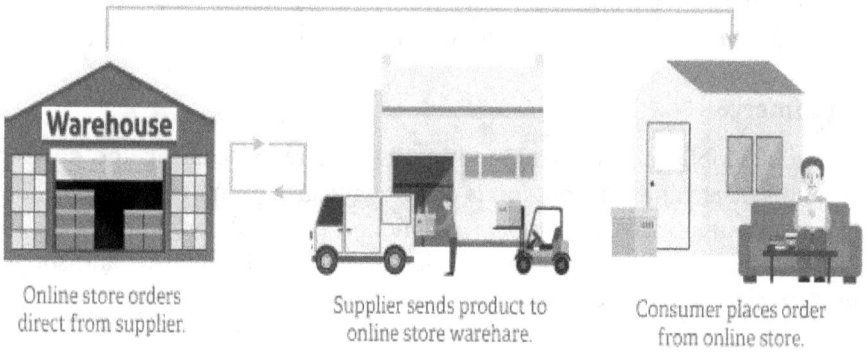

Online store orders direct from supplier.

Supplier sends product to online store warehare.

Consumer places order from online store.

DollarDays is an online wholesaler with a massive product catalog that includes more than 260,000 products. They employ a key strategy for retailers in this space by offering case prices AND piece prices, they can sell to the general public and to retailers. This gives them a higher profit margin than a strictly wholesale model.

Private Labelling and Manufacturing

If you've got an idea for the perfect product, but don't have the cash or desire to build your own factory, this might be the right ecommerce business model for you. Companies that manufacture products offsite for sale send the plans or prototypes to a contracted manufacturer who produces the product to meet customer specifications and can either ship directly to the consumer, to a third party such as Amazon, or to the company selling the final product.

E-Commerce

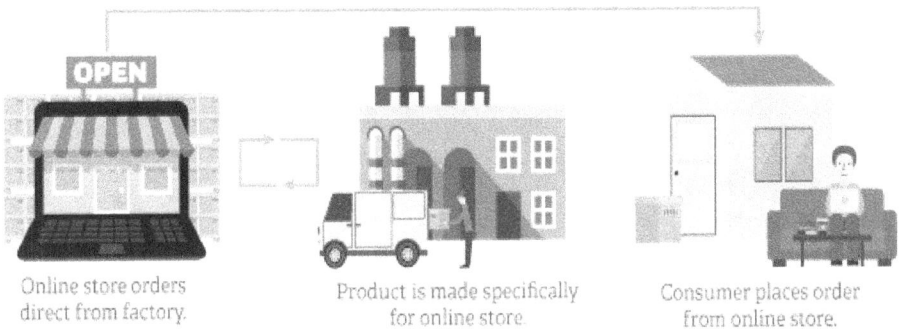

| Online store orders direct from factory. | Product is made specifically for online store. | Consumer places order from online store. |

On-demand manufacturing allows you to quickly change suppliers if you encounter problems with product quality. The startup costs are minimal, and if you're interested in potentially opening your own production facilities later, this is a good way to test a new product or concept.

White Labelling

You choose a product that is already successfully sold by another company, but offers white label options, design your package and label, and sell the product. This is common in the beauty and wellness industries, but more difficult to encounter in other niches.

| Online store orders direct from supplier. | Existing product is relabeled with your branding. | Consumer places order from online store. |

One problem with white labelling is demand. You're stuck with whatever you order, and most of these companies set a minimum production quantity. If you can't sell it, you'll have to live with it. Consider this option when you're willing to work full time on your business and know your product is in demand.

Subscription Ecommerce

One of the most popular and successful pure ecommerce brands is the Dollar Shave Club. Other examples of subscription services include Stitch Fix, Blue Apron, and Nature Box. On the local level, community-supported agriculture boxes are popular.

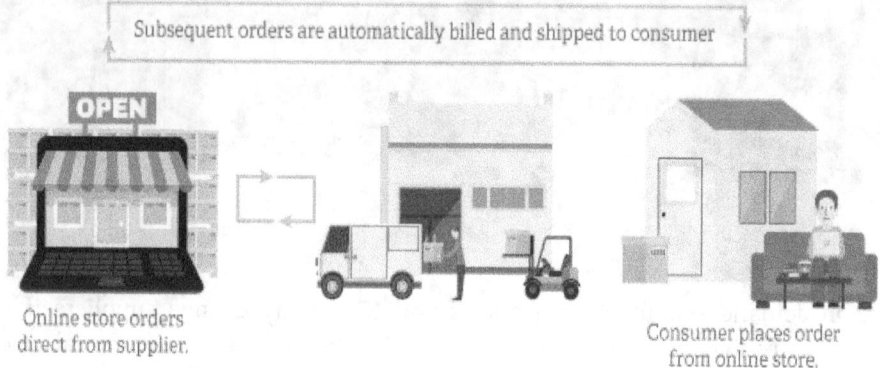

Online store orders direct from supplier.

Consumer places order from online store.

These ecommerce companies rely on a subscription model that delivers customers a box of products at regular, scheduled intervals. Subscription companies have relatively reliable income streams and can easily incentivize customers to purchase additional subscriptions or encourage their contacts to subscribe.

Picking the right products and niches can be difficult. Successful subscription boxes tend to fall into a small handful of product categories: health and grooming, beauty, fashion, and food. Outside of these areas, few subscription companies thrive.

Advantages of E-Commerce

Make Business More Accessible

E-commerce or web-based business has made it less demanding for organizations to contact individuals around the globe and run their business without moving toward their providers straightforwardly. It gives access to the buyers and organizations everywhere throughout the world.

Decreased Cost of Business: Online business decreases the exertion required to work together. It lessens the labour required, stock costs, buying expenses telephone calls etc.

Increases the Sale of the Business: because it increases the access of the customers to the business and hence increases the sale too.

Lessened Work Pressure on Staff: Internet business improves and simplifies the services to the clients without much interaction with the employee of the organisation, in this manner mitigating the staff from one of their activity obligations.

Easy, Secure and Better Payment Option: With the advancements in online payment system, E-business permits encoded and secure online payment

Simplified business administration: With the utilization of effective programming, the vast majority of the business-related assignments are simplified. Sending and accepting logs and different business organization forms are consequently put away.

Disadvantages

Despite of the easy way for the customer to access lot of products with different varieties it has some difficulties too and some of the most difficulties are briefed below:

Tax Collection Difficulties: It is not easy to fix the criteria on which taxes should be charged from the products when the business and the customers are in different countries and states. It is unjustifiable to gather taxes from organizations whose items are not promoted over the Internet and to permit organizations offering their items over the Internet not to pay any tax.

Security: It is a major threat to the e-commerce system where it needs advanced encryption and deception systems to protect the confidential information about their customers or clients.

High Delivery Cost: Deployment of product to the customers is sometimes very costly especially web business and clients have different countries or states.

Lack of Personal Touch and Experience the Product: There is no individual way to deal with the products physically and personally, and denial of the individual touch in online purchase can be the greatest weakness of web-based business.

E-Commerce Delays Goods: Especially when business is in different state delivery of products take a lot longer time to get the goods into your hands even though we are using express shipping services.

All Goods Can't Be Purchased: there are goods that you cannot buy online. Most of these would be in the categories of "perishable" or "odd-sized e.g. ice-cream."

Architecture

E-commerce supports two and three tiers client server architecture. General two and three tier architectures are briefed here.

Two Tier Client -Server Architecture

It has two Tier, one is Client Tier and other is Data Tier as shown in Figure 6.1.

Client Tier

- Clients request the data from the server and server satisfies the request by fetching the data from the server.
- It is two level communication i.e. communications from client to server and server to client.
- Client tier provides an interface to the users through which users interact with the e- commerce vendors.
- It displays products, prices etc. to the customers.

Data Tier

- Stores product data, price data and customer data.

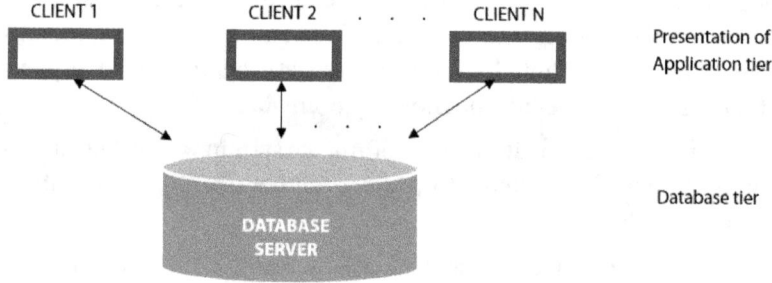

Figure 6.1: *Two tier Architecture*

Three Tier Architecture

It comprises of three layers or tiers namely Presentation layer, application, and Database layer as shown in Figure 6.2.

Presentation Layer: presents information to the user in different formats, communicates with the users, database server and other tier.

Application Layer: Also known as middle tier and controls business logics

Determines how data is to be created, displayed, modified and stored in different layers.

Data Tier: Where data is stored and retrieved and data is independent from the business logic data contains database and file management software. Provides Application programming interface API to application layer to communicate with the database layer.

E-Commerce

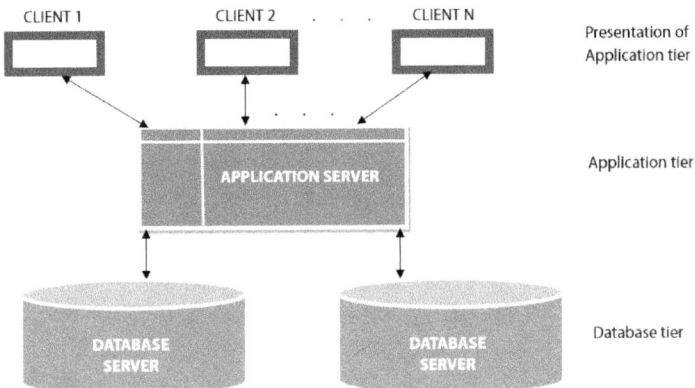

Figure 6.2: *Three tier Architecture*

Note: *All e-commerce companies follow three tier architecture because it is more secure and robust as compared to two tiers.*

The following flow of sequence when a customer places an order is shown below and this flow is supported by all three layers of the architecture.

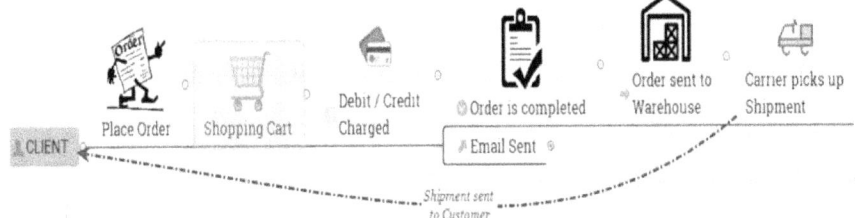

Figure 6.3: *Process of placing an online order [carajaclasses.com]*

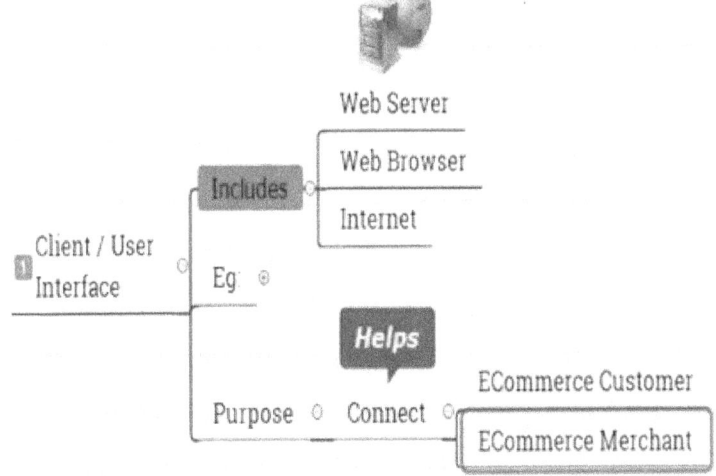

Figure 6.4: *Functions of client layer*

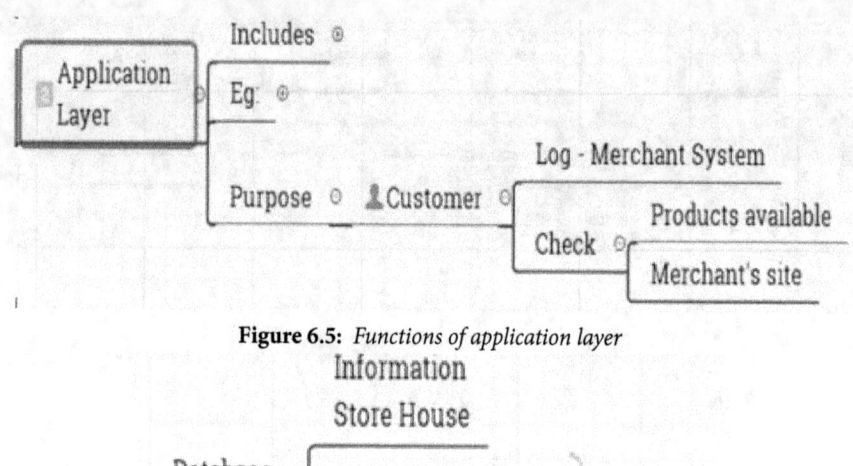

Figure 6.5: *Functions of application layer*

Figure 6.5: *Functions of application layer*

In today's life data security is a major concern and there are high threats from malicious software are called computer viruses, Trojan horses, worms and they have the ability to damage precious computer hardware, corrupt valuable data, tie up limited computing resources.

Chapter 7
Computer Viruses

A computer virus is a small program developed to damage or disrupt the normal functions of our computer and its data. It replicates or spreads itself when an infected file is executed and infecting other programs on the same computer.

How viruses are transmitted from one device to another by email, downloading from the internet, network connections, floppy disks or CDs etc.

Basic Classifications of Viruses

Worm Viruses

Are self-contained man-made programs replicating or spreading themselves that remain hidden and propagate via email or duplication to other computers but, unlike a virus, it does not infect other program files on the computer.

Boot Viruses

They attack the boot sectors on hard drive and disrupt basic operations of computer, stop normal operating system functioning run.

Macro Viruses

They are mainly designed to attack data files, e.g. word documents and spreadsheets.

Trojan Viruses

Trojan viruses pretend to be legitimate software other software, but in reality, it will attack drives, deleting files and modifying system files, making system to become unstable when operating system files are deleted. Although Trojan horse programs are not true viruses, because they do not replicate. Trojan Horses are often found with free downloads since we cannot oppose a free offer. Once loaded onto our machine, it may capture usernames and passwords or may allow a wicked hacker to remotely control our computer.

E-Mail Viruses

E-mail is most likely the common method for replicating and transmitting the virus and email viruses are spread via attachments. To protect against email viruses, it is wise to not open attachments from strangers.

FAT viruses

Use the File Allocation Table or FAT part of a disk which contains important information related to the opened files in the system. It alters the information of FAT and is dangerous because it may change the order of operations leading to unexpected results.

Table 7.1: Summary of some important viruses is given in table

Virus name	Intention	Affects
Program or File Virus	Infects executables (other programs, with affixes such as EXE, BIN, COM, SYS).	Destroys or alters programs and data.
Boot sector Virus	Infects boot sectors on hard and floppy disks.	Destroys or alters programs and data.
Multipartite Virus	A hybrid of a program and boot sector virus.	Destroys or alters programs and data.
Macro Virus	Triggers on a command in Microsoft Office.	Usually damage Word & Excel.
Stealth Virus	Uses various strategies to avoid detection.	Destroys or alters programs and data.
Polymorphic Virus	Uses encryption to halt detection, so that it appears differently in each infection.	Destroys or alters programs and data files.

Steps on How to Minimise Your Exposure to Viruses

- Purchase and install anti-virus software.
- Used software must be compatible with the operating system used.
- Update your antivirus software at regular intervals.
- Regularly Scan computer system and external devices used in computer for viruses by using anti-virus.
- Scan new programs or other files for virus that may contain executable files before you run or open them.
- Avoid open unknown emails or email attachments.

Stages in the Life of a Virus

The lifetime, of a virus is described in terms of four stages:

1. **Dormant Phase**: In this phase, the virus is idle and will be initiated and activated by occurrences of some events such as the system date or the presence of another program or file.
2. **Propagation Phase**: In this stage, the virus places an indistinguishable copy of itself into different programs or into certain territories on the disk. Each contaminated file now contains a clone of the virus, which will itself enter a propagation phase.
3. **Triggering Phase**: Here, it will be activated and perform its intended function. As with the dormant phase, the triggering phase can be caused by a variety of system events.
4. **Execution Phase**: The actual function of the virus is performed in the execution phase i.e. damaging the data files.

Virus Generations

Viruses are classified into five generations and each new generation of viruses has introduced some new features which make the viruses trickier to detect and eradicate.

First generation (Simple): The first generation of viruses consisted of simple viruses. These viruses are simple and do nothing other than replication. Boot sector viruses come under this generation, which could cause a long chain of linked sectors. Many of the new viruses being discovered today still fall in this category. Damages from these simple viruses are usually caused by bugs or incompatibilities in software that were not anticipated by the author of the virus; they don't hide identity and usually can be found simply by noticing an increase in the size of files or the presence of a distinctive pattern in an infected file.

Second generation (Self-recognition): First generation viruses repeatedly infect the host, which leads to depleted memory and then early detection. To prevent this unnecessary growth of infected files, second-generation viruses usually implant a unique signature that signals that the file or system is infected. The virus will check for this signature before attempting infection. If the signature is not present, it will place the signature soon after the infection has taken place; however, if the signature is present, the virus will not re-infect the host.

Third generation (Stealth): They destabilize and interrupt selected system service when they are active. If any operation identifies the presence of the virus, the process is redirected to return false information.

Fourth Generation (Armoured): As anti-virus researchers have developed tools to analyse new viruses, authors have turned to methods to confuse the code of their viruses. This "armouring" is to add extra unnecessary code for confusing and it is more difficult to analyse the virus code. These viruses may attack direct even though anti-virus software installed on the affected system.

Fifth Generation (Polymorphic): Latest class of viruses also called self-mutating viruses. These viruses infect their targets with a customized or encrypted version of themselves. Therefore a simple byte matching algorithm cannot detect the presence of such viruses and to detect the presence of such viruses require more complex algorithms.

Some Important Points:

- First PC virus was developed in 1986 (Pakistan, boot sector) and it was Brain virus.
- First memory resident file virus was discovered in 1987 at Lehigh University called Lehigh virus.
- First anti-virus (1988) was Den Zuk developed in Indonesia and It was designed to handle Brain virus.
- I Love You virus (2000) causes chaos; was communicated via email and, when opened, it robotically sends mail to one and all in the user's address book.
- It is transmitted via e-mail and, When opened, it automatically Sends mail to everyone.

Chapter 8
Computer Networks and Data Communication

What is a Computer Network?

A computer network is a network of computers that are geographically distributed, but are connected in such a way that they are able to transfer and exchange the data among each other. In another word, a computer network is a combination of hardware and software that transfer data from one location to another. Primary objectives of a computer network are:

a. Sharing of information
b. Sharing of resources
c. Processing of load.

Network Topologies

The term network topology tells us how the nodes or devices in a network are connected with each other. The network topology is the geometric representation of the relationship of all the links and connecting devices. It tells us about the possible paths available between any pair of nodes in the network. The main four network topologies are given below:

- Mesh Network topology
- Bus Network Topology
- Star Network Topology
- Ring Network Topology
- Hybrid Network Topology

Mesh Topology

Mesh topology is also known as a completely connected network. In this network every device has a dedicated point-to-point link to every other device. If there are N nodes, then the first node is connected to N-1 nodes, the second node is connected to N-1, the third node is connected to N-1 and so on. Thus, the total number of physical links is N(N-1). If physical links are duplex in nature there are N(N-1)/2 links. Mesh topology is shown in Figure 8.1

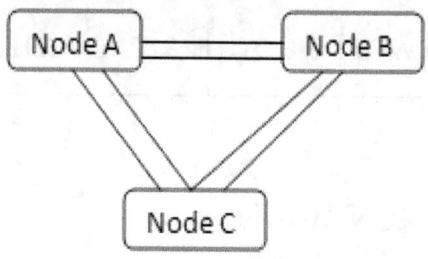

Figure 8.1: *A mesh topology for three nodes.*

All regional telephone offices are connected through mesh topology.

Advantages

1. There is not a single common channel for data transmission, as a result there is no traffic problem.
2. Each connection will carry its own data load i.e. the load of only two devices.
3. It is more robust and reliable.
4. Communication cannot stop due to the failure of the one link, because on failure, another link will be available for data transfer.
5. Because of dedicated links communication is very fast.
6. Point-to-point links make the identification and fault isolation easy.

Disadvantages

1. It requires more cabling.
2. Hardware required is very expensive.
3. The links required are N(N-1).

Bus Topology

A bus topology is known as multipoint topology. Here a single long cable acts as a *backbone* to link all the devices in a network. When a node wishes to send a message or packet to another node, it adds the destination address at the beginning of the message and then check the availability of the link i.e. It checks whether the link is free or not. When line found free, it broadcasts (sends to every other node) the message on the line. Each node will receive the message and check the destination address of the message added at the sender site. If the node found is addressed to it, the received message will be accepted, otherwise it is rejected. After accepting the message, the node sends an acknowledgement to the source node and frees the line. The bus topology is shown in Figure 8.2.

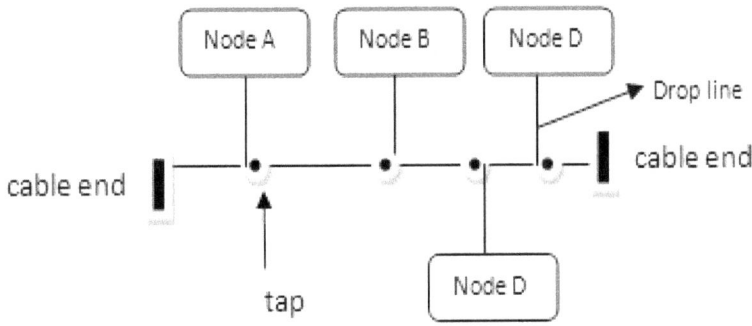

Figure 8.2: *Multipoint bus topology*

Nodes are connected to the bus or cable by drop lines and taps.

Advantages

1. Easy to install.
2. Buses less cabling than star and mesh topologies.
3. Failure of a node does not affect communication among other nodes.

Disadvantages

1. Reconnection and fault isolation is difficult.
2. Adding a new device to the network is not easy.
3. Signal reflection at the taps can cause degradation in quality by creating the noise.
4. Fault or break in the cable stops all transmission, even between devices on the same side of the problem.
5. All nodes in the network must have good communication capabilities.
6. Only one node at a time can send the message.

Star Network Topology

In this topology a special type of node called host node or hub is used. All the nodes in the network are connected to this host node. There is no direct communication between the nodes, and they can communicate via host node by establishing a logical path or connection between them. If a node wants to send data to another node, it sends the data to the hub first, which then forwards the data to the other connecting node. Star topology is shown in Figure 8.3.

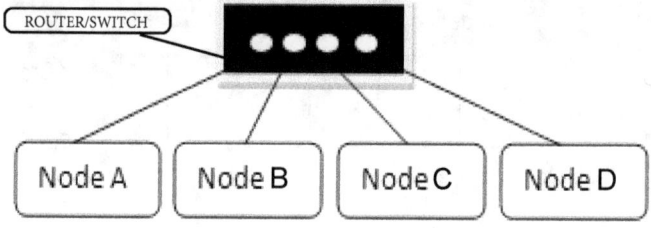

Figure 8.3: *Star topology connecting 4 nodes*

Advantages

1. Star topology is more robust i.e., if one link is failed it will not affect the whole communication.
2. Easy fault identification and isolation.
3. It has minimal line (wire) cost, because for *N* nodes there are *N-1* lines required.
4. Adding more nodes does not increase the delay in transmission.
5. Less expensive than mesh topology.

Disadvantages

1. The biggest disadvantage of this topology is that whole communication is dependent on the hub.
2. Failure of hub means failure of whole communication.
3. More cabling is required as compared to ring and bus topologies.

Ring Network Topology

In ring topology, each device has a dedicated point-to-point connection with only the two devices on either side of it. A signal called a token is passed along the ring in one direction from node to node until it reaches its destination. Each device in this topology is incorporated with a *repeater*. The task of the repeater is to regenerate (increase the strength of the signal) the bits and pass them along. The ring topology is shown in Figure 8.4.

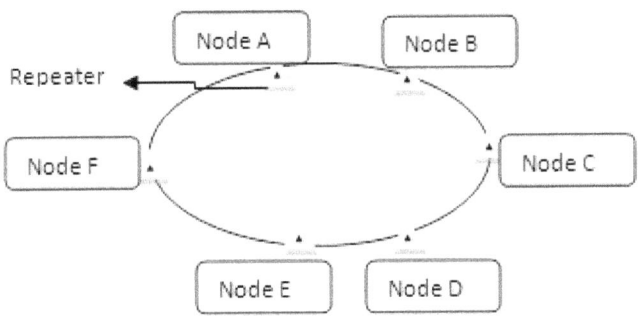

Figure 8.4: *Bus topology*

Advantages

1. Easy to install and reconfigure.
2. There is no central node like star topology.
3. More reliable than star.
4. If a link between any two nodes fails, or node itself is failed, alternate routing is possible (double ring or bidirectional ring).

Disadvantages

1. Communication delay is directly proportional to the number of nodes in the network.
2. Requires more complicated control software.
3. Most of the time it is unidirectional.

Hybrid Topology

In real life, a pure star, ring or bus topologies are rarely used. Instead, an organisation normally uses a hybrid network that is a combination of two or more different network topologies. A hybrid topology is shown in Figure 8.5.

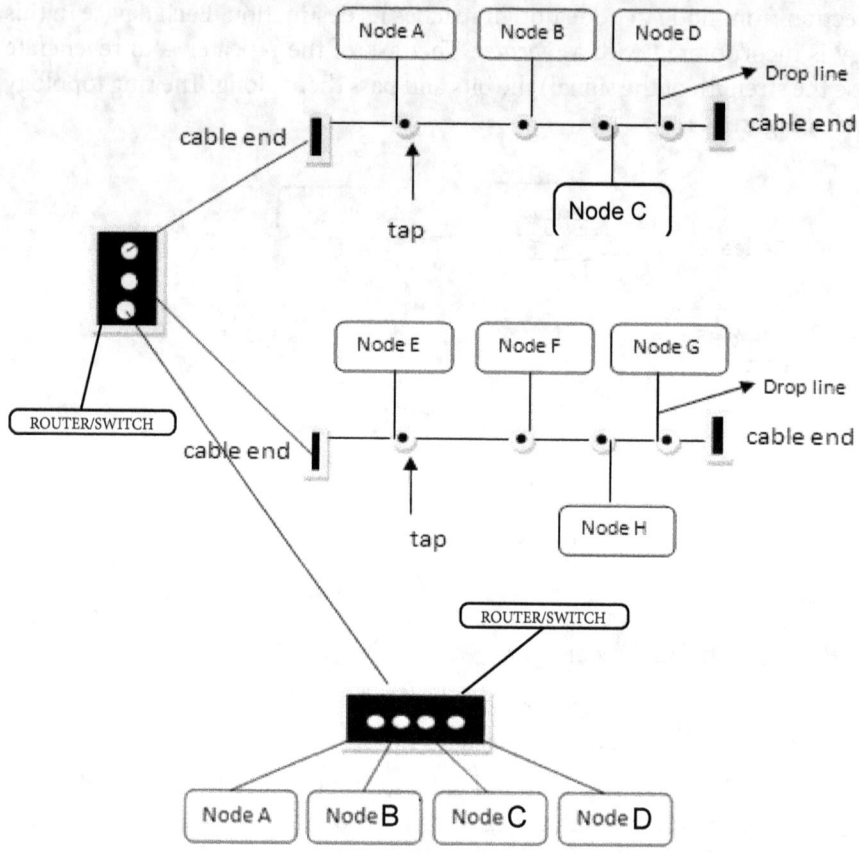

Figure 8.5: *A hybrid topology: two buses and one-star networks*

Types of Computer Network

Computer networks are classified into mainly two categories:
 a. LAN (Local area network)
 b. WAN (Wide Area Network)

LAN (Local Area Network)

LAN is a computer network that is designed for limited geographic areas such as a building or a campus. The examples of LAN technologies are Ethernet, Token Ring, Token Bus, FDDI and ATM (Asynchronous transfer mode) LAN.

Characteristics of a LAN

 a. LAN size is limited to a few kilometres.
 b. It supports the client server model of the network.

c. LAN will prefer only one type of media.
d. Early LANs have data rate of 4 to 16 megabits per second (Mbps) but today it has more than 1000 Mbps.
e. Communication can be twisted pair, coaxial cable, and fibre optics.
f. It belongs to a single organisation.
g. The cost of communication is negligible.

WAN (Wide Area Network)

It provides long- distance transmission of data, image, audio and video information over a large geographic area that may comprise a country, a continent or even the whole world. The examples of such systems are: Switched WAN X.25, ARPANET (Advance Research Project Agency Network), ERNET (Education and Research Network) and NIC (National Informatics Centre).

Characteristics of a WAN

a. WAN may extend over thousands of kilometres and may operate nationwide, continent wide or worldwide.
b. It also supports the client server model of the network.
c. Data transmission rate is less than LAN and is between 1200 bps to 2Mbps.
d. Communication media used here are: telephones lines, microwave links and satellites.
e. It belongs to multiple organisations.
f. Communication cost is high because media used is lease lines.

MAN (Metropolitan-Area Network)

This type of network shares the characteristics of both LAN and WAN and its size is between a LAN and WAN. It usually covers the area inside a town or a city. It is designed for the users who need a high -speed connectivity when the computers (nodes) spread over a city or part of the city. The examples of such systems are: telephone company network and cable TV network.

Characteristics of MAN

a. It covers a geographic area at least up to about 50 km in diameter.
b. It interconnects LANs located in metropolitan cities like Delhi.
c. Communication media usually used here are: coaxial cable and microwave links.

Note: *Data rate of LAN and WAN given here are not updated and are increasing continuously with advancements of technologies.*

Internetwork or Internet

When two more networks (LAN, MAN, WAN) are connected, they make an internet or internetwork. Thus, the internet is a network of networks. The internet uses a common mechanism for addressing or identifying computers called *IP addressing or global addressing*. It uses a common set of protocols (TCP/IP or OSI reference model) for communications between two computers on the network.

History of Internet

A network is a group of connected communicating devices such as computers and printers. When we write *internet* (lower case 'i') then two or more networks are combined to make an internet. Whereas, when we write **Internet** (uppercase 'I') then internet is the collaboration of more than hundreds of thousands interconnected networks.

In the mid 1960s, mainframes computers were mostly used in research organisations and stand-alone systems. the computers from different companies were not able to communicate with these systems. The ARPA (advance research project agency) in the department of defence was interested in finding a way to connect computers so that the researchers could share their findings.

ln 1967, at an association for computing (ACM) meeting ARPA presented its ideas for ARPANET, a small network of connected computers. In 1969, ARPANET was reality. Four nodes, at the University of California at Los Angeles (UCLA), the university of California at Santa Barbara (UCSB), Stanford research institute (SRI), and university of Utah, were connected via a special computer called Inter Message Processor (IMP). The communication software used was network control protocol (NCP).

In 1972, Vint Cerf and Bob Kahn, were the part of the core ARPANET, work together on *inter knitting project*. They gave the concept of TCP (Transmission control protocol) which included encapsulation, datagram, and the functions of a gateway. The internet evolved from basic ideas of ARPANET for interconnecting computers, and was used by research organisations and universities initially to share and exchange information. In 1989, the U.S Government lifted restrictions on use of the Internet, and allowed it to be used for commercial purposes as well. Some facts about internet in India context is given below and the source of these facts is Zee News (*DNA*):

a. Total number of internet users in India are apx.48 crore, where 11 crore users are in rural India.
b. The average internet speed in India is 3.5 Mbps and maximum speed is 25 Mbps.
c. In high-speed ranking India's position is 114 in all over the world.
d. More internet users than America.
e. Currently there are 2G, 3G, 4G and 5G speeds available in the internet world.
f. Today, the Internet is used to transfer more than 6.38 GB data per minute.
g. 47 thousand applications are downloaded per minute from the internet.
h. 701 new Apps are launched per day on the internet.
i. 60 lakhs pages are seen on Facebook in a day.
j. I lakh new tweets can be seen in a day.
k. On YouTube every month users spend 300 crores hrs.

Internet Services

The four primary services provided by the internet are given below:
a. Electronic Mail (E-Mail)
b. Telnet
c. File Transfer Protocol (FTP)
d. Usenet News

Electronic Mail

Email is one of the most popular services of the internet. At the beginning of the internet era, Email was used for text messages only. But today, E-mail is more complex and is used to send audio, video and text messages, the only restriction on data is that it must be in digital form.

It is very much similar to the postal mail service.

All internet users have an E-mail address e.g. *abc@gmail.com*. Each user has a logical *mailbox*. The E-mail service delivers the sent messages to the mailboxes of the users, later on users can retrieve and read the messages from their mailboxes. The receiver can save, delete, forward or respond by sending another message back. A simple architecture of email is given below in Figure 8.6.

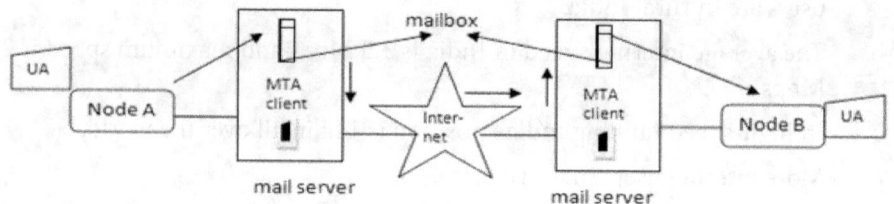

Figure 8.6: *E-mail architecture*

User Agent (UA), User agent program used to prepare the message and store it mailbox of the system at node A's site. Node B uses the same program to retrieve messages stored in the mailbox of the system at its site.

Message Transfer Agent (MTA), MTA at the sender site, takes the message from the mailbox and transfers it to the receiver over the internet, and at the receiver site, it receives the message from the internet and stores it in the mailbox at the receiver site.

Advantages

1. It is faster than postal mail services.
2. Unlike telephone, two communicating persons need to be available at the same time.
3. E-mail documents can be saved, edited and deleted easily.

File Transfer Protocol (FTP)

File transfer protocol is used to transfer files (text, audio, video) from one machine to another on the internet. Moving a file from a remote machine to one's own machine is called *downloading* the file, while moving a file from its own machine to a remote machine is called *uploading* the file. FTP is the standard mechanism provided by TCP/IP for copying a file from one system to another. FTP is different from other client server applications because it uses two connections instead of one. One connection is used to transfer data and other for control information (commands and responses). This separation makes the ftp more efficient. Another hand *Anonymous FTP*, allows a user to access the public information or files without having a *username* and *password*. In this scenario the user can use *anonymous* as the user name and *guest* as the password Architecture of FTP is shown in Figure 8.7.

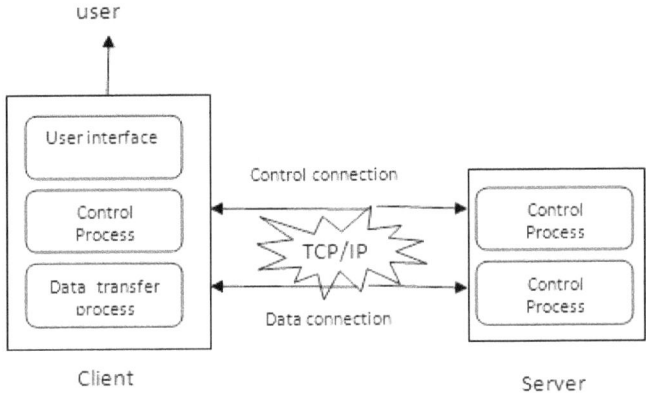

Figure 8.7: *File transfer protocol*

FTP works in the following manner:

a. A user first executes the *ftp* command on his local machine, giving the address of the remote device.

b. A ftp process on the client side establishes a connection with the *ftp* process on the server side.

c. Then the user asked to enter the user's name and password on the remote machine to ensure the authorized access to the remote machine.

d. After successful login, the user can download and upload the files by using *get* and *put* methods respectively from the remote device.

Telnet

Telnet is an abbreviation for TErminal NETwork. It is the standard TCP/IP protocol for virtual terminal service as proposed by the International Organisation for Standards **(ISO)**. ***TELNET*** enables the establishment of connection to a remote system in such a way that the local terminal appears to be a terminal at the remote system. A user can execute the telnet command on his/her local computer to start a login session on a remote machine and this action is called "remote login".

The remote login session can be created by typing the command *telnet* and then the address of the remote machine on his local machine terminal. After this the system asks the user to enter the username and password of the remote machine so that unauthorized access to the system can be avoided. Once the login session is created, *telnet* enters input mode, and anything typed on the local computer can be sent to the remote machine for further processing.

Usenet News

A Usenet service enables a group of Internet users to exchange their views/ideas/information with other members belonging to the same group. Such groups exist on the internet called *newsgroups.*

If a user wants to share his ideas with the other users of the group, he/she creates the message and submits it to the Usenet software running on his/her system. The Usenet software posts the message on the common virtual notice board, and the posted message can be seen by all members of the group.

There are two types of Newsgroups:

a. Moderated Newsgroup
b. Non-Moderated Newsgroup

Moderated Newsgroup: In this type of news group, only few members of the group have the right to post the message directly on the virtual notice board. Here the message first sent to the authorized member, he/she will check the message, if message found appropriate, he/she will posts it.

Non-Moderated NewsGroup: Here any member of the group is authorized to post the message on a common virtual notice board. This method is not preferable, because there is no mechanism to check whether a message is appropriate/readable to other members of the group.

World Wide Web (WWW)

WWW is the most popular method of accessing the internet. Its popularity is based on the concept of hypertext, where information is stored and retrieved in a novel way. A hypertext document has some series of links, and each link points to another document. Hypertexting allows a user to retrieve the information rapidly from large amounts of data on the internet. The linked document can be anywhere on the internet. The example of the hypertext document is shown below.

The Above-Mentioned Document Has two Links

a. Govt. College of Engineering & Technology Jammu,
b. Anna University Chennai.

When we click on a link, Govt. College of Engineering & Technology Jammu,, **a new** document is opened which gives the detailed description of this link. The hypertext documents on the internet are known as *web pages,* and these pages are created with the help of *HyperText Markup Language (HTML) or XML (Extendable Markup Language).* WWW uses a client server model, and the internet protocol used is called HTTP (HyperText Transfer Protocol).

WWW Browser

As we know, in the client-server network model, number machines can act as client- which request the services, and one or may more than one machine can act as server- which provide the services to the client. A system can act as a web client only when it is loaded with a special type of software called *Browser*. *The different benefits of browser are given below:*

a. Browsers do not require a user to log in and log out to the remote server, but the protocol like telnet and ftp require the user to log in and log out the server or remote machine.

b. It allows the user to access the server directly by Uniform Resource Locator (*URL* e.g. www.cukashmir.ac.in).URL is the addressing scheme which is used by the WWW browser to locate a system/server on the internet. No two sites on the internet have the same URL and it is Unique.

c. Browser provides a history feature, which is used to maintain the history of server machines visited in a surfing session.

d. With the help of a browser user can maintain the list of favourite URL addresses which are frequently used in the near future, such a list is called *hotlist*.

e. Most important feature of a browser is that it downloads the information from server to local host in various formats (text, video, audio, PostScript).

Applications/Use of Internet

Nowadays, the internet has worldwide scope. The various areas where internet is widely used are given below:

a. **Sharing:** One of the objectives of the internet is sharing of resources. It provides access to a large number of shareable software (Operating System, Compiler), tools, and utility programs.

b. **On-line Communication:** Nowadays, internet is the most rapid and productive communication tool for billions of users over the globe. Users can use Email service, social media sites like Facebook to exchange the messages with each other in a secure and secret way.

c. **Posting of Information:** Users can post the information on a virtual notice board, so that many users in the group can see the information. Twitter and Facebook are now commonly used platforms for posting and sharing the views and the useful information.

d. **Promotion and Feedback:** Many manufacturing companies make use of the internet to promote their products. Film producers, directors, actors etc are making use of the internet to promote their films. Customers are also making the use of internet to give the rating and feedback of the products of the company. After gathering the feedback about the products from the customers, the companies can do the modification on the existing products to satisfy their customers and it also increases the productivity of the company as well.

e. **Access to on-Line Journal and Magazine:** The internet has thousands of electronic subscriptions found both for free and low cost. For example users can access many research papers on "Google scholar" free of cost, many e-papers like Times of India, Greater Kashmir, Daily Excelsior etc are available free of cost.

f. **On-Line Shopping (E-Commerce):** Internet has facilitated the introduction of new market concepts consisting of virtual shops and these shops available for customers 24/7. As compared to the traditional shopping (physically at shops or malls), here users will have more brands and choice of the products. Examples of such sites are *flipcart.com, jabong.com* etc.

g. **Worldwide Video and Audio Conferencing:** Internet allows a group of users residing around the globe to talk and interact with each other as if they were sitting and discussing in a single room. They can see each other on their computer's screen while talking. The CU-SeeMe software developed at Cornell University is an example of internet based video conferencing software.

Data Communication

When people communicate with each other, they share information. Communication can be local i.e., face to face or it can be remote communication i.e. communication takes place over the long distance.

Telecommunication (*tele* is Greek for "far"), includes telephony, telegraphy, and television, means communication at distance.

The word *data* refers to information presented in whatever form is agreed upon by the parties creating and using the data.

Thus, *data communication* is the process of exchanging the information between two machines via some transmission media. Transmission media can be wired or wireless.

Components of Data Communication System

A communication system is consisting of five components:

1. **Message:** It is the message or data to be communicated and it can be in the form of text, numbers, pictures, audio and video.
2. **Sender:** The sender is a machine which sends the message and it can be a computer telephone, video camera etc.
3. **Receiver:** The receiver is the machine which receives the data or information from the sender.
4. **Transmission media:** Transmission media is the physical path by which a message travels from sender to receiver and it can be wired or wireless. Examples of transmission media include twisted pair, coaxial cable, fibre-optic cable and radio waves (wireless).
5. **Protocol:** A protocol is a set of rules that governs data communication. Without protocol two machines can be connected but cannot communicate, just as a person speaking Hindi cannot be understood by a person who speaks German only. Thus, protocol represents an agreement between two communicating machines. A Communicating system is shown in Figure 8.8.

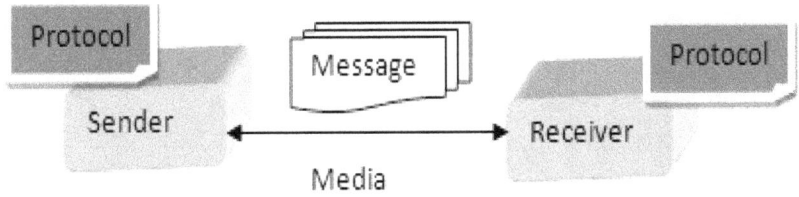

Figure 8.8: *Five components of communication system*

Data Communication IoT and Cloud Computing Modes/Data Flow/Transmission Modes

Communication between two devices can be in:
   a. Simplex Mode
   b. Half Duplex Mode
   c. Full Duplex Mode

Simplex Mode

This type of mode of communication is unidirectional e.g. one-way street. Only one of the two devices on a link can transmit the data, and the other can only receive. There is no acknowledged mechanism, and examples of such systems are keyboards (only introduce the input) and Monitors(only accept output). Because of unidirectional in nature and no acknowledgement mechanism such mode of communication is rarely used. Such a system is shown in Figure 8.9.

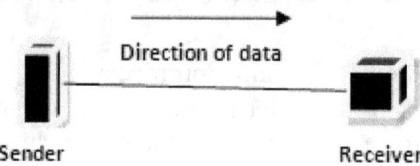

Figure 8.9: *Simplex mode*

Half-Duplex

This type of system is bidirectional in nature i.e. both the devices can send and receive the data, but not at the same time.

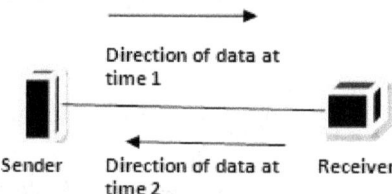

Figure 8.10: *Half duplex mode*

When one device is sending, the other can only receive the data and vice versa. Example of such systems is Walkie-Talkie. Such a system is shown in figure 8.10.

Full-Duplex

It is also called duplex, where both stations can transmit and receive information simultaneously. The duplex mode is like a two-way street with traffic flowing in both directions at the same time. Here, signal going in one direction share the capacity of the channel or link with the signals going in other direction

One example of duplex communication is the telephone network. When persons are communicating by telephone line, both can talk and listen at the same time. Such a system is shown in Figure 8.11.

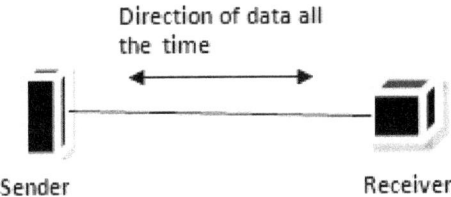

Figure 8.11: *Full duplex*

What is IoT

IoT stands for Internet of Things. It refers to the interconnectedness of physical devices, such as appliances and vehicles that are embedded with software, sensors, and connectivity which enables these objects to connect and exchange data. This technology allows for the collection and sharing of data from a vast network of devices, creating opportunities for more efficient and automated systems.

Internet of Things (IoT) is the networking of physical objects that contain electronics embedded within their architecture in order to communicate and sense interactions amongst each other or with respect to the external environment. In the upcoming years, IoT-based technology will offer advanced levels of services and practically change the way people lead their daily lives. Advancements in medicine, power, gene therapies, agriculture, smart cities, and smart homes are just a very few of the categorical examples where IoT is strongly established.

> *"IoT is a network of interconnected computing devices which are embedded in everyday objects, enabling them to send and receive data."*

Main Components of IOT

- **Low-Power Embedded Systems:** Less battery consumption, high performance are the inverse factors that play a significant role during the design of electronic systems.
- **Sensors:** Sensors are the major part of any IoT application. It is a physical device that measures and detects certain physical quantities and converts it into a signal which can be provided as an input to a processing or control unit for analysis purposes.

Different types of Sensors

1. Temperature Sensors
2. Image Sensors

3. Gyro Sensors
4. Obstacle Sensors
5. RF Sensor
6. IR Sensor
7. MQ-02/05 Gas Sensor
8. LDR Sensor
9. Ultrasonic Distance Sensor

Characteristics of IoT

- Massively scalable and efficient
- IP-based addressing will no longer be suitable in the upcoming future.
- An abundance of physical objects is present that do not use IP, so IoT is made possible.
- Devices typically consume less power. When not in use, they should be automatically programmed to sleep.
- A device that is connected to another device right now may not be connected in another instant of time.
- Intermittent connectivity – IoT devices aren't always connected. In order to save bandwidth and battery consumption, devices will be powered off periodically when not in use. Otherwise, connections might turn unreliable and thus prove to be inefficient.

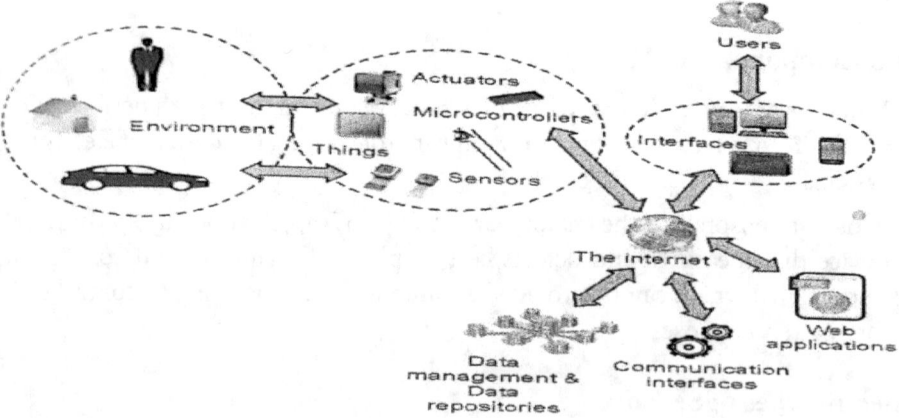

Figure 8.12: *IoT-diagram*

Advantages of IoT

1. Improved efficiency and automation of tasks.
2. Increased convenience and accessibility of information.
3. Better Monitoring and control of devices and systems.
4. Greater ability to gather and analyse data.
5. Improved decision-making.
6. Cost savings.

Disadvantages of IoT

1. Security concerns and potential for hacking or data breaches.
2. Privacy issues related to the collection and use of personal data.
3. Dependence on technology and potential for system failures.
4. Limited standardization and interoperability among devices.
5. Complexity and increased maintenance requirements.
6. High initial investment costs.
7. Limited battery life on some devices.
8. Concerns about job displacement due to automation.
9. Limited regulation and legal framework for IoT, which can lead to confusion and uncertainty.

What is Cloud Computing?

Cloud computing means storing and accessing the data and programs on remote servers that are hosted on the internet instead of the computer's hard drive or local server. Cloud computing is also referred to as Internet-based computing, it is a technology where the resource is provided as a service through the Internet to the user. The data which is stored can be files, images, documents, or any other storable document.

Some operations which can be performed with cloud computing are –

- Storage, backup, and recovery of data.
- Delivery of software on demand.
- Development of new applications and services.
- Streaming videos and audio.

Characteristics of Cloud Computing

- **Scalability:** With Cloud hosting, it is easy to grow and shrink the number and size of servers based on the need. This is done by either increasing or decreasing the resources in the cloud. This ability to alter plans due to fluctuations in business size and needs is a superb benefit of cloud computing, especially when experiencing a sudden growth in demand.
- **Instant:** Whatever you want is instantly available in the cloud.
- **Save Money:** An advantage of cloud computing is the reduction in hardware costs. Instead of purchasing in-house equipment, hardware needs are left to the vendor. For companies that are growing rapidly, new hardware can be large, expensive, and inconvenient. Cloud computing alleviates these issues because resources can be acquired quickly and easily. Even better, the cost of repairing or replacing equipment is passed to the vendors. Along with purchase costs, off-site hardware cuts internal power costs and saves space. Large data centres can take up precious office space and produce a large amount of heat. Moving to cloud applications or storage can help maximize space and significantly cut energy expenditures.
- **Reliability:** Rather than being hosted on one single instance of a physical server, hosting is delivered on a virtual partition that draws its resource, such as disk space, from an extensive network of underlying physical servers. If one server goes offline it will have no effect on availability, as the virtual servers will continue to pull resources from the remaining network of servers.
- **Physical Security:** The underlying physical servers are still housed within data centres and so benefit from the security measures that those facilities implement to prevent people from accessing or disrupting them on-site.
- **Outsource Management:** When you are managing the business, someone else manages your computing infrastructure. You do not need to worry about management as well as degradation.

Chapter 9
GIS (Geographic Information System)

What is GIS?
- A geographic information system (GIS) is a computer system for capturing, storing, checking, and displaying data related to positions on Earth's surface.
- GIS can show many different kinds of data on one map. This enables people to more easily see, analyse, and understand patterns and relationships. With the invention of GIS people can compare the loca-tions of different things in order to discover how they relate to each other. For example, using GIS, the same map could include sites that produce pollution, such as gas stations, and sites that are sensitive to pollution, such as wetlands. Such a map would help people determine which wetlands are most at risk.
- The location in GIS can be represented in many different ways, such as latitude and longitude, address, or ZIP code. The GIS can include data about people, such as population, income, or education level. It can include information about the land, such as the location of streams, different kinds of vegetation, and different kinds of soil.
- The acronym GIS is sometimes used for geographic information science (GIScience) to refer to the academic discipline that studies geographic information systems and is a large domain within the broader academic discipline of geoinformatics.
- Geographic information science is the science underlying geographic concepts, applications, and systems.
- GIS is a broad term that can refer to a number of different technologies, processes, and methods. It is attached to many operations and has many applications related to engineering, planning, management, transport/logistics, insurance, telecommunications, and business.
- It can include information about the sites of factories, farms, and schools, or storm drains, roads, and electric power lines. GIS is the combination of the keywords, Geographic, Information and system, and are explained below:

Geographic: It implies that the locations of the data items are known or calculated with the help of geographic coordinates. The geographic coordinates are *Latitude (horizontal axis on model of earth)* and *longitude (vertical axis on model of earth)*.

Information: It implies that the *data in GIS* are organised so that useful knowledge can be achieved. When the user passes the query to GIS, he/she may get coloured maps, images, Statistical graphs, tables etc.

System: It refers to the physical components of the GIS. It is made up of several interrelated and linked components with different functions. That is why the GIS has the functional capabilities for data capture, input, output, manipulation, visualization transformation, combinations, query, analysis and modelling.

History of GIS Development

The first known use of the term "geographic information system" was by Roger Tomlinson in the year 1968 in his paper "A Geographic Information System for Regional Planning". Tomlinson is also known as the "father of GIS".

Previously, one of the first applications of spatial analysis in epidemiology is the 1832 "*Rapport sur la marche et les effets du choléra dans Paris et le département de la Seine*". The French geographer Charles Picquet represented the 48 districts of the city of Paris by halftone color gradient according to the number of deaths by cholera per 1,000 inhabitants.

In 1854 John Snow determined the source of a cholera outbreak in London by marking points on a map depicting where the cholera victims lived, and connecting the cluster that he found with a nearby water source. The John Snow map was unique, using cartographic methods not only to depict but also to analyse clusters of geographically dependent phenomena.

The early 20th century saw the development of photo zincography, which allowed maps to be split into layers, for example one layer for vegetation and another for water. This was particularly used for printing contours–drawing these was a labour-intensive task but having them on a separate layer meant they could be worked on without the other layers to confuse the draughtsman. This work was originally drawn on glass plates but later plastic film was introduced, with the advantages of being lighter, using less storage space and being less brittle, among others. When all the layers were finished, they were combined into one image using a large process camera. Once color printing came in, the layers idea was also used for creating separate printing plates for each color. While the use of layers much later became one of the main typical features of a contemporary GIS, the photographic process just described is not considered to be a GIS in itself – as the maps were just images with no database to link them to.

Computer hardware development spurred by nuclear weapon research led to general-purpose computer "mapping" applications by the early 1960s.

The year 1960 saw the development of the world's first true operational GIS in Ottawa, Ontario, Canada by the federal Department of Forestry and Rural Development. Developed by Dr. Roger Tomlinson, it was called the Canada Geographic Information System (CGIS) and was used to store, analyze, and manipulate data collected for the Canada Land Inventory– an effort to determine the land capability for rural Canada by mapping information about soils, agriculture, recreation, wildlife, waterfowl, forestry and land use at a scale of 1:50,000.

CGIS was an improvement over "computer mapping" applications as it provided capabilities for overlay, measurement, and digitizing/scanning. It supported a national coordinate system that spanned the continent, coded lines as arcs having a true embedded topology and it stored the attribute and locational information in separate files. As a result of this, Tomlinson has become known as the "father of GIS", particularly for his use of overlays in promoting the spatial analysis of convergent geographic data.

CGIS lasted into the 1990s and built a large digital land resource database in Canada. It was developed as a mainframe-based system in support of federal and provincial resource planning and management. Its strength was continent-wide analysis of complex datasets. The CGIS was never available commercially.

In 1964 Howard T. Fisher formed the Laboratory for Computer Graphics and Spatial Analysis at the Harvard Graduate School of Design (LCGSA 1965–1991), where a number of important theoretical concepts in spatial data handling were developed, and which by the 1970s had distributed seminal software code and systems, such as SYMAP, GRID, and ODYSSEY – that served as sources for subsequent commercial development—to universities, research centres and corporations worldwide.

By the late 1970s two public domain GIS systems (MOSS and GRASS GIS) were in development, and by the early 1980s, M&S Computing (later Intergraph) along with Bentley Systems Incorporated for the CAD platform, Environmental Systems Research Institute (ESRI), CARIS (Computer Aided Resource Information System), MapInfo Corporation and ERDAS (Earth Resource Data Analysis System) emerged as commercial vendors of GIS software, successfully incorporating many of the CGIS features, combining the first generation approach to separation of spatial and attribute information with a second generation approach to organizing attribute data into database structures.

In 1986, Mapping Display and Analysis System (MIDAS), the first desktop GIS product emerged for the DOS operating system. This was renamed in 1990 to

MapInfo for Windows when it was ported to the Microsoft Windows platform. This began the process of moving GIS from the research department into the business environment.

By the end of the 20th century, the rapid growth in various systems had been consolidated and standardized on relatively few platforms and users were beginning to explore viewing GIS data over the Internet, requiring data format and transfer standards. More recently, a growing number of free, open-source GIS packages run on a range of operating systems and can be customized to perform specific tasks. Increasingly geospatial data and mapping applications are being made available via the world wide web.

GIS Model

A model of GIS is shown in Figure 9.1.

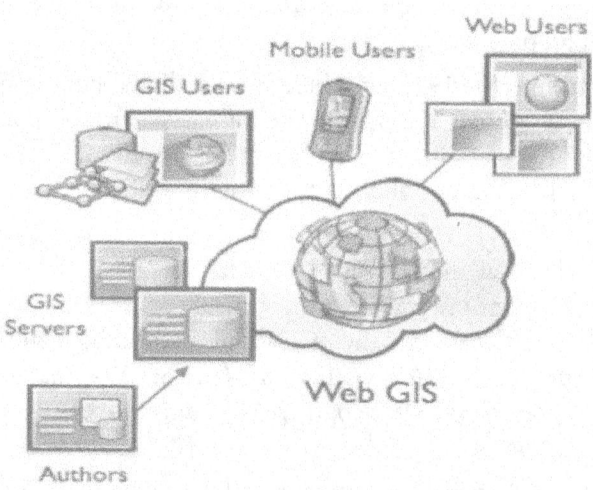

Figure 9.1: *A model of GIS*

GIS Server: Server is the machine where GIS data is present. The sever provides the services requested by the clients.

Users: The various types of users are: Web users, mobile users, and GIS users. These users are connected to the GIS server by internet (Web GIS).

Author: Here the author (May be a technical person) is the owner of the data and is different from a normal user. He /she can directly interact with the GIS server, and can perform the tasks like loading GIS data, modifying the GIS data etc.

Characteristics of GIS Model
a. It allows all users to create interactive queries.
b. Can analyse spatial queries.
c. Can edit data in GIS.
d. It refers to a number of different technologies, processes and methods.
e. It relates unrelated information.
f. It records location or extents in the earth space- time.

Components of GIS
The various Components of GIS are shown in Figure 9.2

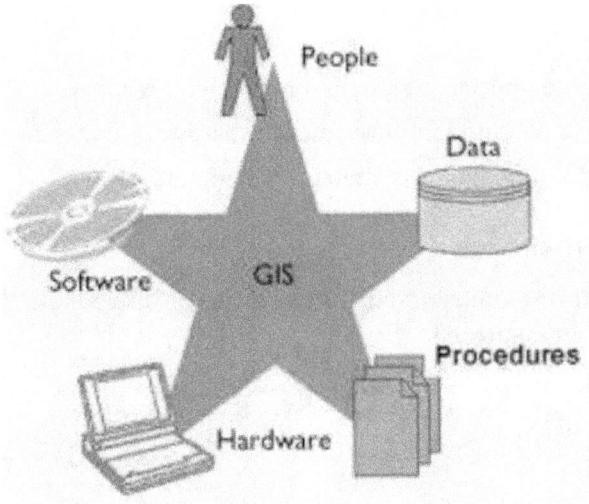

Figure 9.2: *Key Components of GIS*

Hardware
a. It refers to the physical components of the GIS.
b. It is used to control the centralized server of GIS.
c. It is a chief part of GIS e.g. Computer.

Software
a. It refers to a set of programs that are used to perform some specific tasks.
b. They are used to analyse and display GIS information.
c. Provides functions and tools needed.

Data

a. Data refers to *facts, numbers and pictures*.
b. Raw materials in production of information.
c. Key functionality of this component is data collection and data storage.
d. It collects geographic and other tabular data.
e. It integrates spatial data with other existing data sources.

People

a. They are developers or normal users.
b. They can be specialists or normal users.

Procedures

a. Are used to drafting designs and implementing plans.
b. It involves planning for investment in hardware and software.
c. Integration into business strategy and operation.

Contributed Disciplines

The GIS system is the contribution of many fields or disciplines. These disciplines are summarized in Figure 9.3.

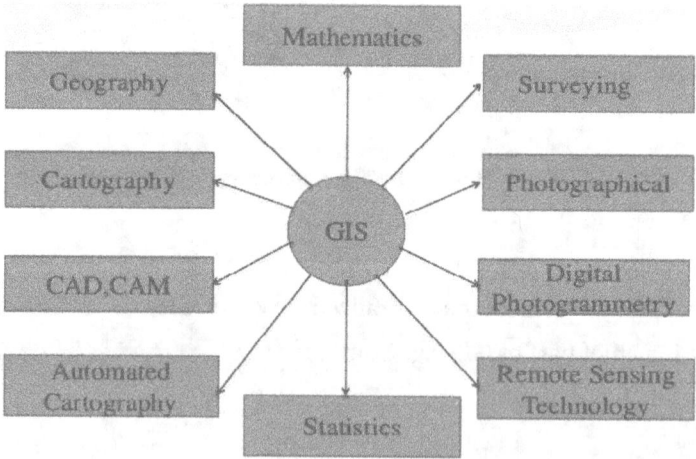

Figure 9.3: *Various disciplines of GIS*

Applications of GIS

Various applications of GIS are given below:
1. **Agriculture**
    a. Farm management
    b. Pest/Disease tracking
    c. Crop Monitoring
    d. Yield prediction
    e. Soil analysis/prediction
2. **Natural resource Management**
    a. Forestry and ecology
    b. Petroleum and mining
    c. Water resources
3. **Planning and Economic Development**
    d. Land use/ Zoning
    e. Population forecasting
    f. Property tax Assessment
    g. Market analysis
    h. Transportation
4. **Geography Matters**
    a. Climate change
    b. Urban growth
    c. Sustainable agriculture
    d. National and international security
    e. Energy
    f. Natural hazards like: Seismicity, weather events
5. **Vehicle Routing**
6. **Land use Planning and Management**
7. **Environmental Applications**
    a. Land use and land cover analysis
    b. Modelling watersheds

c.   Soil erosion
   d.   Forest management
   e.   Conservation and protected areas

Business Application
a.   Retail Store placement
b.   Delivery of goods and services
c.   Traffic flow
d.   Parking location
e.   Location of potential customers

Data and GIS

Data in many different forms can be entered into GIS. Data that are already in map form can be included in GIS. This includes such information as the location of rivers and roads, hills and valleys. Digital, or computerized, data can also be entered into GIS. An example of this kind of information is data collected by satellites that show land use—the location of farms, towns, or forests. GIS can also include data in table form, such as population information. Putting information into GIS is called *data capture*. Data that are already in digital form, such as images taken by satellites and most tables, can simply be uploaded into GIS. Maps must be scanned, or converted into digital information.

Because maps have different scales, a GIS must make the information. A scale is the relationship between the distance on a map and the actual distance on Earth. GIS combines the information from different sources in such a way that it all has the same scale. A *projection* A world map can show either the correct sizes of countries or their correct shapes, but it can't do both. GIS takes data from maps that were made using different projections and combines them so all the information can be displayed using one common projection.

GIS Maps

Once all of the desired data have been entered into a GIS system, they can be combined to produce a wide variety of individual maps, depending on which data layers are included. For instance, using GIS technology, many kinds of information can be shown about a single city. Maps can be produced that relate such information as average income, book sales, and voting patterns. Any GIS data layer can be added or subtracted to the same map.

GIS maps can be used to show information about number and density. For example, GIS can be used to show how many doctors there are in different areas compared with the population. They can also show what is near what, such as which homes and businesses are in areas prone to flooding.

With GIS technology, researchers can also look at change over time. They can use satellite data to study topics such as how much of the polar regions is covered in ice. A police department can study changes in crime data to help determine where to assign officers.

GIS often contains a large variety of data that do not appear in an onscreen or printed map. GIS technology sometimes allows users to access this information. A person can point to a spot on a computerized map to find other information stored in the GIS about that location. For example, a user might click on a school to find how many students are enrolled, how many students there are per teacher, or what sports facilities the school has.

GIS technology makes updating maps much easier. Updated data can simply be added to the existing GIS program. A new map can then be printed or displayed on screen. This skips the traditional process of drawing a map, which can be time-consuming and expensive.

People working in many different fields use GIS technology. Many businesses use GIS to help them determine where to locate a new store. Biologists use GIS to track animal migration patterns. City officials use GIS to help plan their response in the case of a natural disaster such as an earthquake or hurricane. GIS maps can show these officials what neighbourhoods are most in danger, where to locate shelters, and what routes people should take to reach safety. Scientists use GIS to compare population growth to resources such as drinking water, or to try to determine a region's future needs for public services like parking, roads, and electricity. There is no limit to the kind of information that can be analysed using GIS technology. GIS allows multiple layers of information to be displayed on a single map as shown in Figure 9.4.

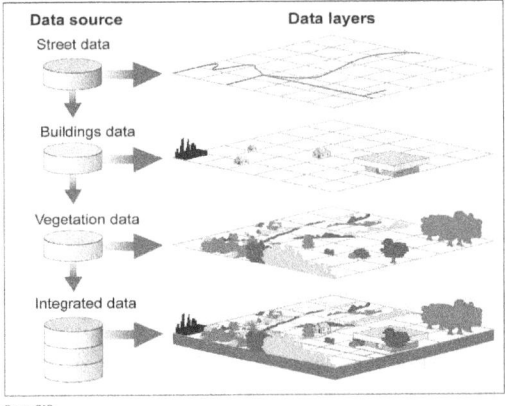

Figure 9.4: *GIS allows multiple layers of information to be displayed on a single map.*

What is GIS Mapping Software?

GIS software lets you produce maps and other graphic displays of geographic information for analysis and presentation. With these capabilities a GIS is a valuable tool to visualize spatial data or to build decision support systems for use in your organization.

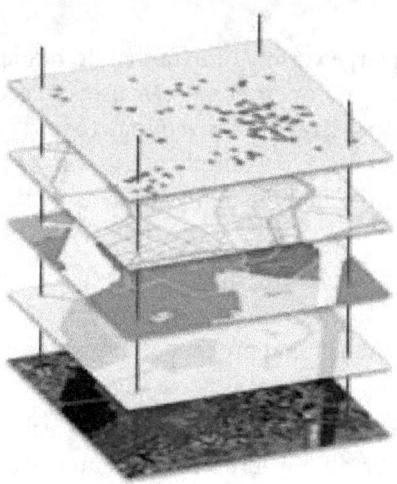

A GIS stores data on geographical features and their characteristics. The features are typically classified as points, lines, or areas, or as raster images. On a map city data could be stored as points, road data could be stored as lines, and boundaries could be stored as areas, while aerial photos or scanned maps could be stored as raster images.

Geographic Information Systems store information using spatial indices that make it possible to identify the features located in any arbitrary region of a map. For example, a GIS can quickly identify and map all of the locations within a specified radius of a point, or all of the streets that run through a territory.

In addition to the above capabilities, Maptitude implements a professional-strength relational database, a feature critical for GIS software.

Properties of GIS Software

The Power of Mapping

A geographic information system (GIS) lets us visualize, question, analyze, and interpret data to understand relationships, patterns, and trends.GIS benefits organizations of all sizes and in almost every industry. There is a growing interest in and awareness of the economic and strategic value of GIS.

Cost Savings from Greater Efficiency: GIS is widely used to optimize maintenance schedules and daily fleet movements. Typical implementations can result in a savings of 10 to 30 percent in operational expenses through reduction in fuel use and staff time, improved customer service, and more efficient scheduling. GIS helped the City of Woodland refine its fleet scheduling, saving fuel and labour.

Better Decision Making: GIS is the go-to technology for making better decisions about location. Common examples include real estate site selection, route/corridor selection, evacuation planning, conservation, natural resource extraction, etc. Making correct decisions about location is critical to the success of an organization.

This GIS-based disaster decision support system helps Taiwan plan for and respond to typhoons.

Improved Communication: GIS-based maps and visualizations greatly assist in understanding situations and in storytelling. They are a type of language that improves communication between different teams, departments, disciplines, professional fields, organizations, and the public. Michels Corporation improved collaboration and communication with GIS.

Better Record Keeping: Many organizations have a primary responsibility of maintaining authoritative records about the status and change of geography. GIS provides a strong framework for managing these types of records with full transaction support and reporting tools. ROI on Montana's GIS-based statewide cadastral system is more than $9 million annually.

Managing Geographically: GIS is becoming essential to understanding what is happening and what will happen in geographic space. Once we understand, we can prescribe action. This new approach to management—managing geographically—is transforming the way organizations operate. Kuwait University used GIS to design and build a multibillion-dollar expansion. GIS can relate unrelated information by using location as the key index variable. Locations or extents in the Earth space-time may be recorded as dates/times of occurrence, and x, y, and z coordinates representing, longitude, latitude, and elevation, respectively.

Implications of GIS in Society: With the popularization of GIS in decision making, scholars have begun to scrutinize the social and political implications of GIS. GIS can also be misused to distort reality for individual and political gain. It has been argued that the production, distribution, utilization, and representation of geographic information are largely related with the social context and has the potential to increase citizen trust in government. A more optimistic social approach to GIS adoption is to use it as a tool for public participation.

Chapter 10
Artificial Intelligence

Introduction

A branch of Computer Science called *Artificial Intelligence* pursues creating computers or machines as intelligent as human beings.

What is Artificial Intelligence (AI)?

According to the father of Artificial Intelligence, John McCarthy, it is *"The science and AI engineering of making intelligent machines, especially intelligent computer programs"*.

Artificial Intelligence is a way of **making a computer, a computer-controlled robot, or software think intelligently**, in a similar manner the intelligent humans think.

AI is accomplished by studying how the human brain thinks, and how humans learn, decide, and work while trying to solve a problem, and then using the outcomes of this study as a basis for developing intelligent software and systems.

Philosophy of AI

While exploiting the power of the computer systems, the curiosity of humans, leads him to wonder, *"Can a machine think and behave like humans do?"*

Thus, the development of AI started with the intention of creating similar intelligence in machines that we find and regard as high in humans.

Goals of AI

a. **To Create Expert Systems:** The systems that exhibit intelligent behavior, learn, demonstrate, explain, and advise its users.

b. **To Implement Human Intelligence in Machines:** Creating systems that understand, think, learn, and behave like humans.

What Contributes to AI?

Artificial intelligence is a science and technology based on disciplines such as Computer Science, Biology, Psychology, Linguistics, Mathematics, and Engineering. A major thrust of AI is in the development of computer functions associated with human intelligence, such as reasoning, learning, and problem-solving.

Out of the following areas, one or multiple areas can contribute to building an intelligent system.

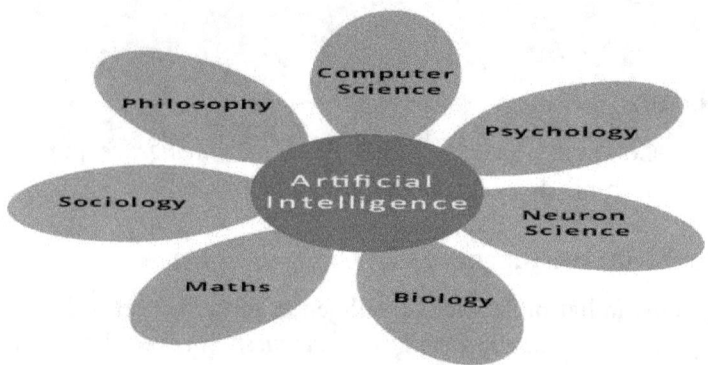

Figure 10.1: *Different areas of AI*

Programming without and with AI

Programming Without AI	Programming With AI
A computer program without AI can answer the **specific** questions it is meant to solve.	A computer program with AI can answer the **generic** questions it is meant to solve.
Modification in the program leads to change in its structure.	AI programs can absorb new modifications by putting highly independent pieces of information together. Hence you can modify even a minute piece of information of program without affecting its structure.
Modification is not quick and easy. It may lead to affecting the program adversely.	Quick and Easy program modification.

What is AI Technique?

In the real world, the knowledge has some unusual properties:
    a. Its volume is huge, next to unimaginable.
    b. It is not well-organized or well-formatted.
    c. It keeps changing constantly.

AI Technique is a manner to organize and use the knowledge efficiently in such a way that:

a. It should be perceivable by the people who provide it.
b. It should be easily modifiable to correct errors.
c. It should be useful in many situations though it is incomplete or inaccurate.

AI techniques elevate the speed of execution of the complex program it is equipped with.

Applications of AI

a. **Gaming:** AI plays a crucial role in strategic games such as chess, poker, tic-tac-toe, etc., where machines can think of a large number of possible positions based on heuristic knowledge.

b. **Natural Language Processing:** It is possible to interact with the computer that understands natural language spoken by humans.

c. **Expert Systems:** There are some applications which integrate machine, software, and special information to impart reasoning and advising. They provide explanations and advice to the users.

d. **Vision Systems:** These systems understand, interpret, and comprehend visual input on the computer. For example,

- A spying aeroplane takes photographs, which are used to figure out spatial information or map of the areas.
- Doctors use a clinical expert system to diagnose the patient.
- Police use computer software that can recognize the face of a criminal with the stored portrait made by a forensic artist.

e. **Speech Recognition:** Some intelligent systems are capable of hearing and comprehending the language in terms of sentences and their meanings while a human talks to it. It can handle different accents, slang words, noise in the background, change in human's noise due to cold, etc.

f. **Handwriting Recognition:** The handwriting recognition software reads the text written on paper by a pen or on screen by a stylus. It can recognize the shapes of the letters and convert it into editable text.

g. **Intelligent Robots:** Robots are able to perform the tasks given by a human. They have sensors to detect physical data from the real world such as light, heat, temperature, movement, sound, bump, and pressure. They have efficient processors, multiple sensors and huge memory, to exhibit intelligence. In addition, they are capable of learning from their mistakes and they can adapt to the new environment.

History of AI

Year	Milestone / Innovation
1923	Karel Čapek's play named "Rossum's Universal Robots" (RUR) opens in London, first use of the word "robot" in English.
1943	Foundations for neural networks laid.
1945	Isaac Asimov, a Columbia University alumnus, coined the term Robotics.
1950	Alan Turing introduced the Turing Test for evaluation of intelligence and published Computing Machinery and Intelligence. Claude Shannon published Detailed Analysis of Chess Playing as a search.
1956	John McCarthy coined the term Artificial Intelligence. Demonstration of the first running AI program at Carnegie Mellon University.
1958	John McCarthy invented the LISP programming language for AI.
1964	Danny Bobrow's dissertation at MIT showed that computers can understand natural language well enough to solve algebra word problems correctly.
1965	Joseph Weinbaum at MIT built ELIZA, an interactive problem that carries on a dialogue in English.
1969	Scientists at Stanford Research Institute Developed Shakey, a robot, equipped with locomotion, perception, and problem solving.
1973	The Assembly Robotics group at Edinburgh University built Freddy, the Famous Scottish Robot, capable of using vision to locate and assemble models.
1979	The first computer-controlled autonomous vehicle, Stanford Cart, was built.
1985	Harold Cohen created and demonstrated the drawing program, Aaron.
1990	**Major advances in all areas of AI –** • Significant demonstrations in learning. • Case-based reasoning. • Multi-agent planning. • Scheduling. • Data mining, Web Crawler. • Natural language understanding and translation. • Vision, Virtual Reality. • Games.
1997	The Deep Blue Chess Program beats the then world chess champion, Garry Kasparov.
2000	Interactive robot pets become commercially available. MIT displays Kismet, a robot with a face that expresses emotions. The robot Nomad explores remote regions of Antarctica and locates meteorites.

While studying artificial intelligence, you need to know what intelligence is. This chapter covers idea of intelligence, types, and components of intelligence.

What is Intelligence?

The ability of a system to calculate, reason, perceive relationships and analogies, learn from experience, store and retrieve information from memory, solve problems, comprehend complex ideas, use natural language fluently, classify, generalize, and adapt new situations.

Types of Intelligence

As described by Howard Gardner, an American developmental psychologist, the Intelligence comes in following types:

Intelligence	Description	Example
Linguistic intelligence	The ability to speak, recognize, and use mechanisms of phonology (speech sounds), syntax (grammar), and semantics (meaning).	Narrators, Orators
Musical intelligence	The ability to create, communicate with, and understand meanings made of sound, understanding of pitch, rhythm.	Musicians, Singers, Composers
Logical-mathematical intelligence	The ability to use and understand relationships in the absence of action or objects. Understanding complex and abstract ideas.	Mathematicians, Scientists
Spatial intelligence	The ability to perceive visual or spatial information, change it, and re-create visual images without reference to the objects, construct 3D images, and to move and rotate them.	Map readers, Astronauts, Physicists
Bodily-Kinesthetic intelligence	The ability to use complete or part of the body to solve problems or fashion products, control over fine and coarse motor skills, and manipulate the objects.	Players, Dancers
Intrapersonal intelligence	The ability to distinguish among one's own feelings, intentions, and motivations.	Gautam Buddha
Interpersonal intelligence	The ability to recognize and make distinctions among other people's feelings, beliefs, and intentions.	Mass Communicators, Interviewers

You can say a machine or a system is **artificially intelligent** when it is equipped with at least one and at most all intelligences in it.

What is Intelligence Composed of?

Intelligence is intangible. It is composed of:

    a. Reasoning

    b. Learning

    c. Problem Solving

    d. Perception

    e. Linguistic Intelligence

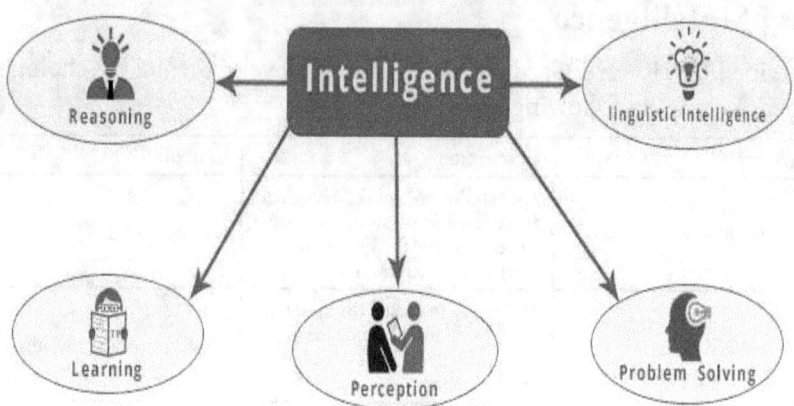

Figure 10.2: *Different types of intelligence in AI*

Source: PP tutorial

a. **Reasoning:** It is the set of processes that enables us to provide basis for judgement, making decisions, and prediction. There are broadly two types:

Inductive Reasoning	Deductive Reasoning
It conducts specific observations to makes broad general statements.	It starts with a general statement and examines the possibilities to reach a specific, logical conclusion.
Even if all of the premises are true in a statement, inductive reasoning allows for the conclusion to be false.	If something is true of a class of things in general, it is also true for all members of that class.
Example – "Nita is a teacher. All teachers are studious. Therefore, Nita is studious."	Example – "All women of age above 60 years are grandmothers. Shalini is 65 years old. Therefore, Shalini is a grandmother."

b. **Learning:** It is the activity of gaining knowledge or skill by studying, practising, being taught, or experiencing something. Learning enhances the awareness of the subjects of the study.

The ability of learning is possessed by humans, some animals, and AI-enabled systems. Learning is categorized as –

- **Auditory Learning:** It is learning by listening and hearing. For example, students listening to recorded audio lectures.
- **Episodic Learning:** To learn by remembering sequences of events that one has witnessed or experienced. This is linear and orderly.
- **Motor Learning:** It is learning by precise movement of muscles. For example, picking objects, Writing, etc.
- **Observational Learning:** To learn by watching and imitating others. For example, a child tries to learn by mimicking her parents.

- **Perceptual Learning:** It is learning to recognize stimuli that one has seen before. For example, identifying and classifying objects and situations.
- **Relational Learning:** It involves learning to differentiate among various stimuli on the basis of relational properties, rather than absolute properties. For Example, Adding 'little less' salt at the time of cooking potatoes that came up salty last time, when cooked with adding say a tablespoon of salt.
- **Spatial Learning:** It is learning through visual stimuli such as ima-ges, colors, maps, etc. For Example, A person can create a roadmap in mind before actually following the road.
- **Stimulus-Response Learning:** It is learning to perform a particular behaviour when a certain stimulus is present. For example, a dog raises its ear on hearing a doorbell.

c. **Problem Solving:** It is the process in which one perceives and tries to arrive at a desired solution from a present situation by taking some path, which is blocked by known or unknown hurdles.

Problem solving also includes decision making, which is the process of selecting the best suitable alternative out of multiple alternatives to reach the desired goal.

d. **Perception:** It is the process of acquiring, interpreting, selecting, and organizing sensory information.

Perception presumes sensing. In humans, perception is aided by sensory organs. In the domain of AI, the perception mechanism puts the data acquired by the sensors together in a meaningful manner.

e. **Linguistic Intelligence:** It is one's ability to use, comprehend, speak, and write the verbal and written language. It is important in interpersonal communication.

Difference between Human and Machine Intelligence

a. Humans perceive by patterns whereas the machines perceive by set of rules and data.
b. Humans store and recall information by patterns, machines do it by searching algorithms. For example, the number 40404040 is easy to remember, store, and recall as its pattern is simple.
c. Humans can figure out the complete object even if some part of it is missing or distorted; whereas the machines cannot do it correctly.

The domain of artificial intelligence is huge in breadth and width. While proceeding, we consider the broadly common and prospering research areas in the domain of AI –

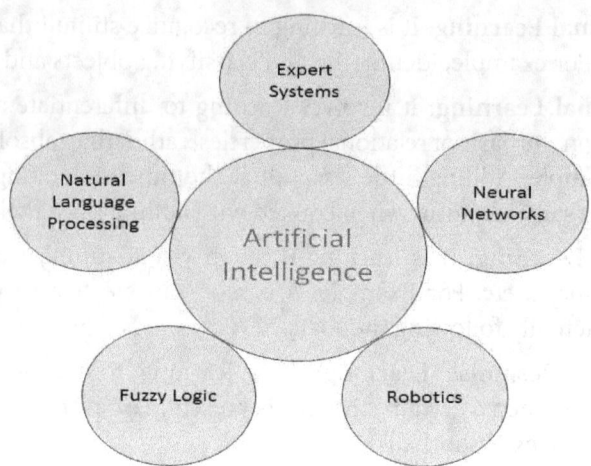

Figure 10.3: *Different disciplines of artificial intelligence*

Source: PP tutorial

Speech and Voice Recognition: These both terms are common in robotics, expert systems and natural language processing. Though these terms are used interchangeably, their objectives are different.

Speech Recognition	Voice Recognition
The speech recognition aims at understanding and comprehending **WHAT** was spoken.	The objective of voice recognition is to recognize **WHO** is speaking.
It is used in hand-free computing, map, or menu navigation.	It is used to identify a person by analysing its tone, voice pitch, and accent, etc.
Machine does not need training for Speech Recognition as it is not speaker dependent.	This recognition system needs training as it is person oriented.
Speaker independent Speech Recognition systems are difficult to develop.	Speaker dependent Speech Recognition systems are comparatively easy to develop.

Real Life Applications of AI Research Areas

There is a large array of applications where AI is serving common people in their day-to-day lives

1. Expert Systems   Examples – Flight-tracking systems, Clinical systems.
2. Natural Language Processing   Examples: Google Now feature, speech recognition, Automatic voice output.
3. Neural Networks   Examples – Pattern recognition systems such as face recognition, character recognition, handwriting recognition.

4. Robotics Examples – Industrial robots for moving, spraying, painting, precision checking, drilling, cleaning, coating, carving, etc.	
5. Fuzzy Logic Systems Examples – Consumer electronics, automobiles, etc.	

Task Classification of AI

The domain of AI is classified into **Formal tasks, Mundane tasks,** and **Expert tasks.**

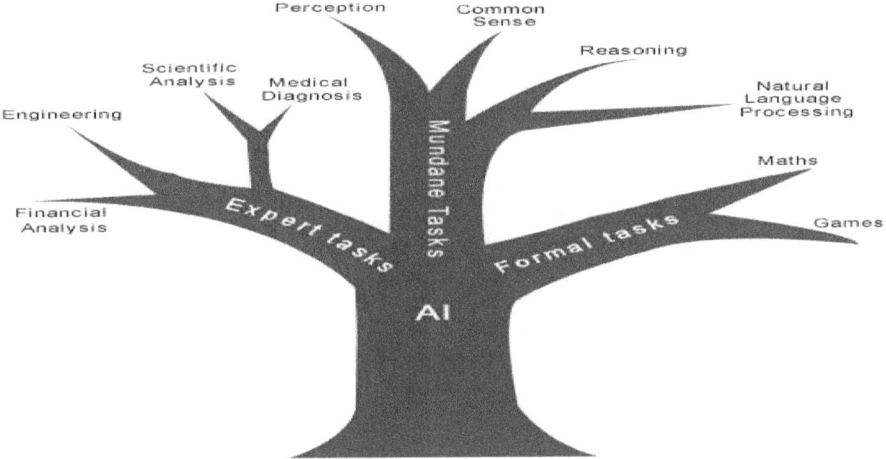

Figure 10.4: *Classification of AI*

Source: PP tutorial

Task Domains of Artificial Intelligence		
Mundane (Ordinary) Tasks	**Formal Tasks**	**Expert Tasks**
Perception • Computer Vision • Speech, Voice	• Mathematics • Geometry • Logic • Integration and Differentiation	• Engineering • Fault Finding • Manufacturing • Monitoring
Natural Language Processing • Understanding • Language Generation • Language Translation	Games • Go • Chess (Deep Blue) • Checkers	Scientific Analysis
Common Sense	Verification	Financial Analysis
Reasoning	Theorem Proving	Medical Diagnosis
Planning		Creativity
Robotics • Locomotive		

Humans have been learning **mundane (ordinary) tasks** since their birth. They learn by perception, speaking, using language, and locomotives. They learn Formal Tasks and Expert Tasks later, in that order.

For humans, the mundane tasks are easiest to learn. The same was considered true before trying to implement mundane tasks in machines. Earlier, all work of AI was concentrated in the mundane task domain.

Later, it turned out that the machine requires more knowledge, complex knowledge representation, and complicated algorithms for handling mundane tasks. This is the reason **why AI work is more prospering in the Expert Tasks domain** now, as the expert task domain needs expert knowledge without common sense, which can be easier to represent and handle.

Language

Artificial Intelligence Markup Language (AIML) is a programming language which is an Extensible Markup Language (XML) specification used by chatbot, verbot, pandorabot, superbot, and other talking robots.

It was developed by Dr. Richard Wallace and followed by other like minded programmers (AIML free software community). An A.L.I.C.E. ("Artificial Linguistic Internet Computer Entity") AIML tag set was released under GNU General Public License (GPL).

Information Technology and IT Acts

Information technology (IT) is the use of any computers, storage, networking and other physical devices, infrastructure and processes to create, process, store, secure and exchange all forms of electronic data. Typically, IT is used in the context of business operations, as opposed to technology used for personal or entertainment purposes. The commercial use of IT encompasses both computer technology and telecommunications.

The *Harvard Business Review* coined the term *information technology* to make a distinction between purpose-built machines designed to perform a limited scope of functions, and general-purpose computing machines that could be programmed for various tasks. As the IT industry evolved from the mid-20th century, computing capability increased, while device cost and energy consumption decreased, a cycle that continues today when new technologies emerge.

What Does Information Technology Encompass?

The IT department ensures that the organization's systems, networks, data and applications all connect and function properly. The IT team handles three major areas:

1. deploys and maintains business applications, services and infrastructure (servers, networks, storage);
2. Monitors, optimizes and troubleshoots the performance of applications, services and infrastructure; and
3. Oversees the security and governance of applications, services and infrastructure.

Most IT staff have different responsibilities within the team that break into several key areas including:

- **Administration:** Administrators handle the day-to-day deployment, operation and Monitoring of an IT environment, including systems, networks and applications. Admins often perform a range of other duties such as software upgrades, user training, software license management, procurement, security, data management and observing adherence to business process and compliance requirements.

- **Support:** Help desk staff specialize in answering questions, gathering information and directing troubleshooting efforts for hardware and software. IT support often includes IT asset and change management, helping admins with procurement, handling backup and recovery of data and applications, Monitoring and analysing logs and other performance Monitoring tools and following established support workflows and processes.

- **Applications:** Businesses rely on software to perform work. Some applications are procured and deployed from third parties, such as email server applications. But many organizations retain a staff of skilled developers that create the applications and interfaces -- such as APIs -- needed to deliver critical business capabilities and services. Applications might be coded in a wide array of popular languages and integrated with other applications to create smooth and seamless interactions between different applications. Developers might also be tasked with creating interactive business websites and building mobile applications. The trend toward agile or continuous development paradigms requires developers to be increasingly involved with IT operations, such as deploying and Monitoring applications.

- **Compliance.** Businesses are obligated to observe varied government- and industry-driven regulatory requirements. IT staff play a major role in securing and Monitoring access to business data and applications to ensure that such resources are used according to established business governance policy that meets regulatory requirements. Such staff are deeply involved with security tasks and routinely interact with legal and business teams to prevent, detect, investigate and report possible breaches.

Examples of Information Technology

So how is IT actually involved in day-to-day business? Consider five common examples of IT and teams at work:

1. **Server Upgrade:** One or more data centre servers near the end of their operational and maintenance lifecycle. IT staff will select and procure replacement servers, configure and deploy the new servers, backup applications and data on existing servers, transfer that data and applications to the new servers, validate that the new servers are working properly and then repurpose or decommission and dispose of the old servers.

2. **Security Monitoring:** Businesses routinely employ tools to Monitor and log activity in applications, networks and system IT staff receive alerts of potential threats or noncompliant behaviour -- such as a user attempting to access a restricted file -- check logs and other reporting tools to investigate and determine the root cause of the alert and take prompt action to address and remediate the threat, often driving changes and improvements to security posture that can prevent similar events in the future.

3. **New Software:** The business determines a need for a new mobile application that can allow customers to log in and access account information or conduct other transactions from smartphones and tablets. Developers work to create and refine a suitable application according to a planned roadmap. Operations staff posts each iteration of the new mobile application for download and deploy the back-end components of the app to the organization's infrastructure.

4. **Business Improvement:** A business requires more availability from a critical application to help with revenue or business continuance strategies. The IT staff might be called upon to architect a high-availability cluster to provide greater performance and resilience for the application to ensure that the application can continue to function in the face of single outages. This can be paired with enhancements to data storage protection and recovery.

5. **User Support:** Developers are building a major upgrade for a vital business application. Developers and admins will collaborate to create new documentation for the upgrade. IT staff might deploy the upgrade for limited beta testing -- allowing a select group of users to try the new version -- while also developing and delivering comprehensive training that prepares all users for the new version's eventual release.

Obligatory for Intermediaries

- No platform can allow **harmful unapproved online games** and their advertisements.
- They should not share false information about the Indian government, **as confirmed by a fact-checking unit.**
  - » An online intermediary – including social media platforms like Facebook, YouTube and Twitter and internet service providers like Airtel, Jio and Vodafone Idea – should make "reasonable efforts" to not host content related to the Central Government that is "identified as fake or misleading" by a "fact check unit" that may be notified by the IT Ministry.

Self-Regulatory Bodies

- Platforms providing online gaming will have to register with a Self-Regulatory Body (SRB) that will determine whether or not **the game is "permissible."**
- The platform should ensure **that online games do not involve any gambling or betting elements.** They should also comply with legal requirements, standards, and safety precautions such as parental controls.

Losing Safe Harbour

- If any piece of information is marked as fake by the upcoming fact check unit, intermediaries will be required to take it down, failing which they would risk losing their safe harbour, which protects them from litigation against third-party content.
  - » Social media sites will have to take down such posts, and internet service providers will have to block URLs of such content.

Readers are requested, for more details about IT ACT 2000 kindly refer this link https://www.indiacode.nic.in/bitstream/123456789/13116/1/it-act-2000-updated.pdf.

What are the Key IT Rules, 2021?

Mandates social media to Exercise Greater Diligence

- Broadly, the IT Rules (2021) mandate social media platforms to exer-cise greater diligence with respect to the content on their platforms.

Ensuring Online Safety and Dignity of Users

- Intermediaries shall remove or disable access within 24 hours of receipt of complaints of contents that expose the private areas of individuals, show such individuals in full or partial nudity or in sexual act or is in the nature of impersonation including morphed images etc.

Educating Users about the Privacy Policies

- The privacy policies of the social media platforms must ensure that users are educated about not circulating copyrighted material and anything that can be construed as defamatory, racially or ethnically objectionable, paedophilic, threatening the unity, integrity, defence, security or sovereignty of India or friendly relations with foreign states, or violative of any contemporary law.

What are the Concerns?

No Clear Definition

- The amendment fails to define **fake news** and allows the government's fact-check unit to declare the veracity of any news "in respect of any business" that involves the state.
- The use of undefined words, especially the phrase "any business", gives the government unchecked power to decide what people can see, hear, and read on the internet.

No Clarity for Fake News

- The IT Rules, 2023 don't **specify what qualifies as false or misleading information** or the qualifications and procedures for the fact-check unit.
- This has raised concerns about the government's arbitrary power to determine what qualifies as fake news, as the rules do not provide a clear definition of the term.

Removable of Information

- Intermediaries will remove information deemed false by the Fact Check Unit, leaving **only the state to determine what is true.**
- The new regulation gives the government the power to decide what information is bogus and exercise censorship by compelling intermediaries to take down posts deemed fake or false.

Violates the Supreme Court's Judgment

- **Shreya Singhal vs Union of India (2015), Supreme Court** held that a law that limits speech can neither be vague nor over-broad.

Way Forward

- To combat misinformation and fake news, the government and intermediaries can use technology solutions like algorithms and fact-checking websites.
- Intermediaries can also implement self-regulatory measures such as Monitoring content and working with fact-checking websites.
- Additionally, raising public awareness about the dangers of censorship and promoting free speech can be achieved through social media campaigns, workshops, and discussions in public forums.

Chapter 11
Microsoft Word

Introduction

A word processor is a computer program that allows you to create, edit and produce text documents, such as letters. Microsoft Word is a word processor created by Microsoft. The first version of Microsoft Word was released in 1983 as a competitor to WordStar, the most popular word processor at the time.

What is Microsoft Office?

The term "Microsoft Office" refers to Microsoft's entire suite of office productivity applications. Microsoft Word is one of the many applications that are grouped under the "Microsoft Office" umbrella.

What is Office 365?

Office 365 is a service where you pay a monthly subscription fee (around $10 a month) to use Microsoft Office programs (as opposed to paying $100 or more up front, as was traditionally done). One benefit to using Office 365 is that software updates are free (for example, if a new version of Microsoft Word comes out, you can upgrade to that new version for free).

In this class, we will be using Word 2016, which is the latest version.

Exploring the Word 2016 Environment

> **Teacher's Note**
> - Mention how the Quick Reference Guide Contains notes on every thing that is covered in class.
> - Mention that the flash drives must stay in the computer lab and are not for students to keep.

Open word by using the search windows box or by double –clicking on the desktop icon for Microsoft

Title Bar

1. **Note** the title bar section which has **window controls** at the right end, as in other Windows programs.
2. **Note** that a blank document opens with a default file name of **Document 1**.

Quick Access Toolbar

The Quick Access Toolbar is located all the way to the left on the title bar. It contains frequently used commands and can be customized using the drop-down menu.

1. **Point** to each small icon to view its ScreenTip.
2. **Be aware** that the **Undo** button is not located anywhere else in the application except for the Quick Access Toolbar.
3. **Click** the **Customize Quick Access Toolbar** button, **click New** on the menu, and **see** the command get added to the Quick Access Toolbar.
4. **Click** the **Customize Quick Access Toolbar** button again, and **click**.

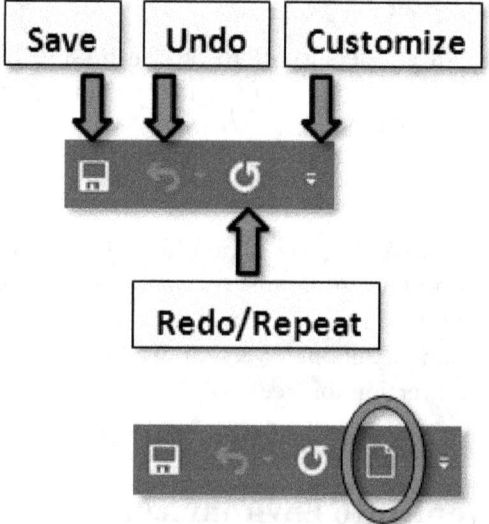

Show Below the Ribbon. Click Show Above the Ribbon to move the Quick Access Toolbar back again.

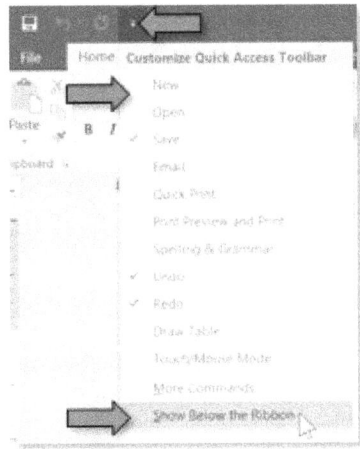

Ribbon

The ribbon contains all of the tools that you use to interact with your Microsoft Word file. It is located towards the top of the window underneath the title bar. All of the programs in the Microsoft Office suite have one.

The ribbon has a number of **tabs**, each of which contains **buttons**, which are organized into **groups**. Depending on the object you have selected in the document, several **contextual tabs** may appear, which provide additional formatting options for the selected object.

Try **clicking** on other **tabs** to view their buttons (do not click the File tab yet), and then **return** to the Home tab.

Active Tab

By default, Word will open with the **Home tab** active on the ribbon. **Note** how the Active tab has a white background and blue letters, and the Inactive tabs have the opposite.

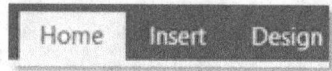

Contextual Tab

Contextual tabs are displayed when certain objects, such as an images and text boxes, are selected. They contain additional options for modifying the object. Contextual tabs stand out because they are darker in color and are located to the right of all the other tabs. As soon as we start being productive in the program, we will see contextual tabs appear.

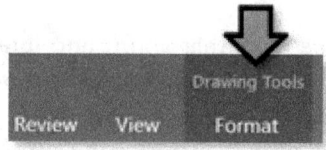

Groups and Buttons

On each **Tab**, the **Buttons** (a.k.a. commands or tools) are organized into **Groups**. The groups have names, but the names are not clickable.

Hover over some of the buttons on the Home tab to **observe** the **ScreenTips**. The ScreenTip displays the name of the button, along with a short description of what the button does.

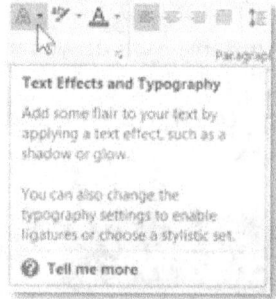

Buttons with Arrows

Note that some buttons have images on them and some have images *and an arrow*. The arrow indicates that more information is needed to carry out the function of the button. Some arrowed buttons have two parts: the button proper and the list arrow.

A **one-part arrowed button**, called a **menu button**, will darken completely when you point to it:
1. In the **Font group, point** to the **Text Effects and Typography** button.
2. **Note** there is no difference in shading between the left and right of the button when you point to each section.

On a **two-part arrowed button**, called a **split button**, only one section at a time will darken when you point to it.
1. In the **Paragraph group, point** to the left part of the **Shading** button. This is the "**button proper**" section of the button. **Note** how it is darkened separately from the arrow portion of the button.

2. **Point** to the **right portion**, the section with the arrow. This is the "**list arrow**" section of the button. **Note** how it is darkened separately from the left portion.

3. The **button proper** is the section of a two-part button that will carry out the default option or the last used option.
4. The **list arrow** section will open an options menu.

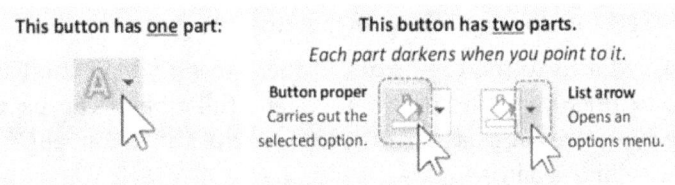

Dialogue Box Launcher

On some groups there is a **launcher** icon which will open a **dialogue box** or a **side panel** with related but less common commands.

Click any Dialogue Box Launcher icon, and then **close** the dialogue box or side panel.

Ribbon Display Options Button

This button provides options that will hide the Ribbon from view. The main benefit to this is that it allows your document to take up more of the screen.

1. **Locate** the **Ribbon Display Options** button (to the left of the window control buttons).

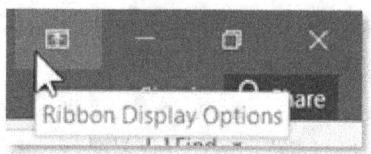

2. **Click** on it. Three options appear.

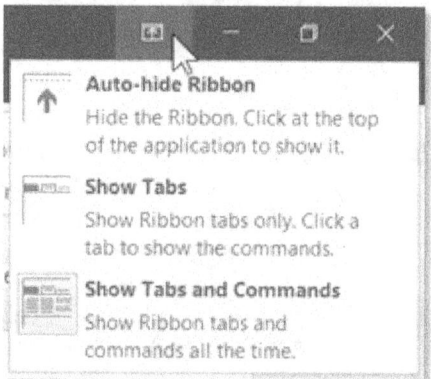

3. **Click Auto-hide Ribbon.** This option essentially makes Word go into "full screen" mode. It hides not only the ribbon, but also the Quick Access Toolbar, title bar, and Window Controls.
4. To get the ribbon to **show** after Auto-hiding it:
    a. **Point** to the **top-center** of the screen and **click**. (Clicking the three dots does the same thing.) The full ribbon can be seen and used. However, as as soon as the body of the document is clicked it will hide again.

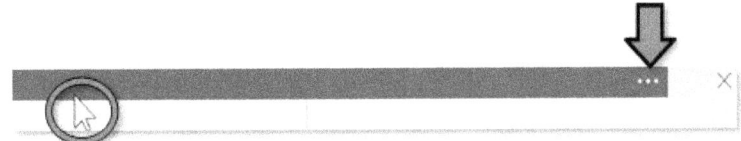

    b.   **Click** in the middle of the document. **Notice** how the ribbon **hides** again.

5.   To get a partial display of the ribbon to stay in view:

    a.   **Click** the "mini" **Ribbon Display Options** button on the top right.

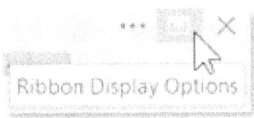

    b.   **Click Show Tabs**. **Note** this option has brought back our Quick Access Toolbar, title bar,

Window Controls, and *part* of the ribbon; only the **Tabs** are visible. The buttons are not.

    a.   **Click** the **Home** tab. **Notice** how the buttons come into view.

    b.   **Click** in the middle of the document. **Notice** how the buttons disappear again.

> **Note:** A shortcut for changing to the "Show Tabs" view is to **double-click** the Active Tab. If the buttons in the ribbon suddenly disappear, then you may have done this by accident.

1.   To get the entire ribbon to stay in view:

    a.   **Click Ribbon Display Options**

    b.   **Click Show Tabs and Commands**. This option keeps **entire** ribbon visible at all times. It is the **default** option. We will keep this option selected for the remainder of class.

Dynamic Resizing

If you use Word on other computers, be aware that the button placement on the ribbon might look **slightly different**. For instance, a button might be a different size or be positioned in a slightly different place. The reason for this is that the ribbon auto-adjusts itself based on the size of the Word window.

1.   On the **Home** tab **notice** what the buttons in the **Editing** group currently look like.

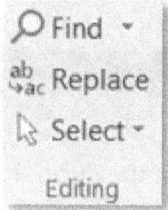

2. **Click Restore Down** to shrink the size of the Word window.

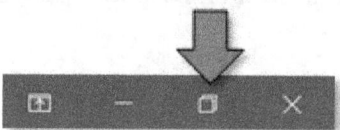

3. **Notice** how the group looks different now. The entire group was collapsed into a **single button**. Click on the button to reveal the contents of the group.

4. **Click Maximize** to bring the window back to full screen.

File Tab

The **File** tab provides a **Backstage** view of your document. The Backstage view exposes information and metadata about the currently active document, lists recently opened documents, and provides a variety of user options, such as opening, saving, and printing. Instead of just a menu, it is a full-page view, which makes it easier to work with.

1. **Click** on the **File** tab.

2. **Notice** that the ribbon and the document are no longer in view. **Note** the commands, listed on the left side of the screen, are ones you would use to perform actions **TO** a document rather than **IN** a document.
3. Other things you can do in the **Backstage** view:
   a. **Click** the **Info** tab. The **Info** section of the **Backstage** view offers an easy-to-use interface for inspecting documents for hidden properties or personal information.
   b. **Click** the **New** tab. In this section you can create a new Blank document, or choose from a large selection of Templates.
   c. **Click** the **Open** tab. The **Open** section is used to open existing files on your computer.
      - It immediately presents you with a list of documents that you have **recently** opened, so you can quickly find and open them again. (This is disabled in the computer lab.)
      - Clicking **Browse** opens a **File Explorer** dialogue, which allows you to find the file on your computer. We will be using this option in class.
   d. **Click** the **Save As** tab. This section allows you to save your file.
4. To return to the document from the Backstage view, **click** the large, left pointing arrow in the top-left corner of the screen.

Workspace

Underneath the ribbon is the workspace.

1. **Note** the **rulers** and **margin** settings.
2. **Note** the **scroll bar** on the right side of the screen.
   a. If the scroll bar is not visible, **move** the mouse and it will come into view.
3. **Note** the **blinking cursor/insertion point,** which is where **new input will display** when entered.
   a. If the insertion point is not blinking, move the mouse and it will start blinking.
4. **Point** somewhere on the blank page and **note** the mouse cursor with the **I-beam shape**, appropriate for a text environment.

Status Bar

The Status bar is located below the document window area.

Current Information

The **left end** displays a variety of information about the document, such as the page number, how many total words are in the document, and whether there are any spelling errors.

Views

At the **right end** are shortcuts to the different **views** that are available. Each view displays the document in a different way, allowing you to carry out various tasks more efficiently.

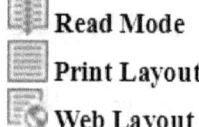

Read Mode	Displays the document full-screen, making it easier to read. You cannot edit the document in this view.
Print Layout	Shows what the document looks like when it's printed. This is overall the best view for editing documents. It is selected by default.
Web Layout	Shows what the document would look like if it were saved as a webpage.

Zoom Slider

Also at the **right end** of the Status bar is the **Zoom Slider**. This allows you to adjust how large the document is displayed on the screen. It does not adjust the actual size of the document—just how big or small it is displayed on the screen (like moving a newspaper away from or closer to your eyes).

Customization

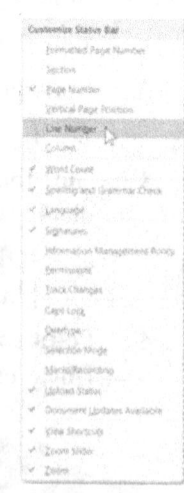

The Status bar can be customized.

1. Right-click on the Status bar to bring up the customize menu. Options that are enabled have a checkmark next to them.
2. Click on "Line Number" to enable this option.
3. Notice how the menu didn't disappear. Click in a clear space to dismiss the menu.
4. Notice how "Line: 1" appears in the Status bar

Microsoft Word

Creating a Document and Saving It

Takes: 20min

Creating a Document

1. When Word opens, it will display a blank document ready for you to type in. The words that you type and the formatting that you use become your document.
2. **Type** "My first document".
3. Each document you create is temporary unless you save it as a **file** with a unique name and location.

Preparing a Save to Location – a USB Device

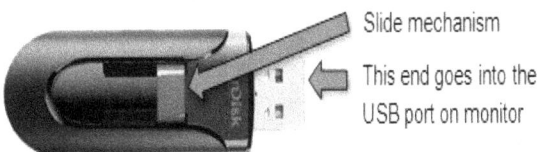

When we save a Word document, all the data in that document is collected and saved as a **file**. Normally files are saved on a computer's hard drive, but due to security restrictions on computer lab machines, files must be saved on removable storage devices.

For this class, we will be using a **USB flash drive** to save our work. This flash drive will remain in the lab between classes.

1. Orient the flash drive as pictured below.

2. **Notice** that there is a **slide mechanism** on the side to retract the USB connector into the body of the drive. **Slide** this all the way to the **right** to **expose the connector**.

3. **Locate** the USB ports on the Monitor. The connector will slide into the port only one way with your **name label facing toward you** and right-side up.

4. **Fit** the connector into the port and **push** it in gently.
5. At this point, you *may* get a notice that the computer is installing a device driver – **wait** until the message disappears.

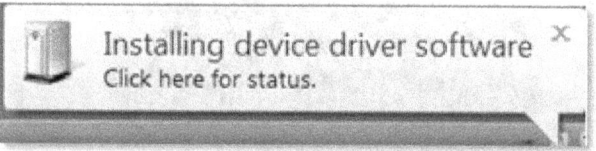

6. A notification may appear in the bottom-right corner of the screen, asking what you want to do with the flash drive. **Close** it by **pointing** to it and clicking its **Close** button.

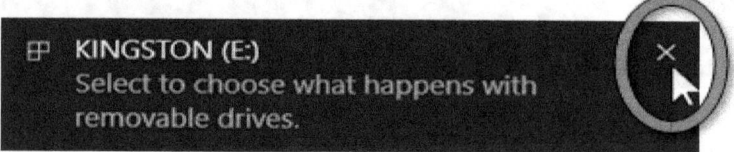

7. You are now ready to begin saving your file.

Saving the File

1. **Click** the **File** tab.
2. **Click Save As**. We use "Save As" instead of "Save" the **first** time we save a file because we need to tell the computer *where* to *put* the file (the file doesn't have a "home" yet).

"Save" assumes you've saved it before.

3. **Click Browse**.
4. **Notice** that a smaller window appears in front of our work. This small window is called a **dialogue box**. Because the computer needs to know more than just "OK, save," the dialogue box is where we tell it *how* we want to save our work.

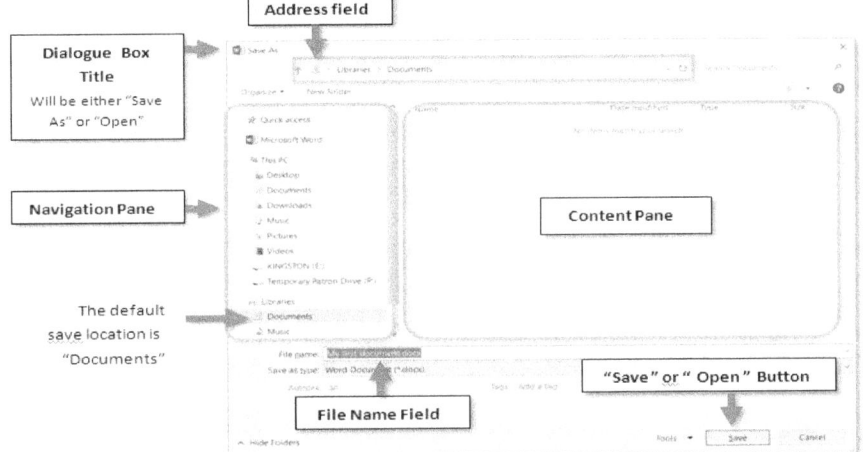

5. When it comes to saving, there are two important things to *identify* for the computer:
   a. The **location** where the file is going to be saved to.
   b. What **name** you want to give the file.
6. The **location** where it will be saved is displayed for us in the **Address field**. In this case, **note** that the **Documents directory** is the **default** save location, but we want to save our file to the **flash drive**.
7. **Notice** other available folders and devices can be seen in the left pane, called the **Navigation pane**. If we wanted to save to one of these alternate locations, we would have to click on it.
8. **Find** the location labeled **KINGSTON (E:)** and **click** it. Kingston is the name of the company that created our flash drive.

> **Note:** If you are taking this class from home and do not have a flash drive, use "Documents" as the location to save your files.

9. Your address field should now read **This PC > KINGSTON (E:)**.

10. Now we need to name our file. **Notice** that the file name field is towards the bottom of the dialogue box. By default, Word names the file after the first few words that were typed into the document.

11. **Click** into this box and the words will be highlighted. Then **type** the word **first** to name your file 'first'.

12. Once we have given the computer **a file name** and a **save location**, we are ready to save. At this point, your Save As dialogue box should look like the image below. To save, you will **click Save**.

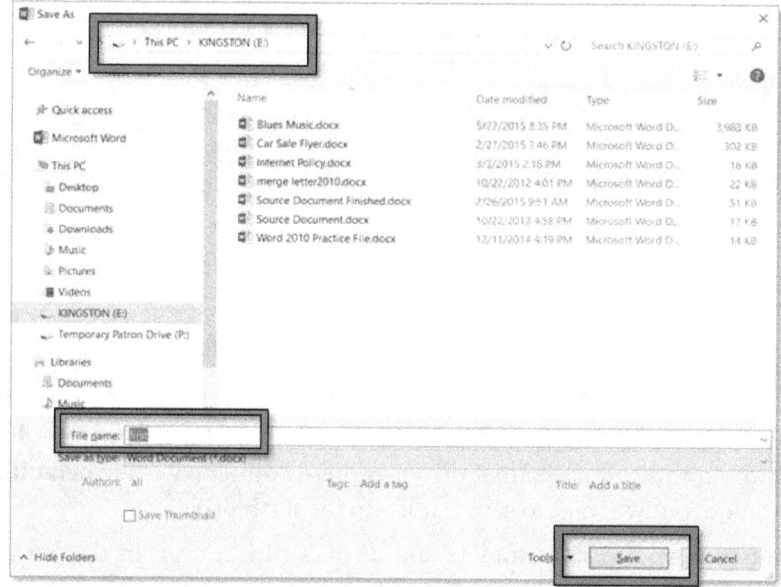

13. Your Word window will still be open but **notice** the **title** bar will now show the file name **first.docx**.

Safe Removal of a USB Device

Before we learn more about creating and saving files, we are going to learn how to safely remove our flash drive. You should never just pull it out because, if the computer is in the middle of writing information to the file, it could corrupt it and make it unreadable!

1. First, and MOST important, be sure to **close** any and all windows that you might have open..**Check** your **taskbar** for buttons very carefully. Remember open programs will have **blue lines** under the taskbar icons.

2. When you first insert an USB device, an **icon** resembling the one circled in the picture below appears in the notification area. This icon will aid in the safe removal of your flash drive from the computer.

3. **Find** the icon with the help of your screen tips. The ScreenTip will say "**Safely Remove Hardware and Eject Media**".

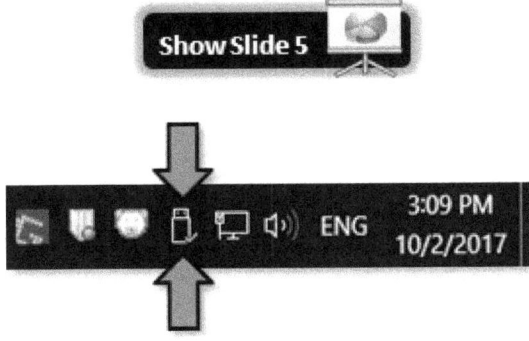

4. Once you **locate** the correct icon, **click** on it.
5. When you do, a menu will appear. **Click** on **Eject Cruzer Glide**. This is the brand name of our flash drives.

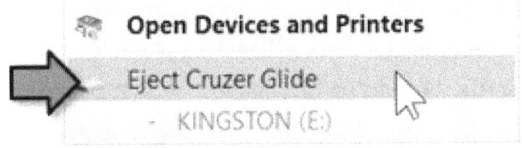

6. You will then see a **confirmation message** that the drive is safe to physically remove from the computer.

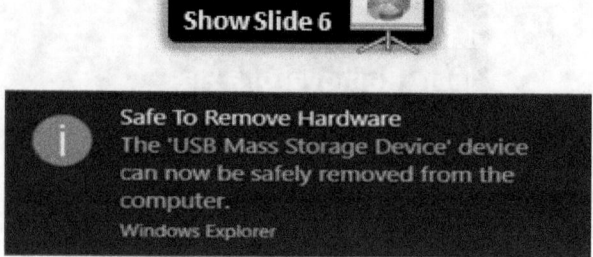

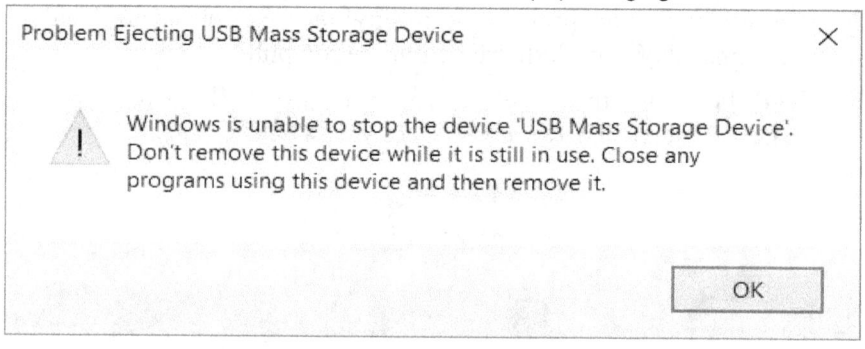

7. Occasionally you might **forget** to close your windows before clicking on the Safely Remove Hardware icon. In that case a dialogue box will appear, saying that the drive cannot be safely ejected because it is in use. It prompts you to close all your windows and then try ejecting again.

8. **Be aware** that performing the safely remove step removes the USB device virtually from the computer. In order to use the drive again however, it must also be physically removed from the port and re-inserted. **Remove your drive from the computer.**

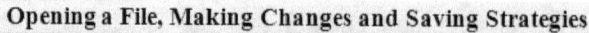 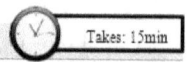

The purpose of saving a file is to bring it back later and that is what we are about to do. Before we attempt to open a saved file, we need to make sure that the storage location for that file is in place.

1. Your file is on the flash drive so **insert** your flash drive.
2. **Open** Word. You should be looking at a new blank document.
3. **Click** on the **File** tab and **click Open**.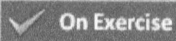

Microsoft Word

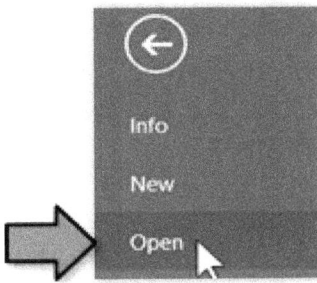

4. Click Browse.

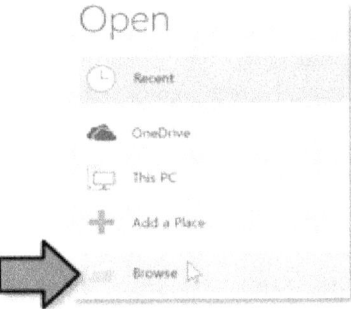

5. A **dialogue box** that looks like the "Save as" window will now appear. **Notice** in fact, the only visible differences are that the **title** bar says **Open** and the **Save button** now says **Open** instead.

6. At first, the computer will be looking for your file in the default location, which is **Libraries > Documents**. But we saved our file on the flash drive.

In order to get the computer to look in the flash drive for your file, you need to **click** on the flash drive entry in the **Navigation pane** (which is on the left side of the dialogue box). The flash drive is listed as **KINGSTON (E:)**.

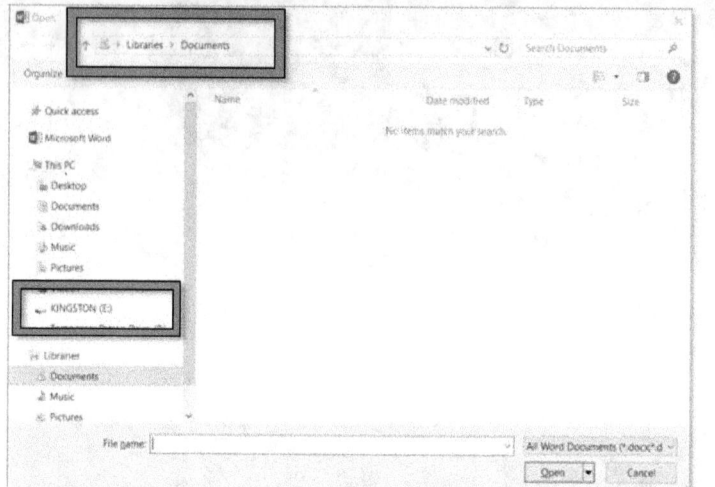

7. **Notice** how the dialogue box now shows the Kingston drive in the address field and our "first" file is displayed in the pane on the right. **Notice** that your "**first**" file has a small icon next to it that looks like the Word icon and the name of the file is '**first.docx**' rather than just "first".

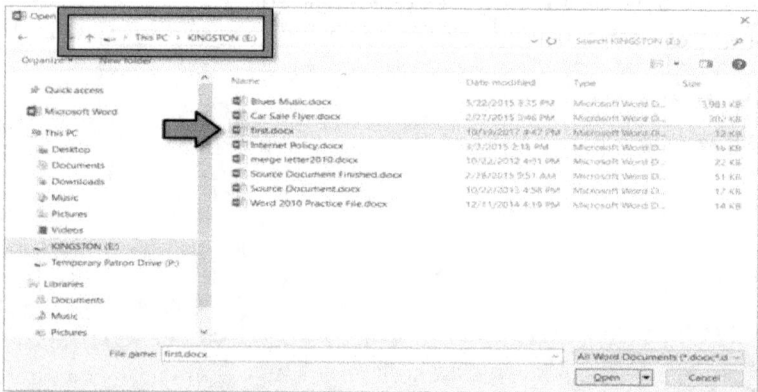

8. Now, you can open the file.
   a. Click once on the icon to select it.
   b. **Click** the **Open** button.

> **Tip:** Another way to open the file is to **double-click** its <u>icon</u>. Do not double-click the file name! If you double-click the file name too slowly, it will think you want to rename the file!

9. **Notice** that Word has opened and you can see your "first" document.

Making Changes in a Document

1. **Note** that **cursor** or **insertion point** is blinking at the beginning of the first line.
2. **Tap** the key End (which is above the arrow keys on the keyboard) to move the cursor to the end of the line.
3. **Tap** the enter key to move the cursor to the beginning of the next line.
4. **Type** your **phone number**.

Using the Save Button to Save Changes

Now, we want to save the new changes we've made.

1. Because we've already given Word a name and location for the file, we can do one of the following:

- **Select** "**Save**" from the File menu, **OR**

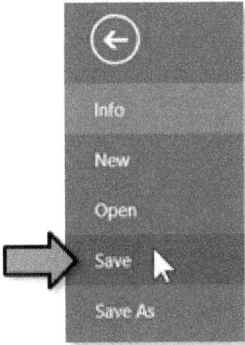

- **Click** on the icon that looks like a **floppy disk** on the Quick Access toolbar.

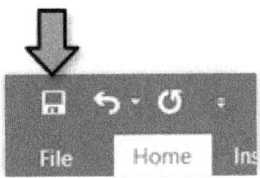

2. **Note** that the "Save As" dialogue box **will not** appear because Word already has a name and location for the file.
3. Now **close** the file by clicking on **File > Close**.

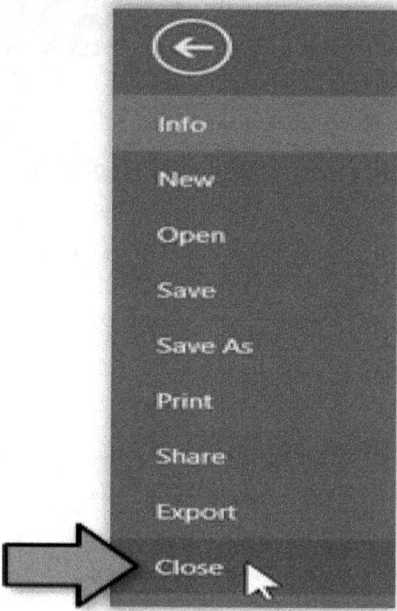

4. Use **File > Open** to **re-open first.docx** to **verify** that the last changes were saved.

Forgetting to Save

1. **Click** at the end of the second line in order to move your cursor there and then **tap. Type** your **street**.
2. **Click** on **File > Close** again. A dialogue box will appear, asking you if you want to save the changes you made.
3. **Click** anywhere **outside** of the dialogue. **Notice** how it **flashes** at you. This means that you **MUST** answer this dialogue box before you can do anything else.
4. Choosing **Don't Save** will **close** the file and **discard** any changes that were made to it since it was last saved.
5. Choosing **Cancel** will dismiss the dialogue and let you continue your work. Clicking the "X" in the top-right corner will do this too.
6. **Click Save**. This will still close the file, but will save it first.

Creating a New Blank Document When Word is Already Open

At this point, the Word program is open, but there is no document to work in.

1. On the **File** tab, **click New**.
2. This screen presents you with a list of **templates** to choose from. **Click Blank document** to create a new, blank document.

> **Tip:** Adding a **New** button to the Quick Access Toolbar would eliminate having to go through the templates page to open a blank document.

3. **Bear in mind** that as long as we don't type anything into the new document we will not be prompted to save it should we close the program.

Moving Around in a Document

> **Teacher's note**
> The changes we make to **Internet Policy.docx** may not be completed in one session. At the end of the session, close the document and **save changes**.

Opening a Practice File

We are now going to open a **pre-typed** file which we will use to explore some features of Word 2016. The file is on your flash drive and is named **Internet Policy.docx**.

- Using **File > Open, navigate** to your flash drive and **open** "**Internet Policy.docx**".

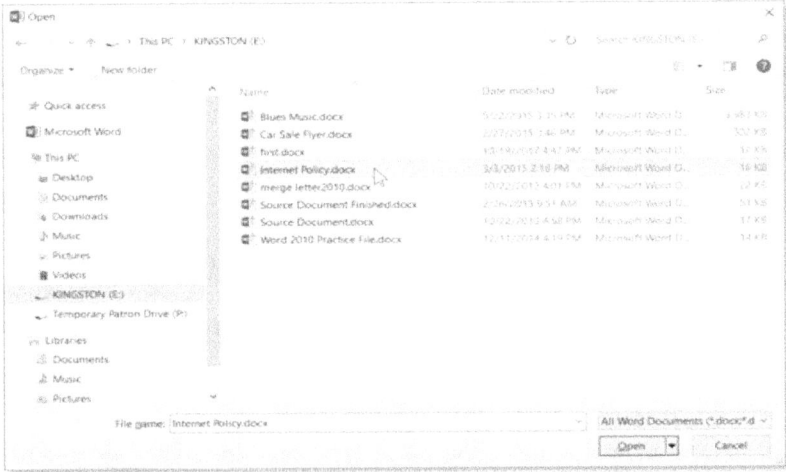

Insertion Point

Sometimes referred to as the **cursor,** insertion point is the name for the blinking line where anything you insert goes. There are several ways to move the insertion point to get it where you want it to be.

1. **Click** in the middle of the first line of the first paragraph of the practice document.
2. **Refer** to the chart below to practice moving the insertion point around using the keyboard.

Press	To Move The Insertion Point
Home	To the beginning of the current line
End	To the end of the current line
Page Up	To the previous screen
Page Down	To the next screen
Left arrow or Right Arrow	Left or right one character at a time
Up arrow or Down Arrow	Up or down one line at a time
Ctrl + Left Arrow	Left one word at a time
Ctrl + Right Arrow	Right one word at a time
Ctrl + Up Arrow	Up one paragraph at a time
Ctrl + Down Arrow	Down one paragraph at a time
Ctrl + Up Arrow Twice	To beginning of previous paragraph
Ctrl + Home	To the beginning of a document
Ctrl + End	To the end of a document
Ctrl + Page Up	To the top of the previous page
Ctrl + Page Down	To the top of the next page

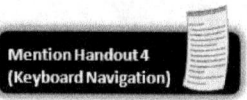
Mention Handout 4
(Keyboard Navigation)

Teacher's note:
Walk the students through some of these key combinations, notably:
- Ctrl + Home (+ Fn on teaching laptop)
- Ctrl + End (+ Fn on teaching laptop) **BEWARE - DO NOT USE THE END KEY ON KEYPAD ON PACS**
- Arrow keys (give you fine-grain control over the cursor)

Paste

Keyboard Keys

There are several other keyboard keys that are important to know.

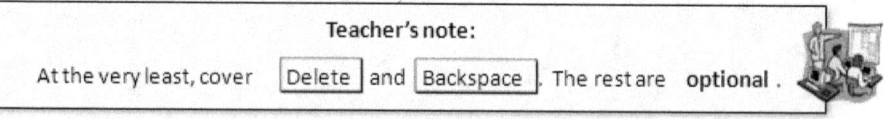
Teacher's note:
At the very least, cover Delete and Backspace . The rest are optional .

1. Enter – Moves the insertion point to a new line, but also creates a new paragraph. When you are typing in Word, the insertion point will move, showing where the next character you type will appear. When the insertion

Microsoft Word

point reaches the right margin, the word you are typing will move to the next line. This is called **word wrap**. Because of this, you should only tap enter to start a new paragraph.

2. Creates a small space between words. Space Bar
   a. **Click** after the word "Library" on the first line of the first paragraph of the practice Space Bar document.
   b. **Try** the.
3. Delete -Removes characters to the **right** of the insertion point.
   a. **Click** in the middle of the word "Library" on the first line of the second paragraph of the practice document.
   b. **Try** Delete the key.
4. Removes characters to the **left** of the insertion point. Backspace
   a. **Try** the Backspace key
5. When typed in conjunction with a letter key, inserts a capital letter. Shift

   Note: Word will *automatically* capitalize the first word of every sentence, as well as the word "I".

6. Makes all letters come out as uppercase.
   Caps Lock

Now that we have made several changes to this document, it is a Good

Undo and Redo

time to learn how to "undo" changes that you regret making or that you have made by accident.

The buttons for doing this are located on the **Quick Access Toolbar**.

Undo

The Undo button reverts changes that you've recently made to the document. The Undo button is a split button:

- Clicking on the **button proper** will undo one change (action) at a time.
- Clicking on the **list arrow** will display the entire history of changes you made to the document. Clicking on a change will undo all changes that were made **up to and including** the selected change.

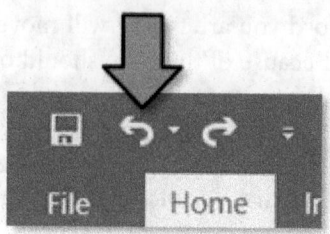

1. **Click** on the **list arrow**.
2. **Notice** the list that appears. This is a **history** of all of the changes you made to your document since you opened it.
3. **Point** to the **last item** in the list (the line **above** where it says "Undo X Actions").

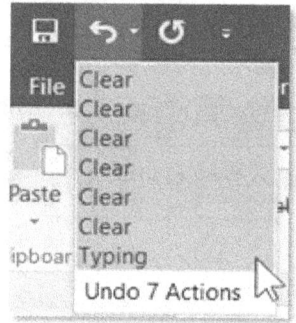

4. **Notice** how all of the items above and including the one we are pointing to are **colored gray**. When we click, all of those changes will be undone.
5. **Click** on the **last item**. Our document is now back to the way it was when we first opened it.

Redo

Similarly, the **Redo** button **re-applies** any changes that were made with the **Undo** button.

The Redo button **only** appears *after* you click Undo!

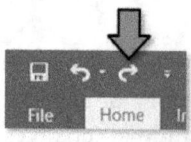

Microsoft Word

"To affect it, you must select it."

Selecting, also referred to as **highlighting**, is the basic first step to modifying text or to copying or cutting text. There are many ways to select text.

Note: Selected text will remain selected until you click somewhere else. To clear a selection (also known as "deselecting"), click anywhere <u>outside</u> selected text or tap an arrow key on the keyboard.

Hold down Ctrl key on the keyboard and tap the Home the key to get to the top of the document.

Let go of the key. Ctrl

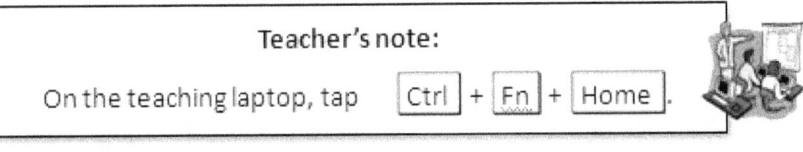

Teacher's note:

On the teaching laptop, tap Ctrl + Fn + Home.

Select a specific section of text

Shift+ click method

Tip: Shift clicking is especially

1. **Click** at the **beginning** of the first paragraph. Effective on laptop **touchpads**.
2. **Hold down** the Shift **key** on the keyboard.
3. **Click** at the **end** of the first paragraph.
4. If you have a selection already highlighted, you can increase or decrease that selection by holding down the key and clicking at a different endpoint. **Decrease** the selection by one sentence.
5. **Select** the text.

Dragging Method

1. **Hold down** the left mouse button while **you drag** the mouse across the first line of the document. Keep the mouse button down and **drag downward to select more lines.**
2. **Let go** of the mouse button when you are done with your selection.
3. Deselect the text.

> **Teacher's note:**
> The **dragging** method can be used in many situations, but often a combination of keyboard and mouse -clicking is more effective.

Select a Single Word

1. **Point** to the word "has" in the first line of the second paragraph. Small words are hard to select using the dragging method.
2. Instead...**double-click** on the word to select it.
3. **Deselect** the text.

Select a Sentence

1. **Point** anywhere on the first sentence of the second paragraph.
2. **Hold down** Ctrl the **key** on the keyboard.
3. **Click** somewhere inside of the sentence to select the Ctrl sentence. **Let go** of the key.
4. **Deselect** the text.

Select a Single Line or Several Lines

1. **Move** the mouse pointer to the **left margin** so the mouse cursor points to the right.
2. Staying within the left margin, **position** the cursor so it is parallel to the first line of the second paragraph.
3. **Single-click** to select that line.
4. **Hold** the mouse button down and **drag downward** to select more lines.
5. **Deselect** the text.

Select a Paragraph

1. **Move** the mouse pointer to the left margin so the mouse cursor points to the right.
2. Staying within the left margin, **position** the cursor so that it is pointed to the middle of the second paragraph.
3. **Double-click** to select the paragraph.
4. **Deselect** the text.

Select Entire Document

1. **Hold down** Ctrl and A **tap** to select the entire document (it doesn't matter where the insertion point is).
2. **Deselect** the text.

Moving Text

Cut and Paste

When you **cut** something, it is removed from its current location and placed on the clipboard. The **clipboard** is a temporary storage area for data that can be accessed by any program on your computer.

1. **Select** the red paragraph.
2. In the **Home** tab on the ribbon, **locate** the **Clipboard** group.
3. **Click Cut**. The paragraph disappears from view, but is saved in the computer's memory.
4. **Move** your insertion point to the space beneath the first paragraph.
5. **Locate** the **Paste** button in the **Clipboard** group. **Hover** over it and **notice** it is a **split button**.
6. **Click** the **Paste button proper** (not the list arrow) to move the selection to the new location.

Copy and Paste

When you **copy** something, it remains in its original location, and is also placed on the clipboard.

> **Tip:** Copying a paragraph is helpful for when you want to make changes to it, but also want to preserve the original in case you want to go back to the way it was.

1. **Select** the red paragraph.
2. In the **Home** tab on the ribbon, **locate** the **Clipboard** group.
3. **Click Copy**.
4. **Move** your insertion point below the third paragraph.
5. **Click** the **Paste** button proper.
6. **Notice** that the same paragraph now appears in two locations.

Formatting Text

Changing Text Attributes

1. **Select** the second line in the first paragraph.
   a. In the **Font** group, **apply** the **Bold**, **Italic** and **Underline** attributes.
   - **Notice** how the **Underline** button is a **split button. Click** the **button properly**.
   b. **Notice** how the buttons darken when they are active. When the buttons are active, it means that these formatting options are applied to the selected text.
   c. **Deselect** the text to see the changes.
2. **Select** the third paragraph.
   a. **Click** the **Font** drop-down list box and **click** a different font (CurlzMT).
   b. **Notice** that the font names are in **alphabetical order**.
   c. **Notice** that, as you move your mouse over various fonts, Word shows you what your selected text will look like with that font. This is called a **Live Preview**.

   > **Tip:** A "font face" can also be referred to as a "**font name**" or just a "**font**".

   d. **Click** the **font size** drop-down combo box and **click** a different font size (20). **Notice** the Live Preview.
3. **Select** the first paragraph.
   a. Using the **list arrow** next to the **Font Color** button **change** the **font color** to **blue**. **Notice** the Live Preview as you mouse over the colors in the palette.
   b. Also **notice** how the **Font Color button proper** changed from red to blue. The button remembers the last color that was selected.

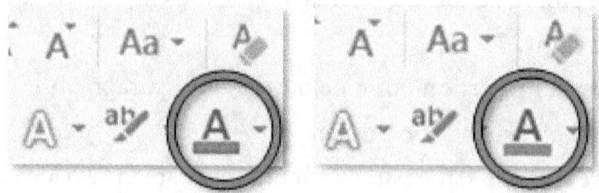

Formatting a Paragraph

Changing Alignment

1. **Select** the **first paragraph**.
2. In the **Paragraph** group**, find** the **Align Text** buttons. **Notice** that the Align Text Left button is selected (it is grey).

3. **Change** the alignment of the paragraph by **clicking** on the other buttons.
   c. **Align Left:** Lines the text up against the left margin.
   d. **Center:** Centers the text on the page. This is good for titles.
   e. **Align Right:** Lines the text up against the right margin.
   f. **Justify:** Lines the text up against the left and right margins, resulting in a cleaner look. It accomplishes this by adding extra space between words as necessary (it doesn't add extra space characters; it just makes the space characters wider). Newspapers use this alignment.

Changing Line Spacing

1. With the first paragraph still selected, in the **Paragraph** group, **click** the **Dialogue Box Launcher** to access more paragraph formatting options.

2. On the **Indents and Spacing** tab, in the **Spacing** section, **click** the **Line spacing** drop-down arrow, and **click Double.**
3. **Click OK.**

Changing Paragraph Indentation

1. With the first paragraph still selected, in the **Paragraph** group, **click Align Left**.
2. In the **Paragraph** group, **click** the **Dialogue Box Launcher** to access more paragraph formatting options.
   a. On the **Indents and Spacing** tab, in the **Indentation** section, **click** the **Special** drop-down arrow, and **click First line.** **Click** ok.

    b.   **Notice** how the first line of the paragraph is now indented.

3.   Hanging indent (all lines of a paragraph are indented except the first line) - using the same instructions as in step 2 above, **change** the **Special Indentation** to **Hanging. Click** ok. Again, **notice** the changes.

4.   **Deselect** the text by **clicking** on a clear area.

Controlling the Appearance of your Document

Changing Page Margins

1.   **Click** the **Layout** tab to access tools to change the appearance of your document.

2.   In the **Page Setup** group, **click Margins**. A list will appear that will have your current settings highlighted. **Click Wide** to *see* how it will affect your document.

3.   **Click Margins** again and **click Custom Margins** at the bottom of the list.

    a.   When the **Page Setup dialogue box** opens, on the **Margins** tab, in the **Margins** section **click** the arrows to **change** the top, left, bottom and right margins to **0.8"**.

    b.   The **Gutter** setting is an extra margin that is only used if you want to **bind** your printed pages together in some way (such as with a three-hole-punch). **Leave** this at **0"**. c. **Click OK**.

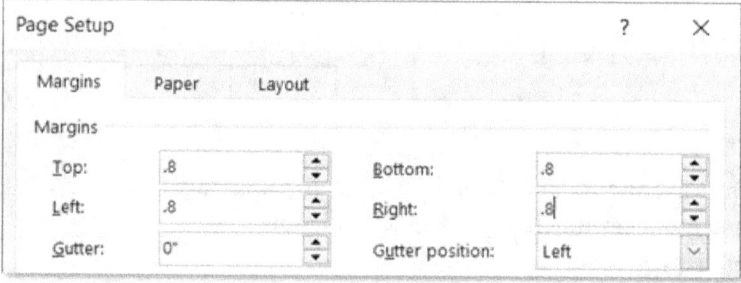

4.   In the **Page Setup** group, **click Margins** again and **notice** how the margin list has now populated with your customization.

Microsoft Word

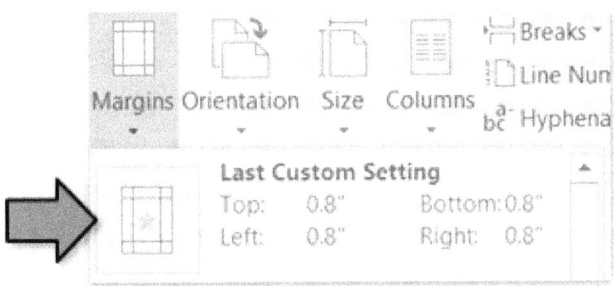

Page Breaks

1. **Place** your insertion point at the end of the blue paragraph.
2. On the **Insert** tab, **find** the **Pages** group and **click Page Break**.

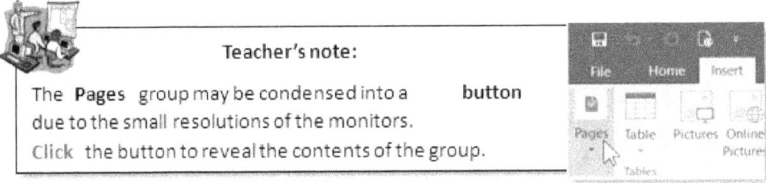

Teacher's note:
The **Pages** group may be condensed into a button due to the small resolutions of the monitors.
Click the button to reveal the contents of the group.

3. **Notice** how the lines below are now on the next page.

Notice how Word Delete has inserted some blank space at the top of the next page.

4. **Tap** the **key** to remove this extra space.

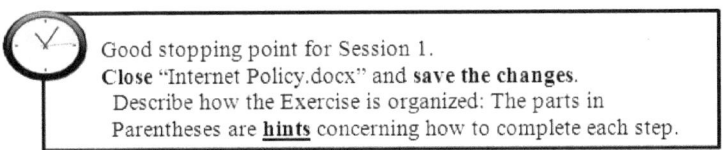

Good stopping point for Session 1.
Close "Internet Policy.docx" and **save the changes**.
Describe how the Exercise is organized: The parts in Parentheses are **hints** concerning how to complete each step.

Headers and Footers

A **header** is text that appears at the **top** of every page in your document. Similarly, a **footer** is text that appears at the **bottom** of every page.

1. First, let's insert a **header**.

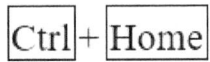

    a. **Open** Internet Policy.docx.
    b. **Tap** to get to the top of the document.
    c. **Click** the **Insert** tab. In the **Header & Footer** group, **click Header** to open a list of different header options.
    d. **Scroll** down the menu to view all the options and **click Blank**.
    e. **Notice** that a new **contextual ribbon** has opened called **Header & Footer Tools**. It has one tab - **Design**.
    f. **Notice** how Word is calling out the header section with a **dotted-line**.
    g. **Notice** the words **"Type here"** enclosed in brackets on the left. This is a **placeholder** for an area of the header into which we can enter content. It is **colored gray**, which means it is already selected and ready for us to populate it with content.
    h. **Type** "Internet Policy".

2. **Close** header. This can be done in two ways:
    a. On the **Header & Footer Tools** contextual ribbon, on the **Design** tab, **click Close Header and Footer**.

    b. By **double-clicking** anywhere within the body of the document. (We'll try this in a minute)

3. **Scroll down** and **notice** that "Internet Policy" appears at the top of every page.

4. Also **notice** that the font color of the text in the header is light gray. This is not the **actual** font color. Microsoft Word makes the header text display in light grey to show that the header is **not currently active**.

5. **Double-click** on the header to make it active. **Notice** how the font color has changed to its real color (black) and the document body text is now dimmed. Again, this is to show that the header/footer is **active**, and the document body is **not active**.

6. Next, let's insert a **footer**.
    a. **Note** that, when the header is active, the footer is active as well. **Scroll down** to the bottom of the current page and notice that there is a **Footer** section called-out with a dotted-line.

Microsoft Word

    b.   On the **Header & Footer Tools** contextual ribbon, on the **Design** tab, locate the **Header & Footer** group. **Click Footer** to open a list of different footer options.

    c.   Again, **scroll down** the list to view all the options and then **click Blank (Three Columns).**

    d.   What we're going to do is, put our **name** in the left placeholder, the **current date** in the center placeholder, and the **page number** in the right placeholder. There are tools on the Header & Footer Tools contextual ribbon to facilitate this.

    e.   **Click** on the **left** placeholder to select it and **type** your name. *Do not tap Enter.*

    f.   Let's make our name bold. How would we do this? Because there is no Bold button visible, we have to switch to another ribbon. **Click** the **Home** tab, **locate** the **Font** group and **click**

Bold (No need to highlight the name)

    a.   **Note** how our Header & Footer Tools contextual ribbon is no longer active since we switched to the Home tab. To bring the Header & Footer Tools contextual ribbon back, **click** on its **Design** tab.

    b.   **Click** on the middle placeholder in the footer to select it. On the **Header & Footer Tools** ribbon, **locate** the **Insert** group and **click Date & Time**. When the dialogue box opens, **click** any date format you wish under the **Available Formats** in the left pane.

    c.   **Note** the empty checkbox that says "Update automatically". This would need to be checked if you want the inserted date to change to the current date every time you open this document.

- **Click OK**
- **Click** on the **right** placeholder. On the **Header & Footer Tools** ribbon, **locate** the **Header & Footer** group and **click Page Number**. A list of options will be shown about where you want to insert the page numbers (see table below).

Top of Page	Puts the page number in the header.
	Warning: This will replace your entire header with a new header!
	Warning: This will replace your entire footer with a new footer

| Page Margins | Puts the page number in the left or right margins. |
| Current Position | Puts the page number wherever your insertion point is. |

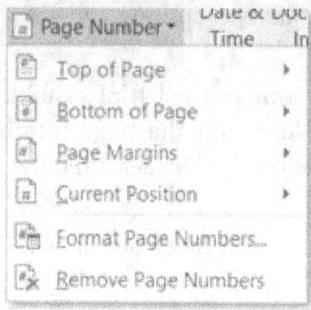

- **Bottom of Page** Puts the page number in the footer.
- **Move** your pointer to **Current Position** and a list of options will open. **Scroll down** the list to the "**Page X of Y**" section and **click Bold Numbers**.

- **Double-click** in the body of the document to close the Header and Footer Tools.

Adding Visual Interest

Changing the **Page Background**

a. On the **Design** tab, in the **Page Background** group, **click Page Color** to display a palette of colors.

b. **Mouse-over** the colors and **observe Live Preview** changes to your document.

c. **Click** a color that is **fairly dark** (fourth row of Theme Colors).

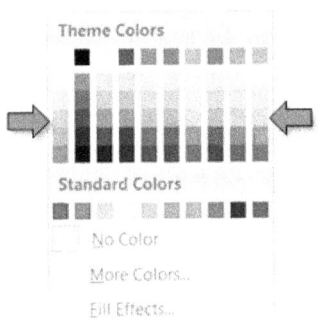

Tip: The document's text color automatically changes to white when a dark background color is selected.

Adding a Watermark

a. On the **Design** tab, in the **Page Background** group, **click Watermark** to see a list of semi-transparent messages that can be added to your document. **Click** on one of the messages and **note** its insertion into the document. These messages will be printed should you print the document.

b. You can also **customize** the watermark text. **Click Watermark** again and **click** "Custom Watermark". In the Printed Watermark dialogue box, find the Text field, **click** into it, **delete** the existing text, and **type** some different text. **Click** OK.

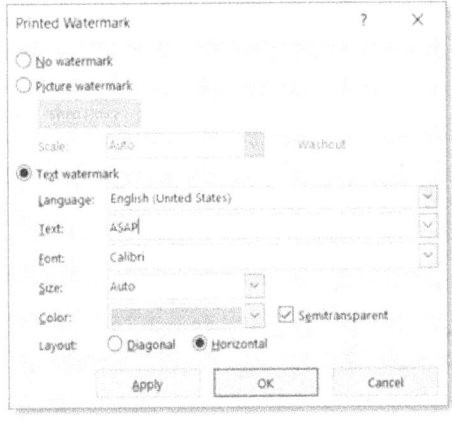

What's the difference between the "Apply" and "OK" buttons?

- **Apply** will commit your changes and **keep** the dialogue box **open**.
- **OK** will commit your changes and **close** the dialogue box.

Adding a Page Border

a. To place a border around your document, on the **Design** tab, in the **Page Background** group, **click Page Borders**. A **Borders and Shading Dialogue Box** will open.

b. In the **Borders and Shading Dialogue Box,** on the **Page Border tab,** there are options for customizing a border. As you **click** on different settings, styles, colors, etc. in the left and center panes, **note** a preview in the right pane.

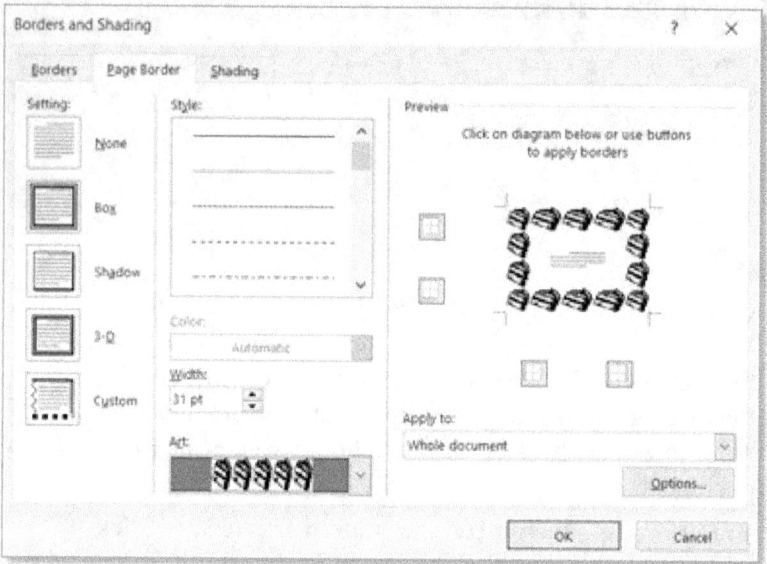

c. In the **Borders and Shading Dialogue Box,** on the **Page Border tab,** in the *left* pane, click on the **Box** setting.

d. In the **Borders and Shading Dialogue Box,** on the **Page Border tab,** in the *center* pane, in the **Art** drop-down list box, **click** the drop-down arrow. **Scroll down** and **click** a border style that you like. **Click** OK to add the border.

Note that, depending on how large the border is, it may **cover up** your **header and/or footer.** To fix this, you can adjust the distance between the edge of the page and the header/footer.

- **Double-click** on the **header** to make it active.

- On the **Header & Footer Tools** contextual ribbon, on the **Design** tab, in the **Position** group, there are two text boxes:
  » The **top** one controls the distance between the **header** and the edge of the page.

- » The **bottom** one controls the distance between the **footer** and the edge of the page.
- Increase the values in both of these text boxes until you can see your header and footer. Note – you will need to click into the footer before you adjust the bottom control.

- » **Save** the document and then **close** Word.

Opening a File Using "File Explorer"

File Explorer is Windows software that allows you to access the drives or storage locations on your computer.

1. On the **Taskbar, find** the **File Explorer** icon and **click** it.

2. **File Explorer** is comprised of two panes. **Notice** this window looks like a save as or open dialogue window but lacks a name in the title bar.
   a. The **left** pane is called the **navigation pane**. This is where you would select a drive or folder in order to see what it contains. Normally you would see the C drive (hard drive) displayed in the navigation pane, but it is blocked on the lab computers for security reasons.
   b. The **right** pane is called the **content pane**. This displays the contents of the folder that is selected in the navigation pane.
   c. The **address bar** at the top of the window displays the hierarchy of the folder that you are currently viewing in the content pane.
3. **Look** in the **navigation pane** for our flash drive listing. Many flash drives are named after the manufacturer of the flash drive. Our flash drives are named "KINGSTON". The computer itself assigns the drive letter. The letter could change depending on how many devices are plugged in at the same time. On most computers Drive C: designates the hard drive. Other drive letters get assigned as more devices get installed or plugged in.

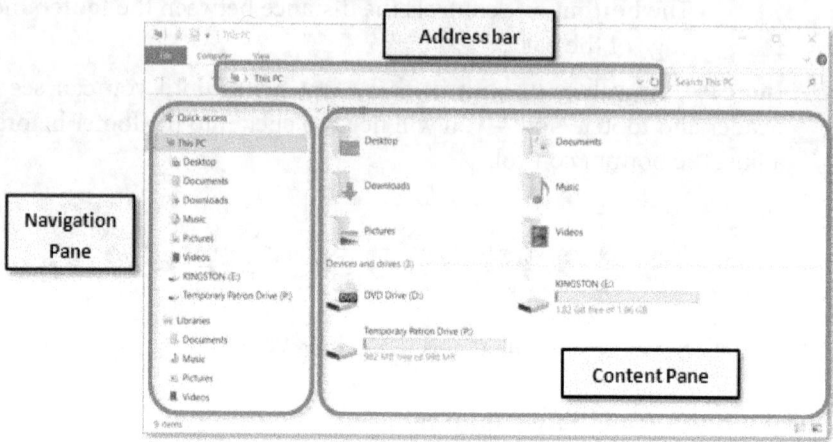

4. **Click KINGSTON (E:)** in the **navigation pane**.
5. **Note** the **address bar** in the **Computer window** has updated to reflect the selected drive, which is the **(E:) drive**, your Kingston flash drive in particular. The address field even shows the navigational path to your drive.

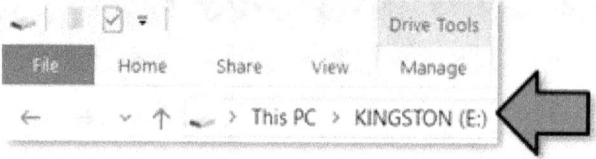

6. In the **right pane**, you are now looking at a directory of all of the files on your flash drive.
7. We are going to open the file called **Blues Music.docx**. To open it, **point** to the **icon** next to the file name and **double-click**. **Notice** that the Word program is launched and your file opens.

> Note: It is also possible to double click on the file name to open the file. However, if you double-click too slowly, Windows will think that you are trying to rename the file! So, it's best to double-click on the **icon** instead.

Correction and Editing Tools

For this section, we will be using the file that we opened in the previous section (**Blues Music.docx**).

> **Teacher's note**
>
> **Blue Music.docx** will be used to demo **Spell Check** and **Printing**. It is _not necessary to save changes_ if either task is not completed by the end of a session.

Find/Replace

Scenario: In this document, we consistently misspelled a common jazz term. Instead of manually correcting each misspelling, we will use Word's find & replace tool to fix all of them at once.

1. Tap 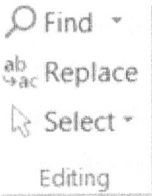 + Home to move your **insertion point** to the beginning of the document.

2. On the **Home** tab, in the **Editing** group, **click** the **Find** button proper.

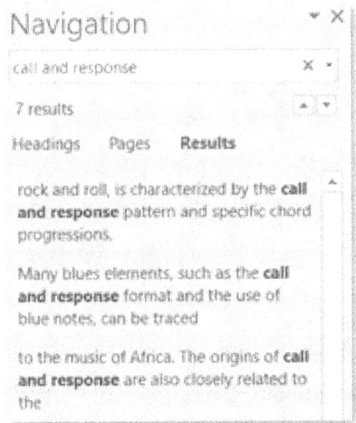

3. A **Navigation task pane** will open on the left. **Click** into the **Search document** field and **type** "**call and response**".

4. **Notice** how the Navigation task pane displays each match, along with the text surrounding the matched phrase.
5. **Scroll** down the body of the document. **Notice** all instances of the phrase "call and response" are highlighted in yellow to make them easy to see.

   ie call and response format
   origins of call and response a
   mmunity, the spirituals. The

6. In the **Editing** group, **click Replace**. This opens the **Find and Replace** dialogue.
7. In the **Find and Replace** dialogue, on the **Replace tab**, in the **Replace with** field, **type** "**call-and response**" (the same phrase, but with dashes in between each word). **Click Replace All** to perform the operation.

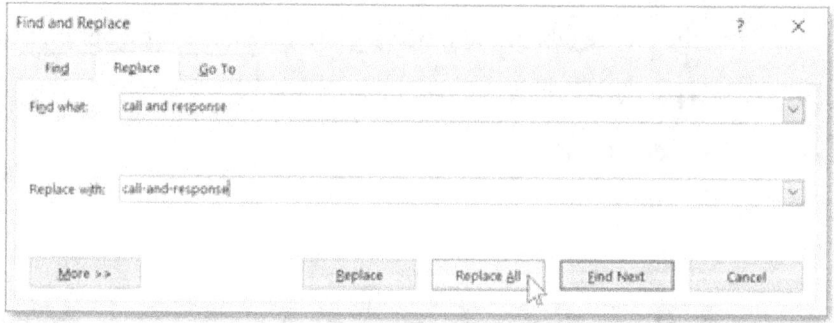

8. A dialogue box will appear telling you how many words have been replaced. **Click OK**.
9. **Close** the **Find and Replace** dialogue box.
10. **Click** the **X** to close the **Navigation task pane**.

Spelling & Grammar Check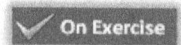

As you type a document, Word automatically checks your spelling and grammar.

1. **Scroll down** the document and **notice** how some words have wavy red and green lines beneath them. This indicates that Word detects possible spelling (red) or grammar (blue) errors.

2. These lines are just visual indicators. If we were to print our document, the lines would not appear in the printout.

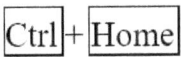

3. **Tap** to get to the top of the document.

Correcting Individual Words

Words can be individually corrected by right-clicking on them.
1. **Right-click** on the first word that is misspelled ("**sogns**").
2. A **context menu** appears with suggested spelling corrections. **Click songs** from the list.

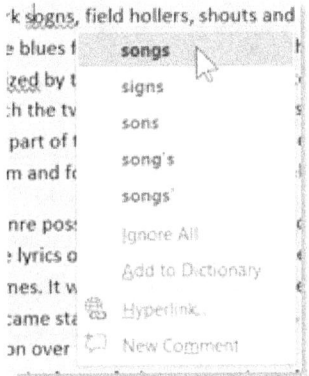

Reviewing the Entire Document

You can also have Word step you through all of the spelling and grammar mistakes in the entire document.
1. **Click** the **Review** tab.
2. In the **Proofing** group, **click Spelling & Grammar**. This will start a spelling and grammar check starting from wherever the insertion point is.

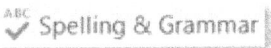

3. **Notice** a **task pane** that opens on the **right**. This pane allows you to address every misspelling or grammar mistake that Word finds. At this point, the spell checker is active.
4. **Note** that if you click into the document while the spell checker is active, it will cause the spell checker to **pause** (this is a common mistake first-time

students make). You should avoid doing this. Let's see what happens when we do this and then describe how to recover from it.

5. **Note** once again that our spell checker is **currently active**, due to the presence of the task pane on the right.
6. **Click** where it says "Blues Music" at the top of the document.
7. **Notice** how there is now a button labeled **Resume** in the task pane on the right. The presence of this button means that our spell checker has been **paused**. We cannot continue spell checking our document until we click "Resume".

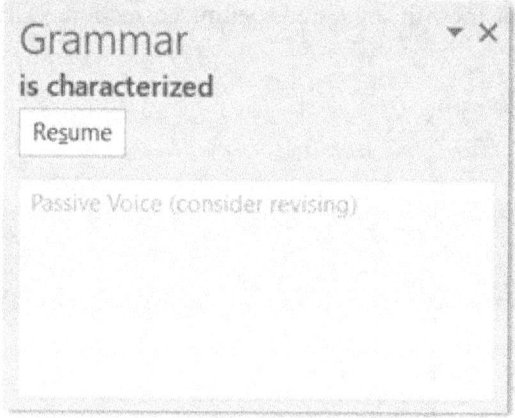

8. **Click Resume** to re-activate the spell checker.
9. Now, let us continue with spell checking our document. **Notice** at the top of the task pane that Word is telling us it found a **Grammar** issue having to do with the words "**is characterized**" in the document.

   a. **Notice** that the sentence containing the text in question is **highlighted** in the document on the left.
   b. **Notice** the button labeled **Ignore** in the task pane. It is only giving us the option of ignoring the grammar issue. If we wanted to fix it, we would have to revise the sentence ourselves. Many grammar check issues do not give you an automatic fix option like the spell checker does.
   c. **Notice** the **white box** underneath the Ignore button. This is where Word puts **suggestions** for how to fix it. **Notice** it is telling us that the sentence is in Passive Voice.
   d. **Notice** how it gives us a **description** of what Passive Voice is below the white box.

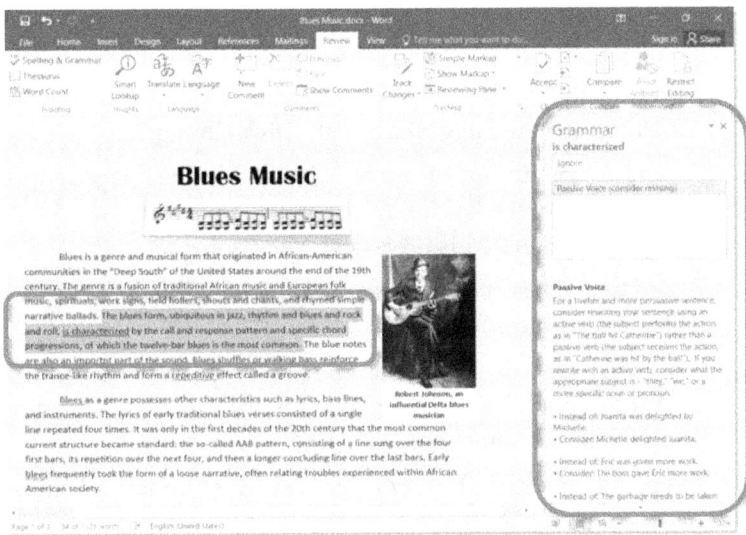

10. **Click Ignore** to move on to the next issue.

11. **Correct** the remaining spelling and grammar issues in the document as follows:

    a. Ignore all Passive Voice grammar errors.

    b. "importnt": This should be spelled "important".

       Click important in the **Suggestions** list. **Click Change**.

    c. "Blees": This should be spelled "Blues".

       Click Blues in the **Suggestions** list. **Click Change All**.

    d. "blees": This should be spelled "blues" too. But we clicked Change All the last time we corrected this word. Why didn't it change this instance of the misspelling too? Because it starts with a lower-case "b", not a capital "B".

       Click blues in the **Suggestions List**. **Click Change All**.

    e. "blues rock": The grammar checker thinks this should be a Compound Word, spelled "blues rock".

       Click blues-rock in the **Suggestions** list. **Click Change**.

    f. "lyrics": The grammar checker thinks there should be a comma after this word.

       Click lyrics, in the **Suggestions** list. **Click Change**.

g. "4": The grammar checker is suggesting that we spell out this number. Read the description below the suggestion box. It says any number below 10 should be spelled out.

   Click four in the **Suggestions** list. **Click Change**.

h. "Handy's": Notice how the word "Handy" in the image caption on the right is not marked as being misspelled, but "Handy's" *IS* marked as being misspelled. This is because Microsoft

   Word treats these two words as **completely different words** (just like "Blees" and "blees").

i. "Handy" was not marked as misspelled probably because Word is treating "Handy" as an adjective (the word "handy" meaning "to be useful"), not as someone's last name.

j. Word has marked "Handy's" as misspelled because it doesn't make sense to put an apostrophe "s" after an adjective.

k. *Bottom line:* We know that this is a valid spelling because it is the possessive version of someone's last name. **Click Add**. This will add "Handy's" to Word's dictionary.

l. This dictionary item is saved on the hard drive of your computer.

m. "a": It should say "**an** African American".

   Click an in the **Suggestions** list. **Click Change**.

n. "But": The grammar check is saying you shouldn't start a sentence with "but".

   Click However, in the **Suggestions** list. **Click Change**.

o. "Odum": This is somebody's last name. Last names are often not in Word's dictionary. **Click Add**.

12. A "spell check complete message" will appear when all has been ⌈Ctrl⌉ + ⌈End⌉ corrected. **Click** OK.

13. Testing Spelling & Grammar check features

14. **Tap** to **move** your ⌈Enter⌉ insertion point to the end of the document

15. **Tap** to go to a new line.

    a. **Type** the word "jazz" with a lower-case "j" and ⌈Space Bar⌉ **tap** the **Notice** how it **automatically capitalized** the word.

    b. **Type** the name "Odum" with a capital "O" and **tap** the ⌈Space Bar⌉

       Notice how the word **does not receive red squiggly lines**. That's because we added this word to Word's dictionary.

c. On the same line **type** "odum" again, but with a lower-case "o" and **tap** the Space Bar .

Notice how this word is **flagged as misspelled**. Microsoft Word treats it as a different word because it does not have a capital "O".

d. Word is programmed with many common spelling errors and fixes them automatically as you type. **Staying** on the same line, **Type** "teh" and **tap** the.

Notice how it automatically changed to "the".

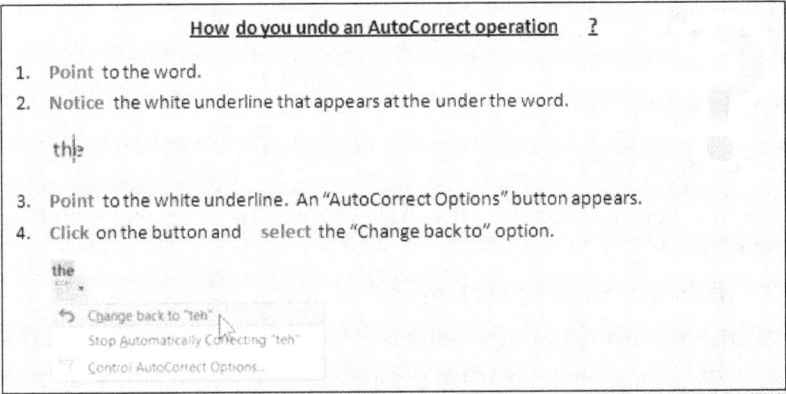

Pick up Where you Left Off Feature

"Word has a neat 'Pick up where you left off' feature. When you close a document, Word bookmarks the exact location you were last working on within that file. It does so by identifying where the insertion point was when you closed the document. When you open it again, Word offers to let you pick up where you left off". - Fatima Wahab

1. In the **Lyrics section** on the second page, **click** at the end of the first paragraph to move your insertion point there.
2. **Close Blues Music.docx** and **save** changes.
3. **Reopen Blues Music.docx**.
4. **Notice** the message on the right. It invites us to continue where we left off the last time we had this document open.

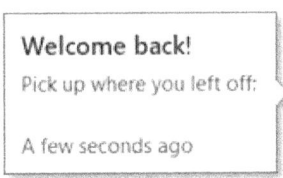

5. After a moment, the message will disappear and be replaced with a "bookmark" icon.

6. **Point** to the icon. The message **reappears**. **Click** on it.
7. **Notice** how it **scrolls down** to the *general vicinity* of where we were the last time we had this document open.

Printing a Word Document

Print Preview

Still in Blues Music.docx

Always preview before you print. That way, you won't waste paper or ink printing unwanted pages.

1. **Click** the **File tab**, and **click Print**.
2. **Notice** the **Print Preview pane** on the right. This shows you what your document will look like when printed.
3. **Note** that the document's **blue background** does not show up in the Print Preview. This is because Word will **not** print a document's background color unless you specifically instruct it to do so (in order to save printer ink). This setting is located in Word's Options screen.
4. **Check** the number of pages in your document by **looking** in the lower left of the Print Preview pane.

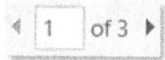

5. **Scroll** down or use the right arrow to **see** page 2.
6. To see two pages of your document side by side, **lower** the zoom using the zoom slider at the bottom right of the Print Preview pane.

7. If you need to amend your document, **click** the **Back** button to return to your document and make all necessary changes.

Microsoft Word

Adjusting Print Settings

1. **Click** the **File tab**, and **click Print**.
2. In the **center pane** are **options** for printing. At the **top** is where you can designate a printer.
3. The **Settings** section is where you can decide other things about how you would like your document to print. For this class, we will cover how to designate which pages of your document you want to print.
4. By default, Word prints **all the pages** in the document. However, this is not always what you want. You can use the "**Pages:**" field to choose which specific pages you want to print. **Point** to the **Pages:** field and **note** the large ScreenTip that describes how pages can be entered.

   a. **Single page numbers** can be entered if you just want to print 1 page.
   Example: 2

   b. **Non-consecutive page numbers** can be separated by commas.
   Example: 1, 3

   c. A **range of page numbers** can be expressed with the use of a dash between two numbers. Example: 3-6

5. In order to launch the print job (which we are **NOT** going to do), you would click the large Print button at the top of the center section.

6. **Close** Word without saving changes to the file.

Saving a Document under a Different Name

Sometimes, you want to save changes to a document, but you want to keep the original version of the document. In this case, you can save your changes under a **different file name**.

   Story: You and your family members are helping a relative sell his car by creating a flyer for him.

> **Teacher's note:**
> Car Sale Flyer.docx will be used to demo saving files under a different name and as different versions. All changes will be saved.

1. **Use File Explorer** to **open Car Sale Flyer.docx** from your flash drive.
2. You think the **price** should have some extra effects to make it stand out more.
   a. **Select** the text that reads $18,000.
   b. On the **Home** tab, in the **Font** group, **click Text Effects and Typography.**

   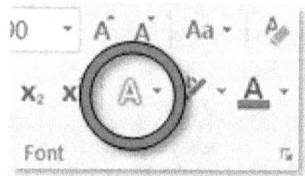

   c. Click the effect with the white text and red outline in the bottom row.

3. We want to send this updated document to everyone to get their opinion on how it looks. **Think** about how we want to save this file. If we just click **Save**, the older version of the file will be lost. If nobody likes it, we will have lost the original version!
4. Instead, we can save the file under a **different name**.
   a. **Click File**, and then **click Save As**.
   b. **Click Browse** and in the **Save As dialogue box**, in the **navigation pane, click** KINGSTON (E:).
   c. In the **Save As dialogue box**, in the **file name field, type Car Sale Flyer Revised**, then **click Save**.
   d. **Notice** how the **title bar** contains the new name of the file.
5. **Click** on the taskbar button for File Explorer and **note** the new file at the bottom of the list.
6. **Note** that the original **Car Sale Flyer.docx** file is still there.

Saving a Document in Different formats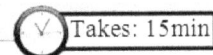

Older Microsoft Word File Format (.doc)

Story: We want to send this new version, **Car Sale Flyer Revised.docx,** out to all our family members for them to review. But not all of them have the same version of Word that we do. Some of them have older versions.

If you send a Word document to someone using a previous version of Word, they may not be able to open it if you save it formatted as a Word 2016 (*.docx) document. Word 2016 provides an option to save the file in a format that can be opened by previous versions of Word. However, this may result in some loss of formatting.

1. **Click** the **File tab. Click Save As**, and then **click Browse**.
2. In the **Save As dialogue box**, in the **navigation pane, click** KINGSTON (E:).
3. In the **Save as type:** field, **click** to open a list of file types:

4. In the list of file types, **click Word 97-2003 Document (*.doc).**

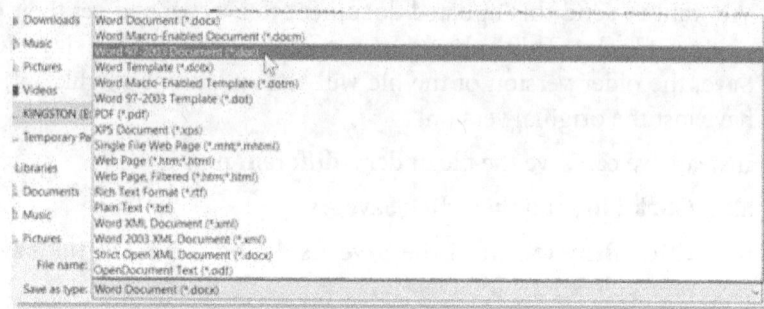

5. **Notice** how the file name now has an extension of **.doc**. **Click Save**.

6. A **Microsoft Word Compatibility Checker** window pops up. This alerts us to the fact that some formatting may be lost when we save in an older file format. **Click Continue**.

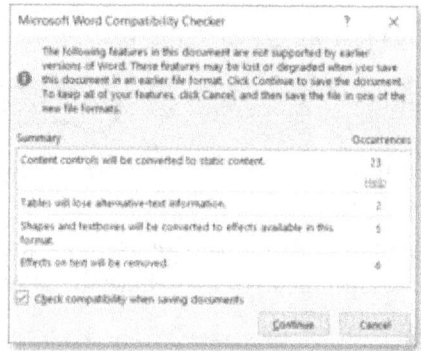

7. **Notice** what happened to the price text. **The formatting is completely gone!** The page background also turned gray. What happened?

8. **Notice** that the file name in the title bar says **Compatibility Mode**. This means it is showing you what the document looks like when viewed in an older version of Microsoft Word.

![Car Sale Flyer Revised.doc [Compatibility Mode] - Word]

9. **Also notice** how the **Text Effects and Typography** button that we used before looks grayed out. **Click** on it. Nothing happens. **Point** to the button

and **look** at its **screen tip**. This feature is not available in older versions of Word. That is why the price text lost its formatting. Certain tools are unavailable in this document because it is saved in an older file format.

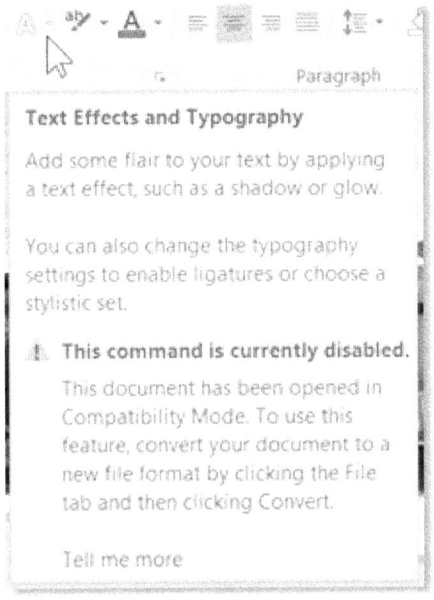

PDF

Another saving option is to save a Word document formatted as a PDF (Portable Document Format). One benefit to using this format is that it is widely supported across all computer and mobile devices. Nearly all computers come pre-installed with software that can open PDF files. If your computer does not have this software, you can download software called "**Adobe Acrobat Reader DC**" for free. This  makes PDF an ideal choice for sharing files with people who do not have Microsoft Word.

Another benefit to using PDFs is that they retain ALL of the formatting in your Word document. PDFs are designed to represent **printed pieces of paper**, so they act like an electronic "print-out."

But the main downside is that PDF files **cannot be edited** unless you purchase special software called **Adobe Acrobat DC**. If you want to make a change to a PDF, you must open the original Word document, make the change there, then **re-save** it as a PDF.

1. **Open Car Sale Flyer Revised.docx**.
2. **Use** the **Save As** function again but **choose PDF** as the file format.
3. Before clicking **Save, notice** the checkbox that says **Open file after publishing**. If checked, then the PDF file will be opened in Adobe Reader as soon as the Save operation is complete. This gives you the chance to inspect the PDF file to make sure it looks OK. **Leave** it checked.
4. **Click Save.**
5. **Notice** how **Adobe Acrobat Reader** opens after a few moments.
6. **Be aware** that the PDF file you've created does NOT automatically update whenever your Word document updates! This means that, if you change your Word document, you will need to **re-save** it as a PDF.
7. **Close** the PDF window.

Protected View	🛡 PROTECTED VIEW

8. **Close** all open Word documents.

Protected View is a security feature that helps to protect your computer from viruses that reside inside Word documents (notably, from files that were downloaded from the Internet, such as from email attachments). Protected View protects your computer from viruses, but **prevents** you from **editing** or **printing** the document. If you trust the source of the document, you can **deactivate** Protected View in order to edit and print the document like normal.

1. We are going to **download** a Word document from the **Internet** to demonstrate this.

    a. **Double-click** the **Class Resources** link on the Desktop.

    > **Home Students:** Open a web browser and go to www.mc-npl.org/class-resources.

    b. **Scroll** to the section for Microsoft Word. Underneath the Supporting Files subsection, **click volunteer application.doc**.

    c. A **dialogue box** appears, asking what we want to do with the file. **Click Save As** because if you just click Save, it won't tell you where it's being saved to.

    > **Teacher's note:**
    > It is important that they click "Save As". If they just click "Open", then the document might not open in Protected View.

d. In the Save As dialogue box, **navigate** to your **flash drive** and **click Save**.

e. Internet Explorer will display a toolbar at the bottom of the screen that has a button to open the downloaded file in its native program, Word. **Click Open**.

f. A security warning appears stating that opening files from the Internet can harm your computer. **Click Allow**.

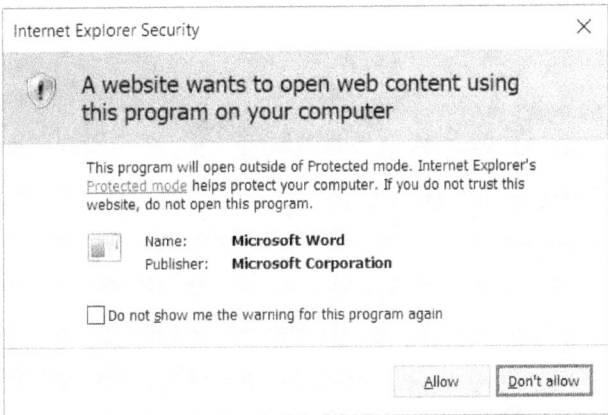

2. **Notice** the **title bar** and **warning**. The document has opened in **Protected View** because we downloaded it from the Internet.

3. **Notice** how we have **two columns** of text and the text is **very large**.

a. **Look** at the **Status Bar** at the bottom of the screen and **notice** we are currently in **Read Mode**. Documents that open in Protected View are opened in Read Mode by default.

b. **Click Print Layout** to see what the document "actually" looks like.

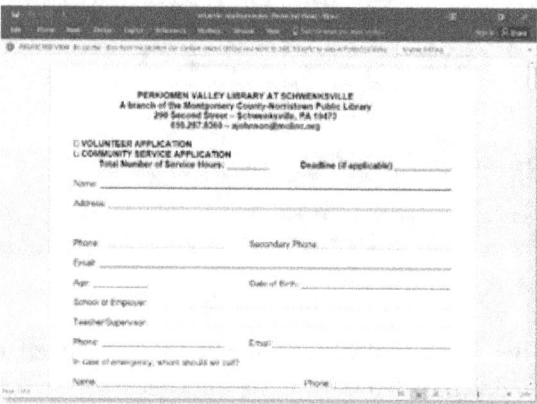

4. **Click** the **File** tab, then **click Print**.
5. **Notice** the warning about printing a **Protected View** document. It is not possible to print without clicking that "Enable Printing" button first. Clicking this button will also enable editing and take the document out of protected mode.

6. **Close Word.**

Microsoft Word

 Good stopping point for Session 2.
Describe how the Exercise is organized: The parts in parentheses are **hints** concerning how to complete each step.

When you want to present a list of items in a document, you will usually want to put each item on its own line. There are several different types of lists in Word:

Bulleted Lists

Use **Bulleted Lists** when the **order** of the items **is not important** (for example, a shopping list).

1. **Open** a new blank Word document.
2. **Type** "Grocery List" and **tap** Enter to get to a new line.
3. On the **Home** tab, in the **Paragraph** group, **click** the **Bullets** button proper. This tells Word to create a new list.
4. Let's populate our list with some items:
    a. **Type** "milk"; **tap** Enter
    b. **Type** "bread"; **tap** Enter
    c. **Type** "eggs"; **tap** Enter
5. **Click** the **Bullets** button proper again. This will end your list.
6. **Notice** how each word is on a separate line and proceeded by a bullet.

Numbered Lists

Use **Numbered Lists** when the **order** of the items **is important** (for example, a recipe).

1. **Type** "Cookie Recipe", then **tap** Enter to get to a new line.
2. On the **Home** tab, in the **Paragraph** group, **click** the **Numbering** button proper.
3. Let's populate our list with some items:
    a. **Type** "Preheat oven"; **tap** Enter
    b. **Type** "Mix ingredients"; **tap** Enter
    c. **Type** "Bake for 1 hour"; **tap** Enter
    d. **Click** the **Numbering** button proper to end your list.

> Cookie Recipe
> 1. Preheat oven
> 2. Mix ingredients
> 3. Bake for 1 hour

Multilevel Lists

Use **Multilevel Lists** when you want to create an **outline** of items, where each item can have its own sub-list of items.

1. **Type** "Inventory" and **tap** .
2. On the **Home** tab, in the **Paragraph** group, **find** the **Multilevel List** button.

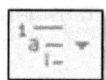

   a. **Notice** how this is a **one-part** button, unlike the others which were split buttons.
   b. **Click** on the Multilevel **list**. A menu of styles will open. **Hover** your mouse pointer over the various styles to view them.
   c. In the **List Library** section, **click** the option which is **next to "None"**.

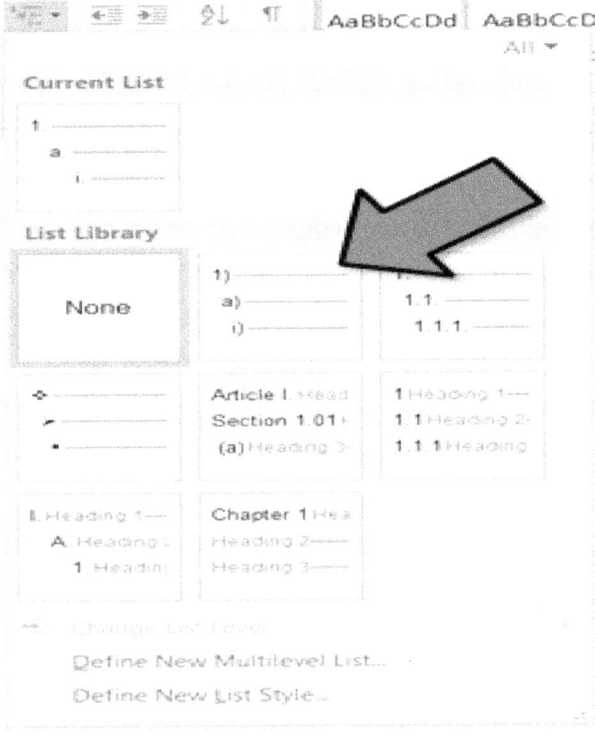

3. Multi-level lists are trickier than normal lists because you have to tell Word what **level** to place each list item on.
   a. Using Enter the key will create a new item at the **same** level.
   b. Using Tab the key will move an item to a **lower** level. (indented more)
   c. Using Shift + Tab will move an item to a **higher** level. (indented less)
4. Let's try this by populating our list with some items.
   a. **Type** "Office"; **tap** Enter
      Tab ; type "Desk"; tap Enter
   b. **Tap** Tab ; type "Top drawer"; tap Enter
   c. **Tap** Tab ; type "Pencils"; tap Enter
   d. **Tap** Tab ; type "Top drawer"; tap Enter
   e. **Type** "stapler"; **tap** Enter
   f. **Type** "ruler"; **tap** Enter
      Shift and tap Tab

    g.   **Hold** to move to **one** higher level

    h.   **Type** "Middle drawer"; **tap** `Enter`

    i.   **Tap**

    j.   **Type** "tax forms"; **tap** `Enter` `Shift` and tap `Tab`.

    k.   **Hold twice** to move to **two** higher levels

    l.   **Type** "Filing cabinet"

5.   When finished `Enter` with your list, **tap** until no more bullets appear. This is another way of ending a list.

```
Inventory
1) Office
    a) Desk
        i)  Top drawer
            (1) Pencils
            (2) Stapler
            (3) Ruler
        ii) Middle drawer
            (1) Paper
            (2) Tax forms
    b) Filing cabinet
```

Modifying an Existing List

1.   To **insert** a new list item:

    a.   We will insert a new item below "Ruler".

    b.   **Click** after the word "Ruler" to move your insertion point there.

    c.   **Tap**

    d.   **Notice** that a new list entry was created.

    e.   **Type** "paper clips".

2.   To **delete** a list item:

    a.   We will delete the "Stapler" list item.

    b.   **Click** after the word "Stapler" to move your insertion point there.

Microsoft Word

    c.   **Use** to Backspace delete the word.

    d.   once the list item is blank, Backspace **continue** to tap until your insertion point is after the word "Pencils". Do not tap it too many times or else you will delete "Pencils" as well.

3.   To change the style of bullets or numbers:

    a.   **Select** all of the list items in the **Grocery List** list.

    b.   **Note** that the **bullets** do not appear selected when you select a list. This is normal.

    c.   In the **Paragraph** group, **click** the drop-down arrows on the **Bullets or Numbering** buttons and hover over each option to see a live preview of changes.

4.   To change the indent level:

    a.   **Select** all of the items in the **Cookie Recipe** list.

    b.   In the **Paragraph** group, **click Increase Indent** or **Decrease Indent** to make changes.

Teacher's note:
The next few sections use a new blank document to demonstrate inserting several different kinds of objects. If they are not completed by the end of the class session, save the file, naming it "Objects".

Tables

Word allows you to insert **tables** into your document. Tables consist of the following elements:

- **Row**: Runs horizontally (left to right)

- **Column**: Runs vertically (up and down, like on a Roman building)
- **Cell**: The intersection of a row and column. You can type text into each cell.

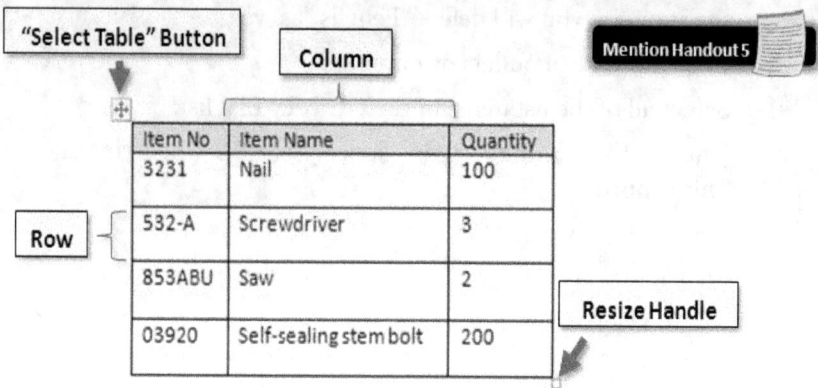

Inserting a Table
1. Open a new blank document in word.
2. Click the insert tab and in the Tables group, click Table.
3. Move your Pointer over the squares in the Table Pane to determine the size of your table. Notice how the squares change color and the dimensions are given at the top. The dimensions list the number of columns first, then the number of rows.

4. When you have a **7 column x 5 row** table, **click** the left mouse button. Your table will be inserted wherever your insertion point was located in the document.

Microsoft Word

Moving Around a Table

You can move between cells in a number of ways:

1. **Confirm** that your blinking cursor/ insertion point is inside of the **first cell**. Tab key. This moves your insertion point one cell to the right. Tapping Tab.
2. **Tap** the at the end of a row will move the insertion point to the first cell of the next row.
3. You can also use the **directional arrows** to move the insertion point from cell to cell. **Try it**.
4. Lastly, you can **click** in a cell to move the insertion point. **Try it**.
5. **Move** the insertion point to the **very last cell** of the table and Tab then **tap**. **Notice** how it created a **new row**.

Entering Information into a Table

We are going to enter the **days of the week** in the cells in the **first row**. An **autocomplete** feature will assist in this task.

1. **Click** in the first cell (the left-most cell) of the first row.
2. **Type the first 4 letters** of Monday.

    a. **Notice** the **autocomplete** feature which pops up after Enter typing the 4th letter. **Tap** to take accept the autocomplete suggestion.

    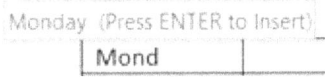

    b. *Before you continue,* **note** that this is the **only advisable time** to tap in a cell. Otherwise you will create a new line in the cell. **Tap** again. **Notice** how it inserted a new line underneath Monday. This is what happens when Enter is tapped without an autocomplete suggestion. **Tap** to delete the new line.

    c. **Tab** the Tab key to move to the next cell, and **use** autocomplete again to type the next day of the week. Keep going through Sunday.

Selecting Parts of a Table

To format your table, you must know how to select individual cells, columns, and rows, as well as the entire table.

1. **Selecting a Cell: Move** your pointer to the left edge of an empty cell in the second column until a small black arrow appears, then **click**. **Note** the inside of the cell becomes **grey**. This means the cell is selected. Use the **select cell cursor** to **click and drag** across several cells to select multiple cells.

2. **Selecting a Column: Move** your pointer to the top of a column until a small downward pointing black arrow appears. This is the **select column cursor**. When you see this cursor, **click** to select the column. **Click and drag** to select several columns.

3. **Selecting a Row: Move** your pointer to an area to the left of the second row until the pointer changes to a **right pointing white arrow**. This **select row cursor** allows you to select an entire row with a **click**. If you have clicked in the right place every cell in the row should be selected.

You may note that when you click to select the row, new items appear on the screen. You may see a **mini toolbar** offering a toolset that can be used to perform actions upon the selected row. The other object is an **Insert Control** feature which we will be covering further on.

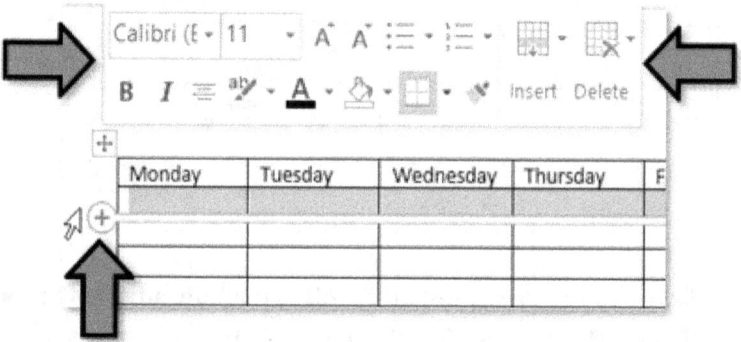

4. **Click** the **select row cursor** and **drag** to select several rows.

5. **Selecting the entire table**: **Click** the **Select Table** button that appears at the top left corner of the table. **Click** in a clear area off the table to deselect the table.

Teacher's note:
<u>**Do NOT move the table yet**</u>. <u>If you move the table, then you can no longer click in the left margin to select an entire row.</u>

Resizing Rows and Columns

1. To adjust the **width of a column, point** to the **vertical border** between two columns so your pointer changes into a **double arrow**. Then you click and drag the line where you want it. **Use** this **resizing cursor** to make the first column wider.

2. To adjust the **height of a row, point** to the **horizontal border** between two rows so your pointer changes into a **double arrow. Use** this **resizing cursor** to make the first row higher.

> **Tip:** If you **double-click** when your mouse pointer has changed to the "adjust width" or "adjust height" pointers, the row/column will **auto-adjust**, based on the size of your text.

Inserting Rows and Columns

Insert Control Feature

The insert control feature utilizes an interface we noticed when we were in the process of selecting various sections of the table. The tool will appear when pointing to the left or top border of the table and in the general vicinity between two rows or two columns. As opposed to other insertion methods, this tool facilitates an insertion without having to select any particular portion of the table. When the tool is completely in focus, it will turn from grey to blue and can then be clicked to perform an insertion. It will insert a row **below** the insert control tool or a column to the **right** of it. *Let's try it.*

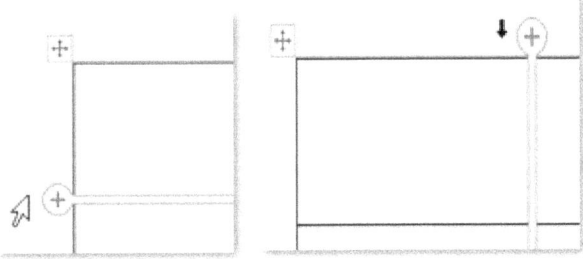

1. **Point** to the **left** border of the table and move your mouse until you see the **blue insert control tool** on the border between the **first** and **second row**. Click the +. **Note** it inserts a row **below** the first row. **Click Undo.**

2. **Point** to the **top** border of the table and move your mouse until you see the **blue insert control tool** on the border between the **first** and **second column** and **click** the **+**. **Note** it inserts a column to the **right** of the first column.
3. **Click Undo**.

Ribbon Method

Note that, when you have any part of a table selected, a new **contextual ribbon** appears called **Table Tools**. This contextual ribbon has two tabs, **Design** and **Layout**.

Unlike the limited functionality of the insertion control feature, there are tools on the ribbon which will allow the insertion of a row **above** an existing row or to the **left** of a column *as well as* insertion below and to the right. However, prior to using the ribbon tools, the insertion point must be inside a cell in the table. The ribbon tools will delete rows above or below the selected cell and columns to the left or right of it.

1. **Click** in the first cell in the first row (it has Monday in it).
2. On the **Table Tools** contextual ribbon, **click** the **Layout** tab.
3. In the **Rows & Columns** group, **click Insert Left**. **Note** the new column inserted to the left of the first column. **Click** Undo.
4. In the **Rows & Columns** group, **click Insert Above**. **Note** the new row inserted above the second row.
5. **Click** Undo.

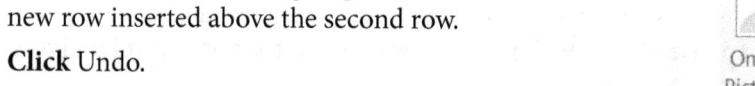

Right-Click Menu

Row and column insertion tools are also available on a right-click menu. Again the insertion point must be inside a cell.

1. **Click** in the first cell in the first row.
2. **Maintain** cursor focus on the selected cell and **right-click**.
3. **Point** to **Insert** and then **click Insert Rows Above**. **Note** the new row inserted above.
4. **Click** Undo.

Microsoft Word

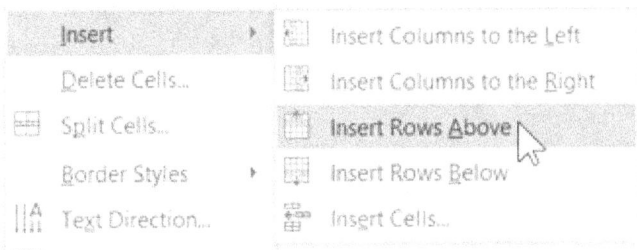

Deleting Rows and Columns

Both the ribbon and the right-click menu have tools to delete rows and columns. The **ribbon** tool, named **Delete**, can be accessed when the insertion point is in a cell in the row or column to be deleted. The **right-click menu** offers a *specific* delete button when the row or column is selected first.

Ribbon Method

1. **Click in** the **third cell** in the **first row (Wednesday)**.
2. On the **Table Tools** contextual ribbon, **click** the **Layout** tab.
3. In the Rows & Columns group, **click Delete**. On the menu click **Delete Columns**. **Note** the column with the Wednesday cell disappears. **Click** Undo.
4. In the Rows & Columns group, **click Delete**. On the menu click **Delete Rows**. **Note** the row with the Wednesday cell disappears. **Click** Undo.

Right-Click Menu

1. **Select** the row with the Wednesday cell in it.
2. **Maintain** cursor focus on the selected row and **right-click**.
3. **Click Delete Rows**. **Note** the deletion. **Click** Undo.

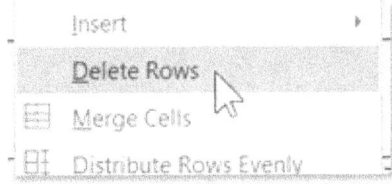

4. **Select** the column with the Wednesday cell in it.
5. **Maintain** cursor focus on the selected column and **right-click**.

6. **Click Delete Columns. Note** the deletion. **Click** Undo.

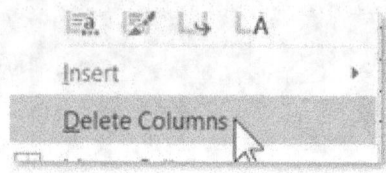

Formatting a Table

1. **Insert** a new row above the first row.
2. **Select** the first row.
3. Let's apply some formatting to the first row.
   a. On the **Table Tools** contextual ribbon, **click** the **Layout** tab. In the **Merge** group, **click Merge Cells.** Those seven selected cells will now function as a single cell.
   b. **Type** the word "**schedule**" into the still selected cell.
   c. On the **Layout** tab, In the **Alignment** group, **use** the ScreenTips to **find Align Center. Note** there are several different options for aligning text in a cell.
   d. **Click Align Center.**
   e. On the **Table Tools** contextual ribbon, **click** the **Design** tab. In the **Table Styles** group, **click** the **list arrow** section of the **Shading** split button. A menu of colors will appear.
   f. **Move** your pointer over the colors to see a **Live Preview** and then **click** on any color you like. **Notice** that only the selected cell is shaded.
4. **Select** the **entire table** by **clicking** on the **Select Table** button.
5. On the **Table Tools** contextual ribbon, on the **Design** tab (you may need to make the Design tab active), in the **Borders** group, **click** the **Dialogue Box Launcher.** This dialogue gives you **fine-grain** control over your table's borders.
   a. In the **Borders** tab, under **Setting, make sure All** is selected.
   b. **Scroll** through the **Style Menu** and as you **click** on different options, see the preview in the preview pane on the right. **Click** whatever style you prefer.
   c. **Click** the **Color** list arrow and **choose** a color from the menu.
   d. **Click** the **Width** list arrow and **choose** a width.

e. **Click Ok** to apply your changes.

f. **Deselect** the table so you can view the border better.

6. To **move** your table, **click** on the **Select Table** button and **drag** your table down the page a little.

   Then **drag** it back to where it was.

   Do NOT move the table into the top margin, or else it could get stuck.

7. To **resize** your table, **locate** the small square at the bottom right of the table. This is a **Resize handle**. **Point** to it and **notice** that the pointer changes to a **white arrow with two ends**. **Click** and **drag** towards the **center** of the table. This action resizes the entire table **proportionally**, so all the row and columns get resized by the same amount.

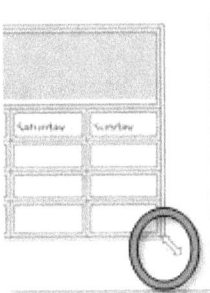

8. **Click Undo** to return the table to its original size and position. You may have to click it multiple times.

Online Pictures, Shapes, Text Boxes, and Other Pictures

The insertion of specialized objects into a document can add visual interest. We will explore a few different types of objects in this section and also learn how to format the objects.

Online Pictures

The former name for this type of object was Clip Art. **Clip art** are small pictures and symbols made available for computer users to add to their documents. They can be used to enhance a narrative.

Inserting Online Pictures

1. **Click** in a clear area underneath the table to move your insertion point off of the table.

> **Teacher's note:**
> If the student's table is too far down the page, the cursor will get stuck above the table. If this happens, the student can **double-click** below the table to place their insertion point there.

2. On the **Insert** tab, in the **Illustrations** group, **click Online Pictures**.
3. A dialogue box opens that prompts us to enter a search term.

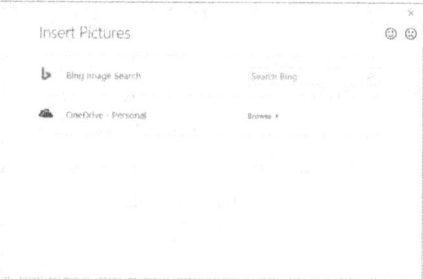

4. **Note** the words **Bing Image Search**. Microsoft Word will search the Internet for images using its search engine, Bing (it is a competitor to Google).

5. **Type helmet** in the search field [Enter] and tap.

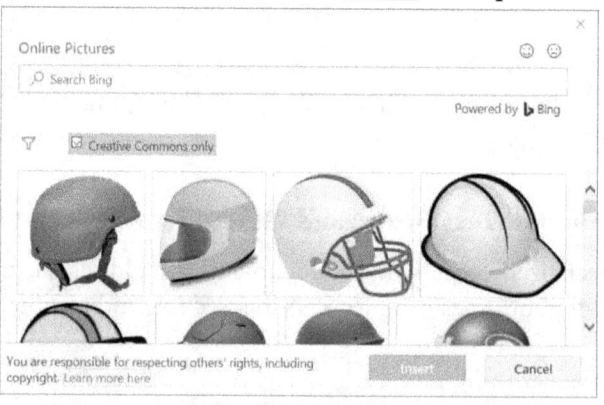

6. **Note** the gray checkbox labeled "Creative Commons only". Word has filtered the search results to only show images that are licensed under **Creative Commons** licenses.

a. **What is Creative Commons?** It is a type of copyright license that is frequently used on the internet. In general, it is a liberal license that gives you permission to use the image for free.

b. **HOWEVER,** Creative Commons allows content creators to add "gotchas" such as "cannot use for commercial purposes" or "must provide attribution to the original author". **MICROSOFT WORD DOES NOT SHOW YOU THESE.** So, at the end of the day, it is up to **you** to verify that you are abiding by the author's **SPECIFIC** license terms—and finding the specific license terms is not always an easy task.

c. For this reason, if you are planning to use clip art for any professional purpose, we recommend using a clip art website that contains only **public use** images. One such website is **pixabay.com**. Public use images give you **complete control** over how you may use them. *Later in the lesson we will learn how to insert a picture from pixabay.com into a Word document.*

d. Another alternative is to **purchase** clipart (also called "stock images"). This is how businesses typically obtain clip art.

7. **Find** a picture you like.
8. **Point** to the image.
9. **Click** on the **three dots** in the bottom-right corner of the image. A screen tip appears above the image containing additional information about the image, including its pixel dimensions and Internet URL.

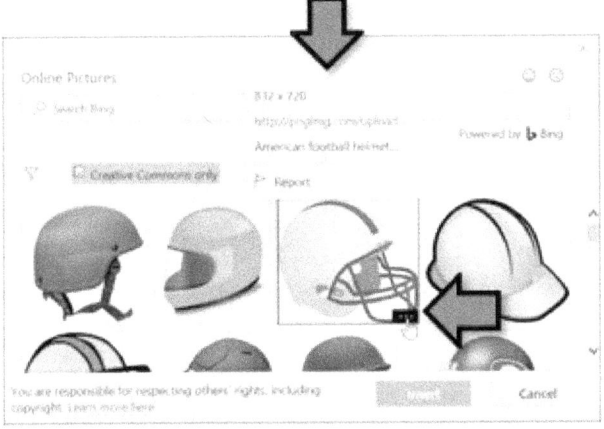

10. Click in a clear space to dismiss the screen tip.
11. Now, we will insert the image into our document.

a. **Click** on the picture to **select** it.
b. **Notice** the check mark that appears in the **top-right** corner of the picture.
c. **Notice** how the Insert button indicates that **one picture** is selected. d. **Click Insert (1).**

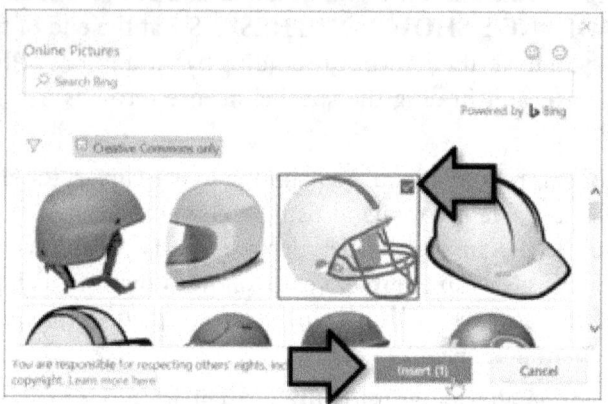

Resizing Inserted Objects

Objects can be resized by using "**handles**" that appear around a selected object.

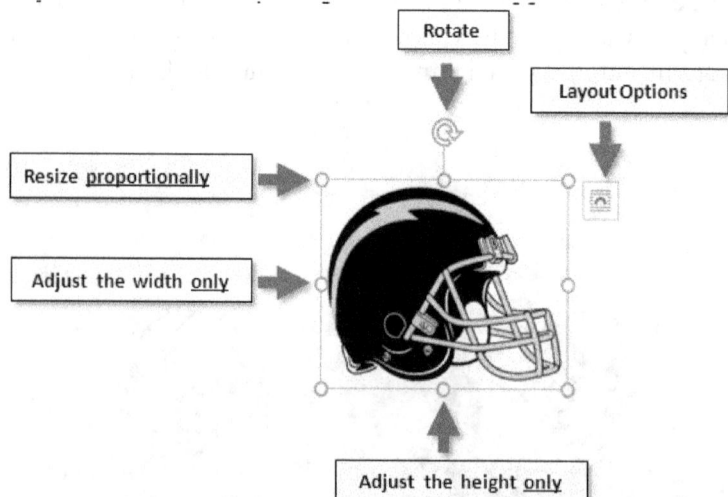

1. If you cannot already see a border and small circles around your picture, **click** on the picture to select it.
2. **Point** your mouse to one of the circles. These circles are called **resizing**

handles. **Notice** the pointer shape changes to a **white arrow with two ends**. As we learned before, this is a **resizing cursor**.

3. Using one of the **corner circles, click** and **drag** towards the center of the picture and **note** it resizes the picture **proportionately**. This does not always work with ⌈Shift⌉ other types of objects. Other objects require you to hold down while resizing to retain the original proportions.

Warning: Increasing the size of an online picture can result in a **distorted look** when printed. To avoid this, try not to make an online picture any larger than it was when you originally inserted it into the document.

4. **Click** and **drag** from one of the **side circles** and **note** the change in shape of the picture. These circles do **not** resize the picture proportionally. **Click Undo**.

5. **Click** and **drag** the **circular arrow icon** above the picture to note how the picture **rotates**. **Click Undo** to get it back to its original rotation.

6. **Using** the **rulers** on the top and left edges of the document as a reference, **resize** the object proportionally to approximately 1 ½" square.

7. **Deselect** the object by clicking in a **blank area**.

Applying Wrapping Styles

"Objects can be placed in your document in two ways: either inline or floating. Inline objects are those that reside on the same layer as your text and are positioned within the stream of text that surrounds the object. Floating objects are those that are placed on a layer over the text". –Allen Wyatt

This positioning of objects is called the **text wrapping style.** The wrapping style can affect how difficult it is to move an object on the page. If it seems difficult to move an object where you want to, then you may need to change the wrapping style:

1. **Select** the picture object and **move** your pointer around on it until you see a **Move** cursor shape.

2. When you see this cursor, **click** and **drag**. You should **notice** that it is hard to move the object. We need **to change the wrapping style** so it is easier to move. The default wrapping style for pictures is **In Line with Text**, which means that only text can move it around. This can be very restricting.

3. **Click Layout Options** to the **right** of the selected object.

a. It presents you with a set of icons, each of which represent a **wrapping style**.

b. You can get an idea of what each wrapping style does by looking at the icons. The blue, horizontal lines represent your document's text, and the gray arch represents the image.

c. **Point** to the icons to see a **ScreenTip** containing their names. **Click In Front of Text**.

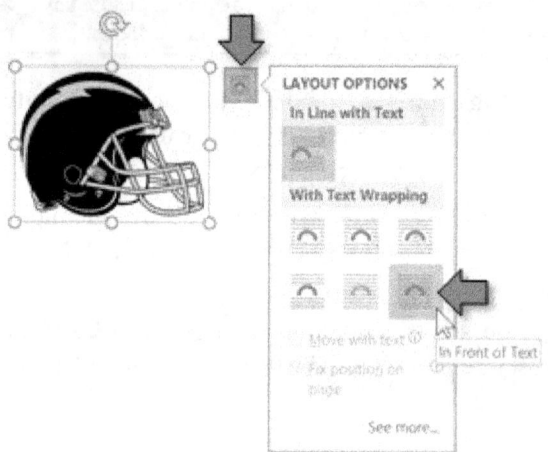

4. **Notice** the small "anchor" symbol that has appeared after we changed the wrapping style to a "floating" style. This is called an **object anchor** and it indicates where a floating object is located in relation to the text in your document. If we were to insert multiple lines of text somewhere in our document above the anchor, it would cause our object to get "bumped" down, even though it is floating.

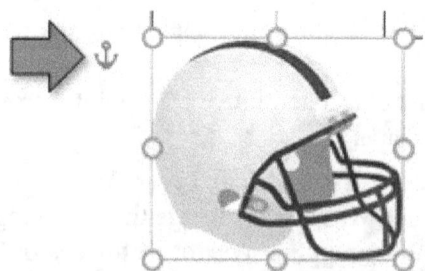

5. **Using** the **move cursor**, **move** your object slightly to the left. You should **see** a **green line** appear. This green line helps you to align your object against the left margin of the document.

6. **Move** the object so it is on top of the last column in your table.
7. **Notice** how there are now **two** contextual ribbons: **Table Tools** and **Picture Tools**. This is because our picture object is selected *and* it is on top of the table.
    a. **Picture Tools** has one tab: **Format**
    b. **Table Tools** has two tabs: **Design** and **Layout**

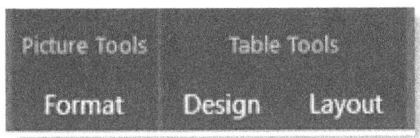

Applying Formatting to Pictures

1. **Click** the picture to select it if it is not already selected.
2. On the **Picture Tools** contextual ribbon, **click** the **Format** tab and, in the **Picture Styles** group, **move** your pointer over the predefined **Picture Styles** thumbnails to see a **Live Preview** of their effects.
3. **Click** the **More** button to see more predefined styles. As you point to the different styles **note** the ScreenTips that appear which contain the name of the style. **Click** on the **Metal Oval** style.

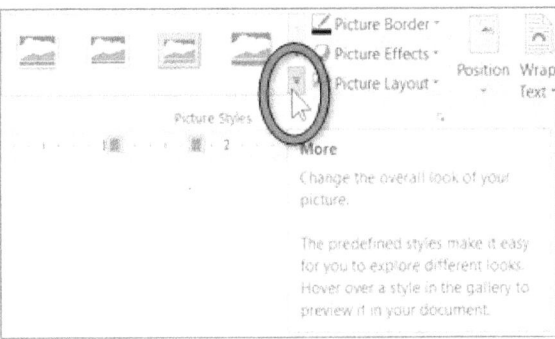

4. In the **Picture Styles** group, **click** on **Picture Border** and **click** on any color that you like.
5. **Deselect** the picture.

Shapes

A shape is another type of object that can be inserted into a Word document.

Let's insert an **arrow shape** into our document.

1. On the **Insert** tab, in the **Illustrations** group, **click Shapes.** A menu of shapes will open. The shapes are organized by type of shape.
2. In the **Line** section, **mouse** over the line shapes until you see a ScreenTip that says **Double Arrow**  . **Click** the shape.
3. **Find** your mouse cursor in the document and **note** that it is shaped like a crosshair ✛.
4. We are going to "**draw**" an arrow from our **helmet picture** to the word "**Monday**" in our table. a. **Point** to the helmet picture.
   a. **Click** and **drag** to the word Monday.
   b. **Let go** of the mouse button.
5. **Note** the arrow is **selected**. You can tell by the **resize handles** at the ends.
6. With the arrow still selected, **note** the **Drawing Tools** contextual ribbon. It has one tab: **Format. Click** the Format tab.
7. In the **Shape Styles** group, **click Shape Outline. Point** to **Weight** and, on the sub-menu, **click 6 pt**.
8. **Click Shape Outline** again. **Mouse over** the colors to see a live preview on your arrow. **Click** a color to select it.
9. **Point** your mouse at the **body** of the arrow until you see a **Move cursor**. **Click** and **drag** to move the arrow to another place.
10. **Deselect** your arrow.

Microsoft Word

11. **Insert** your cursor beneath the table.

> **Tip**: To change the **default line styling** that is used when you create a new line, **right-click** on the line whose style you want to make the default and **click "Set as Default Line"**.

*Next, we will insert a **star shape**.*

1. On the **Insert** tab, in the **Illustrations** group, **click Shapes**.
2. In the **Stars and Banners** section, **mouse over** the shapes until you see **5-point Star** and **click** it.
3. **Find** your cursor in the document and note that it is shaped like a crosshair ✛.
4. **Click** next to the insertion point and **drag** diagonally down and to the right. Don't let go of the mouse until the star is about 3" square (**use** the document rulers as a guide). **Let go** of the mouse button when you finish dragging.

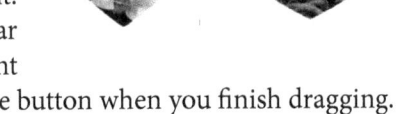

5. **Remember** that as long as you don't let go of the mouse button, you have **full control** over the size and shape of the drawing.

> **Tip**: Using the corner resize handles on a shape will **NOT** resize the shape proportionally, like with clipart. To resize a shape proportionally, you must hold down Shift while resizing.

6. **Find** the **move cursor** on the star object and **move** the star to the right side of the document.

   Use the green line to **align** it to the right margin of the document.

7. On the **Drawing Tools** contextual ribbon, on the **Format** tab, in the **Shape Styles** group, **click More** to see a gallery shape styles that could be used. **Mouse over** these Quick Styles to **see** a **live preview of the different styles**. **Scroll** down the gallery and **click** a quick style in the last row.

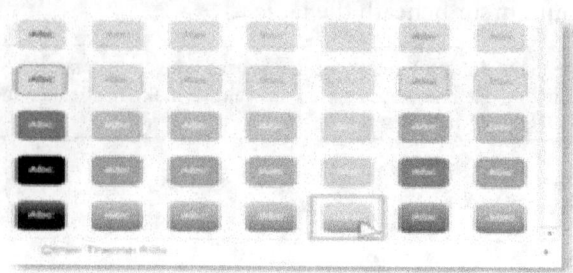

Clicking between objects may make tabs inactive

1. **Click** on the helmet object again. **Note** that your star shape object has become deselected and the Drawing Tools contextual ribbon associated with it has disappeared.
2. **Note** that **two contextual ribbons** now appear; one associated with the online picture object (Picture Tools) and one with the table (Table Tools). However, none of the tabs on either contextual ribbon are active.

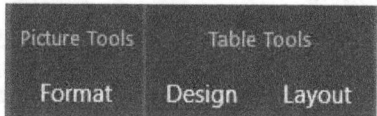

3. **Click** on the **Design** tab and **note** the background color of the tab is **white**. This is how you can tell it is active.

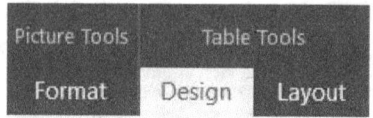

4. **Click** on the star object again. **Note** that while the Drawing Tools contextual ribbon may appear, its **Format** tab might not be active. If you don't see the tools you expected to see, you may have to **click** on the tab to activate the tool selection.

Text Boxes

A text box is a freestanding object that can contain words. *Let's insert a text box.*

1. **Deselect** the star object.
2. **Click** on the **Insert** tab. In the **Text** group, **click Text Box**. A menu of Built-in text box styles will appear. However, to have more control over format, placement and size, we will draw our own text box. **Click Draw Text Box.**
3. **Click** into your document where you want the text box to start and **drag** diagonally and to the right to where you want it to end.

4. The insertion point within the text box indicates that what you type will be inserted there. **Type your name**.
5. **Resize** the text box to just fit around your name.
6. To move your text box, **make sure** it is selected, then **move** your pointer to the edge of the box until a **move cursor** appears. Then **click** and **drag** your text box to the **center** of the **star shape**.
7. **Note** that the text box has a **black border** and it is also **filled** with white color.
8. You can change the formatting of the text box by using tools on the **Drawing Tools** contextual ribbon.
    a. With the text box selected, on the **Drawing Tools** contextual ribbon, **click** the **Format** tab. In the **Shape Styles** group, **click Shape Outline**, and **click No Outline.**
    b. Next, In the **Shape Styles** group, **click Shape Fill** and **click No Fill**. **Deselect** the text box.

Other Pictures

In addition to inserting pictures via Online Pictures, you can also insert images of your own into a document. These images can be ones that you've made yourself (like photos taken with a camera) or ones that you've downloaded from the Internet. We have placed a couple of pictures on the flash drive for you to use in this section.

Inserting a Picture

1. **Open** a new blank Word document.
2. **Click** the **Insert** tab. In the **Illustrations** group, **click Pictures**.
3. In the Insert Picture dialogue box, **navigate** to the flash drive and **click Orchid.jpg**.

4. In the dialogue box, **click Insert.**

Color Effects and Artistic Effects

1. To prep for this section, let's move our picture to the right side of the page. See if you can remember how to do this. This is an important thing to know!

   a. **Change** the Text wrapping style to "In front of text".

   b. **Click** and **drag** your picture to the right side of your document.

2. On the **Picture Tools** contextual ribbon, on the **Format** tab, **find** the **Adjust** group, and **click** on **Color. Mouse over** the coloring effects that could be applied to your picture.

3. **Click** on the **title bar** to dismiss the gallery.

4. In the **Adjust** group, **click** on **Artistic Effects** and **mouse over** the artistic effects that could be applied to your picture.

5. **Click** on the **title bar** to dismiss the gallery.

Remove Background Effect

1. To prep for this section, we are going add a **dark background color** to the document.

   - **Click** on the **Design** tab, and in the **Page Background** group, **click** on **Page Color**. b. **Click** a dark color.

   > Note: By default, Word will **not print** a page's background color because of the amount of ink required.

2. On the **Picture Tools** contextual ribbon, **click** the **Format** tab and, in the **Adjust** group, **click Remove Background**. Your picture will look like the picture below. Also, a new contextual tab named **Background Removal** will open.

3. On the **Background Removal** tab, in the **Refine** group, **click Mark Areas to Keep**.

Microsoft Word

4. The pointer will change to the **shape of a pencil** when you point to the picture. **Use** the **tip** of the pencil to "**click away**" the bright pink sections.
5. In the **Close** group, **click Keep changes**.
6. **Deselect** your picture.

Crop Picture Effect

1. **Open** a new blank Word document.
2. **Insert** another picture from your flash drive. It is named **red-roses-photo.jpg**.

3. On the **Picture Tools** contextual ribbon, on the **Format** tab, **find** the **Size** group and **click** on the **list arrow** part of the **Crop** split button.
4. **Point** to **Crop to Shape**. In the **Basic Shapes** section of the Shapes menu, click **Heart** ♡ .

Format Painter

The Format Painter is used to **copy** the **formatting** of a piece of text or picture and **apply** it to something else. For instance, in the case of text, the formatting would be the font face, size, and color. We will use the Format Painter to apply the formatting of one object to another.

1. **Deselect** the **red roses** object which we just cropped to a heart shape (**click** the right margin).
2. **Insert** the **Orchid.jpg** picture from your flash drive again.
3. **Resize** each object **proportionally** (use the corner handles) until they appear side by side. (make them about **3" wide**).
4. **Select** the **red roses** object.
5. **Click** the **Home** tab and in the **Clipboard** group, **click Format Painter**.

6. **Move** the mouse pointer around the screen. **Notice** how the mouse cursor has changed to an arrow with a paintbrush next to it.

7. **Click** on the orchid object that you just inserted. **Notice** how it now has the same cropped shape as the red roses object.

8. **Deselect** the orchid object and **note** your cursor shape has returned to an **I-beam shape**.

   Double-Clicking Format Painter makes it possible to apply a format to more than one object. *Let's try it.*

   1. **Insert** your cursor to the right of the orchid object Enter and tap .
   2. **Search** for **Online Pictures** pictures using the search term **flowers**.
   3. In the search results, **locate** two pictures of **flowers** that do not have white backgrounds. Since the search dialogue allows the insertion of multiple objects at one time, **click** each of the two pictures and then **click Insert.**

4. **Resize** each image so they are each about **3" in width**.
5. **Click** one of the objects that is formatted with a heart shape.
6. **Double-click Format Painter**.
7. **Click** on one of the flower objects and **notice** it adopts the heart-shaped format.
8. **Deselect** the flower object and **notice** that the cursor does not change back to an I-beam.
9. **Click** on the **second flower object** and **notice** it adopts the heart-shaped format.
10. In order to **"turn off"** the Format Painter, **single-click** on its button in the Home ribbon.

Inserting a Picture from a Webpage

You can also insert images from a webpage into your document. However, be aware that many images on the internet are **protected by copyright**. When you find an image you like, you should read the website's fine print to determine if you can use the image or not. This is especially important if you are making a presentation for commercial purposes (for example, as part of your job).

1. **Open** a new, blank document.
2. Using the Start Menu, **open Firefox**.
3. **Click** into the **address bar** at the top of the screen and **type www.pixabay.com**. Pixabay is a website that contains images that you can download and use for free, without restriction.
4. **Type** "healthy food" into the search box Enter and **tap** .
5. **Click** on an image you like (except for the ones in the first row—those cost money).

6. On the next screen, **notice** the **copyright notice** on the right. It says "**CC0 Creative Commons**". This means you can use the image however you want. You don't even have to give the original author credit.
7. **Right-click** in the **middle** of the image and **select Copy Image**.

CC0 Creative Commons
Free for commercial use
No attribution required

> **Tip:** If you're planning on printing the document, it's best to use a **high-resolution** version of the image. To do this, click the green "Free Download" button on the right. This will download an image file to your hard drive. Then, follow the instructions found in the "Inserting a Picture" section to insert the image file into the presentation.

8. Using the **taskbar, switch back** to **Word**.
9. In the **Home** tab, in the **Clipboard** group, **click** the **Paste button proper**.
10. **Close** Firefox.

Quick Parts (Supplemental)

Quick Parts allows you to add preformatted portions of text. The portions of text can be reused as many times as you like. If you are constantly typing the same text such as a company name or an address, you can create a quick part out of it and in a couple of keystrokes insert the text into your document. Quick Parts can save you a lot of time when you're creating documents.

Creating a Quick Part

1. **Close** any Word documents you have open and open a new, blank document.

> **Teacher's note:**
> It is important that all Word documents are closed; otherwise they will not get the message about saving their building blocks.

2. **Type** Montgomery County-Norristown Public Library into the document and **highlight** it.
3. **Bold** it and **change** the font size to 14. Do not deselect the text.
4. On the **Insert** tab, in the **Text** group, **click** the **Explore Quick Parts** button and **click Save Selection to Quick Part Gallery**.

Microsoft Word

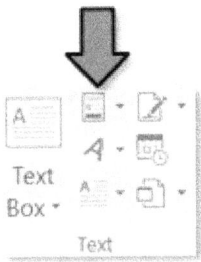

5. A dialogue box opens. In the **Name** field, **replace** the content with a code such as **m1**. The code is very important because this is what you will type to retrieve your quick part. Make it **short** but **understandable**.

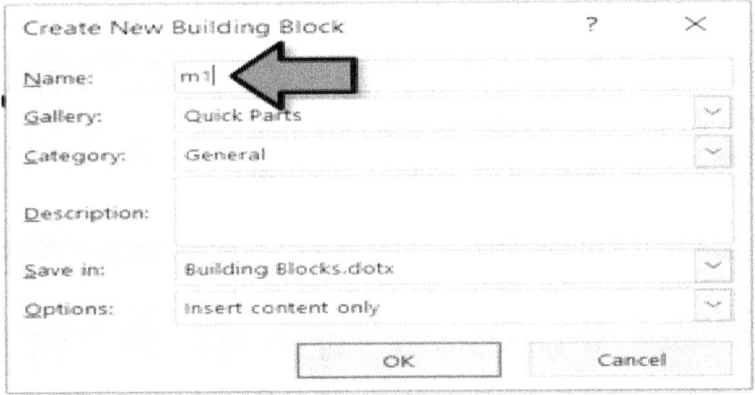

6. Leave other fields at the default setting.
7. **Click OK.**

Inserting a Quick Part (Method1)

1. **Insert** your cursor at another spot in your document.
2. **Type m1** and then **tap** F3 the key.

Inserting a Quick Part (Method2)

1. **Click** the **Insert** tab on the ribbon.
2. In the **Text** group, **click Explore Quick Parts.**
3. The Quick Part you created will be listed at the top. **Click** it.

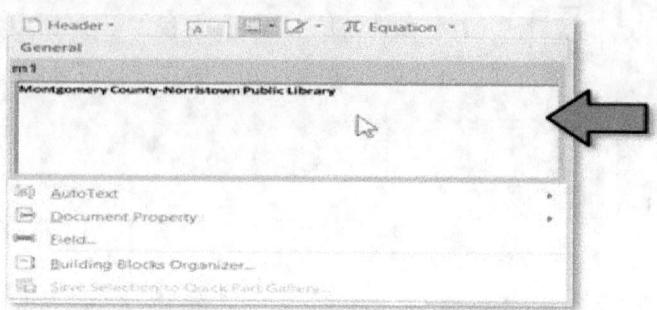

Saving the Building Block

The Quick Part Building Block gets saved to a Word template which contains all of the settings contained in a new document. When you exit out of Word, you may be prompted to save the building block to **Normal.dotm** or **Building Blocks.dotx**. You should respond in the affirmative.

1. **Close** the document without saving changes.
2. Next, it will prompt you to save your building blocks. At home or work, you should always click Save. However, since we are on a public computer, we will **click Don't Save**.

Repeat (supplemental)

The Repeat button is located in the Quick Access Toolbar. It repeats the last action you performed.

1. **Open** "Blues Music.docx" on your flash drive.
2. In the first paragraph, **select** the word "Blues".
3. On the **Home** tab, in the **Font** group, **click Text Effects and Typography** and **click** a style of your choice.

Microsoft Word

4. **Notice** the **Repeat** button in the Quick Access Toolbar.

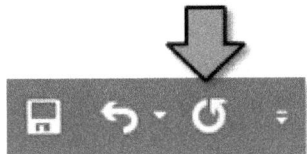

5. **Find** another instance of the word "blues" in the document and **select** it.
6. Click **Repeat**. **Notice** how the text effect was applied to the selected text.
7. **Click Undo**. **Notice** how the Repeat button was **replaced** with the Redo button. The Repeat button **disappears** when you undo something.

8. **Click Redo** to reapply our text effect. The Repeat button appears again.
9. **Close** Blues Music.docx and don't save changes.

> **Why would you use Repeat instead of Format Painter?**
> Repeat only repeats the last action you performed. For instance, if you applied Bold and then Underline formatting to a word, repeat would only repeat the Underline action.
> **Could we have used Repeat with the previous crop-to-shape exercise?**
> Since there were multiple steps involved, (inserting a picture, resizing, moving, then cropping), Repeat would not have helped us in that situation.

Templates (Supplemental)

Calendar Wizard

1. **Open** Word.
2. On the **File** tab, **click New**.

3. In the **New** pane there is a selection of **featured** templates. *However, we're going to search for one.*
4. **Click** in the text box where it says "Search for online templates", **type** "**calendar**", then **tap** Enter on the keyboard to commit the search.
5. **Click** the **Family photo calendar** that looks like this (4th or 5th row).

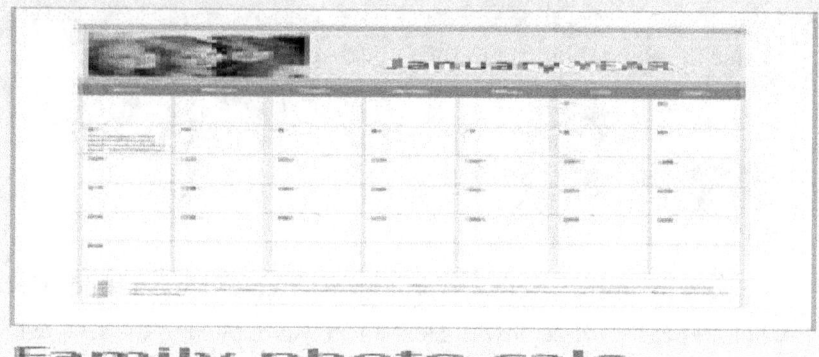

6. A dialogue appears with more information. **Click Create**.
7. Next, a dialogue prompts you to select a month for the calendar. It defaults to the current month. **Click OK**.

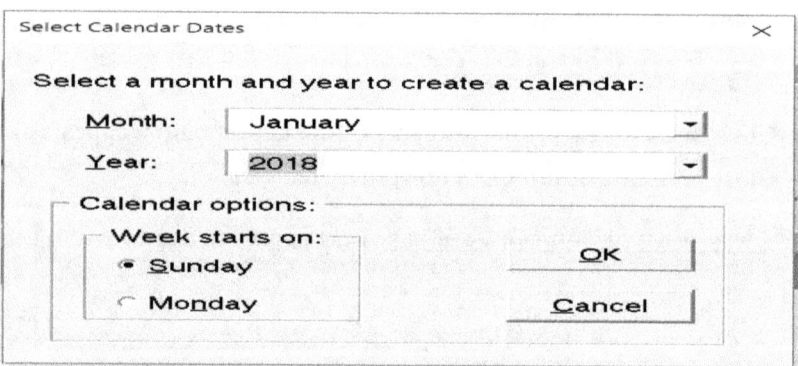

8. Next, a message appears with instructions on how to change the month. **Click OK**.
9. **Note** that a **new tab** has opened up named **Calendar**.
10. On the Calendar tab, in the Themes group, **click Themes**. **Mouse over** some of the themes for a live preview of how your calendar could look. **Click** a theme you like.
11. **Notice** how the **first Sunday** of the month has some content in it. Word is giving us a hint that we can type content into the calendar if we want.

Microsoft Word

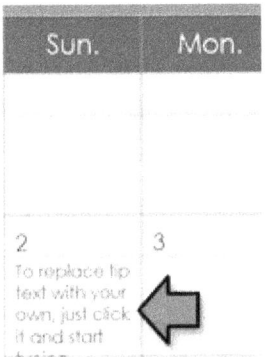

12. If we were to print out this calendar, this "tip text" would appear on our printout. Let's **remove** it.
    a. **Click** once on top of the text. The text turns gray.
    b. **Tap** on the keyboard.
    c. **Remove** the tip text from Backspace the "Notes" section at the bottom of the page.
13. **Click** into one of the dates on the calendar and **type** "Blood Test 11 AM". Be sure to click **underneath** the number, **not** to the right of the number.
14. Next, let's change the picture.
    a. **Right-click** on the picture and **click Change Picture**.
    b. **Click From a file**.
    c. **Navigate** to your flash drive and **open red-roses-photo.jpg**.

15. **Close** the document and **don't save** changes.

Raffle Tickets

1. On the **File tab, click New**.
2. **Search** for **tears**.
3. **Click** the **Raffle tickets** template.

Raffle tickets

4. **Click Create** in the dialog box that appears.
5. This template contains **five raffle tickets**. They are identical to each other except for the ticket number.
6. **Notice** how the words **Name of Raffle Event** are repeated throughout the page.
7. **Click** on any of the Name of Raffle Event headings.
   a. **Notice** how it turns gray.
   b. **Notice** a name for the object you clicked on ("Event Name") appears above the header.
   c. These are both clues that what you clicked on may be a **field** with some **special programming** behind it.

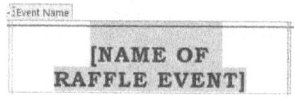

8. **Type State Fair Giveaway**, then **click** in the **right margin** to deselect.
9. **Notice** how the headings of each ticket were automatically populated with the new name.
10. The prize amounts work the same way. **Change** the 1st place prize to **$700**. **Notice** how all the tickets change.
11. **Close** and don't save.

Mail Merge (Supplemental)

Mail merge is a feature of Word processing programs that enables you to generate form letters. Form letters are sent out en masse to people where much of the letter is the same for each recipient. What changes in the letter are the recipient's name, address, and maybe certain other items specific to each recipient.

To use a mail-merge system, you would first create a **data file** with a set of information, like a list of names and addresses. In a Word document, you would create a **sample letter**, substituting special symbols in place of names and addresses (or whatever other information will come from the first file). Through a series of small steps, you can create form letters that are personalized for each recipient.

The data file can be created with various programs such as Word, Excel, or Access. The beauty of the mail merge feature is that, while you can create your own data source in Word, if you already have a spreadsheet of data created in Excel or some other program, it makes sense to use that.

Steps to Create a Mail Merge Document

1. To save time, we have already created a data file in Excel and a sample letter in Word and placed them on your flash drive.
    a. **Insert** your **flash drive.**
    b. **Use File Explorer** to **open Donations List.xlsx.**
    c. **Use File Explorer** to **open merge letter.docx.**
2. Before we start the mail merge process, let's look at the donations list that was created in Excel.
    a. **Notice** that the **list** is on the worksheet named Sheet 1.
    b. Notice that the **first row** of the worksheet contains headings.
    c. **Close Donations List.xlsx**
3. In **merge letter.docx, notice** that the **address** of the establishment, the **body** of the letter and the **closing** are all in place. We will use mail merge to personalize each letter with an **address block**, a **salutation**, and a **donation** amount for each person in our list.
4. **Click** the **Mailings** tab.
5. **Find** the **Start Mail Merge** group. **Click Start Mail Merge** and then **click Step-by-Step Mail Merge Wizard.**

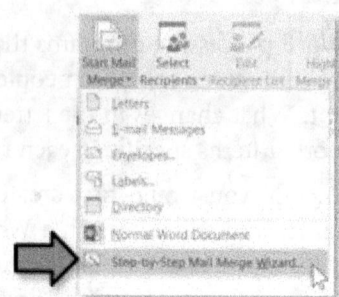

6. A **Mail Merge pane** will open on the right that will take you through the mail merge process in 6 steps.

7. **Step 1 - Notice Select document type** prompt. By default, the radio button for letters is checked, which is what we want. **Click** on **Next: Starting Document** at the bottom of the Mail Merge pane.

8. **Step 2 - Notice** the **Select starting document** prompt. Since we will be using this letter, do not change the default selection of use in the current document. **Click** on **Next: Select Recipients** at the bottom of the Mail Merge pane.

9. **Step 3 - Notice** the **Select recipients** prompt

    a. The default selection, Use an existing list is the one we need. To find the list, **click** on the Browse button.

    b. A **Select Data Source** dialogue box will open. **Navigate** to your flash drive and **open**

       Donations List.xlsx

    c. A **Select Table** dialogue box will open. We need to provide some information about our document.

    d. **Notice** that by default, Sheet 1 is selected.

    e. **Remember** that when we examined our Excel file our data was on the Worksheet entitled Sheet 1.

    f. Also **be sure** that the **check box** before the First row of data contains column headers is **checked**.

    g. **Click OK.**

Microsoft Word

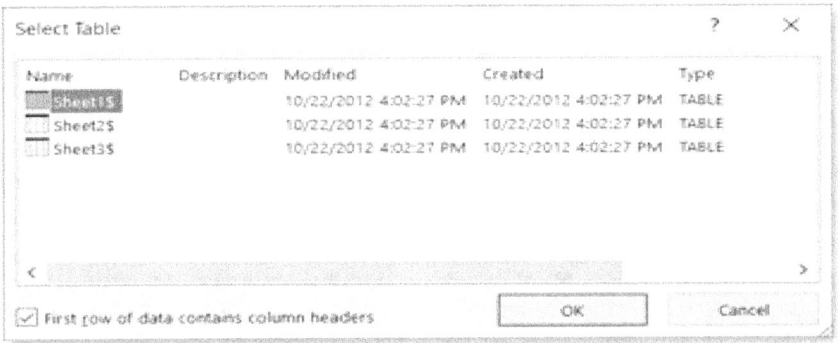

    h. A **Mail Merge Recipients** dialogue box will open which will allow you to review, delete or change your list. Since we are not making any changes, **click OK**.

    i. **Click Next: Write your letter** at the bottom of the Mail Merge pane.

10. **Step 4 - Notice** the **Write your letter** prompt. Since we are using an existing letter, we merely have to click into a location within the letter to insert different items.

    a. **Place** your insertion point below the return address for the Animal Shelter, then **click** Address block in the Mail Merge pane.

    b. An **Insert Address Block** Dialogue box will appear with a **preview** of how your address block will look in the letter. If you select a different format, your preview will change. Make no changes. **Click** OK.

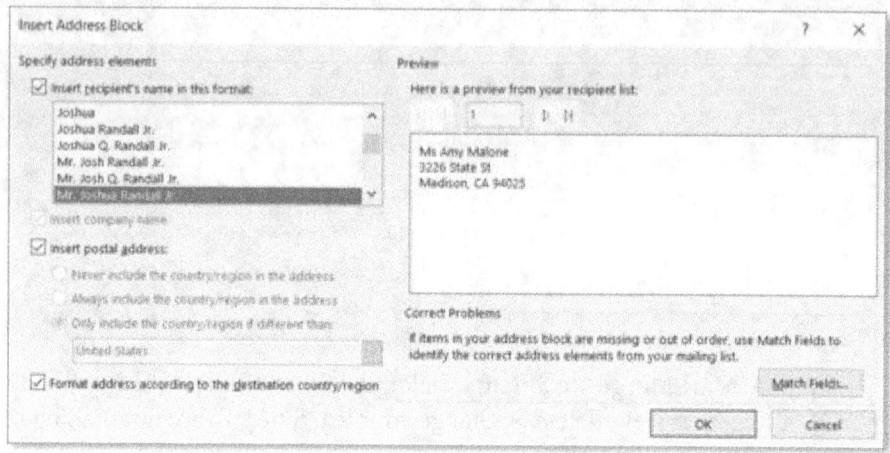

c. **Notice** how the text «**AddressBlock**» has appeared. This will be replaced with an actual address when we complete the mail merge.

d. **Place** your insertion point below the address block and **click** Greeting Line in the Mail Merge Pane.

e. An **Insert Greeting Line** dialogue box will appear to allow you to control the way you want your greeting to appear.

f. **Click** on the **list arrow** next to the box that reads "Mr . Randall" and **click** "Joshua". This will use the person's first name as the greeting.

g. **Click OK.**

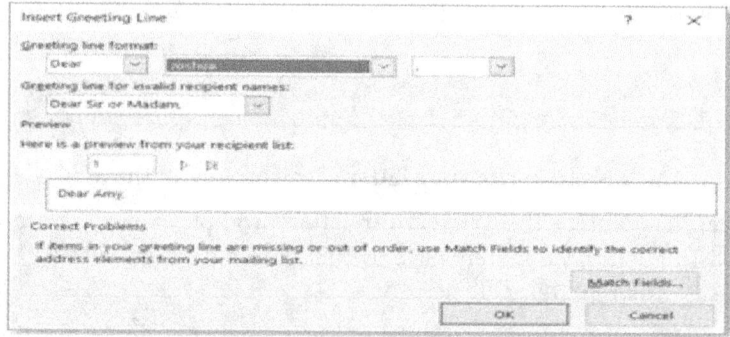

h. Within the body of the letter, **place** your insertion point immediately after the word's **contribution in** the first sentence. **Click** on **More items** in the Mail Merge pane.

i. An **Insert Merge Field** dialogue box will appear.

- **Click donation**

- **Click Insert**.
- **Click Close**.

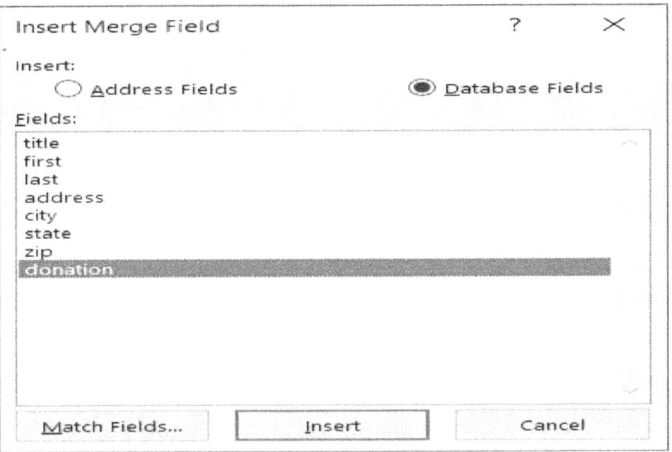

j. **Be sure** that there is a space before and after «**donation**».

k. **Click Next: Preview your letters** at the bottom of the Mail Merge pane.

11. **Step 5 – Notice** the **Preview your letters** prompt.

a. The letter to the first person on your list will appear.

b. Use the **arrows** to **scroll** through each succeeding letter.

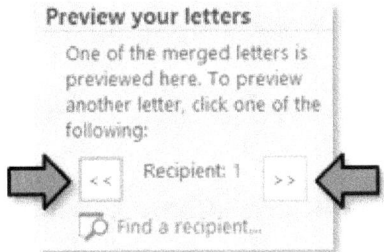

c. **Notice** how the addresses and greetings are all clumped together. Let's insert some blank lines to separate them. Even though only one person's letter is showing, these changes will affect each letter.

d. **Click** at the end of the **first zip code** of the first address and press Enter . .

e. **Click** after the **second zip code** and press Enter .

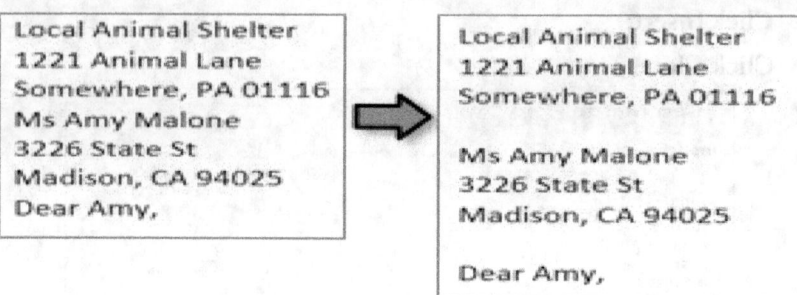

f. **Notice** that there is no $ before the donation amount in your letter. **Place** your insertion point directly before the donation amount, and **type** a $. This change will affect each letter.

g. **Click Next: Complete the merge** at the bottom of the Mail Merge pane.

12. **Step 6 – Notice** the choices on the **Complete the merge** prompt.

    a. **Click** on the **Edit individual's letters** choice.

    b. This will open a **Merge to New Document** dialogue which allow us to merge all our records into a specific new document, separate and apart from the merge letter.docx, rather than just printing the letters out, so that in future we can have a record of to whom we sent letters. **Click OK**.

    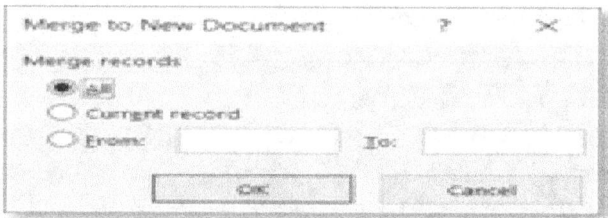

    c. A **new document** called "Letters1" opens with each letter on a separate page.

    d. **Scroll down** the document to see the other pages.

    e. **Save** your file as **Fall Thank You Letters**. **Close** the file.

    f. **Click Print** in the Mail Merge pane. The **Merge to Printer** dialogue box will open allowing you to select which records you wish to print letters for. Be warned: This option sends the records directly to the printer without showing you a print preview.

    g. We will not be printing. **Click Cancel**.

Microsoft Word

h. **Close** Word. Do not save changes to merge letter.docx.

Steps to Use Mail Merge for Address Labels

1. To save time, we will use **Donations List.xlsx** again.
2. **Open** a new Word document
3. **Click** the **Mailings** tab.
4. **Find** the **Start Mail Merge** group. **Click Start Mail Merge** to **open** the menu and then **click Step-byStep Mail Merge Wizard**.
5. A Mail Merge pane will open on the right that will take you through the mail merge process in 6 steps.
6. **Step 1** - **Notice Select document type** prompt. By default, the radio button for letters is checked, **check** the radio button next to **Labels**. **Click** on **Next: Starting Document** at the bottom of the Mail Merge pane.
7. **Step 2** - **Notice** the **Select starting document** prompt. Accept the default selection of Change document layout. **Click Label Options**.
   a. A dialogue box will open allowing you to select the type of printer (dot matrix or laser), the type of label product (such as Avery), and the product number.
   b. **Click Avery US Letter** and product number **15513** for this lesson.
   c. **Click OK**. (If you are using a custom label, click **Details**, and then type the size of the label.)

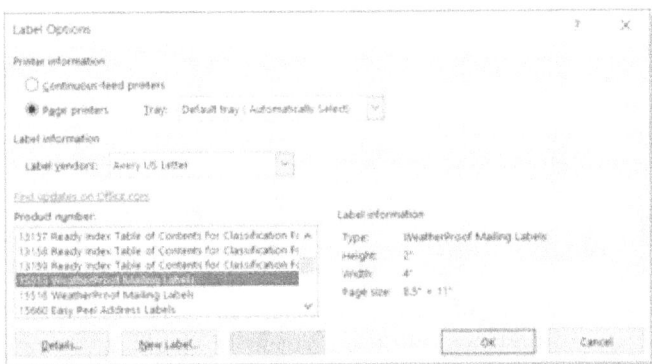

   d. **Click** on **Next: Select Recipients** at the bottom of the Mail Merge pane.
8. **Step 3** –**Select recipients** prompt
   a. The default selection, Use an existing list is the one we need. To find the list, **click Browse**.

b. A **Select Data Source** dialogue box will open. **Navigate** to your flash drive and **open**

DonationsList.xlsx

c. A **Select Table** dialogue box will open. We need to provide some information about our document. **Notice** that by default, Sheet 1 is selected. **Remember** that when we examined our Excel file our data was on the Worksheet entitled Sheet 1. Also **be sure** that the **check box** before First row of data contains column headers is selected. Click OK.

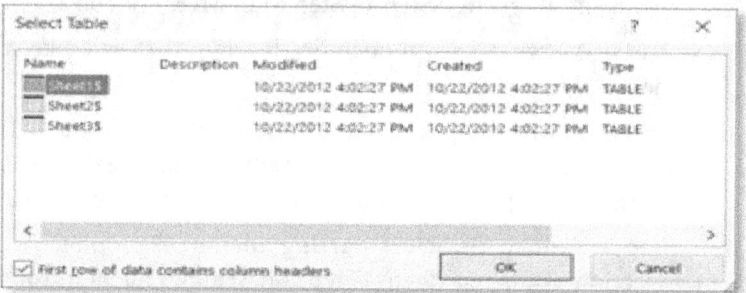

d. A **Mail Merge Recipients** dialogue box will open which will allow you to review, delete or change your list. Since we are not making any changes, **click OK**.

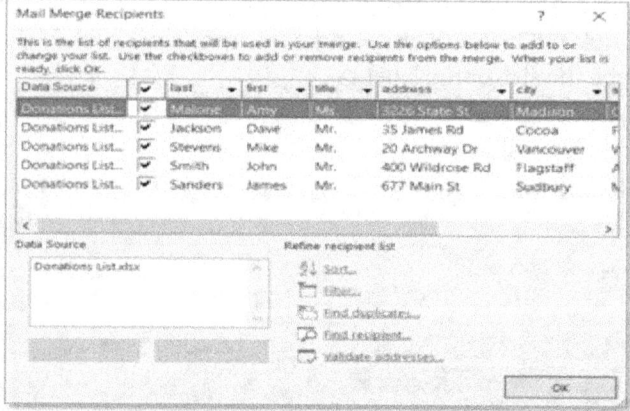

e. You will now see that the first label is blank and every other label has «**Next Record**». This is because the first label begins on the first record. The other labels must be instructed to move on to the next record.

f. **Click Next: Arrange your labels** at the bottom of the Mail Merge pane

9. **Step 4 – Arrange your labels** prompt

a. **Scroll** to the **left** and **notice** the insertion point is in the first label.
   b. Since these are address labels, **click Address block**.
   c. An insert address block dialogue box will appear allowing you to make the same kinds of choices as is the merge letter above. **Click OK**.
   d. **Notice** how «**Address**» gets inserted into only the **first label**.
   e. Under the **Replicate labels** prompt, **click Update all labels**. This causes the address block to propagate into the other labels.
   f. **Click Next: Preview your labels** at the bottom of the Mail Merge pane
10. **Step 5 – Notice** the **Preview your labels** prompt
    a. **Check** your labels
    b. **Click Next: Complete the merge** at the bottom of the Mail Merge pane.
11. **Step 6 – Notice** the choices on the **Complete the merge** prompt.
    a. The same options apply as for Merge letters above.

Steps to Use Mail Merge for Envelopes

1. To save time, we will use **Donations List.xlsx** again.
2. **Open** a new Word document
3. On the **ribbon, click** on the **Mailings** tab.
4. **Find** the **Start Mail Merge** group. **Click Start Mail Merge** to **open** the menu and then **click Step-by Step Mail Merge Wizard**.

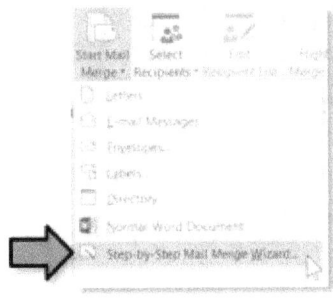

5. A Mail Merge pane will open on the right that will take you through the mail merge process in 6 steps.
6. **Step 1 - Notice Select document type** prompt. By default, the radio button for letters is checked, **check** the radio button next to Envelopes. **Click** on **Next: Starting Document** at the bottom of the Mail Merge pane.

7. **Step 2 - Select starting document** prompt. **Accept** the default selection of Change document layout. **Click** on **Envelope Options**.

   a. A dialogue box will open allowing you to select the envelope size, the type of font and position. **Select Size 10** (the default setting) for this lesson. **Click OK.**

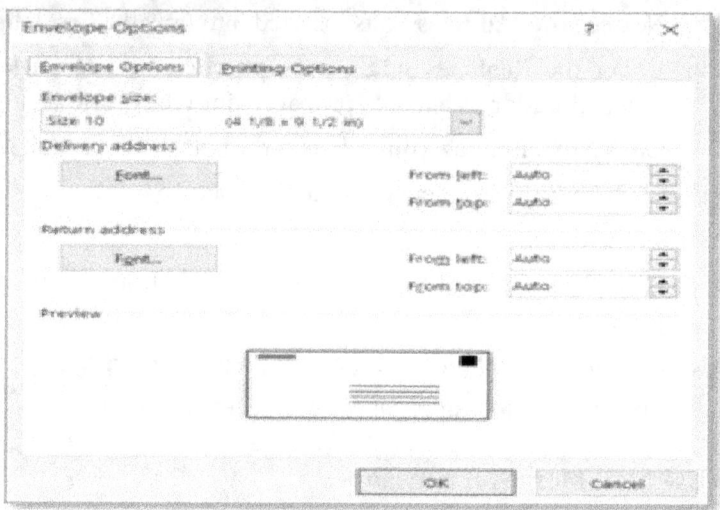

   b. **Click** on **Next: Select Recipients** at the bottom of the Mail Merge pane.

8. **Step 3 – Notice** the **Select recipients** prompt

   a. The default selection, **Use an existing list** is the one we need. To find the list, **click Browse.**

   b. A **Select Data Source** dialogue box will open. **Navigate** to your flash drive and **open**

      Donations List.xlsx

   c. A **Select Table** dialogue box will open. We need to provide some information about our document. **Notice** that by default, Sheet 1 is selected. **Remember** that when we examined our Excel file our data was on the Worksheet entitled Sheet 1. Also **be sure** that the **check box** before the First row of data contains column headers is *selected*. **Click OK.**

Microsoft Word

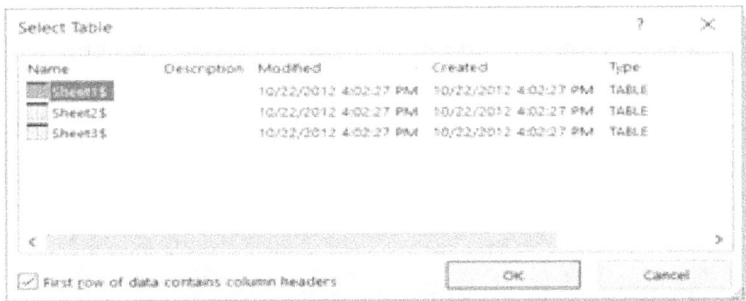

d. A **Mail Merge Recipients** dialogue box will open which will allow you to review, delete or change your list. Since we are not making any changes, **click OK**.

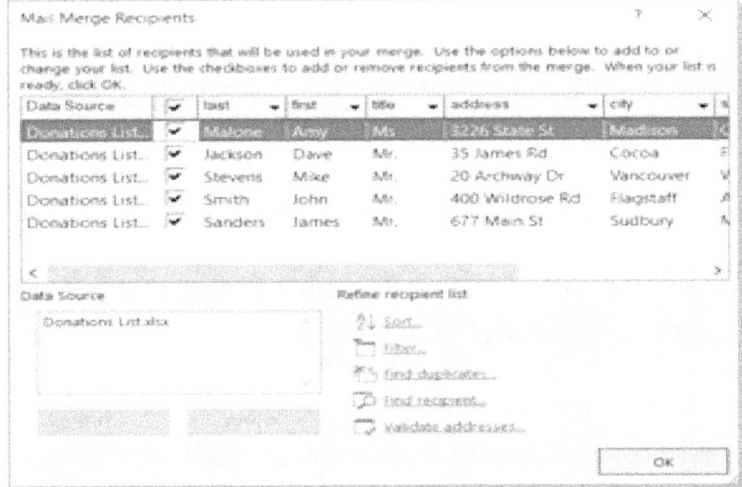

e. **Click** on **Next: Arrange Your Envelope** at the bottom of the Mail Merge pane.

9. **Step 4 – Notice** the **Arrange your Envelope** prompt

a. The insertion point will be located where a return address should be placed. Most businesses will have preprinted envelopes. If yours do not, **type** your **return address**.

b. **Click around** in the center of the envelope towards the bottom until a **text box** appears.

c. **Click Address block** in the Mail Merge pane.

d. An insert address block dialogue box will appear allowing you to make the same kinds of choices as in the merge letter above. **Click OK**.

e. **Click Next: Preview your envelopes** at the bottom of the Mail Merge pane.

10. **Step 5 – Notice** the **Preview your envelopes** prompt
    a. **Check** your envelopes.
    b. **Click Next: Complete the merge** at the bottom of the Mail Merge pane.
11. **Step 6 – Notice** the choices on the **Complete the merge** prompt.
    a. The same options apply as for Merge letters above

Long Document (Supplemental)

In this section, we are going to learn how to manage a long document, giving it a Cover Page and a Table of Contents. Creating a long document requires some forethought in terms of how the content is going to be organized. We have created a document which organizes content for a Manual of Operations into a basic outline using multi-level list functionality. This will serve as a jumping off point.

The document, named **Source Document.docx** has been placed on your flash drive. **Use File Explorer** to **open** it. The outline structure of this document will assist us as we make decisions on formatting the content.

Creating a Cover Page

1. **Place** your insertion point in front of the word Services.
2. **Click** on the **Insert** tab. In the **Pages** group, **click Cover Page**. **Click** the **Integral** template.

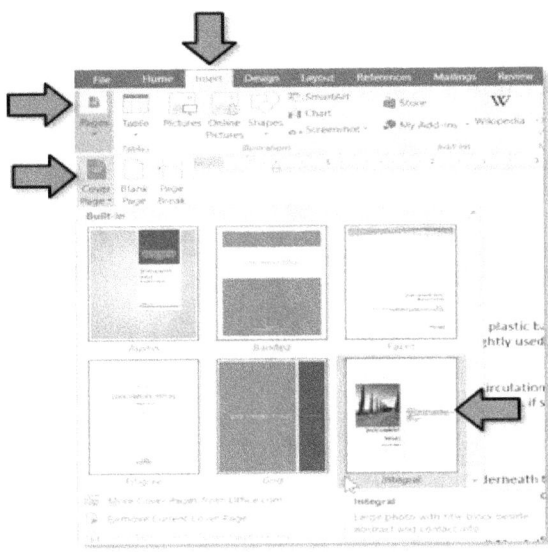

3. **Click** into the [**Document title**] field (be sure you click on the words "Document" or "title" and not an empty space). The field becomes selected and you can **type** "Manual of Operations". **Note** that this field is formatted to display all letters in **capitals**.

4. **Type** "Circulation Desk" into the [**Document subtitle**] field.

5. On the right side, **note** the section labeled ABSTRACT.

    a. **Click** in the bracketed field underneath the word Abstract. **Note** a label appears with the name of the field, Abstract.

    b. **Replace** the text in the [Enter] brackets with "Defines the duties of the circulation staff." Do not tap. Just **leave the insertion point where it is**.

6. **Click** on the word all underneath the abstract field. **Note** a label appears with the name of the field, **Author**.

    a. Unlike the other fields, this field came pre-populated. It contains the word "all" because that's the name of the Windows profile on the lab computers.

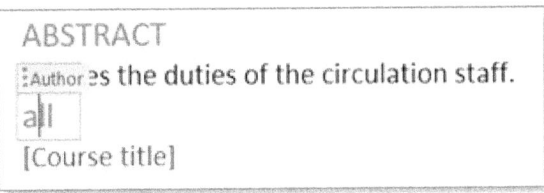

b. **Change** the author field to "Adult Services Department".

We are going to delete the Course Title Field. To do this **Right-click** on the field and **click Remove Content Control**.

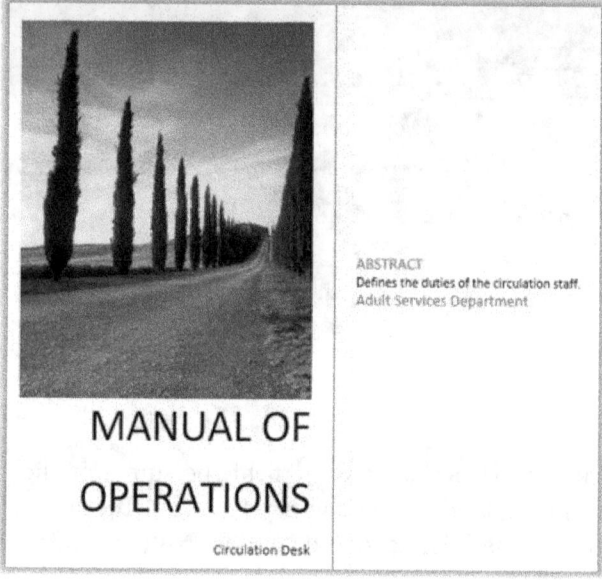

Creating a Header & Footer

1. On the next page of our document, **place** the insertion point in front of the word Services.
2. On the **Insert** tab, **locate** the **Header & Footer** group and **click Header**. **Scroll down** the alphabetical list of Built-in styles until you **see Integral**. **Click** the **Integral** style. **Note** how the header automatically populates with the title we typed on the cover page. This is because we typed the title into a **field** and the header is **referencing** the same field.
3. On the **Header & Footer Tools** ribbon, **find** the **Footer** button and **click** it. **Click** the **Integral** style.

    Similar to the title in the header, it **auto-populated** the footer with the contents of the **author field**.
4. **Close** the **Header and footer** ribbon.

Creating a Table of Contents

A **table of contents** can be generated when certain sections of the text in a long document are assigned a "Heading Style". Our outline format helps us to determine the heading styles we want to use. We are going to create a table of contents which will display four levels of content in our outline.

1. **Observe** the two pages of our document and **note** that the highest levels content in our outline are "1. Services" and "2.Closing Procedures". We will assign a **Heading 1** style to them.
    a. **Make sure** the **Home** tab is active.
    b. **Click** on the word "Services" and in the **Styles** group, **click** on **Heading 1**. **Note** how the numbering is removed.
    c. **Click** on the word "Closing Procedures" and in the **Styles** group, **click** on **Heading 1**
2. Second level content is under the **letters** in the outline.
    a. Under the **Services** section, **click** (one at a time) the second level content "Book Bags", "Book Sale", and "Check-Out" and in the **Styles** group, **click** on **Heading 2** for each.
- **Note** as you eliminate some of the numbered list items, replacing them with heading styles, the list loses some integrity (numbering can become continued from previous sections when that was not the original intent). Eventually we will eliminate most numbering so that shouldn't be an issue.
    b. Under the **Closing Procedures** section, click (one at a time) "Book Bag and Book Sales", "Z Report", "Turn off machines", and "Closing Announcements" and **click on Heading 2** for each.
3. We are not done assigning our headers yet, but let's create a **Table of Contents** to see what the outline of the document looks like so far.
    a. We want our Table of Contents to go at the very top of our document so **move** the insertion point to the top of the first page (at the beginning of the **Services** header).
    b. **Click** on the **References** tab on the ribbon.
    c. In the **Table of Contents** group, **click Table of Contents** and **click Custom Table of Contents**. This option will allow us to add as many levels of content as we want.

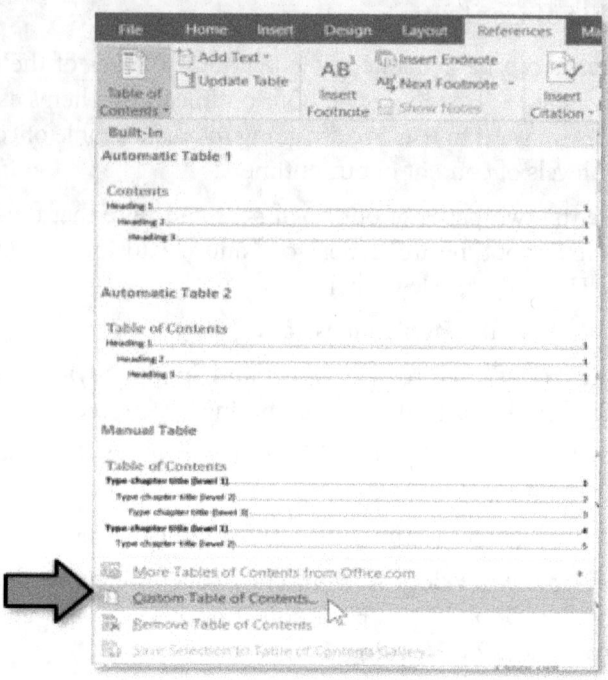

d. In the **Table of Contents** dialogue box, on the Table of Contents tab, in the General section, on the **Format** menu, **click Distinctive**.

e. Then, **spin** the **Show levels** button to "5". This means that the table of contents will show headers that have up to the "Header 5" style.

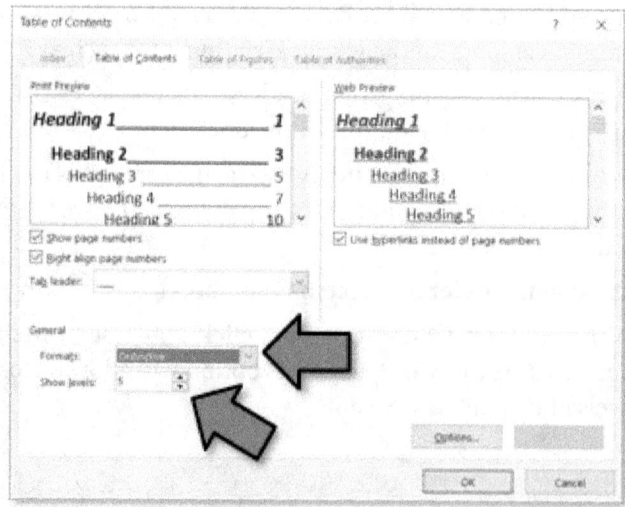

f. **Click OK** in the dialogue box and **observe** the Table of Contents.

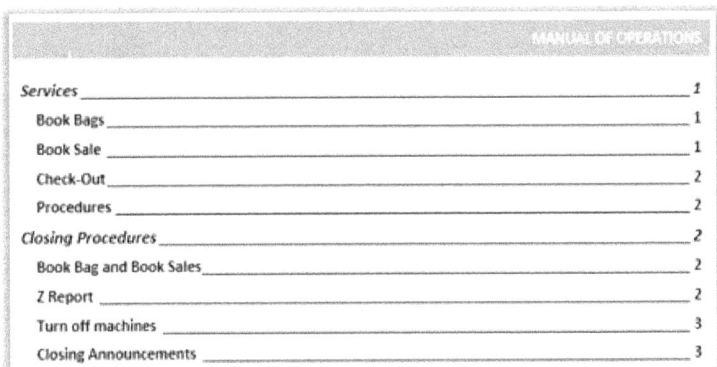

4. Now, let's assign our third level headers. **Assign** the **Heading 3** style to all of the **Roman numeral** list items underneath the **Services** section (to save time, **do not** format the ones underneath Closing Procedures).

5. In order for the table of contents to show the document's updated outline, it must be updated.

   a. **Click** the **References** tab and **locate** the **Table of Contents** group. **Click Update Table**.

   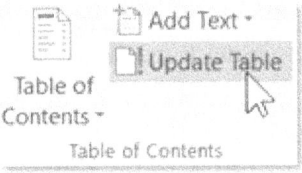

   b. A dialogue box appears, asking us what parts of the table of contents we want to update.

   Because we've modified the outline of the document by adding some headings, **click Update entire table** and **click** OK. This is usually the option you always want to choose because it ensures that the entire table is completely up to date.

   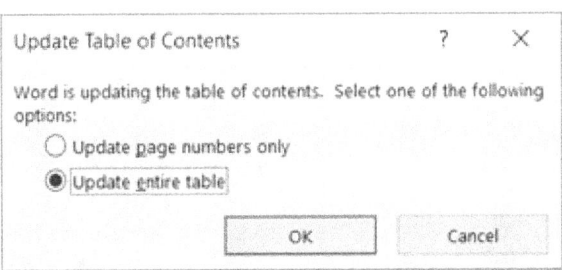

c. **Scroll** to the top of the document to **view** the updated Table of Contents.

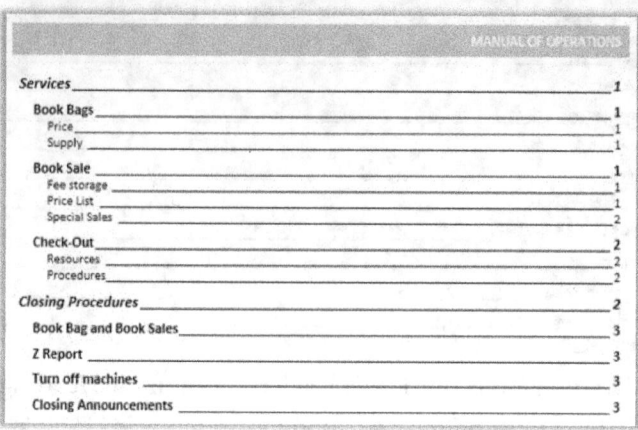

Changing the Header Styles

If you don't like how the headers are formatted (for example, you don't like the font size or the color), you can change them. Let's add a background color to the "Heading 1" style and increase its font size, so that it stands out better.

1. In the **Home** tab, **locate** the **Styles** group.
2. **Right-click** on the **Heading 1** style and click **Modify….**
3. A dialogue opens that allows you to edit the basic formatting settings of the style. **Change** the font size to "20".
4. **Click Format**, and click on **Border….**
5. **Click** the **Shading** tab and **click** a fill color.
6. **Click OK** to close the **Border** dialogue box.
7. **Click OK** again to close the **Modify Style** dialogue box.

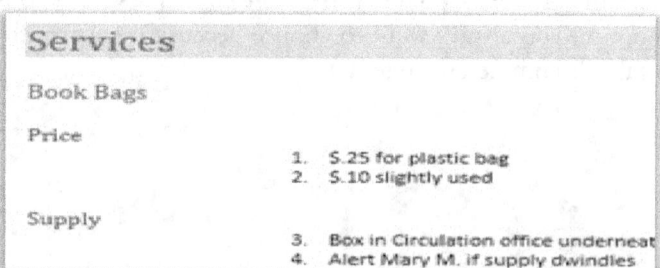

Navigating the Document

By organizing your document using Header styles, not only can you create a Table of Contents, but you can also jump around to specific sections with ease.

Using the Table of Contents
1. **Scroll** to the **Table of Contents**.
2. **Hold down** the Ctrl key.
3. **Click** on the "**Closing Procedures**" section.
4. **Notice** how the screen has jumped down to that section.

Using the Navigation Task Pane
1. **Click** on the **View** tab.
2. In the **Show** group, **click** the **Navigation Pane** checkbox.
3. **Notice** an outline of the document has appeared on the left.

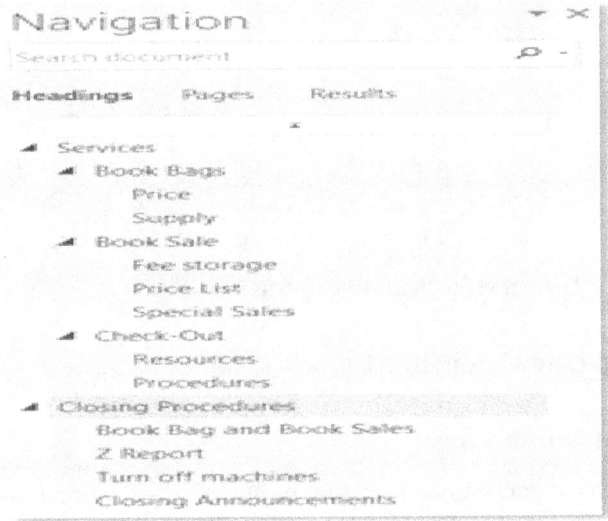

4. **Click** on the **Services** heading in the Navigation task pane.
5. **Notice** how the screen has jumped up to that section.

The Navigation task pane also shows you what section your insertion point is in:

1. **Move** the insertion point to somewhere inside of the **Resources** section.
2. **Notice** how the **Resources** section lights up in the Navigation task pane.
3. **Close** the navigation pane.

Collapsing a Section

1. **Scroll up** to the **Services section header** and **point** to it.
2. **Notice** the **triangle** on the left. This is called a **chevron**. **Notice** how it is **colored gray**.

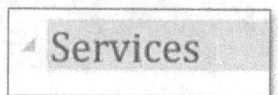

3. **Click** on the chevron.
4. **Notice** how the content in that section has **disappeared**. The section is now **collapsed**, meaning it is hidden. **Also notice** how the chevron has changed to a **white color**. (In addition, the table of contents and the section header have become highlighted. We are not sure why it does this, but it does not harm anything.)

5. **Click** on the chevron again to **expand** the section.

Cleaning up our Document

Fixing the List Numbering

Notice how each list continues its starting number from the previous list, as if they were a part of the same list. We want each list to begin at "1".

1. Under the **Supply** section, **right-click** on the "3".
2. **Click Restart At 1** from the context menu.
3. **Repeat** these steps for the other lists in the Services section.

Changing the List Style

We also want to change the Roman numeral lists in the Closing Procedures section to numbers.

1. **Select** the list in the **Book Bag and Book Sales** section
2. In the **Home** tab, in the **Paragraph** group, **click** on the drop-down arrow next to the **Numbering** button.
3. **Select** a numeric style.
4. **Repeat** these steps for the rest of the Roman numerals lists.

Adjusting the Indentation

1. **Select** the two list items under the **Price** heading.
2. In the **Home** tab, in the **Paragraph** group, **click dialogue box launcher** icon.
3. Under the **Indentation** section, **change** the **Left** text box to "0.3" and click OK.

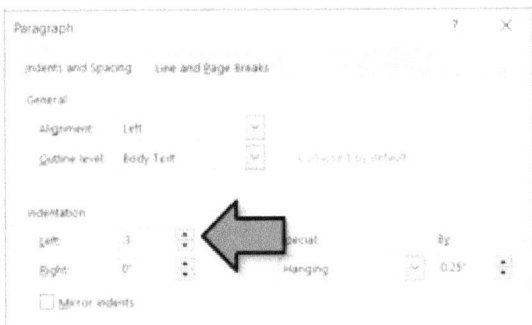

4. **Repeat** these steps for every section.

> **Tip:** Use **region selecting** (holding down the Ctrl key while you select the lists with the mouse) to select all of the lists and change all of their settings at once.

Mail Merge

It effectively conveys that mail merge links a primary document with a dataset to produce personalized form letters, mailing labels, and envelopes based on a predefined template.

Basic steps of mail merger are as follows:

Prepare Your Data Source

Gather the data you want to use in your mail merge. This data could be stored in an Excel spreadsheet, a CSV file, a Microsoft Access database, or even an Outlook contacts list.

Organize your data source so that each piece of information (e.g., recipient names, addresses, etc.) is stored in separate columns or fields.

Create Your Template Document

Open Microsoft Word and create a new document or use an existing one as your template.

Design the layout of your document, including any text, graphics, or formatting you want to include.

Identify the areas within your document where you want to insert personalized information from your data source. These areas are typically called "merge fields" and will be replaced with data from your data source during the merge process.

Start the Mail Merge Process in Word

Navigate to the "Mailings" tab in Microsoft Word.

Click on the "Start Mail Merge" button and select the type of document you want to create (e.g., letters, envelopes, labels).

Select Recipients

Choose the option to "Select Recipients" from the Mail Merge menu.

Specify the data source you prepared earlier (e.g., Excel spreadsheet, CSV file, etc.).

Select the specific records from your data source that you want to include in the merge, or choose to merge all records.

Insert Merge Fields

Place your cursor in the template document where you want to insert merge fields.

Click on the "Insert Merge Field" button in the Mail Merge menu.

Select the fields from your data source that you want to insert into the document. These fields will represent the personalized information for each recipient (e.g., <<First Name>>, <<Last Name>>, <<Address>>, etc.).

Preview Your Document

Use the "Preview Results" button in the Mail Merge menu to preview how the merged document will appear for each recipient.

Check for any errors or formatting issues and make adjustments as needed.

Complete the Merge

Once you're satisfied with the preview, click on the "Finish & Merge" button in the Mail Merge menu.

Choose whether you want to print the merged documents, save them as individual files, or send them directly via email.

Follow the prompts to complete the merge process, making any final adjustments as necessary.

By following these steps, you can efficiently perform a mail merge in Microsoft Word, creating personalized form letters, mailing labels, envelopes, or other documents for a list of recipients.

An Example of Mail merger

The mail merge process involves the following:

1. **The Main Document** – contains the text and graphics that are the same for each version of the merged document.
2. **Data Source** – a file that contains the information to be merged into a document. For example, the names and addresses of the recipients of a letter.

Mail Merge – Form Letters

1. Open **Word** and create a new blank document
2. Type the letter with all needed text and formatting, leaving room for the data from the data source (example: name, address, etc.)
3. Click the **Mailings** tab
4. Click **Start Mail Merge**
5. Click **Step-by-Step Mail Merge Wizard**

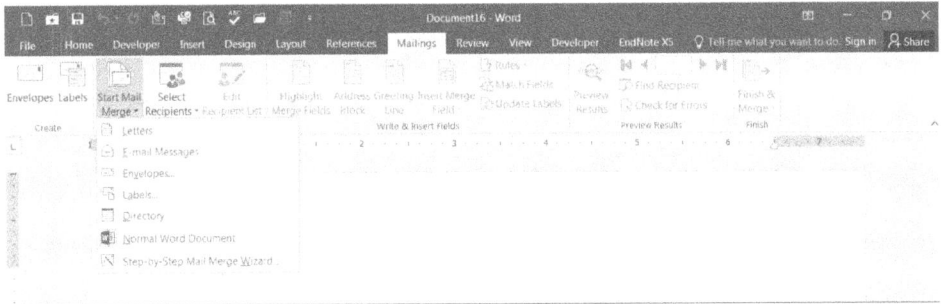

The **Mail Merge task pane** appears on the right of your screen. Note there are 6 steps.

Step 1 – Select Document Type

1. Click **Letters** for the document type
2. Click **Next: Starting document**

Step 2 – Select Starting Document

1. Click **Use the current document** under **Select starting document**
2. Click **Next: Select recipients**

Step 3 - Select Recipients

The recipients can come from either an existing Excel file, an Access table or you can create a new list in Word.

If Using an Existing List:

1. Click **Use an existing list** under **Select recipients**
2. Click **Browse**
3. Select the file
4. Click **Open**
5. Select the worksheet tab name that contains the data
6. Click **OK (Mail Merge Recipients** opens showing the file data)
7. Click **OK**

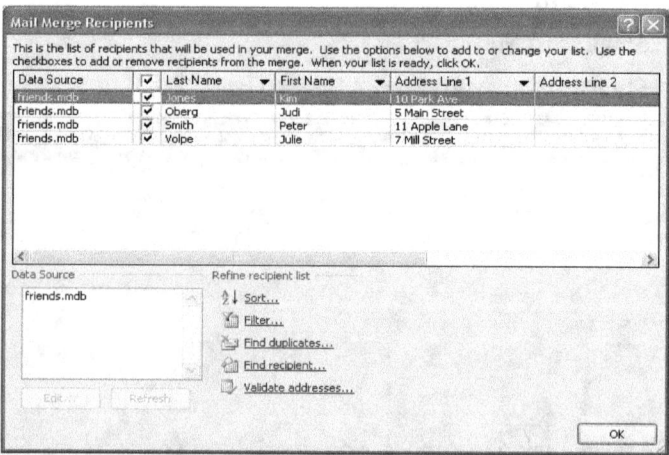

8. Click **Next: Write your letter**

If Creating a New List:

1. Click **Type a new list** under **Select recipients**
2. Click **Create**

3. Click **Customize Columns** to modify the list of fields

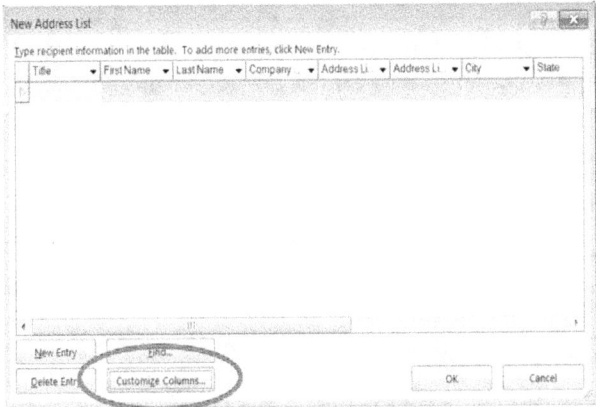

4. Delete any unnecessary field names and/or add new ones 5) Click **OK**

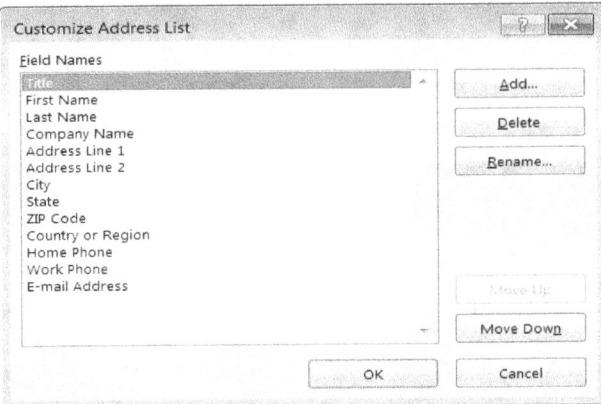

5. Begin typing records, hitting **TAB** to advance to the next field and to continue adding new records

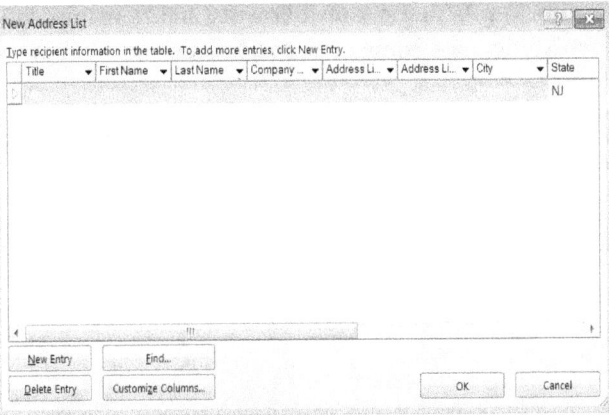

6. Click **OK**
7. Click **Save**

The recipients list will be saved as a separate file as a Microsoft Access file type. It is saved in the **My Data Sources** folder. It is recommended to save the file in this folder.

8. Click **Next: Write your letter**

Step 4 - Write Your Letter

1. If including an address, click the location in your document where the address data will be inserted
2. Click **Address block...**
3. Select the address elements you want included
4. Click **OK**

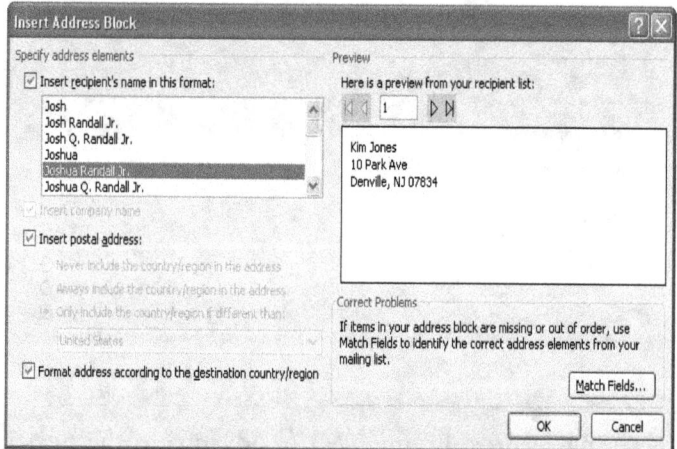

The field name will look like this: <<**AddressBlock**>>

The address block will insert the following fields including any necessary punctuation: First Name, Last Name, Company, Address 1, Address 2, City, State, Postal Code.

If your fields do not match the ones listed above or you are not using address fields, click **More items...**

Microsoft Word

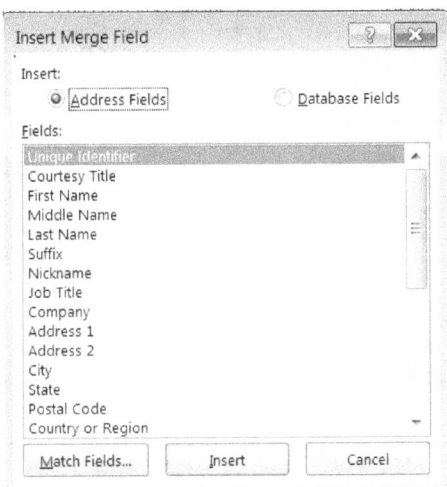

5. Click on the field from the list
6. Click **Insert**
7. Click **Close**

The field name will look like this - «**First_Name**»

8. Repeat this step until all fields have been inserted.

Remember to put spaces and punctuation where needed.

9. Click **Next: Preview your letters**

Step 5 - Preview Your Letters

Here is where you can preview the first page with the fields filled in.

Click **Next: Complete the merge**

Step 6 – Complete the Merge

1. Click **Print** to send directly to the printer
2. Click **Edit individual letters** to create a new file

Remember to save your document as you go. The next time you open your document and click on **Step-by-Step Mail Merge**, the data source file will be attached.

Mail Merge – Labels

1. Create a new blank document
2. Click the **Mailings** tab
3. Click **Start Mail Merge**
4. Click **Step-by-Step Mail Merge Wizard**

Step 1 – Select Document Type

1. Click **Labels** for the document type
2. Click **Next: Starting document**

Step 2 – Select Starting Document

1. Click **Use the current document**
2. Click **Label options** under **Change document layout**
3. Choose the label style you are using
4. Click **OK**

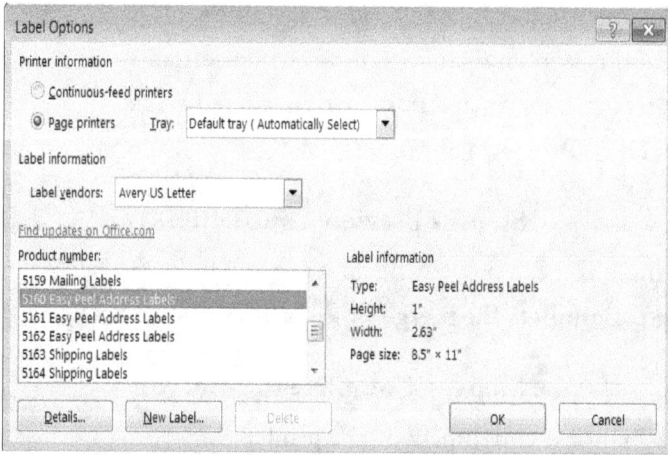

5. Click **Next: Select recipients**

Step 3 – Select Recipients

1. Click **Use an existing list** under **Select recipients** (or you can create a new list)
2. Click **Browse**

Microsoft Word

3. Select the file
4. Click **Open**
5. Select the worksheet tab name that contains the data
6. Click **OK**
7. Click **Next: Arrange your labels**

Step 4 – Arrange Your Labels

1. Click in the first label box and click on either **Address block** or **More items** to insert the data fields
2. Click **Update all labels** to include the fields on all labels
3. Click **Next: Preview your labels**

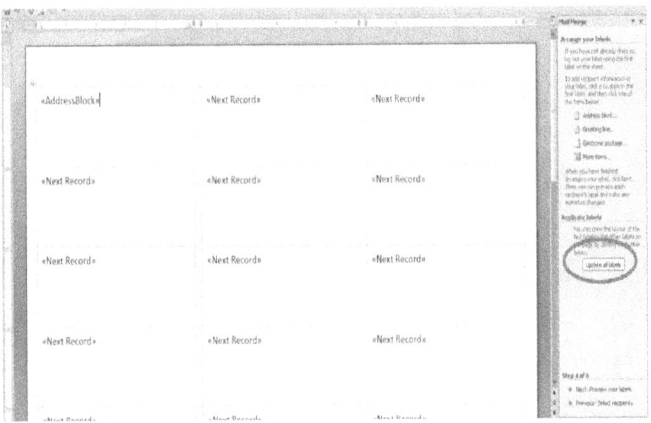

Step 5 – Preview Your Labels

Here is where you can preview the labels.

Click **Next: Complete the merge**

Step 6 – Complete the Merge

Click **Print** to send directly to the printer

OR

Click **Edit individual labels** to create a new file

Chapter 12
Microsoft Excel

Microsoft Excel is an electronic spreadsheet. You can use it to organize your data into rows and columns. You can also use it to perform mathematical calculations quickly. This course teaches Microsoft Excel basics as a prelude to the use of Statistical Analysis System (SAS) software in carrying out more complex statistical analysis. Although knowledge of how to navigate in a Windows environment is helpful, this manual is created for the computer novice.

At the end of the course, participants are expected to know how to use Microsoft Excel to:

1. Enter text and numbers in a spreadsheet
2. Enter Excel formulas
3. Format data
4. Create Excel functions
5. Fill cells automatically
6. Print results
7. Create Charts, and
8. Enter advanced Excel formulas

Accordingly, the course is divided into the following five (5) sections.

Section 1: Entering Text and Numbers

Section 2: Entering Excel Formulas and Formatting Data

Section 3: Creating Excel Functions, Filling Cells, and Printing

Section 4: Creating Charts

Section 5: More on Entering Excel Formulas

Section 1: Entering Text and Numbers

The Microsoft Excel Window

This Section will introduce you to the Excel window. To begin this Section, start Microsoft Excel 2007 as follows:

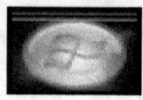

1. Click on Microsoft Start Button
2. Point the mouse on All Programs
3. Click on Microsoft Office
4. Click on Microsoft Excel 2007

The Microsoft Excel window appears and your screen looks similar to the one shown here.

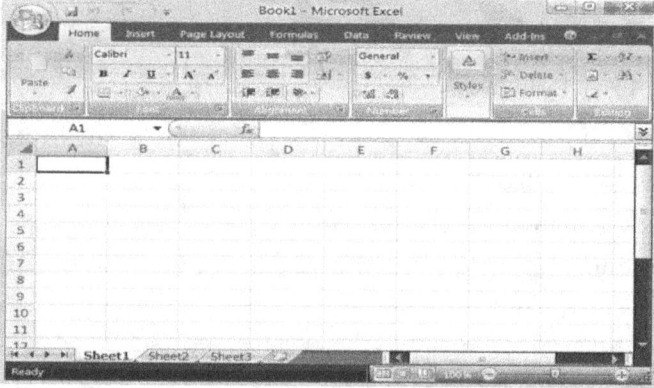

The Microsoft Office Button

In the upper-left corner of the Excel 2007 window is the Microsoft Office button. When you click the button, a menu appears. You can use the menu to create a new file, open an existing file, save a file, print and perform many other tasks.

The Quick Access Toolbar

Next to the Microsoft Office button is the Quick Access toolbar. The Quick Access toolbar gives you quick access to commands you frequently use.

The Title Bar

Next to the Quick Access toolbar is the Title bar. On the Title bar, Microsoft Excel displays the name of the workbook you are currently using. At the top of the Excel window, you should see "Book 1 - Microsoft Excel" or a similar name.

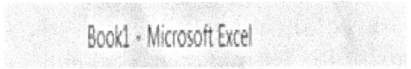

The Ribbon

In Microsoft Excel 2007, you use the Ribbon to issue commands. The Ribbon is located near the top of the Excel window, below the Quick Access toolbar.

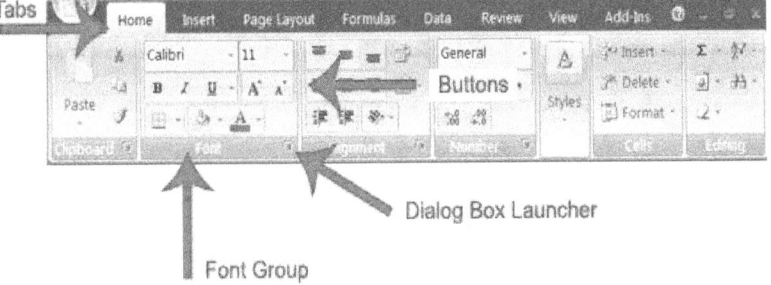

Worksheets

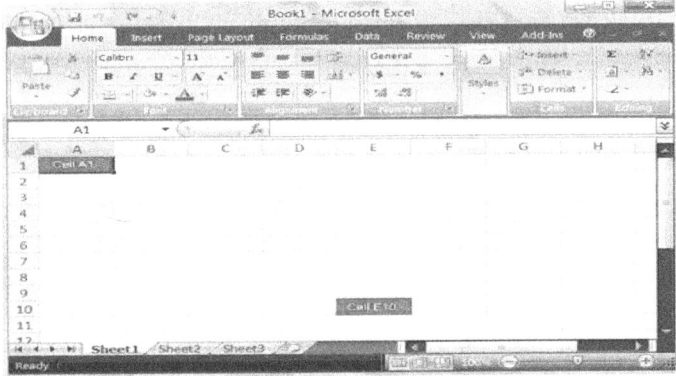

Microsoft Excel consists of worksheets. Each worksheet contains columns and rows. The columns are lettered A to Z and then continuing with AA, AB, AC and so on; the rows are numbered 1 to 1,048,576.

The combination of a column coordinate and a row coordinate make up a cell address. For example, the cell located in the upper-left corner of the worksheet is cell A1, meaning column A, row 1. Cell E10 is located under column E on row 10. You enter your data into the cells on the worksheet.

The Formula Bar

If the Formula bar is turned on, the cell address of the cell you are in displays in the Name box which is located on the left side of the Formula bar. Cell entries display on the right side of the Formula bar.

The Status Bar

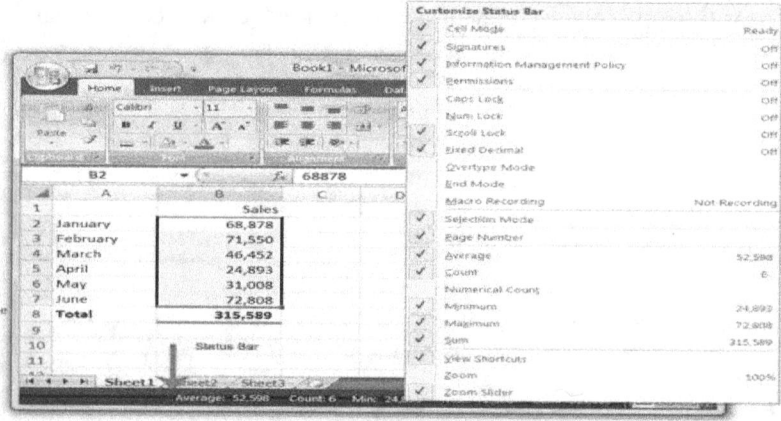

The Status bar appears at the very bottom of the Excel window and provides such information as the sum, average, minimum, and maximum value of selected numbers.

Move Around a Worksheet

By using the arrow keys, you can move around your worksheet. You can use the down arrow key to move downward one cell at a time. You can use the up arrow key to move upward one cell at a time. You can use the Tab key to move across the page to the right, one cell at a time. You can hold down the Shift key and then press the Tab key to move to the left, one cell at a time. You can use the right and left arrow keys to move right or left one cell at a time. The Page Up and Page Down keys move up and down one page at a time. If you hold down the Ctrl key and then press the Home key, you move to the beginning of the worksheet.

Exercise 1

Move around the Worksheet using the Down and Up Arrow Keys, the Right and Left Arrow Keys, the Tab Key, the Page Up and Page Down Keys and the (Ctrl) Home Key.

Go to Cells Quickly

The following are shortcuts for moving quickly from one cell in a worksheet to a cell in a different part of the worksheet.

Exercise 2 Go to -- F5

Press F5. The Go to dialog box opens.

Type **J3** in the Reference field.

Press Enter. Excel moves to cell J3.

Go to -- Ctrl+G

1. Hold down the Ctrl key while you press "g" (Ctrl+g). The Go To dialog box opens.
2. Type **C4** in the Reference field.
3. Press Enter. Excel moves to cell C4.

Go to -- The Name Box

You can also use the Name box to go to a specific cell. Just type the cell you want to go to in the Name box and then press Enter.

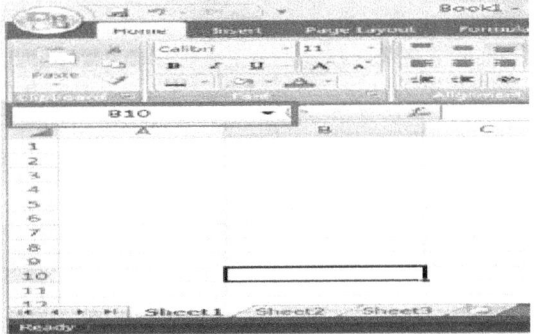

1. Type **B10** in the Name box.
2. Press Enter. Excel moves to cell B10.

Select Cells

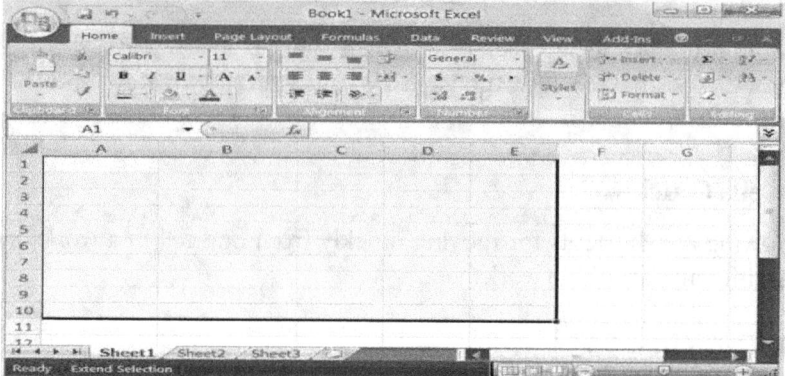

If you wish to perform a function on a group of cells, you must first select those cells by highlighting them. The exercises that follow teach you how to select.

Exercise 3

Select Cells – F8 To select cells A1 to E7:
1. Go to cell A1.
2. Press the F8 key. This anchors the cursor.
3. Note that "Extend Selection" appears on the Status bar in the lower-left corner of the window. You are in the Extend mode.
4. Click in cell E7. Excel highlights cells A1 to E7.
5. Press Esc and click anywhere on the worksheet to clear the highlighting.

Alternative Method: Select Cells by Dragging

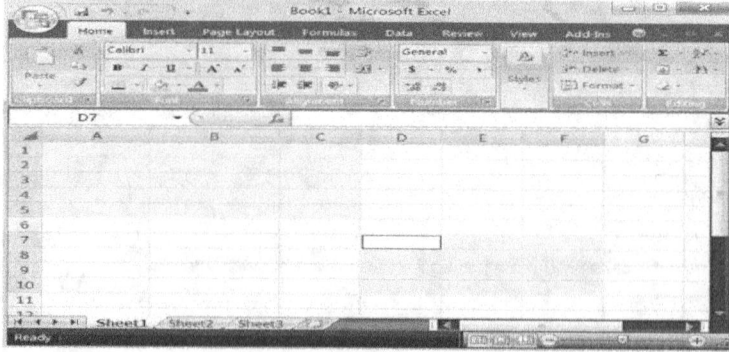

Microsoft Excel

1. Go to cell A1.
2. Press the left mouse button.
3. While holding down the left mouse button, use the mouse to move from cell A1 to C5.
4. Release the left mouse button.
5. Hold down the Ctrl key until step 9.
6. Using the mouse, place the cursor in cell D7.
7. Press the left mouse button.
8. While holding down the left mouse button, move to cell F10. Release the left mouse button.
9. Release the Ctrl key. Cells A1 to C5 and cells D7 to F10 are selected.
10. Press Esc and click anywhere on the worksheet to remove the highlighting.

Enter Data

In this section, you will learn how to enter data into your worksheet. First, place the cursor in the cell in which you want to start entering data. Type some data, and then press Enter. If you need to delete, press the Backspace key to delete one character at a time.

Exercise 4

Enter Data

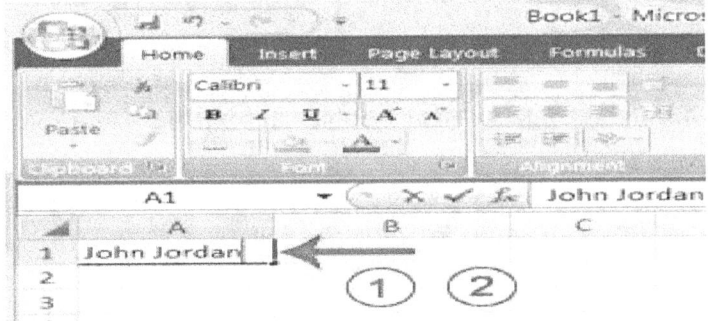

1. Place the cursor in cell A1.
2. Type **John Jordan**. Do not press Enter at this time.

Edit a Cell – F2

After you enter data into a cell, you can edit the data by pressing F2 while you are in the cell you wish to edit.

Exercise 5

Change "John" to "Jones."

1. Move to cell A1.
2. Press F2.
3. Use the Arrow and Backspace keys to change John to Jones
4. Press Enter.

Alternate Method: Editing a Cell by Using the Formula Bar

You can also edit the cell by using the Formula bar. You change "Jones" to "Joker" in the following exercise.

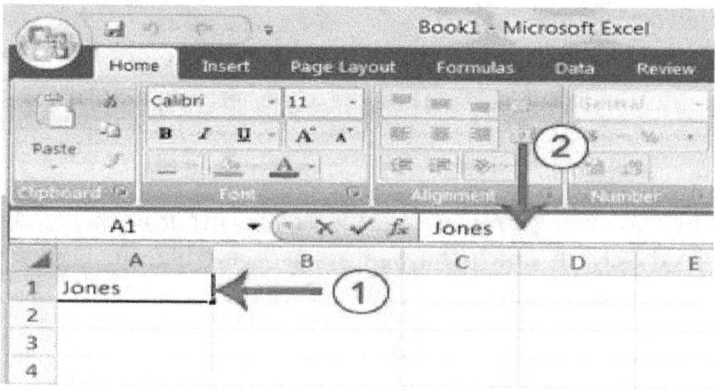

1. Move the cursor to cell A1.
2. Click in the formula or entries area of the Formula bar, and change Jones to Joker.
3. Press Enter.

Alternate Method: Edit a Cell by Double-Clicking in the Cell You can change "Joker" to "Johnson" as follows:

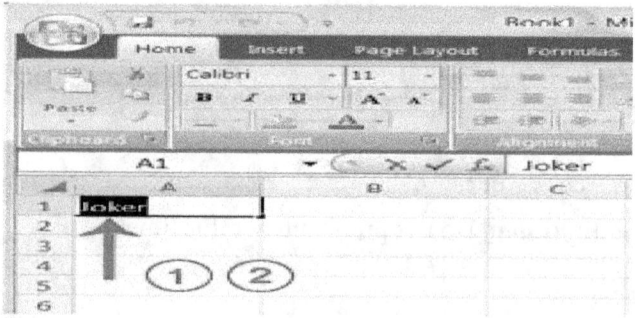

1. Move to cell A1.
2. Double-click in cell A1.
3. Use the Arrow and Backspace keys to change Joker to Johnson.
4. Press Enter.

Change a Cell Entry

Typing in a cell replaces the old cell entry with the new information you type.

1. Move the cursor to cell A1.
2. Type **Cathy**.
3. Press Enter. The name "Cathy" replaces "Johnson Jordan"

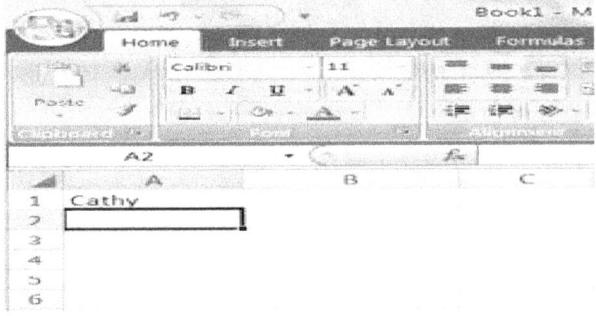

Wrap Text

When you type text that is too long to fit in the cell, the text overlaps the next cell. If you do not want it to overlap the next cell, you can wrap the text.

Exercise 6

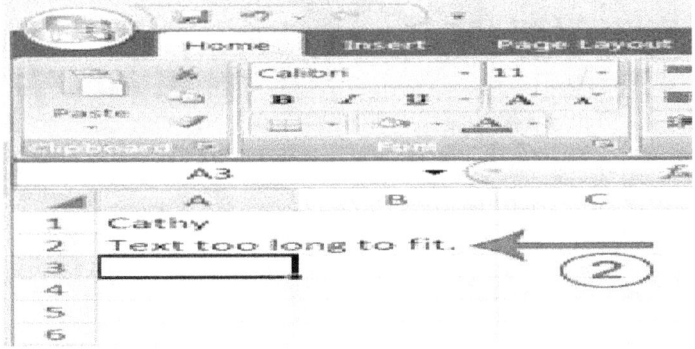

1. Move to cell A2.
2. Type **Text too long to fit.**
3. Press Enter.

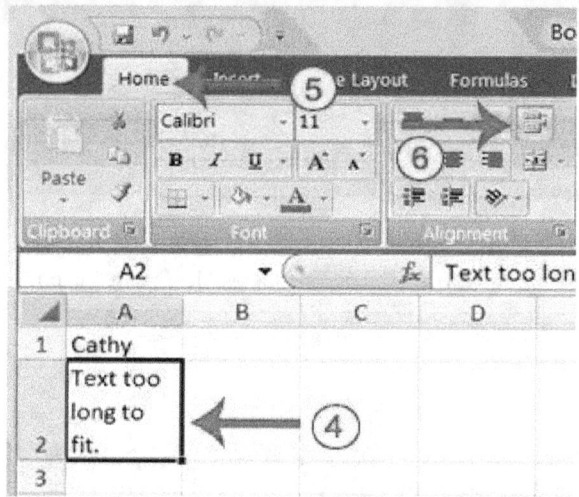

4. Return to cell A2.
5. Choose the Home tab.
6. Click the Wrap Text button. Excel wraps the text in the cell. ab Wrap Text

Delete a Cell Entry

To delete an entry in a cell or a group of cells, you place the cursor in the cell or select the group of cells and press Delete.

Exercise 7 Delete A Cell Entry

1. Select cells A1 to A2.
2. Press the Delete key.

Save a File

This is the end of Section 1. To save your file:

1. Click the Office button. A menu appears.

2. Click Save. The Save As dialog box appears.
3. Go to the directory in which you want to save your file.
4. Type **Section 1** in the File Name field.
5. Click Save. Excel saves your file.

Close Excel

Close Microsoft Excel.

1. Click the Office button. A menu appears.
2. Click Close. Excel closes.

Section 2: Entering Excel Formulas and Formatting Data

Section 1 familiarizes you with the Excel 2007 window, teaches you how to move around the window, and how to enter data. A major strength of Excel is that you can perform mathematical calculations and format your data. In this Section, you will learn how to perform basic mathematical calculations and how to format text and numerical data. To start this Section, open Excel.

Perform Mathematical Calculations

In Microsoft Excel, you can enter numbers and mathematical formulas into cells. Whether you enter a number or a formula, you can reference the cell when you perform mathematical calculations such as addition, subtraction, multiplication, or division. When entering a mathematical formula, precede the formula with an equal (=) sign. Use the following to indicate the type of calculation you wish to perform:

- \+ Addition
- – Subtraction
- * Multiplication
- / Division
- ^ Exponential

In the following exercises, you practice some of the methods you can use to perform mathematical calculations.

Exercise 1

Addition, Subtraction, Multiplication and Division of Numbers

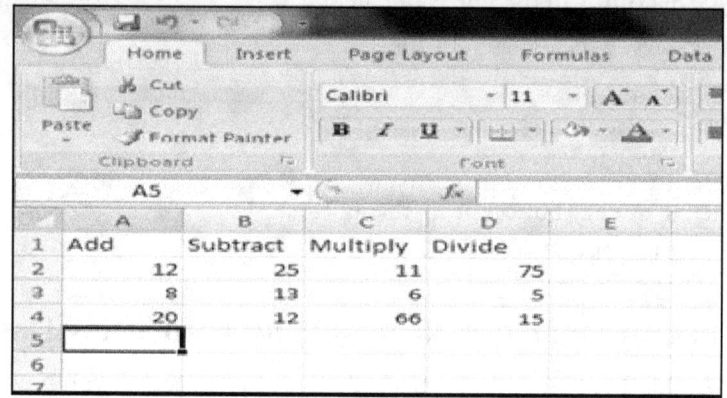

1. Type: Add, Subtract, Multiply, and Divide in cells A1, B1, C1, and D1 respectively
2. Type: 12, 25, 11 and 75 in cells A2, B2, C2 and D2 respectively
3. Type: 8, 13, 6 and 5 in cells A3, B3, C3 and D3 respectively
4. Type: = A2 + A3 in cell A5 and press Enter
5. Type: = B2 + B3 in cell A5 and press Enter
6. Type: = C2 + C3 in cell A5 and press Enter
7. Type: = D2 + D3 in cell A5 and press Enter

When creating formulas, you can reference cells and include numbers. All of the following formulas are valid:

   a.   =A2/B2;
   b.   =A2+12-B3;
   c.   =A2*B2+12;
   d.   =24+53/B2

Perform Advanced Mathematical Calculations

When you perform mathematical calculations in Excel, be careful of precedence. Calculations are performed from left to right, with multiplication and division performed before addition and subtraction.

Microsoft Excel

Exercise 2 Advanced Calculations

1. Move to cell A7.
2. Type =3+3+12/2*4.
3. Press Enter.

Note: Microsoft Excel divides 12 by 2, multiplies the answer by 4, adds 3, and then adds another 3. The answer, 30, displays in cell A7.

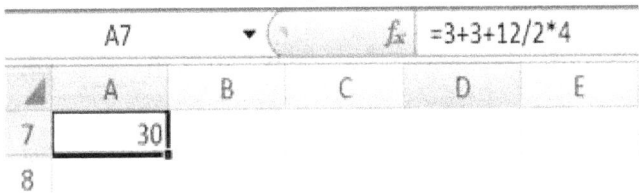

To change the order of calculation, use parentheses. Microsoft Excel calculates the information in parentheses first.

1. Double-click in cell A7.
2. Edit the cell to read =(3+3+12)/2*4.
3. Press Enter.

Note: Microsoft Excel adds 3 plus 3 plus 12, divides the answer by 2, and then multiplies the result by 4. The answer, 36, displays in cell A7.

AutoSum

You can use the AutoSum button Σ on the Home tab to automatically add a column or row of numbers. When you press the AutoSum button Σ Excel selects the numbers it thinks you want to add. If you then click the check mark on the Formula bar or press the Enter key, Excel adds the numbers. If Excel's guess as to which numbers you want to add is wrong, you can select the cells you want.

Exercise 3 Autosum

The following illustrates AutoSum:

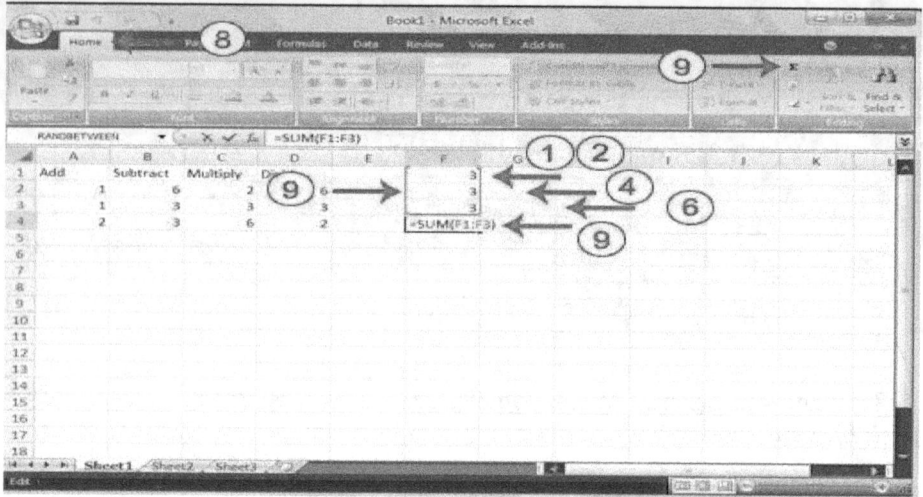

1. Go to cell F1.
2. Type **3**.
3. Press Enter. Excel moves down one cell.
4. Type **3**.
5. Press Enter. Excel moves down one cell.
6. Type **3**.
7. Press Enter. Excel moves down one cell to cell F4.
8. Choose the Home tab.
9. Click the AutoSum button Σ in the Editing group. Excel selects cells F1 through F3 and enters a formula in cell F4.

E	F	G
	3	
	3	
	3	
	9	

10. Press Enter. Excel adds cells F1 through F3 and displays the result in cell F4.

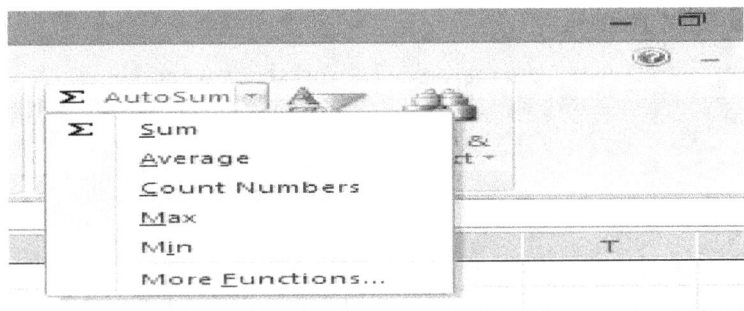

Note that you can click on the arrow next to AutoSum to access other automatic calculations like average, minimum and maximum values, count numbers, etc.

Align Cell Entries

When you type text into a cell, by default your entry aligns with the left side of the cell. When you type numbers into a cell, by default your entry aligns with the right side of the cell. You can change the cell alignment. You can center, left-align, or right-align any cell entry. Look at cells A1 to D1. Note that they are aligned with the left side of the cell.

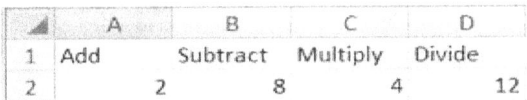

Exercise 4

To centre cells A1 to D1:

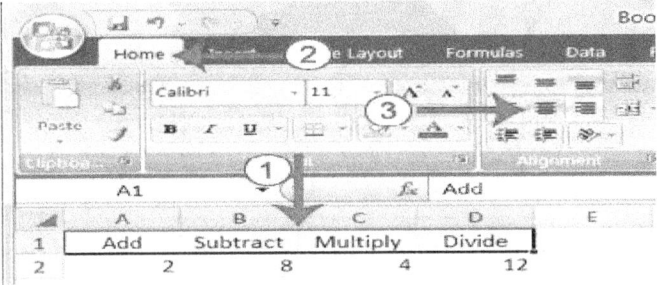

1. Select cells A1 to D1.
2. Choose the Home tab.
3. Click the Center button in the Alignment group. Excel centers each cell's content.

Note that left and right alignment can be carried out in a similar manner.

Copy, Cut and Paste

You can copy or cut data from one area of a worksheet to another.

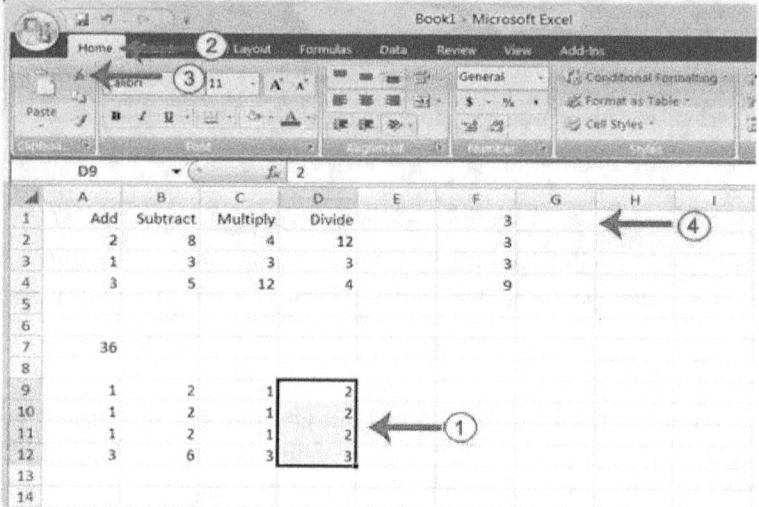

1. Select cells D9 to D12
2. Choose the Home tab.
3. Click the Cut button.
4. Move to cell G1.

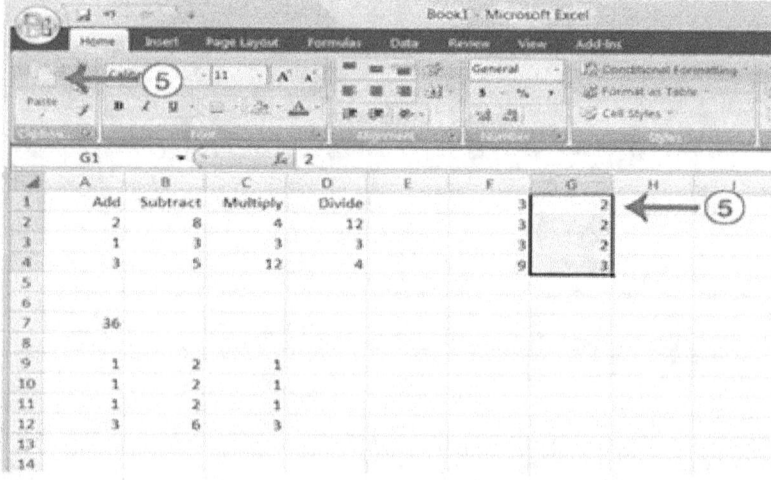

5. Click the Paste button. Excel moves the contents of cells D9 to D12 to cells G1 to G4.

Insert and Delete Columns and Rows

You can insert and delete columns and rows. When you delete a column, you delete everything in the column from the top of the worksheet to the bottom of the worksheet. When you delete a row, you delete the entire row from left to right. Inserting a column or row inserts a completely new column or row.

Exercise 5

Insert and Delete Columns and Rows *To delete columns F and G:*

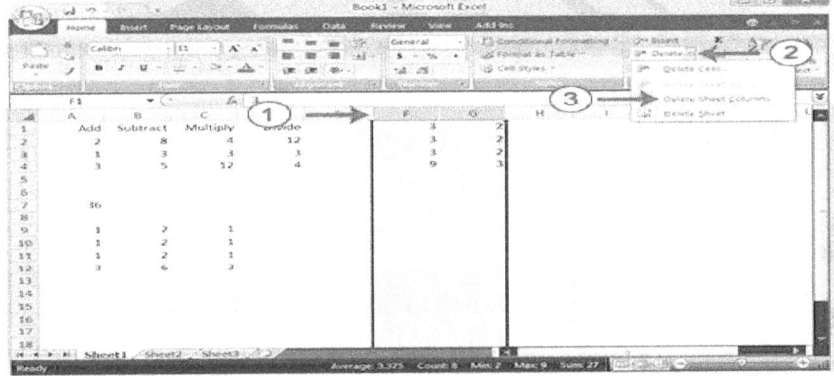

1. Click the column F indicator and drag to column G.
2. Click the down arrow next to Delete in the Cells group. A menu appears.
3. Click Delete Sheet Columns. Excel deletes the columns you selected.
4. Click anywhere on the worksheet to remove your selection.

To delete rows 7 through 12:

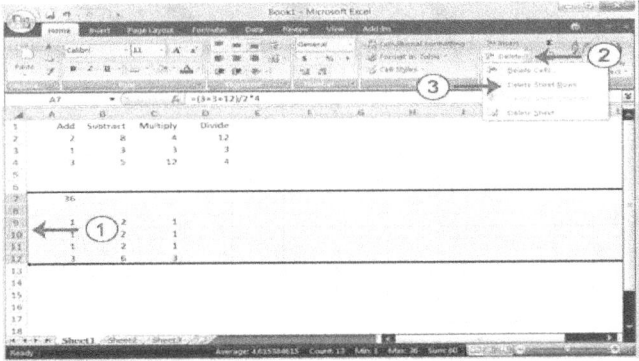

1. Click the row 7 indicator and drag to row 12.
2. Click the down arrow next to Delete in the Cells group. A menu appears.
3. Click Delete Sheet Rows. Excel deletes the rows you selected.
4. Click anywhere on the worksheet to remove your selection.

To Insert a Column

1. Click on A to select column A.
2. Click the down arrow next to Insert in the Cells group. A menu appears.
3. Click Insert Sheet Columns. Excel inserts a new column.
4. Click anywhere on the worksheet to remove your selection.

To Insert Rows

1. Click on 1 and then drag down to 2 to select rows 1 and 2.
2. Click the down arrow next to Insert in the Cells group. A menu appears.
3. Click Insert Sheet Rows. Excel inserts two new rows.
4. Click anywhere on the worksheet to remove your selection.

Work with Long Text

Whenever you type text that is too long to fit into a cell, Microsoft Excel attempts to display all the text. It left-aligns the text regardless of the alignment you have assigned to it, and it borrows space from the blank cells to the right. However, a long text entry will never write over cells that already contain entries—instead, the cells that contain entries cut off the long text. The following exercise illustrates this.

Exercise 6 Work with Long Text

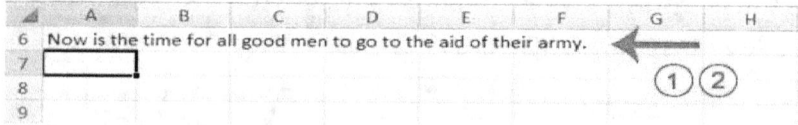

1. Move to cell A6.
2. **Now is the time for all good men to go to the aid of their army**.
3. Press Enter. Everything that does not fit into cell A6 spills over into the adjacent cell.

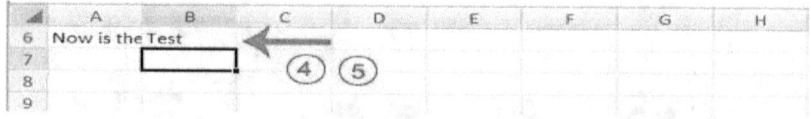

4. Move to cell B6.
5. Type **Test**.
6. Press Enter. Excel cuts off the entry in cell A6.

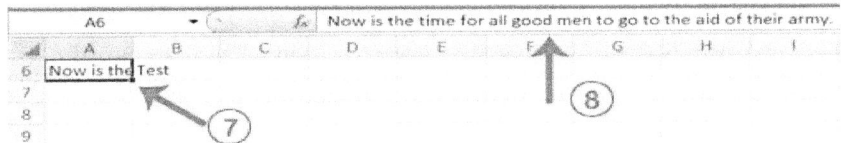

7. Move to cell A6.
8. Look at the Formula bar. The text is still in the cell.

Change A Column's Width

You can increase column widths. Increasing the column width enables you to see the long text.

Exercise 7 Change Column Width

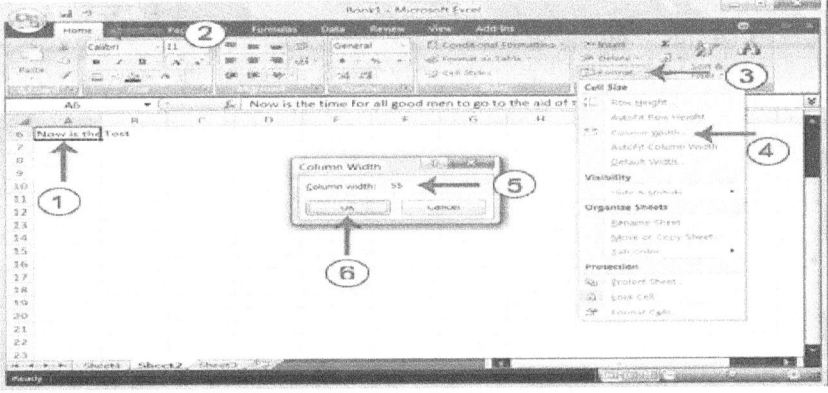

1. Make sure you are in any cell under column A.
2. Choose the Home tab.
3. Click the down arrow next to Format in the Cells group.
4. Click Column Width. The Column Width dialog box appears.
5. Type **55** in the Column Width field.
6. Click OK. Column A is set to a width of 55. You should now be able to see all of the text.

Change a Column Width by Dragging

You can also change the column width with the cursor.

1. Place the mouse pointer on the line between the B and C column headings. The mouse pointer should look like the one displayed here ✛, with two arrows.
2. Move your mouse to the right while holding down the left mouse button. The width indicator Width: 20.00 (247 pixels) appears on the screen.
3. Release the left mouse button when the width indicator shows approximately
4. Excel increases the column width to 20.
5. Change a Column Width by AutoFit Column Width
6. Select the column or column you want to change the column width.
7. Choose the Home tab.
8. Click the down arrow next to Format in the Cells group.
9. Click on AutoFit Column Width. You should now be able to see all of the text.

Format Numbers

You can format the numbers you enter into Microsoft Excel. For example, you can add commas to separate thousands, specify the number of decimal places, place a dollar sign in front of a number, or display a number as a percent.

Exercise 8

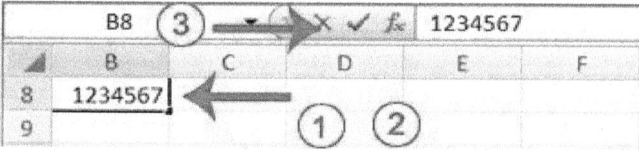

1. Move to cell B8.
2. Type **1234567**.
3. Click the check mark [√] on the Formula bar.

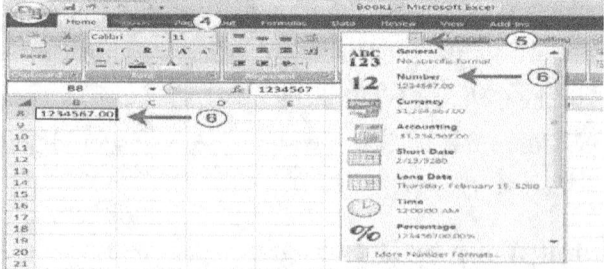

Microsoft Excel

4. Choose the Home tab.
5. Click the down arrow next to the Number Format box. A menu appears.
6. Click Number. Excel adds two decimal places to the number you typed.

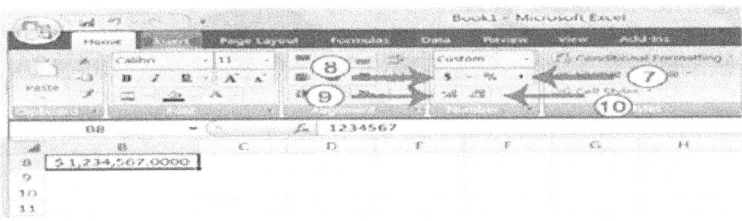

7. Click the Comma Style button . Excel separates thousands with a comma.
8. Click the Accounting Number Format button $. Excel adds a dollar sign to your number.
9. Click twice on the Increase Decimal button to change the number format to four decimal places.
10. Click the Decrease Decimal button , if you wish to decrease the number of decimal places.

Change a Decimal to A Percent.

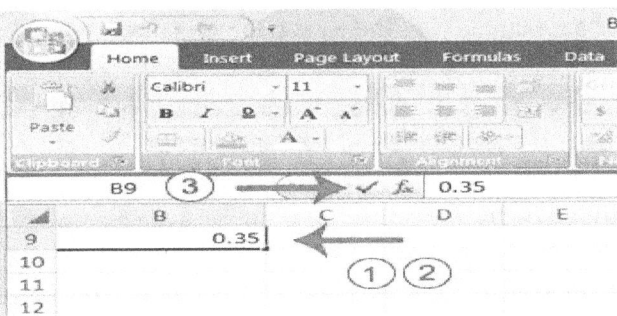

1. Move to cell B9.
2. Type **0.35** (note the decimal point).
3. Click the check mark [√] on the formula bar.

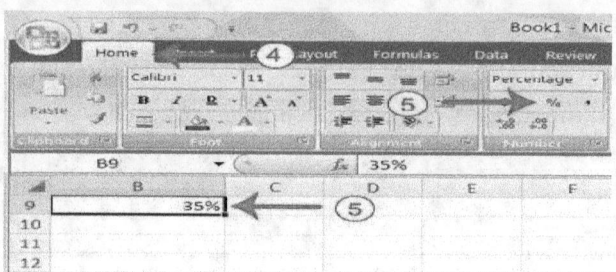

4. Choose the Home tab.
5. Click the Percent Style button % . Excel turns the decimal to a percent.

This is the end of Section 2. You can save and close your file. See Section 1 (Subsections 1.23 and 1.24) to learn how to save and close a file.

Section 3: Creating Excel Functions, Filling Cells, and Printing

By using functions, you can quickly and easily make many useful calculations, such as finding an average, the highest number, the lowest number, and a count of the number of items in a list. Microsoft Excel has many functions that you can use.

Using Reference Operators

To use functions, you need to understand reference operators. Reference operators refer to a cell or a group of cells. There are two types of reference operators: *range* and *union*.

A range reference refers to all the cells between and including the reference. A range reference consists of two cell addresses separated by a colon. The reference A1:A3 includes cells A1, A2, and A3. The reference A1:C3 includes cells A1, A2, A3, B1, B2, B3, C1, C2, and C3.

A union reference includes two or more references. A union reference consists of two or more numbers, range references, or cell addresses separated by a comma. The reference A7,B8:B10,C9,10 refers to cells A7, B8 to B10, C9 and the number 10.

Understanding Functions

Functions are prewritten formulas. Functions differ from regular formulas in that you supply the value but not the operators, such as +, -, *, or /. For example, you can use the SUM function to add. When using a function, remember the following:

1. Use an equal sign to begin a formula.
2. Specify the function name.
3. Enclose arguments within parentheses. Arguments are values on which

you want to perform the calculation. For example, arguments specify the numbers or cells you want to add.

4. Use a comma to separate arguments.

Here is an example of a function:

=SUM(2,13, A1,B2:C7)

In this function, known as the SUM function:

1. The equal sign begins the function.
2. SUM is the name of the function.
3. 2, 13, A1, and B2:C7 are the arguments. Parentheses enclose the arguments.
4. Commas separate the arguments.

After you type the first letter of a function name, the AutoComplete list appears. You can double-click on an item in the AutoComplete list to complete your entry quickly. Excel will complete the function name and enter the first parenthesis.

Exercise 1 Functions

The SUM function adds argument values.

	A	B	C	D	E
1		12			
2		27			
3		24			
4		63			
5					
6					

B4 — =SUM(B1:B3)

1. Open Microsoft Excel.
2. Type **12** in cell B1.
3. Press Enter.
4. Type **27** in cell B2.
5. Press Enter.
6. Type **24** in cell B3.
7. Press Enter.
8. Type **=SUM(B1:B3)** in cell A4.
9. Press Enter. The sum of cells B1 to B3, which is 63, appears.

Alternate Method: Enter a Function with the Ribbon

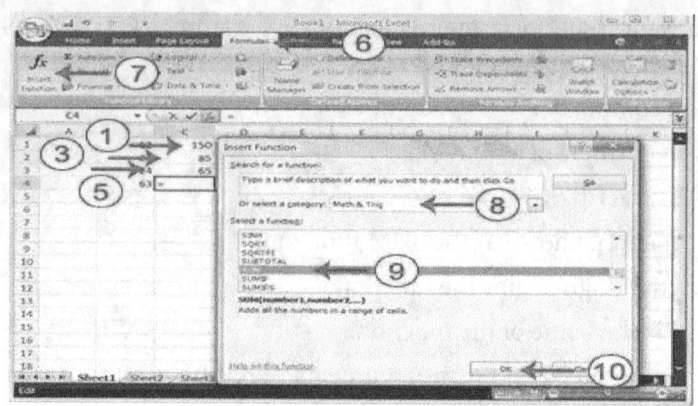

1. Type **150** in cell C1.
2. Press Enter.
3. Type **85** in cell C2.
4. Press Enter.
5. Type **65** in cell C3, and Press Enter
6. Choose the Formulas tab.
7. Click the Insert Function button. The Insert Function dialog box appears.
8. Choose Math & Trig in the Or Select A Category box.
9. Click Sum in the Select A Function box.
10. Click OK.
11. The Function Arguments dialog box appears with C1:C3 displayed in the Number1 field.

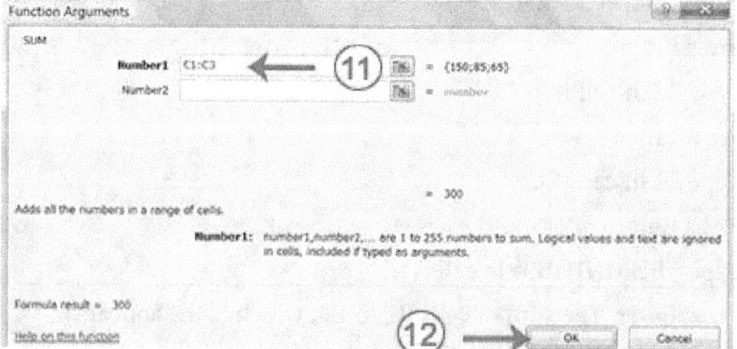

12. Type **C1:C3** in the Number1 field, if it does not automatically appear.
13. Click OK. The sum of cells C1 to C3, which is 300, appears.

Microsoft Excel

Calculate an Average

You can use the AVERAGE function to calculate the average of a series of numbers.

	A	B	C	D	E	F
		B6		=AVERAGE(B1:B3)		
1			12	150		
2			27	85		
3			24	65		
4	Sum		63	300		
5						
6	Average		21			
7						

1. Move to cell A6.
2. Type **Average**. Press the right arrow key to move to cell B6.
3. Type =**AVERAGE(B1:B3)**.
4. Press Enter. The average of cells B1 to B3, which is 21, appears.

Find the Lowest Number

You can use the MIN function to find the lowest number in a series of numbers.

	A	B	C	D	E	F
		B7		=MIN(B1:B3)		
1			12	150		
2			27	85		
3			24	65		
4	Sum		63	300		
5						
6	Average		21	100		
7	Min		12			
8						
9						

1. Move to cell A7.
2. Type **Min**. Press the right arrow key to move to cell B7.
3. Type =**MIN (B1:B3)**.
4. Press Enter. The lowest number in the series, which is 12, appears.

Find the Highest Number

You can use the MAX function to find the highest number in a series of numbers.

	B8			f_x	=MAX(B1:B3)		
	A	B	C	D	E	F	
1		12	150				
2		27	85				
3		24	65				
4	Sum	63	300				
5							
6	Average	21	100				
7	Min	12					
8	Max	27					
9							

1. Move to cell A8.
2. Type **Max**. Press the right arrow key to move to cell B8.
3. Type =MAX(B1:B3).
4. Press Enter. The highest number in the series, which is 27, appears.

Count the Numbers in a Series of Numbers

You can use the count function to count the number of numbers in a series.

	A	B	C	D	E
1		12	150		
2		27	85		
3		24	65		
4	Sum	63	300		
5					
6	Average	21	100		
7	Min	12			
8	Max	27			
9	Count	3			
10					
11					

1. Move to cell A9.
2. Type **Count**. Press the right arrow key to move to cell B9.
3. Type =COUNT(B1:B3).

Microsoft Excel

4. Press Enter. The number of items in the series, which is 3, appears.

Fill Cells Automatically

You can use Microsoft Excel to fill cells automatically with a series. For example, you can have Excel automatically fill your worksheet with days of the week, months of the year, years, or other types of series.

Exercise 2 (a) Fill Cells Automatically

The following demonstrates filling the days of the week:

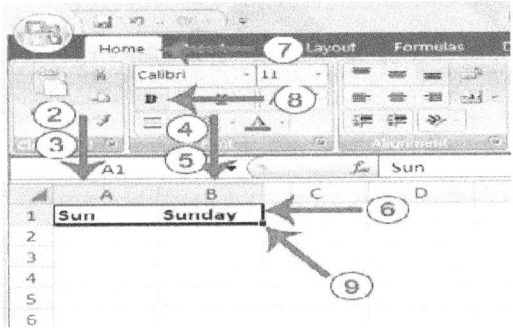

1. Click the Sheet2 tab. Excel moves to Sheet2.
2. Move to cell A1.
3. Type **Sun**.
4. Move to cell B1.
5. Type **Sunday**.
6. Select cells A1 to B1.
7. Choose the Home tab.
8. Click the Bold button **B**. Excel bolds cells A1 to B1.
9. Find the small black square in the lower-right corner of the selected area. The small black square is called the fill handle.
10. Grab the fill handle and drag with your mouse to fill cells A1 to B14. Note how the days of the week fill the cells in a series. Also, note that the Auto Fill Options button appears.

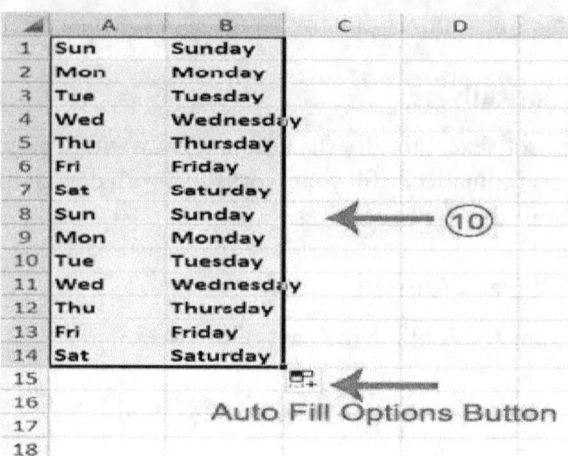

Auto Fill Options Button

(b) Fill Times

The following demonstrates filling time

1. Type **1:00** into cell C1.
2. Grab the fill handle and drag with your mouse to highlight cells C1 to C14. Note that each cell fills, using military time.
3. Press Esc and then click anywhere on the worksheet to remove the highlighting.

To change the format of the time:

1. Select cells C1 to C14.
2. Choose the Home tab.
3. Click the down arrow next to the number format box General. A menu appears.
4. Click Time. Excel changes the format of the time.

(c) Fill Numbers

You can also fill numbers.

1. Type a **1** in cell D1.
2. Type a **2** in cell D2.
3. Select cells D1:D2
4. Grab the fill handle and drag with your mouse to highlight cells D1 to D14.
5. The cells fill as a series, starting with 1, 2, 3.

Here is another interesting fill feature.

1. Go to cell E1.
2. Type **Section 1**.
3. Grab the fill handle and drag with your mouse to highlight cells E1 to E14. The cells fill in as a series: Section 1, Section 2, Section 3, and so on.

Set Print Options

There are many print options. You set print options on the Page Layout tab. Among other things, you can set your margins, set your page orientation, and select your paper size.

Margins define the amount of white space that appears on the top, bottom, left, and right edges of your document. The Margin option on the Page Layout tab provides several standard margin sizes from which you can choose.

Paper comes in a variety of sizes. Most business correspondence uses 8½ by 11 papers, which is the default page size in Excel. If you are not using 8 ½ by 11 papers, you can use the Size option on the Page Layout tab to change the Size setting.

Exercise 3 Set the

Page Layout (Margins)

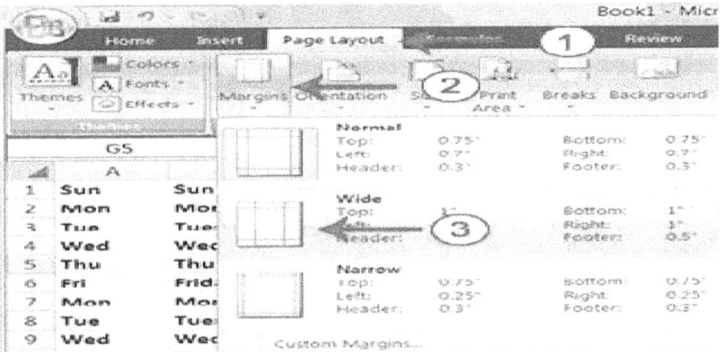

1. Choose the Page Layout tab.
2. Click Margins in the Page Setup group. A menu appears.
3. Click Wide. Excel sets your margins to the Wide settings.

Set the Page Orientation

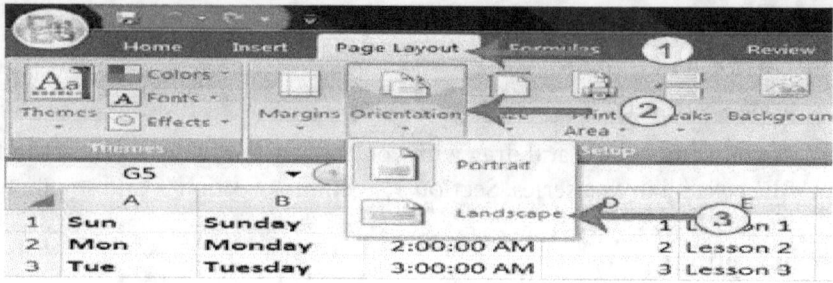

1. Choose the Page Layout tab.
2. Click Orientation in the Page Setup group. A menu appears.
3. Click Landscape. Excel sets your page orientation to landscape.
4. Set the Paper Size

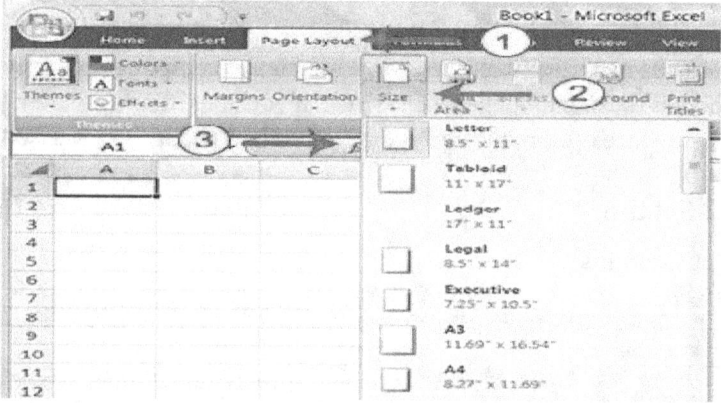

1. Choose the Page Layout tab.
2. Click Size in the Page Setup group. A menu appears.
3. Click the paper size you are using. Excel sets your page size.

Print

The simplest way to print is to click the Office button, highlight Print on the menu that appears, and then click Quick Print in the Preview and Print the Document pane. Dotted lines appear on your screen, and your document prints. The dotted lines indicate the right, left, top, and bottom edges of your printed pages. To print from Microsoft Excel, you can proceed as follows:

1. Click on **Microsoft Office Button**
2. Highlight or point the mouse on **Print.**
3. Click on **Print.**
4. In the **Name** box, under the Printer option, choose an appropriate printer.
5. Under the **Print Range** option, choose the appropriate range of pages to be printed.
6. Under the Copies option, choose the appropriate number of copies of each page to be printed.
7. Click on **OK** when ready.

Exercise 4 Print Preview

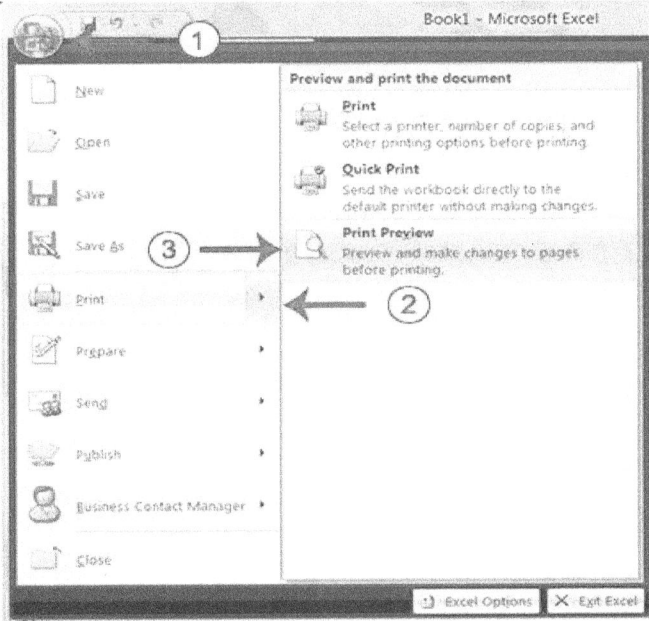

1. Click the Office button. A menu appears.
2. Highlight Print. The Preview and Print The Document pane appears.
3. Click Print Preview. The Print Preview window appears, with your document in the center.

Exercise 5
Print

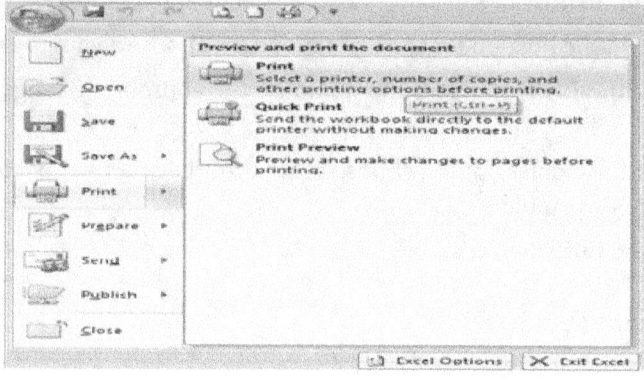

1. Click on **Microsoft Office Button**
2. Highlight or point the mouse on **Print.**
3. Click on **Print.** The Print dialog box appears

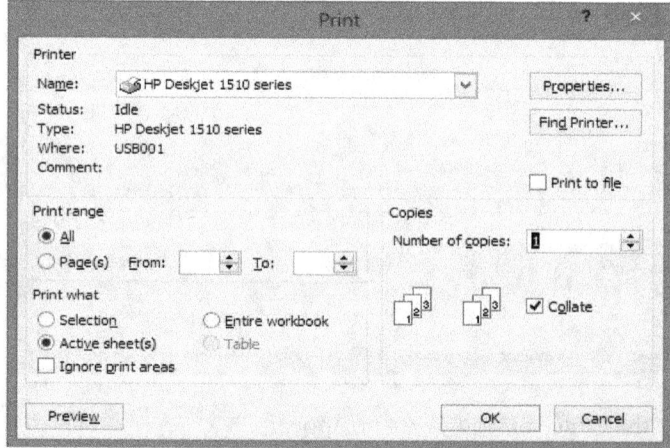

4. In the **Name** box, under the Printer option, choose an appropriate printer.
5. Under the **Print Range** option, choose the appropriate range of pages to be printed.
6. Under **Copies** option, choose appropriate number of copies of each page to be printed.

Microsoft Excel

7. Click on **OK** when ready.
8. This is the end of Section 3. You can save and close your file.

Section 4: Creating Charts

In Microsoft Excel, you can represent numbers in a chart. On the Insert tab, you can choose from a variety of chart types, including column, line, pie, bar, area, and scatter. The basic procedure for creating a chart is the same no matter what type of chart you choose. As you change your data, your chart will automatically update.

You select a chart type by choosing an option from the Insert tab's Chart group. After you choose a chart type, such as column, line, or bar, you choose a chart subtype. For example, after you choose a Column Chart, you can choose to have your chart represented as a two-dimensional chart, a three-dimensional chart, a cylinder chart, a cone chart, or a pyramid chart. There are further sub-types within each of these categories. As you roll your mouse pointer over each option, Excel supplies a brief description of each chart sub-type.

Create a Chart

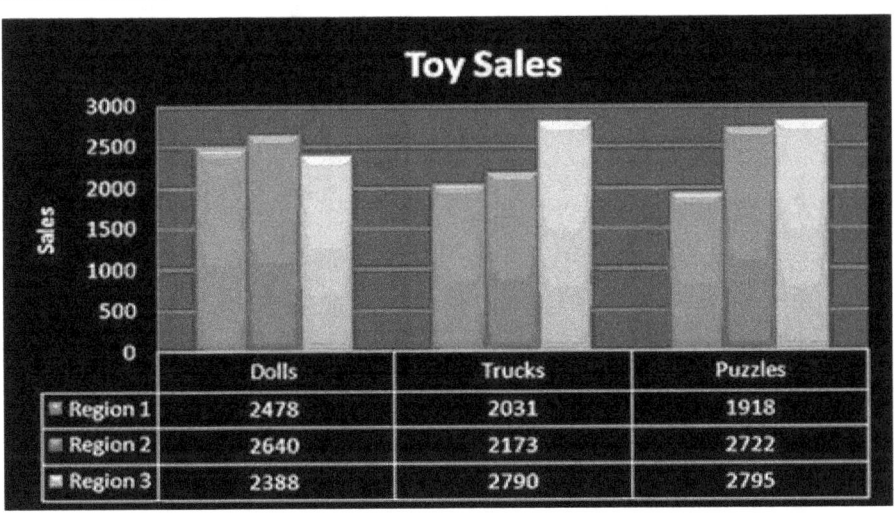

To create the column chart shown above, start by creating the worksheet below exactly as shown.

	A	B	C	D	E
1		Toy Sales			
2					
3	Products	Region 1	Region 2	Region 3	
4	Dolls	2478	2640	2388	
5	Trucks	2031	2173	2790	
6	Puzzles	1918	2722	2795	
7	Total	6427	7535	7973	
8					

After you have created the worksheet, you are ready to create your chart.

Exercise 1

Create a Column Chart

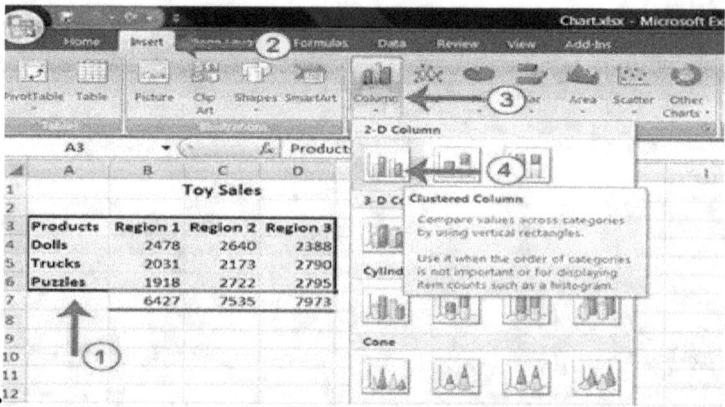

1. Select cells A3 to D6. You must select all the cells containing the data you want in your chart. You should also include the data labels.
2. Choose the Insert tab.
3. Click the Column button in the Charts group. A list of column chart sub-types appears.
4. Click the Clustered Column chart sub-type. Excel creates a Clustered Column chart and the Chart Tools context tabs appear.

Apply a Chart Layout

Context tabs are tabs that only appear when you need them. Called Chart Tools, there are three chart context tabs: **Design, Layout,** and **Format**. The tabs become available when you create a new chart or when you click on a chart. You can use these tabs to customize your chart.

Exercise 2 Apply a Chart Layout

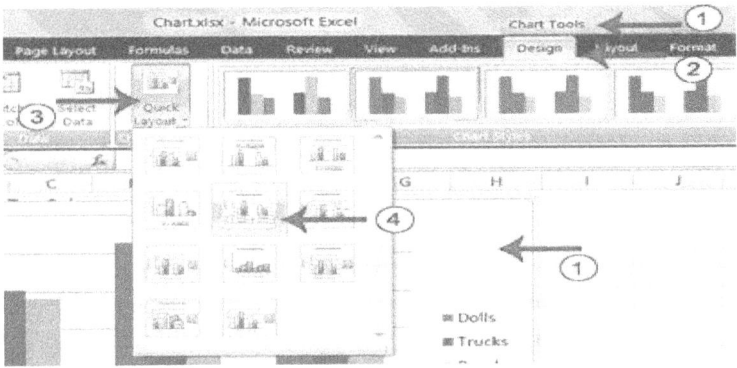

1. Click your chart. The Chart Tools become available.
2. Choose the Design tab.
3. Click the Quick Layout button in the Chart Layout group. A list of chart layouts appears.
4. Click Layout 5. Excel applies the layout to your chart.

Change the Style of a Chart

A style is a set of formatting options. You can use a style to change the color and format of your chart. Excel 2007 has several predefined styles that you can use. They are numbered from left to right, starting with 1, which is located in the upper left corner.

Exercise 3

1. Click your chart. The Chart Tools become available.
2. Choose the Design tab.
3. Click the More button in the Chart Styles group. The chart styles appear.

Change the Style of a Chart

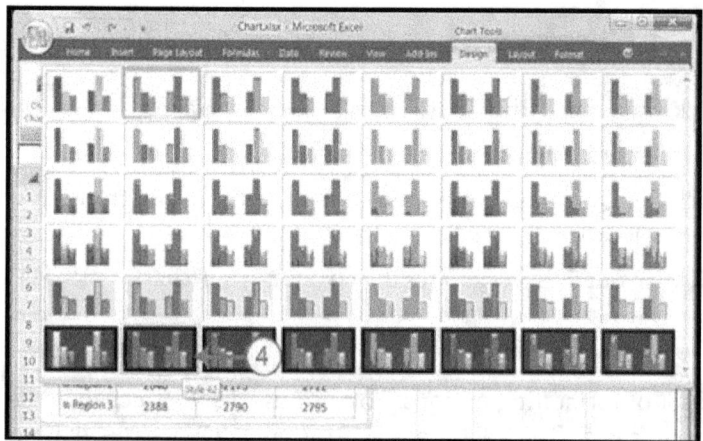

4. Click Style 42. Excel applies the style to your chart.

Change the Size and Position of a Chart

When you click a chart, handles appear on the right and left sides, the top and bottom, and the corners of the chart. You can drag the handles on the top and bottom of the chart to increase or decrease the height of the chart. You can drag the handles on the left and right sides to increase or decrease the width of the chart. You can drag the handles on the corners to increase or decrease the size of the chart proportionally. You can change the position of a chart by clicking on an unused area of the chart and dragging.

Microsoft Excel

Exercise 4 Change the Size and Position of a Chart

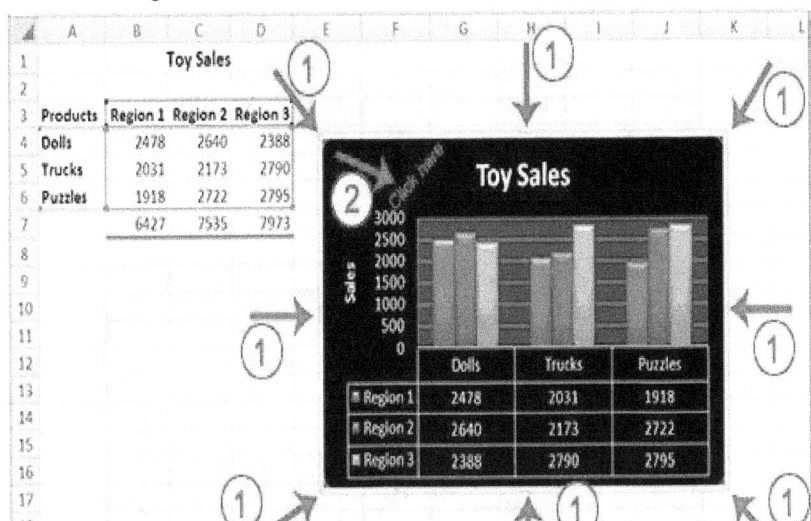

1. Use the handles to adjust the size of your chart.
2. Click an unused portion of the chart and drag to position the chart beside the data.

Move a Chart to a Chart Sheet

By default, when you create a chart, Excel embeds the chart in the active worksheet. However, you can move a chart to another worksheet or to a chart sheet. A chart sheet is a sheet dedicated to a particular chart. By default, Excel names each chart sheet sequentially, starting with Chart1. You can change the name.

Exercise 5

1. Click your chart. The Chart Tools become available.
2. Choose the Design tab.
3. Click the Move Chart button in the Location group. The Move Chart dialog box appears.

Move a Chart to a Chart Sheet

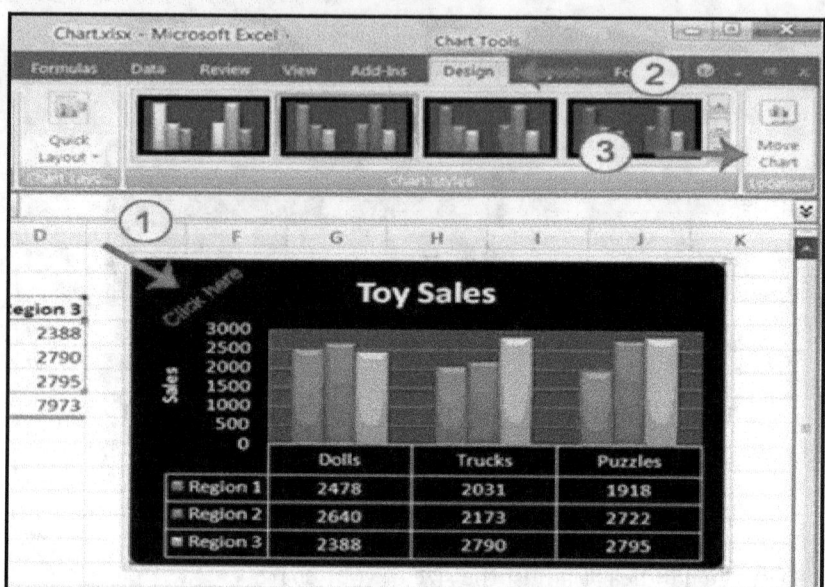

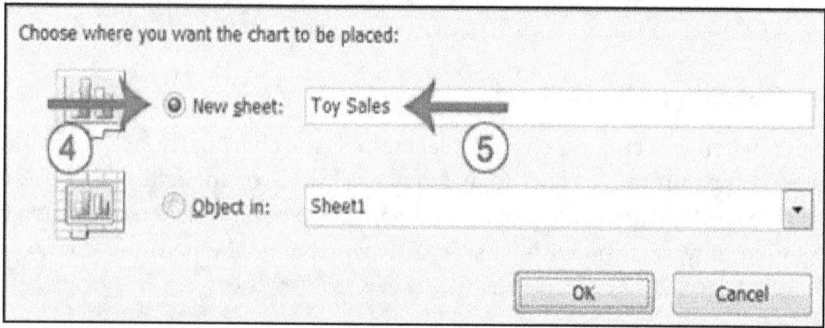

4. Click the New Sheet radio button.
5. Type Toy Sales to name the chart sheet. Excel creates a chart sheet named Toy Sales and places your chart on it.

Change the Chart Type

Any change you can make to a chart that is embedded in a worksheet, you can also make to a chart sheet. For example, you can change the chart type from a column chart to a bar chart.

Exercise 6 Change the Chart Type

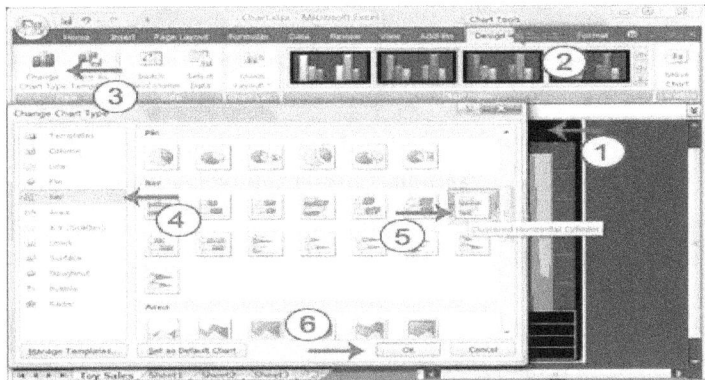

1. Click your chart. The Chart Tools become available.
2. Choose the Design tab.
3. Click Change Chart Type in the Type group. The Chart Type dialog box appears.
4. Click Bar.
5. Click Clustered Horizontal Cylinder.
6. Click OK. Excel changes your chart type.

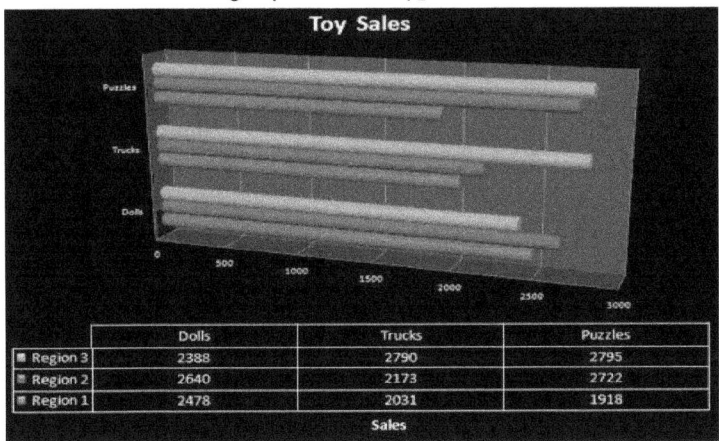

You have reached the end of Section 4. You can save and close your file.

Section 5: More on Entering Excel Formulas

This Section looks at more examples of how to enter and execute Excel Formulas.

The SUMIF Function Syntax SUMIF (range, criteria, sum_range)

The range is the range of cells where Excel searches for the criteria that you want to be evaluated. Cells in each range must be numbers or names, arrays, or references that contain numbers. Blank and text values are ignored.

Criteria are the criteria in the form of a number, expression, or text that defines which cells will be added. For example, criteria can be expressed as 32, "32", ">32", or "apples".

The sum range is the actual cells to add if their corresponding cells in the range match the criteria. If the sum range is omitted, the cells in the range are both evaluated by criteria and added if they match the criteria.

Note: The SUMIF function can be read as:

"Sum or add up the sum **range** if the **range** meets **criteria**."

Example

	A	B
1	Property Value	Commission
2	100,000	7,000
3	200,000	14,000
4	300,000	21,000
5	400,000	28,000
	Formula	Description (Result)
	=SUMIF(A2:A5,">160000",B2:B5)	Sum of the commissions property values over(63,000)
	=SUMIF(A2:A5,">160000")	Sum of the property values over 160,000 (900,000)
	=SUMIF(A2:A5,"=300000",B2:B3)	Sum of the commissions property values equal to 300,000 (21,000)

The AVERAGEIF Function

Returns the average (arithmetic mean) of all the cells in a range that meets a given criteria.

Syntax AVERAGEIF (range, criteria, **average range**)

The range is one or more cells to average, including numbers or names, arrays, or references that contain numbers.

Criteria is the criteria in the form of a number, expression, cell reference, or text that defines which cells are averaged. For example, criteria can be expressed as 32, "32", ">32", "apples", or B4.

The average range is the actual set of cells to average. If omitted, the range is used.

Note: The AVERAGEIF function can be read as:

"Average **average range** if **range** meets **criteria**."

Example: Averaging profits from regional offices

	A	B
1	Region	Profits (Thousands)
2	East	45,678
3	West	23,789
4	North	-4,789
5	South (New Office)	0
6	Midwest	9,678
	Formula	Description (result)
	=AVERAGEIF (A2:A6,"=*West",B2:B6)	Average of all profits for the West and Midwest regions (16,733.5)
	=AVERAGEIF (A2:A6,"<>*(New Office)", B2:B6)	Average of all profits for all regions excluding new offices (18,589)

The COUNTIF Function

Counts the number of cells within a range that meet the given criteria.

Syntax: COUNTIF (range, criteria)

The range is one or more cells to count, including numbers or names, arrays, or references that contain numbers. Blank and text values are ignored.

Criteria are the criteria in the form of a number, expression, cell reference, or text that defines which cells will be counted. For example, criteria can be expressed as 32, "32", ">32", "apples", or B4.

Note: The COUNTIF function can be read as:

"Count frequency or number of times or cells if **range** contains **criteria**."

Remark

You can use the wildcard characters, question mark (?), and asterisk (*), in the criteria. A question mark matches any single character; an asterisk matches any sequence of characters. If you want to find an actual question mark or asterisk, type a tilde (~) before the character.

Example 1: Common COUNTIF formulas

	A	B
1	Data	Data
2	apples	32
3	C	54
4	peaches	75
5	apples	86

Formula	Description (result)
=COUNTIF(A2:A5,"apples")	Number of cells with apples in the first column above (2)
=COUNTIF (A2:A5,A4)	Number of cells with peaches in the first column above (1)
=COUNTIF(A2:A5,A3)+COUNTIF (A2:A5,A2)	Number of cells with oranges and apples in the first column above (3)
=COUNTIF (B2:B5,">55")	Number of cells with a value greater than 55 in the second column above (2)
=COUNTIF (B2:B5,"<>"&B4)	Number of cells with a value not equal to 75 in the second column above (3)
=COUNTIF (B2:B5,">=32")-COUNTIF (B2:B5,">85")	Number of cells with a value greater than or Equal to 32 and less than or equal to 85 in the second column above (3)

Example 2: COUNTIF formulas using wildcard characters and handling blank values

	A	B
1	Data	Data
2	apples	Yes
3	oranges	No
4	peaches	No
5	apples	Yes

Formula	Description (result)
=COUNTIF (A2:A7,"*es")	Number of cells ending with the letters "es" in the first column above (4)
=COUNTIF (A2:A7,"????? es")	Number of cells ending with the letters "es" and having exactly 7 letters in the first column above (2)
=COUNTIF(A2:A7,"*")	Number of cells containing text in the first column above (4)
=COUNTIF(A2:A7,"<>"&"*")	Number of cells not containing text in the first column above (2)
=COUNTIF(B2:B7,"No")/ROWS (B2:B7)	The average number of No Votes including blank cells in the second column formatted as a percentage with no decimal places (33%)

	=COUNTIF(B2:B7,"Yes")/(ROWS (B2:B7)- COUNTIF (B2:B7,= "<>" &"*"))	The average number of Yes votes excluding blank cells in the second column formatted as a percentage with no decimal places (50%)

Note: *You can view the number as a percentage. Select the cell, and then on the* **Sheet** *tab in the* **Number** *group, click* **Percentage Style** % *.*

The IF Function

Returns one value if a condition you specify evaluates to TRUE and another value if it evaluates to FALSE.

Syntax IF(logical_test,value_if_true,value_if_false)

A logical test is any value or expression that can be evaluated to TRUE or FALSE. For example, A10=100 is a logical expression; if the value in cell A10 is equal to 100, the expression evaluates to TRUE. Otherwise, the expression evaluates to FALSE.

Value_if_true is the value that is returned if the logical test is TRUE.

Value_if_false is the value that is returned if the logical test is FALSE.

Remarks: Up to 64 IF functions can be nested as value_if_true and value_if_false arguments to construct more elaborate tests.

Note: The IF function can be read as:

"If **Logical_test** then **Value_if_true** otherwise **Value_if_false**"

Example

	A	
1	Score	
2	45	
3	90	
4	78	

Formula	Description (Result)
=IF(A2<50,"FAIL","PASS")	Assigns either a pass or fail remark to the first score (FAIL)
=IF(A2>89,"A",IF(A2>79,"B", IF(A2>69,"C",IF(A2>59,"D", "F"))))	Assigns a letter grade to the first score (F)
=IF(A3>89,"A",IF(A3>79,"B", IF(A3>69,"C",IF(A3>59,"D", "F"))))	Assigns a letter grade to the second score (A)
=IF(A4>89,"A",IF(A4>79,"B", IF(A4>69,"C", IF(A4>59,"D","F"))))	Assigns a letter grade to the third score (C)

The AND Function

Returns TRUE if all its arguments are TRUE; returns FALSE if one or more argument is FALSE.

Syntax

AND (logical1,logical2, ...)

Logical1, logical2, ... are 1 to 255 conditions you want to test that can be either TRUE or FALSE.

Example 1

	A	B
1	Formula	Description (Result)
2	=AND(TRUE, TRUE)	All arguments are True (True)
3	=AND(TRUE, FALSE)	One argument is False (False)
4	=AND (2+2=4, 2+3=5)	All arguments evaluate to True (True)

Example 2

	A	
1	Data	
2	50	
3	104	

Formula	Description (Result)
=AND(1<A2,A2<100)	Because 50 is between 1 and 100 (TRUE)
=IF(AND(1<A3,A3<100),A3, "The value is out of range.")	Displays the second number above, if it is between 1 and 100 otherwise displays a message (The value is out of range.)
=IF(AND(1<A2,A2<100),A2, "The value is out of range.")	Displays the first number above, if it is between 1 and 100, otherwise displays a message (50)

The FREQUENCY Function

Calculates how often values occur within a range of values, and then returns a vertical array of numbers. For example, use FREQUENCY to count the number of test scores that fall within ranges of scores. Because FREQUENCY returns an array, it must be entered as an array formula.

Syntax: FREQUENCY(data_array, bins_array)

Data_array is an array of or reference to a set of values for which you want to count frequencies. If the data array contains no values, FREQUENCY returns an array of zeros.

Bins_array is an array of or reference to intervals into which you want to group the values in data_array. If bins_array contains no values, FREQUENCY returns the number of elements in data_array.

Remarks

1. FREQUENCY is entered as an array formula after you select a range of adjacent cells into which you want the returned distribution to appear.
2. The number of elements in the returned array is one more than the number of elements in bins_array.

Example

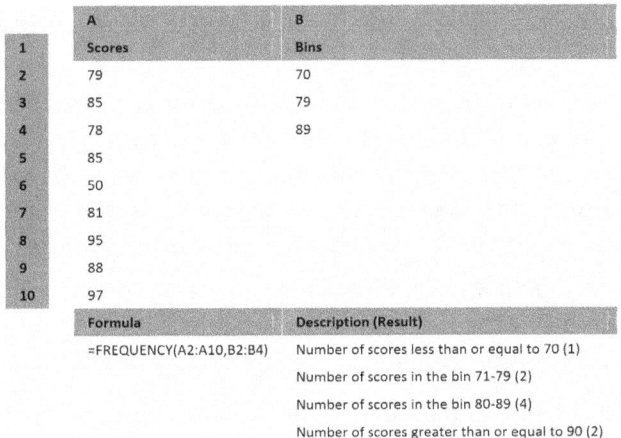

Note: *The formula in the example must be entered as an array formula. After copying the example to a blank worksheet, select the range A12:A15, press F2, and then press CTRL+SHIFT+ENTER. If the formula is not entered as an array formula, there will be only one result in cell A12 (1).*

The TREND Function

Returns values along a linear trend. Fits a straight line (using the method of least squares) to the arrays known_y's and known_x's. Returns the y-values along that line for the array of new_x's that you specify.

Syntax

TREND(known_y's,known_x's,new_x's,const)

Known_y's is the set of y-values you already know in the relationship y = mx + b.

1. If the array known_y's is in a single column, then each column of known_x's is interpreted as a separate variable.
2. If the array known_y's is in a single row, then each row of known_x's is interpreted as a separate variable.

Known_x's is an optional set of x-values that you may already know in the relationship $y = mx + b$.

1. The array known_x's can include one or more sets of variables. If only one variable is used, known_y's and known_x's can be ranges of any shape, as long as they have equal dimensions. If more than one variable is used, known_y's must be a vector (that is, a range with a height of one row or a width of one column).
2. If known_x's is omitted, it is assumed to be the array {1, 2, 3,...} that is the same size as known_y's.

New_x's are new x-values for which you want TREND to return corresponding y-values.

1. New_x's must include a column (or row) for each independent variable, just as known_x's does. So, if known_y's is in a single column, known_x's and new_x's must have the same number of columns. If known_y's is in a single row, known_x's and new_x's must have the same number of rows. If you omit new_x's, it is assumed to be the same as known_x's.
2. If you omit both known_x's and new_x's, they are assumed to be the array {1,2,3,...} that is the same size as known_y's.

Const is a logical value specifying whether to force the constant b to equal 0.

1. If const is TRUE or omitted, b is calculated normally.
2. If const is FALSE, b is set equal to 0 (zero), and the m-values are adjusted so that $y = mx$.

Remarks

1. You can use TREND for polynomial curve fitting by regressing against the same variable raised to different powers. For example, suppose column A contains y-values and column B contains x-values. You can enter x^2 in column C, x^3 in column D, and so on, and then regress columns B through D against column A.
2. Formulas that return arrays must be entered as array formulas.
3. When entering an array constant for an argument such as known_x's, use commas to separate values in the same row and semicolons to separate rows.

Example

	A	B	C
1	Month	Cost	Formula (Corresponding Cost)
2	1	$133,890	=TREND(B2:B13,A2:A13)
3	2	$135,000	
4	3	$135,790	
5	4	$137,300	
6	5	$138,130	
7	6	$139,100	
8	7	$139,900	
9	8	$141,120	
10	9	$141,890	
11	10	$143,230	
12	11	$144,000	
13	12	$145,290	
	Month	Formula (Predicted Cost)	
	13	=TREND(B2:B13,A2:A13,A15:A19)	
	14		
	15		
	16		
	17		

Note: *The formula in the example must be entered as an array formula. After copying the example to a blank worksheet, select the range C2:C13 or B15:B19 starting with the formula cell. Press F2, and then press CTRL+SHIFT+ENTER. If the formula is not entered as an array formula, the single results are 133953.3333 and 146171.5152.*

The ZTEST Function

Returns the one-tailed probability-value of a z-test. For a given hypothesized population mean, µ0, ZTEST returns the probability that the sample mean would be greater than the average of observations in the data set (array) — that is, the observed sample mean.

To see how ZTEST can be used in a formula to compute a two-tailed probability value, see "Remarks" below.

Syntax ZTEST(array,µ0,sigma)

Array is the array or range of data against which to test µ0 **µ0** is the value to test.

Sigma is the population (known) standard deviation. If omitted, the sample standard deviation is used.

Remarks:

1. If array is empty, ZTEST returns the #N/A error value.
2. ZTEST is calculated as follows when sigma is not omitted:

$ZTEST(array, \mu_0) = 1 - NORMSDIST((\bar{x} - \mu_0)/(sigma/\sqrt{n}))$ or when sigma is omitted:

$ZTEST(array, \mu_0) = 1 - NORMSDIST((\bar{x} - \mu_0)/(s/\sqrt{n}))$ where x is the sample mean AVERAGE (array); s is the sample standard deviation STDEV(array); and n is the number of observations in the sample COUNT(array).

3. ZTEST represents the probability that the sample mean would be greater than the observed value AVERAGE (array), when the underlying population mean is µ0. From the symmetry of the Normal distribution, if AVERAGE (array) < µ0, ZTEST will return a value greater than 0.5.

4. The following Excel formula can be used to calculate the two-tailed probability that the sample mean would be further from µ0 (in either direction) than AVERAGE (array), when the underlying population mean is µ0: =2 * MIN(ZTEST(array,µ0,sigma), 1 - ZTEST(array,µ0,sigma)).

Example

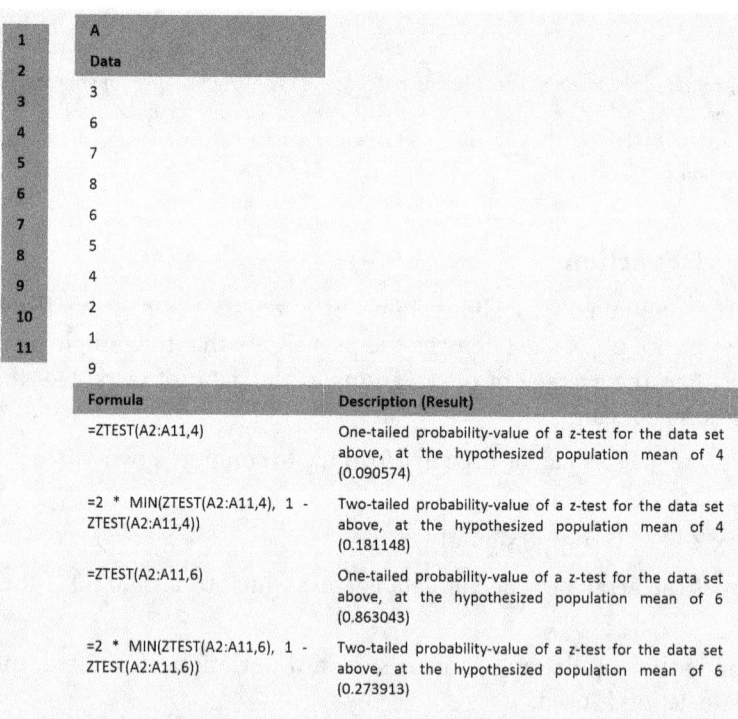

	A
1	Data
2	3
3	6
4	7
5	8
6	6
7	5
8	4
9	2
10	1
11	9

Formula	Description (Result)
=ZTEST(A2:A11,4)	One-tailed probability-value of a z-test for the data set above, at the hypothesized population mean of 4 (0.090574)
=2 * MIN(ZTEST(A2:A11,4), 1 - ZTEST(A2:A11,4))	Two-tailed probability-value of a z-test for the data set above, at the hypothesized population mean of 4 (0.181148)
=ZTEST(A2:A11,6)	One-tailed probability-value of a z-test for the data set above, at the hypothesized population mean of 6 (0.863043)
=2 * MIN(ZTEST(A2:A11,6), 1 - ZTEST(A2:A11,6))	Two-tailed probability-value of a z-test for the data set above, at the hypothesized population mean of 6 (0.273913)

Note: *The Excel Functions that discuss this chapter are only a few of the numerous Excel Functions available in Microsoft Office 2010. More assistance and exposure can be obtained through the Microsoft Excel Help (F1)*

Chapter 13
Number System and Codes

Introduction
- The term digital refers to a process that is achieved by using a discrete unit.
- In the number system there are different symbols and each symbol has an absolute value and also has place value.

Radix or Base
The radix or base of a number system is defined as the number of different digits which can occur in each position in the number system.

Radix Point
The generalized form of a decimal point is known as a radix point. In any positional number system the radix point divides the integer and fractional part.

   N_r = [Integer part. Fractional part]

   Radix point

Number System
In general a number in a system having base or radix 'r' can be written as

$a_n \, a_{n-1} \, a_{n-2} \, ... \, a_0 \, a_{-1} \, a_{-2} \, ... \, a_{-m}$

This will be interpreted as

$Y = a_n \times r^n + a_{n-1} \times r^{n-1} + a_{n-2} \times r^{n-2} + ... + a_0 \times r^0 + a_{-1} \times r^{-1} + a_{-2} \times r^{-2} + ... + a_{-m} \times r^{-m}$

where Y = value of the entire number

   a_n = the value of the nth digit

   r = radix

Types of Number System

There are four types of number systems. They are
1. Decimal number system
2. Binary number system
3. Octal number system
4. Hexadecimal number system

Decimal Number System

- The decimal number system contains ten unique symbols 0,1,2,3,4,5,6,7,8 and 9.
- In the decimal system 10 symbols are involved, so the base or radix is 10.
- It is a positional weighted system.
- The value attached to the symbol depends on its location with respect to the decimal point.

In general, is given by

$d_n\, d_{n-1}\, d_{n-2}\, \ldots\, d_0\, .\, d_{-1}\, d_{-2}\, \ldots\, d_{-m}$

$(d_n \times 10^n) + (d_{n-1} \times 10^{n-1}) + (d_{n-2} \times 10^{n-2}) + \ldots + (d_0 \times 10^0) + (d_{-1} \times 10^{-1}) + (d_{-2} \times 10^{-2}) + \ldots + (d_{-m} \times 10^{-m})$

For Example

$9256.26 = 9 \times 1000 + 2 \times 100 + 5 \times 10 + 6 \times 1 + 2 \times (1/10) + 6 \times (1/100)$

$= 9 \times 10^3 + 2 \times 10^2 + 5 \times 10^1 + 6 \times 10^0 + 2 \times 10^{-1} + 6 \times 10^{-2}$

Binary Number System

- The binary number system is a positional weighted system.
- The base or radix of this number system is 2.
- It has two independent symbols.
- The symbols used are 0 and 1.
- A binary digit is called a bit.
- The binary point separates the integer and fraction parts.

In general, is given by

$d_n\, d_{n-1}\, d_{n-2}\, \ldots\, d_0\, .\, d_{-1}\, d_{-2}\quad d_{-k}$

$(d_n \times 2^n) + (d_{n-1} \times 2^{n-1}) + (d_{n-2} \times 2^{n-2}) + \ldots + (d_0 \times 2^0) + (d_{-1} \times 2^{-1}) + (d_{-2} \times 2^{-2}) + \ldots + (d_{-k} \times 2^{-k})$

Number System and Codes

Octal Number System

- It is also a positional weighted system.
- Its base or radix is 8.
- It has 8 independent symbols 0,1,2,3,4,5,6 and 7.
- Its base $8 = 2^3$, every 3-bit group of binary can be represented by an octal digit.

Hexadecimal Number System

- The hexadecimal number system is a positional weighted system.
- The base or radix of this number system is 16.
- The symbols used are 0,1,2,3,4,5,6,7,8,9,A,B,C,D,E and F
- The base $16 = 2^4$, every 4 – bit group of binaries can be represented by an hexadecimal digit.

Conversion from One Number System to Another

1. **Binary Number System**

   a. **Binary to Decimal Conversion:** In this method, each binary digit of the number is multiplied by its positional weight and the product terms are added to obtain a decimal number.

For example

- Convert $(10101)_2$ to decimal.

   Solution:

   (Positional weight) $2^4\ 2^3\ 2^2\ 2^1\ 2^0$

   Binary number 10101

   $= (1 \times 2^4) + (0 \times 2^3) + (1 \times 2^2) + (0 \times 2^1) + (1 \times 2^0)$

   $= 16 + 0 + 4 + 0 + 1$

   $= (21)_{10}$

- Convert $(111.101)_2$ to decimal.

   Solution:

   $(111.101)_2 = (1 \times 2^2) + (1 \times 2^1) + (1 \times 2^0) + (1 \times 2^{-1}) + (0 \times 2^{-2}) + (1 \times 2^{-3})$

$= 4 + 2 + 1 + 0.5 + 0 + 0.125$

$= (7.625)_{10}$

b. **Binary to Octal Conversion:** For conversion binary to octal the binary numbers are divided into groups of 3 bits each, starting at the binary point and proceeding towards left and right.

Octal	Binary	Octal	Binary
0	000	4	100
1	001	5	101
2	010	6	110
3	011	7	111

For example

- Convert $(101111010110.110110011)_2$ into octal.

    Solution:

Group of 3 bits are	101	111	010	110	.110	110	011
Convert each group into octal = The result is $(5726.663)_8$	5	7	2	6	.6	6	3

- Convert $(10101111001.0111)_2$ into octal.

    Solution:

Binary number	10	101	111	001	.	011	1
Group of 3 bits are =	010	101	111	001	.	011	100
Convert each group into octal = The result is $(2571.34)_8$	2	5	7	1	.3		4

c. **Binary to Hexadecimal Conversion:** For conversion binary to hexadecimal number the binary numbers starting from the binary point, groups are made of 4 bits each, on either side of the binary point.

Hexadecimal	Binary	Hexadecimal	Binary
0	0000	8	1000
1	0001	9	1001
2	0010	A	1010
3	0011	B	1011
4	0100	C	1100
5	0101	D	1101
6	0110	E	1110
7	0111	F	1111

For example

- Convert $(1011011011)_2$ into hexadecimal.

    Solution:

Given Binary number	10	1101	1011
Group of 4 bits are	0010	1101	1011
Convert each group into hex =	2	D	B
The result is $(2DB)_{16}$			

- Convert $(01011111011.011111)_2$ into hexadecimal.

Solution:

Given Binary number	010	1111	1011	.	0111	11
Group of 3 bits are =	0010	1111	1011	.	0111	1100
Convert each group into octal =	2	F	B	.	7	C
The result is $(2FB.7C)_{16}$						

2. **Decimal Number System**

    a. **Decimal to Binary Conversion:** In the conversion the integer number are converted to the desired base using successive division by the base or radix.

For example

- Convert $(52)_{10}$ into binary.

    Solution:

    Divide the given decimal number successively by 2 and read the integer part remainder upwards to get an equivalent binary number. Multiply the fraction part by 2. Keep the integer in the product as it is and multiply the new fraction in the product by 2. The process is continued and the integers are read in the products from top to bottom.

    ```
    2 | 52
    2 | 26    — 0
    2 | 13    — 0
    2 | 6     — 1
    2 | 3     — 0
    2 | 1     — 1
        0     — 1
    ```

Result of $(52)_{10}$ is $(110100)_2$

- Convert $(105.15)_{10}$ into binary.

    Solution:

Integer part			Fraction part
2 ⌊ 105			0.15 x 2 = 0.30
2 ⌊ 52 -		1	0.30 x 2 = 0.60
2 ⌊ 26 -		0	0.60 x 2 = 1.20
2 ⌊ 13 -		0	0.20 x 2 = 0.40
2 ⌊ 6 -		1	0.40 x 2 = 0.80
2 ⌊ 3 -		0	0.80 x 2 = 1.60
2 ⌊ 1 -		1	
0 -		1	

Result of $(105.15)_{10}$ is $(1101001.001001)_2$

b. **Decimal to Octal Conversion:** To convert the given decimal integer number to octal, successively divide the given number by 8 till the quotient is 0. To convert the given decimal fractions to octal successively multiply the decimal fraction and the subsequent decimal fractions by 8 till the product is 0 or till the required accuracy is obtained.

For example

- Convert $(378.93)_{10}$ into octal.

    Solution:

8 ⌊ 378			0.93 x 8 = 7.44
8 ⌊ 47	-	2	0.44 x 8 = 3.52
8 ⌊ 5	-	7	0.52 x 8 = 4.16
0	-	5	0.16 x 8 = 1.28

Result of $(378.93)_{10}$ is $(572.7341)_8$

c. **Decimal to Hexadecimal Conversion:** The decimal to hexadecimal conversion is the same as octal.

For example

- Convert $(2598.675)_{10}$ into hexadecimal.

    Solution:

Remainder

	Decimal	Hex		Hex
16 ⌊ 2598			0.675 x 16 = 10.8	A
16 ⌊ 162	− 6	6	0.800 x 16 = 12.8	C
16 ⌊ 10	− 2	2	0.800 x 16 = 12.8	C
0	− 10	A	0.800 x 16 = 12.8	C

Result of $(2598.675)_{10}$ is $(A26.ACCC)_{16}$

3. **Octal Number System**

   a. **Octal to Binary Conversion:** To convert a given octal number to binary, replace each octal digit by its 3-bit binary equivalent.

   Convert $(367.52)_8$ into binary

   Solution

   Given Octal number is   3   6   7   .   5   2
   Convert each group octal to binary=   011   110   111   .   101   010

   Result of $(367.52)_8$ is $(011110111.101010)_2$

   b. **Octal to Decimal Conversion:** For conversion octal to decimal number, multiply each digit in the octal number by the weight of its position and add all the product terms

   For example

   Convert $(4057.06)_8$ to decimal

   Solution:

   $(4057.06)_8 = 4 \times 8^3 + 0 \times 8^2 + 5 \times 8^1 + 7 \times 8^0 + 0 \times 8^{-1} + 6 \times 8^{-2}$

   $= 2048 + 0 + 40 + 7 + 0 + 0.0937$

   $= (2095.0937)_{10}$

   Result is $(2095.0937)_{10}$

   c. **Octal to Hexadecimal Conversion:** For conversion of octal to Hexadecimal, first convert the given octal number to binary and then binary number to hexadecimal.

   For example

   Convert $(756.603)_8$ to hexadecimal.

   Solution:

Given octal no.	7	5	6 .	6	0	3
Convert each octal digit to binary =	111	101	110 .	110	000	011
Group of 4 bits are =	0001	1110	1110 .	1100	0001	1000
Convert 4 bits to hex. =	1	E	E .	C	1	8

Result is (1EE.C18)$_{16}$

4. **Hexadecimal Number System**

a. **Hexadecimal to Binary Conversion:** For conversion of hexadecimal to binary, replace hexadecimal digit by its 4-bit binary group.

For example

Convert (3A9E.B0D)$_{16}$ into binary.

Solution:

Given Hexadecimal number is	3	A	9	E .	B	0	D
Convert each hexadecimal =	0011	1010	1001	1110 .	1011	0000	1101
Digit to 4 bit binary							

Result of (3A9E.B0D)$_8$ is (0011101010011110.101100001101)$_2$

Hexadecimal to Decimal Conversion: For conversion of hexadecimal to decimal, multiply each digit in the hexadecimal number by its position weight and add all those product terms.

For example

Convert (A0F9.0EB)$_{16}$ to decimal

Solution:

$(A0F9.0EB)_{16} = (10 \times 16^3) + (0 \times 16^2) + (15 \times 16^1) + (9 \times 16^0) + (0 \times 16^{-1}) + (14 \times 16^{-2})$
$+ (11 \times 16^{-3})$

$= 40960 + 0 + 240 + 9 + 0 + 0.0546 + 0.0026$

$= (41209.0572)_{10}$

Result is (41209.0572)$_{10}$

Hexadecimal to Octal Conversion: For conversion of hexadecimal to octal, first convert the given hexadecimal number to binary and then binary number to octal.

For example

Convert (B9F.AE)$_{16}$ to octal.

Solution

Number System and Codes

Given hexadecimal no. is	B	9		F	.	A	E	
Convert each hex. digit to binary =	1011	1001		1111	.	1010	1110	
Group of 3 bits are =	=101	110	011	111	.	101	011	100
Convert 3 bits group to octal. =	=5	6	3	7	.	5	3	4

Result is $(5637.534)_8$

Binary Arithmetic Operation

1. Binary Addition

The binary addition rules are as follows

$0 + 0 = 0\ ;\ 0 + 1 = 1\ ;\ 1 + 0 = 1\ ;\ 1 + 1 = 10$, i.e. 0 with a carry of 1

For example

Add $(100101)_2$ and $(1101111)_2$.

Solution:
```
  1 0 0 1 0 1
+1 1 0 1 1 1 1
───────────────
1 0 0 1 0 1 0 0
```
Result is $(10010100)_2$

2. Binary Subtraction

The binary subtraction rules are as follows

$0 - 0 = 0\ ;\ 1 - 1 = 0\ ;\ 1 - 0 = 1\ ;\ 0 - 1 = 1$, with a borrow of 1

For example

Subtract $(111.111)_2$ from $(1010.01)_2$.

Solution:
```
   1 0 1 0 . 0 1 0
 -   1 1 1 . 1 1 1
 ──────────────────
   0 0 1 0 . 0 1 1
```
Result is $(0010.011)_2$

3. Binary Multiplication

The binary multiplication rules are as follows

$0 \times 0 = 0$; $1 \times 1 = 1$; $1 \times 0 = 0$; $0 \times 1 = 0$

For example

Multiply $(1101)_2$ by $(110)_2$. Solution:

```
    1101
X    110
    ————
    0000
    1101
 +  1101
  ———————
  1001110
```

Result is $(1001110)_2$

4. Binary Division

The binary division is very simple and similar to the decimal number system. The division by '0' is meaningless. So we have only 2 rules

$0 \div 1 = 0$

$1 \div 1 = 1$

For example

Divide $(10110)_2$ by $(110)_2$.

Solution:

```
110) 101101 (111.1
   -  110
      ————
      1010
       110
       ————
       1001
        110
        ————
        110
        110
        ————
        000
```

Result is $(111.1)_2$

1's Complement Representation

The 1's complement of a binary number is obtained by changing each 0 to 1 and each 1 to 0.

For example

Find $(1100)_2$ 1's complement.

Solution:

Given	1	1	0	0
1's complement is	0	0	1	1

Result is $(0011)_2$

2's Complement Representation

The 2's complement of a binary number is a binary number which is obtained by adding 1 to the 1's complement of a number i.e.

2's complement = 1's complement + 1

For example

Find $(1010)_2$ 2's complement.

Solution:

Given	1	0	1	0
1's complement is	0	1	0	1
			+	1
2's complement	0	1	1	0

Result is $(0110)_2$

Signed Number

In sign – magnitude form, an additional bit called the sign bit is placed in front of the number. If the sign bit is 0, the number is positive. If it is a 1, the number is negative.

For example

0 1 0 1 0 0 1 = +41

↑

Sign bit

1 1 0 1 0 0 1 = −41

↑

Sign bit

Subtraction Using Complement Method

1's Complement: In 1's complement subtraction, add the 1's complement of subtrahend to the minuend. If there is a carry out, then the carry is added to the

LSB. This is called end around carry. If the MSB is 0, the result is positive. If the MSB is 1, the result is negative and is in its 1's complement form. Then take its 1's complement to get the magnitude in binary.

For example

Subtract $(10000)_2$ from $(11010)_2$ using 1's complement.

Solution:

```
   1 1 0 1 0              1 1 0 1 0                       =   -26
 - 0 1 0 0 0x     =>    + 0 1 1 1 1  (1's complement)     =   -16
                Carry → 1 0 1 0 0 1                       +    10
                        +       1
                        ─────────────
                          0 1 0 1 0     = +10
```

Result is +10

2's Complement: In 2's complement subtraction, add the 2's complement of subtrahend to the minuend. If there is a carry out, ignore it. If the MSB is 0, the result is positive. If the MSB is 1, the result is negative and is in its 2's complement form. Then take its 2's complement to get the magnitude in binary.

For example

Subtract $(1010100)_2$ from $(1010100)_2$ using 2's complement.

Solution:

```
  1 0 1 0 1 0 0          1 0 1 0 1 0 0                      =   84
 -1 0 1 0 1 0 0   =>   + 0 1 0 1 1 0 0  (2's complement)    = - 84
                       1 0 0 0 0 0 0 0  (Ignore the carry)    ────
                 =         0 (result = 0)                       0
```

Hence MSB is 0. The answer is positive. So, it is +0000000 = 0

Digital Codes

In practice the digital electronics are required to handle data which may be numeric, alphabets and special characters. This requires the conversion of the incoming data into binary format before it can be processed. There are various possible ways of doing this and this process is called encoding. To achieve the reverse of it, we use decoders.

Weighted and Non-Weighted Codes

There are two types of binary codes
1. Weighted binary codes
2. Non- weighted binary codes

In weighted codes, for each position (or bit), there is specific weight attached.

For example, in binary numbers, each bit is assigned a particular weight $2n$ where 'n' is the bit number for n = 0,1,2,3,4 the weights are 1,2,4,8,16 respectively.

Example: BCD

Non-weighted codes are codes which are not assigned with any weight to each digit position, i.e., each digit position within the number is not assigned a fixed value.

Example: Excess – 3 (XS -3) code and Gray codes

Binary Coded Decimal (BCD)

BCD is a weighted code. In weighted codes, each successive digit from right to left represents weights equal to some specified value and to get the equivalent decimal number add the products of the weights by the corresponding binary digit. 8421 is the most common because 8421 BCD is the most natural amongst the other possible codes.

For example

$(567)_{10}$ is encoded in various 4 bit codes.

Solution:

Decimal	→	5	6	7
8421 code	→	0101	0110	0111
6311 code	→	0111	1000	1001
5421 code	→	1000	0100	1010

BCD Addition

Addition of BCD (8421) is performed by adding two digits of binary, starting from the least significant digit. In case if the result is an illegal code (greater than 9) or if there is a carry out of one then add 0110 (6) and add the resulting carry to the next most significant.

Solution:

```
  679.6              0110 0111 1001 . 0110    (679.6 in BCD)
+ 536.8         => + 0101 0011 0110 . 1000    (536.8 in BCD)
 1216.4             1011 1010 1111 . 1110    (All are illegal codes)
                  + 0101 +0011 +0110 . +1000  (Add 0110 to each)
                   0001 0010 0001 0110 . 0100
                     1    2    1    6  .  4   (corrected sum = 1216.4)
```

Result is **1216.4**

BCD Subtraction

The BCD subtraction is performed by subtracting the digits of each 4 – bit group of the subtrahend from corresponding 4 – bit group of the minuend in the binary starting from the LSD. If there is no borrow from the next higher group then no correction is required. If there is a borrow from the next group, then 610 (0110) is subtracted from the difference term of this group.

For example

Subtract 147.8 from 206.7 using 8421 BCD code.

Solution

```
  206.7              0010 0000 0110 . 0111    (206.7 in BCD)
+ 147.8         => - 0001 0100 0111 . 1000    (147.8 in BCD)
   58.9             0000 1011 1110 . 1111    (Borrows are present)
                        -0110 -0110 .-0110
                    0101 1000 . 1001
                      5    8  .  9            (corrected difference = 58.9)
```

Result is $(58.9)_{10}$

Excess Three (XS-3) Code

The Excess-3 code, also called XS-3, is a non- weighted BCD code. This derives its name from the fact that each binary code word is the corresponding 8421 code word plus 0011(3). It is a sequential code. It is a self-complementing code.

Xs-3 Addition

In XS-3 addition, add the XS-3 numbers by adding the 4 bit groups in each column starting from the LSD. If there is no carry out from the addition of any of the 4 bit groups, subtract 0011 from the sum term of those groups. If there is a carry out, add 0011 to the sum term of those groups

For example

Add 37 and 28 using XS-3 code.

Solution:

```
    37              0010 1010         (37 in XS-3)
  + 28         =>  +0101 1011         (28 in XS-3)
    65              1011 11010        (Carry is generated)
                  +      1            (Propagate carry)
                    1100 0101         (Add 0110 to correct 0101 and
                   -0011 +0011         subtract 0011 to correct 1100)
                    1001  1000        (corrected sum in XS-3 = 65₁₀)
```

XS-3 Subtraction

To subtract in XS-3 number by subtracting each 4-bit group of the subtrahend from the corresponding 4-bit group of the minuend starting from the LSD. If there is no borrow from the next 4-bit group add 0011 to the difference term of such groups. If there is a borrow, subtract 0011 from the difference term.

For example

```
    267             0101 1010 1010    (267 in XS-3)
  - 175        => - 0100 1010 1000    (175 in XS-3)
    092             0000 1111 0010    (Correct 0010 and 0000 by adding 0011
                  + 0011 -0011 +0011   and correct 1111 by substracting 0011)
                    0011 1100 0101    (Corrected difference in XS-3 = 9210)
```

ASCII CODE

The American Standard Code for Information Interchange (ASCII) pronounced as 'ASKEE' is a widely used alphanumeric code. This is basically a 7 bit code. The number of different bit patterns that can be created with 7 bits is 2⁷ = 128, the ASCII can be used to encode both the uppercase and lowercase characters of the alphabet (52 symbols) and some special symbols in addition to the 10 decimal digits. It is used extensively for printers and terminals that interface with small computer systems. The table shown below shows the ASCII groups.

The ASCII codes:

LSBs	MSBs							
	000	001	010	011	100	101	110	111
0000	NUL	DEL	Space	0	@	P	p	
0001	SOH	DC1	!	1	A	Q	a	q
0010	STX	DC2	"	2	B	R	b	r
0011	ETX	DC3	#	3	C	S	c	s
0100	EOT	DC4	$	4	D	T	d	t
0101	ENQ	NAK	%	5	E	U	e	u
0110	ACK	SYN	&	6	F	V	f	v
0111	BEL	ETB	'	7	G	W	g	w
1000	BS	CAN	(	8	H	X	h	x
1001	HT	EM	)	9	I	Y	i	y
1010	LF	SUB	*	:	J	Z	j	z
1011	VT	ESC	+	;	K	[	k	{
1100	FF	FS	,	<	L	\	l	|
1101	CR	GS	-	=	M	]	m	}
1110	SO	RS	.	>	N	^	n	~
1111	SI	US	/	?	O	_	o	DLE

EBCDIC Code

The Extended Binary Coded Decimal Interchange Code (EBCDIC) pronounced as 'eb – si- dik' is an like 4-bit alphanumeric code. Since $2^8 = 256$ bit patterns can be formed with 8 bits. It is used by most large computers to communicate in alphanumeric data. The table shown below shows the EBCDIC code.

The EBCDIC code:

LSD (Hex)	MSD(Hex)															
	0	1	2	3	4	5	6	7	8	9	A	B	C	D	E	F
0	NUL	DLE	DS		SP	&							[	]	\	0
1	SOH	DC1	SOS				/		a	j	~		A	J		1
2	STX	DC2	FS	SYN					b	k	s		B	K	S	2
3	ETX	DC3							c	l	t		C	L	T	3

4	PF	RES	BYP	PN				d	m	u		D	M	U	4
5	HT	NL	LF	RS				e	n	v		E	N	V	5
6	LC	BS	EOB	YC				f	o	w		F	O	W	6
7	DEL	IL	PRE	EOT				g	p	x		G	P	X	7
8		CAN						h	q	y		H	Q	Y	8
9		EM						i	r	z		I	R	Z	9
A	SMM	CC	SM		Ø	!	I	:							
B	VT				.	$	,	#							
C	FF	IFS		DC4	<	*	%	@							
D	CR	IGS	ENQ	NAK	(	)	_	'							
E	SO	IRS	ACK		+	;	>	=							
F	SI	IUS	BEL	SUB	I	'	?	'							

Gray Code

The Gray code is a non-weighted code. It is not a BCD code. It is cyclic code because successive words in this differ in one bit position only i.e it is a unit distance code.

Gray code is used in instrumentation and data acquisition systems where linear or angular displacement is measured. They are also used in shaft encoders, I/O devices, A/D converters and other peripheral equipment.

BINARY- TO – GRAY CONVERSION: -

If an n-bit binary number is represented by $B_n B_{n-1} - - - - - B_1$ and its gray code equivalent by $G_n G_{n-1} - - - - - - - - - - - - - - - - G_1$, where B_n and G_n are the MSBs, then gray code bits are obtained from the binary code as follows

$$G_n = B_n$$
$$G_{n-1} = B_n \oplus B_{n-1}$$
.
.
.
.
$$G_1 = B_2 \oplus B_1$$

Where the symbol $\oplus$ stands for Exclusive OR (X-OR)

For example:

Convert the binary 1001 to the Gray code.

Solution:

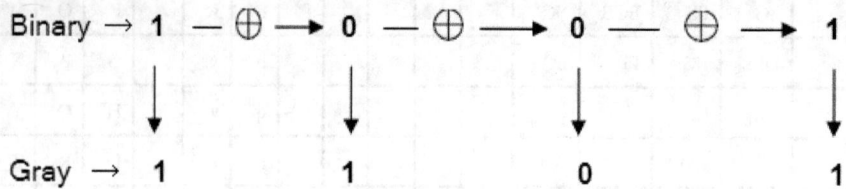

The gray code is 1101

Gray- To - Binary Conversion

If an n-bit gray number is represented by $G_n\ G_{n-1}\ \text{-------}\ G_1$ and its binary equivalent by $B_n\ B_{n-1}\ \text{-----------}\ B_1$,

$$B_n = G_n$$
$$B_{n-1} = B_n \oplus G_{n-1}$$
$$\vdots$$
$$B_1 = B_2 \oplus G_1$$

For example

Convert the Gray code 1101 to the binary.

Solution:

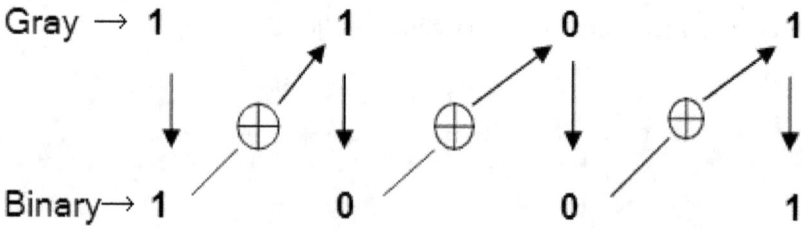

Chapter 14
Logic Gates

Logic Gates
- Logic gates are the fundamental building blocks of digital systems.
- There are 3 basic types of gates AND, OR and NOT.
- Logic gates are electronic circuits because they are made up of a number of electronic devices and components.
- Inputs and outputs of logic gates can occur only in 2 levels. These two levels are termed HIGH and LOW, or TRUE and FALSE, or ON and OFF or simply 1 and 0.
- The table which lists all the possible combinations of input variables and the corresponding outputs is called a truth table.

Level Logic: A logic in which the voltage levels represent logic 1 and logic 0. Level logic may be positive or negative logic.

Positive Logic: A positive logic system is the one in which the higher of the two voltage levels represents the logic 1 and the lower of the two voltages level represents the logic 0.

Negative Logic: A negative logic system is the one in which the lower of the two voltage levels represents the logic 1 and the higher of the two voltages level represents the logic 0.

Different Types of Logic Gates

Not Gate (Inverter)
- A NOT gate, also called an inverter, has only one input and one output.
- It is a device whose output is always the complement of its input.
- The output of a NOT gate is the logic 1 state when its input is in logic 0 state and the logic 0 state when its input is in logic 1 state.

IC No.: 7404

Logic Symbol

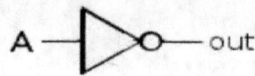 A — ⊳o — out

Truth table

INPUT A	OUTPUT $\overline{A}$
0	1
1	0

Timing Diagram

```
        1    0    0    1
A    ___|‾‾‾‾|____|‾‾‾‾

Ā    ‾‾‾|____|‾‾‾‾|____
        0    1    1    0
```

And Gate

- An AND gate has two or more inputs but only one output.
- The output is logic 1 state only when each one of its inputs is at logic 1 state.
- The output is logic 0 state even if one of its inputs is at logic 0 state.

IC No.: 7408

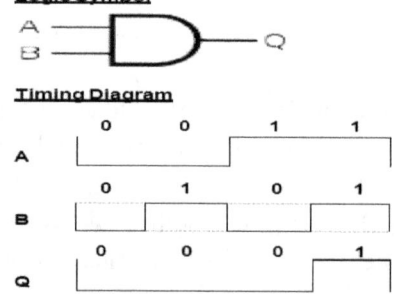

Truth Table

A	B	OUTPUT Q=A. B
0	0	0
0	1	0
1	0	0
1	1	1

OR Gate

- An OR gate may have two or more inputs but only one output.
- The output is logic 1 state, even if one of its inputs is in logic 1 state.
- The output is logic 0 state, only when each one of its inputs is in logic state.

IC No.: 7432

Logic Gates

Logic Symbol

Truth Table

INPUT		OUTPUT
A	B	Q=A + B
0	0	0
0	1	1
1	0	1
1	1	1

Timing Diagram

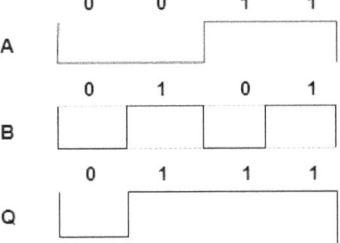

Nand Gate

- NAND gate is a combination of an AND gate and a NOT gate.
- The output is logic 0 when each of the inputs is logic 1 and for any other combination of inputs, the output is logic 1.

IC No.: 7400 two input NAND gate

        7410 three input NAND gate

        7420 four input NAND gate

        7430 eight input NAND gate

Logic Symbol

Truth Table

INPUT		OUTPUT
A	B	Q= $\overline{A.B}$
0	0	1
0	1	1
1	0	1
1	1	0

Timing Diagram

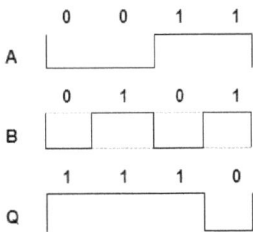

Nor Gate

- NOR gate is a combination of an OR gate and a NOT gate.
- The output is logic 1, only when each one of its inputs is logic 0 and for any other combination of inputs, the output is a logic 0 level.

IC No.: 7402 two input NOR gate

       7427 three input NOR gate

       7425 four input NOR gate

Logic Symbol   **Truth Table**

INPUT		OUTPUT
A	B	$Q = \overline{A + B}$
0	0	1
0	1	0
1	0	0
1	1	0

Timing Diagram

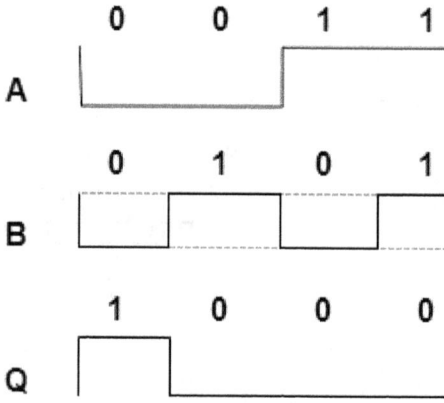

Logic Gates

Exclusive – OR (X-OR) Gate

- An X-OR gate is a two input, one output logic circuit.
- The output is logic 1 when one and only one of its two inputs is logic 1. When both the inputs are logic 0 or when both the inputs is logic 1, the output is logic 0.

IC No.: 7486

Logic Symbol

INPUTS are **A** and **B**

OUTPUT is $Q = A \oplus B$

$= A\bar{B} + A\bar{B}$

Truth Table

INPUT		OUTPUT
A	B	$Q = A \oplus B$
0	0	0
0	1	1
1	0	1
1	1	0

Timing Diagram

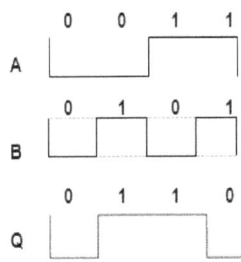

Exclusive – NOR (X-NOR) Gate

- An X-NOR gate is the combination of an X-OR gate and a NOT gate.
- An X-NOR gate is a two input, one output logic circuit.
- The output is logic 1 only when both the inputs are logic 0 or when both the inputs are 1.
- The output is logic 0 when one of the inputs is logic 0 and other is 1.

IC No.: 74266

Logic Symbol

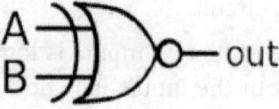

OUT = A B + $\bar{A}$ $\bar{B}$

= A XNOR B

INPUT		OUTPUT
A	B	OUT = A XNOR B
0	0	1
0	1	0
1	0	0
1	1	1

Timing Diagram

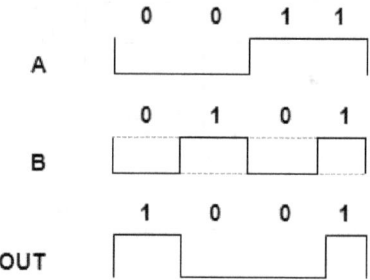

Universal Gates

There are 3 basic gates AND, OR and NOT, there are two universal gates NAND and NOR, each of which can realize logic circuits single handedly. The NAND and NOR gates are called universal building blocks. Both NAND and NOR gates can perform all logic functions i.e. AND, OR, NOT, EXOR and EXNOR.

Nand Gate

a. Inverter from NAND gate

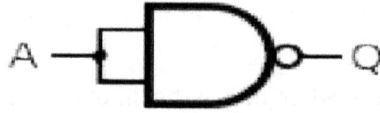

Input = A

Output Q = A

b. AND gate from NAND gate

Logic Gates

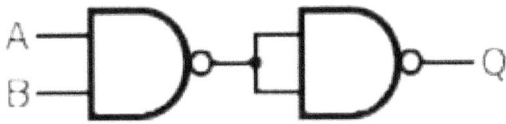

Inputs are A and B

Output Q = A.B

c. OR gate from NAND gate

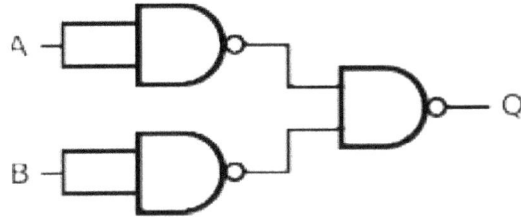

Inputs are A and B

Output Q = A+B

d. NOR gate from NAND gate

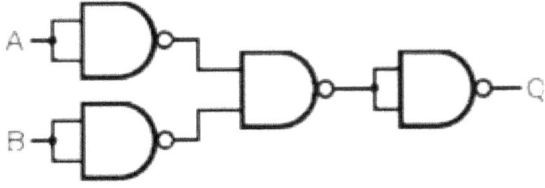

Inputs are A and B

Output Q = A+B

e. EX-OR gate from NAND gate

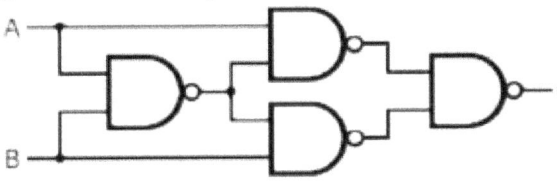

Inputs are A and B

Output Q = A B + AB

f. EX-NOR gate From NAND gate

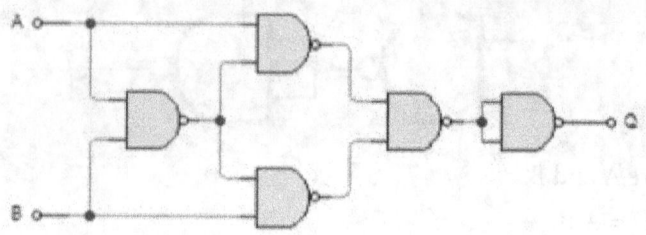

Inputs are A and B

Output Q = A B + A B

Nor Gate

a.   Inverter from NOR gate

Input = A

Output Q = $\overline{A}$

b.   AND gate from NOR gate

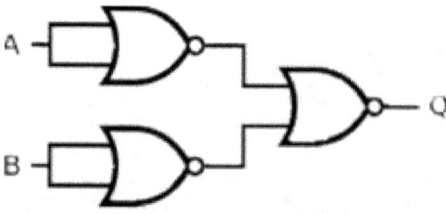

Input s are A and B

Output Q = A.B

c.   OR gate from NOR gate

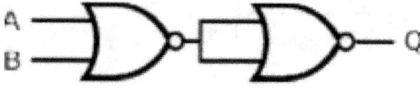

Inputs are A and B

Output Q = A+B

d.   NAND gate from NOR gate

Logic Gates

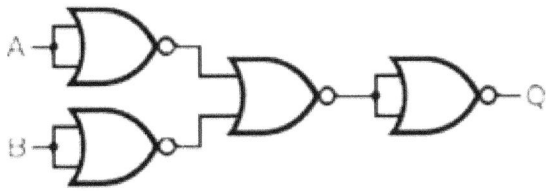

Inputs are A and B

Output Q = A.B

e. EX-OR gate from NOR gate

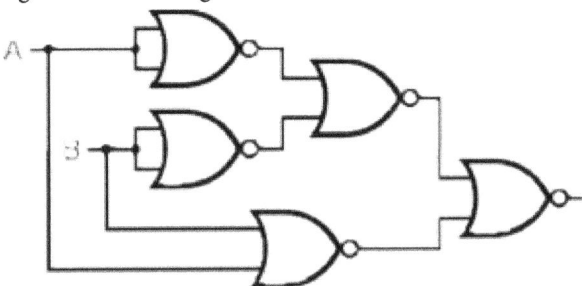

Inputs are A and B

Output Q = A B + A B

f. EX-NOR gate From NOR gate

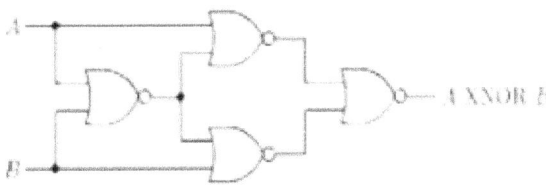

Inputs are A and B

Output Q = A B + A B

Threshold Logic

Introduction

- The threshold element, also called the threshold gate (T-gate) is a much more powerful device than any of the conventional logic gates such as NAND, NOR and others.
- Complex, large Boolean functions can be realized using much fewer threshold gates.

- Frequently a single threshold gate can realize a very complex function which otherwise might require a large number of conventional gates.
- T-gate offers incomparably economical realization; it has not found extensive use with the digital system designers mainly because of the following limitations.
  » It is very sensitive to parameter variations.
  » It is difficult to fabricate it in IC form.
  » The speed of switching of threshold elements is much lower than that of conventional gates.

The Threshold Elements

- A threshold element or gate has 'n' binary inputs $x_1, x_2, ..., x_n$; and a single binary output F. But in addition to those, it has two more parameters.
- Its parameters are a threshold T and weights $w_1, w_2, ..., w_n$. The weights $w_1, w_2, ..., w_n$ are associated with the input variables $x_1, x_2, ..., x_n$.
- The value of the threshold (T) and weights may be real, positive or negative numbers.
- The symbol of the threshold element is shown in fig.(a).
- It is represented by a circle partitioned into two parts, one part represents the weights and other represents T.
- It is defined as

$$F(x_1, x_2, ..., x_n) = 1 \text{ if and only if } \sum_{i=1}^{n} w_i x_i \geq T$$

otherwise

$$F(x_1, x_2, ..., x_n) = 0$$

- The sum and product operation avre normal arithmetic operations and the
- sum $\sum_{i=1}^{n} w_i x_i \geq T$ is called the weighted sum of the element or gate.

Logic Gates

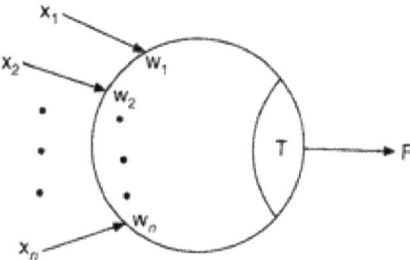

Example:

Obtain the minimal Boolean expression from the threshold gate shown in figure.

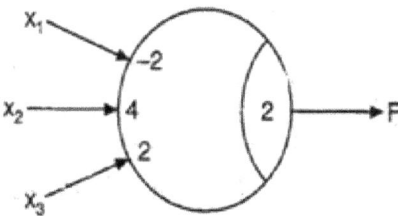

Solution:

The threshold gate has three inputs x_1, x_2, x_3 with weights -2 (w_1), 4 (w_2) and 2 (w_3) respectively. The value of threshold is 2 (T). The table shown is the weighted sums and outputs for all input combinations. For this threshold gate, the weighted sum is

$$w = w_1 x_1 + w_2 x_2 + w_3 x_3$$
$$= (-2)x_1 + (4)x_2 + (2)x_3$$
$$= -2x_1 + 4x_2 + 2x_3$$

The output F is logic 1 for $w \geq 2$ and it is logic 0 for $w < 2$

Input Variables			Weighted Sum	Output
x_1	x_2	x_3	$w = -2x_1 + 4x_2 + 2x_3$	F
0	0	0	0	0
0	0	1	2	1
0	1	0	4	1
0	1	1	6	1
1	0	0	-2	0
1	0	1	0	0

| 1 | 1 | 0 | 2 | | 1 |
| 1 | 1 | 1 | 4 | | 1 |

From the input – output relation is given in the table, the Boolean expression for the output is $F=\Sigma\, m\,(1, 2, 3, 6, 7)$.

The K-map for F is

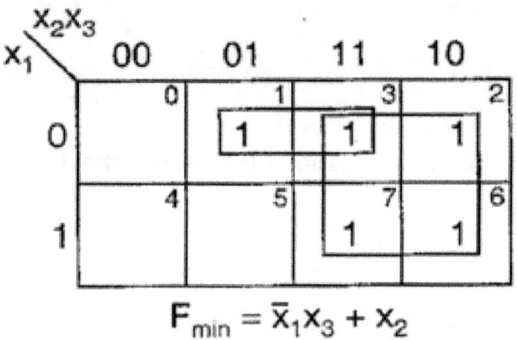

$$F_{min} = \overline{X}_1 X_3 + X_2$$

Universality of A T-Gate

- A single T-gate can realize a large number of functions by merely changing either the weights or the threshold or both, which can be done by altering the value of the corresponding resistors.

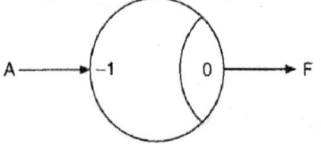

Input	Weighted sum	Output
A	W = –A	F
0	0	1
1	–1	0

(a) NOT gate $F = \overline{A}$

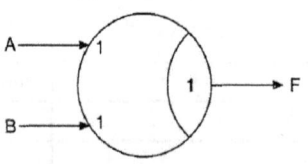

Inputs		Weighted sum	Output
A	B	W = A + B	F
0	0	0	0
0	1	1	1
1	0	1	1
1	1	2	1

(b) OR gate $F = A + B$

Inputs		Weighted sum	Output
A	B	W = A + B	F
0	0	0	0
0	1	1	0
1	0	1	0
1	1	2	1

(c) AND gate $F = AB$

- Since a threshold gate can realize universal gates, i.e., NAND gates and NOR gates, a threshold gate is also a universal gate.
- Single threshold gate cannot realize by a single T-gate
- Realization of logic gates using T-gates is shown in the below figure.

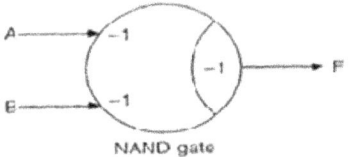

NAND gate
(d) $F = \bar{A} + \bar{B} = \overline{AB}$

Inputs		Weighted sum	Output
A	B	w = -A - B	F
0	0	0	1
0	1	-1	1
1	0	-1	1
1	1	-2	0

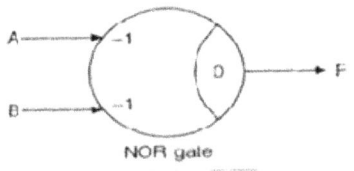

NOR gate
(e) $F = \bar{A} \cdot \bar{B} = \overline{A + B}$

Inputs		Weighted sum	Output
A	B	w = -A - B	F
0	0	0	1
0	1	-1	0
1	0	-1	0
1	1	-2	0

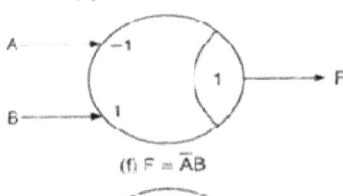

(f) $F = \bar{A}B$

Inputs		Weighted sum	Output
A	B	w = -A + B	F
0	0	0	0
0	1	1	1
1	0	-1	0
1	1	0	0

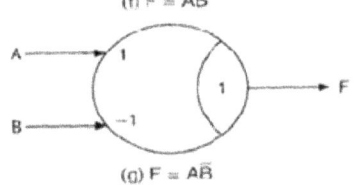

(g) $F = A\bar{B}$

Inputs		Weighted sum	Output
A	B	w = A - B	F
0	0	0	0
0	1	-1	0
1	0	1	1
1	1	0	0

Chapter 15
Boolean Algebra

Introduction
- Switching circuits are also called logic circuits, gates circuits and digital circuits.
- Switching algebra is also called Boolean algebra.
- Boolean algebra is a system of mathematical logic. It is an algebraic system consisting of the set of elements (0,1), two binary operators called OR and AND and a unary operator called NOT.
- It is the basic mathematical tool in the analysis and synthesis of switching circuits.
- It is a way to express logic functions algebraically.
- Any complex logic can be expressed by a Boolean function.
- The Boolean algebra is governed by certain well developed rules and laws.

Axioms and Laws of Boolean Algebra

Axioms or postulates of Boolean algebra are a set of logical expressions that are accepted without proof and upon which we can build a set of useful theorems. Actually, axioms are nothing more than the definitions of the three basic logic operations AND, OR and INVERTER. Each axiom can be interpreted as the outcome of an operation performed by a logic gate.

AND operation	OR operation	NOT operation
Axiom 1: $0 \cdot 0 = 0$	Axiom 5: $0 + 0 = 0$	Axiom 9: $\overline{1} = 0$
Axiom 2: $0 \cdot 1 = 0$ Axiom 3: $1 \cdot 0 = 0$ Axiom 2: $1 \cdot 1 = 1$	Axiom 6: $0 + 1 = 1$ Axiom 7: $1 + 0 = 1$ Axiom 8: $1 + 1 = 1$	Axiom 10: $\overline{0} = 1$

1. **Complementation Laws:** The term complement simply means to invert, i.e. to change 0s to 1s and 1s to 0s. The five laws of complementation are as follows:

Law 1: $\overline{0} = 1$

Law 2: $\overline{1} = 0$

Law 3: if $A = 0$, then $\overline{A} = 1$

Law 4: if $A = 1$, then $\overline{A} = 0$

Law 5: $\overline{\overline{A}} = 0$ (double complementation law)

2. **OR Laws:** The four OR laws are as follows

   Law 1: $A + 0 = 0$ (Null law)

   Law 2: $A + 1 = 1$ (Identity law)

   Law 3: $A + A = A$

   Law 4: $A + \overline{A} = 1$

3. **AND Laws:** The four AND laws are as follows

   Law 1: $A \cdot 0 = 0$ (Null law)

   Law 2: $A \cdot 1 = 1$ (Identity law)

   Law 3: $A \cdot A = A$

   Law 4: $A \cdot \overline{A} = 0$

4. **Commutative Laws:** Commutative laws allow change in position of AND or OR variables. There are two commutative laws.

   Law 1: $A + B = B + A$

   Proof:

A	B	A + B
0	0	0
0	1	1
1	0	1
1	1	1

   =

B	A	B + A
0	0	0
0	1	1
1	0	1
1	1	1

   Law 2: $A \cdot B = B \cdot A$

   Proof:

A	B	A . B
0	0	0
0	1	0
1	0	0
1	1	1

   =

B	A	B . A
0	0	0
0	1	0
1	0	0
1	1	1

This law can be extended to any number of variables. For example
A.B. C = B. C. A = C. A. B = B. A. C

5. **Associative Laws:** The associative laws allow grouping of variables. There are 2 associative laws.

Law 1: $(A + B) + C = A + (B + C)$

Proof:

A	B	C	A+B	(A+B)+C
0	0	0	0	0
0	0	1	0	1
0	1	0	1	1
0	1	1	1	1
1	0	0	1	1
1	0	1	1	1
1	1	0	1	1
1	1	1	1	1

=

A	B	C	B+C	A+(B+C)
0	0	0	0	0
0	0	1	1	1
0	1	0	1	1
0	1	1	1	1
1	0	0	0	1
1	0	1	1	1
1	1	0	1	1
1	1	1	1	1

Law 2: $(A. B) C = A (B .C)$

Proof:

A	B	C	AB	(AB)C
0	0	0	0	0
0	0	1	0	0
0	1	0	0	0
0	1	1	0	0
1	0	0	0	0
1	0	1	0	0
1	1	0	1	0
1	1	1	1	1

=

A	B	C	B.C	A(B.C)
0	0	0	0	0
0	0	1	0	0
0	1	0	0	0
0	1	1	1	0
1	0	0	0	0
1	0	1	0	0
1	1	0	0	0
1	1	1	1	1

This law can be extended to any number of variables. For example, A(BCD) = (ABC)D = (AB) (CD)

6. **Distributive Laws:** The distributive laws allow factoring or multiplying out of expressions. There are two distributive laws.

Law 1: $A (B + C) = AB + AC$

Proof:

A	B	C	B+C	A(B+C)
0	0	0	0	0
0	0	1	1	0
0	1	0	1	0
0	1	1	1	0
1	0	0	0	0
1	0	1	1	1
1	1	0	1	1
1	1	1	1	1

=

A	B	C	AB	AC	A+(B+C)
0	0	0	0	0	0
0	0	1	0	0	0
0	1	0	0	0	0
0	1	1	0	0	0
1	0	0	0	0	0
1	0	1	0	1	1
1	1	0	1	0	1
1	1	1	1	1	1

Law 2: A + BC = (A+B) (A+C)

Proof:

RHS = (A+B) (A+C)

= AA + AC + BA + BC

= A + AC + AB + BC

= A (1+ C + B) + BC

= A . 1 + BC   (1 +C + B = 1 + B = 1)

= A + BC

= LHS

7. **Redundant Literal Rule (RLR):**

Law 1: A + AB = A + B

Proof:

A + AB = (A + A) (A + B)

= 1 . (A + B)

= A +B

Law 2: A(A + B) = AB

Proof:

A(Ā+B) = AĀ+AB

= 0+AB

= AB

8. **Idempotence Laws:**

Idempotence means the same value.

Law 1: A . A = A

Boolean Algebra

Proof:

If A = 0, then A. A = 0. 0 = 0 = A

If A = 1, then A. A = 1. 1 = 1 = A

This law states that AND of a variable with itself is equal to that variable only.

Law 2: A + A = A

Proof:

If A = 0, then A + A = 0 + 0 = 0 = A

If A = 1, then A + A = 1 + 1 = 1 = A

This law states that OR of a variable with itself is equal to that variable only.

9. **Absorption Laws:** There are two laws:

Law 1: A + A · B = A

Proof: A + A · B = A (1 + B) = A · 1 = A

A	B	AB	A+AB
0	0	0	0
0	1	0	0
1	0	0	1
1	1	1	1

Law 2: A (A + B) = A

Proof:

A (A + B) = A · A + A · B = A + AB = A(1 + B) = A · 1 = A

A	B	A+B	A(A+B)
0	0	0	0
0	1	1	0
1	0	1	1
1	1	1	1

10. **Consensus Theorem (Included Factor Theorem):**

Theorem 1:

AB + AC + BC = AB + AC

Proof:

LHS = AB + $\underline{A}$C + BC

= AB + AC + BC ($\bar{A}$+A)

$$= AB + AC + BCA + BCA$$
$$= AB(1+C) + AC(1+B)$$
$$= AB(1) + AC(1)$$
$$= AB + AC$$
$$= RHS$$

Theorem 2:

$(A+B)(\bar{A}+C)(B+C) = (A+B)(\bar{A}+C)$

Proof

LHS $= (A+B)(\bar{A}+C)(B+C)$
$= (A\bar{A}+AC+B\bar{A}+BC)(B+C)$
$= (AC+B\bar{C}+AB)(B+C)$
$= ABC+B\bar{C}+AB+AC+B\bar{C}+ABC$
$= AC+B\bar{C}+AB$

RHS $= (A+B)(\bar{A}+C)$
$= A\bar{A}+AC+B\bar{C}+AB$
$= AC+B\bar{C}+AB$
$= LHS$

11. **Transposition Theorem**

    Theorem:

    $AB + \bar{A}C = (A+C)(\bar{A}+B)$

    Proof:

    RHS $= (A+C)(\bar{A}+B)$
    $= A\bar{A}+C\bar{A}+AB+CB$
    $= 0+\bar{A}C+AB+BC$
    $= \bar{A}C+AB+BC(A+\bar{A})$
    $= AB+ABC+\bar{A}C+\bar{A}BC$
    $= AB+\bar{A}C$
    $= LHS$

12. **De Morgan's Theorem**

    De Morgan's theorem represents two laws in Boolean algebra.

Law 1: $\overline{A+B} = \bar{A} + \bar{B}$

Proof:

A	B	A + B	$\overline{A + B}$
0	0	0	1
0	1	1	0
1	0	1	0
1	1	1	0

=

A	B	$\bar{A}$	$\bar{B}$	$\bar{A}\bar{B}$
0	0	1	1	1
0	1	1	0	0
1	0	0	1	0
1	1	0	0	0

This law states that the complement of a sum of variables is equal to the product of their individual complements.

Law 2: $\overline{A \cdot B} = \bar{A} + \bar{B}$

Proof:

A	B	A.B	$\overline{A.B}$
0	0	0	1
0	1	0	1
1	0	0	1
1	1	1	0

=

A	B	$\bar{A}$	$\bar{B}$	$\bar{A}+\bar{B}$
0	0	1	1	1
0	1	1	0	1
1	0	0	1	1
1	1	0	0	0

This law states that the complement of a product of variables is equal to the sum of their individual complements.

Duality

The implication of the duality concept is that once a theorem or statement is proved, the dual also thus stands proved. This is called the principle of duality.

$[f(A, B, C,...., 0, 1, +, \cdot)]d = f(A, B, C, ... 1, 0, \cdot, +)$

Relations between complement and dual

$f_c(A, B, C, ...) = f(\bar{A}, \bar{B}, \bar{C}, ...) = f_d(\bar{A}, \bar{B}, \bar{C},....)$

$f_d(A, B, C, ...) = f(\bar{A}, \bar{B}, \bar{C}, ...) = f_c(\bar{A}, \bar{B}, \bar{C}, ...)$

The first relation states that the complement of a function f(A, B, C, ...) can be obtained by complementing all the variables in the dual function f_d (A, B, C, ...).

The second relation states that the dual can be obtained by complementing all the literals in f (A, B, C, ...).

Duals

Given expression	Dual
1. $\bar{0} = 1$	$\bar{1} = 0$
2. $0 \cdot 1 = 0$	$1 + 0 = 1$
3. $0 \cdot 0 = 0$	$1 + 1 = 1$
4. $1 \cdot 1 = 1$	$0 + 0 = 0$
5. $A \cdot 0 = 0$	$A + 1 = 1$
6. $A \cdot 1 = A$	$A + 0 = A$
7. $A \cdot A = A$	$A + A = A$
8. $A \cdot \bar{A} = 0$	$A + \bar{A} = 1$
9. $A \cdot B = B \cdot A$	$A + B = B + A$
10. $A \cdot (B \cdot C) = (A \cdot B) \cdot C$	$A + (B + C) = (A + B) + C$
11. $A \cdot (B + C) = AB + AC$	$A + BC = (A + B)(A + C)$
12. $A(A + B) = A$	$A + AB = A$
13. $A \cdot (\bar{A} \cdot B) = A \cdot B$	$A + \bar{A} + B = A + B$
14. $\overline{AB} = \bar{A} + \bar{B}$	$\overline{A + B} = \bar{A} \bar{B}$
15. $(A + B)(\bar{A} + C)(B + C) = (A + B)(\bar{A} + C)$	$AB + \bar{A}C + BC = AB + \bar{A}C$
16. $A + \bar{B}C = (A + \bar{B})(A + C)$	$A(\bar{B} + C) = A\bar{B} + AC$
17. $(A+C)(\bar{A}+B) = AB + \bar{A}C$	$AC + \bar{A}B = (A+B)(\bar{A}+C)$
18. $(A+B)(C+D) = AC + AD + BC + BD$	$(AB+CD) = (A+C)(A+D)(B+C)(B+D)$
19. $A + B = AB + \bar{A}B + A\bar{B}$	$AB = (A+B)(\bar{A}+B)(A+\bar{B})$
20. $\overline{AB} + \bar{A} + AB = 0$	$\overline{A + B} \cdot \bar{A} \cdot (A + B) = 1$

Sum - of - Products Form

- This is also called Disjunctive Canonical Form (DCF) or Expanded Sum of Products Form or Canonical Sum of Products Form.
- In this form, the function is the sum of a number of products terms where each product term contains all variables of the function either in complemented or uncomplemented form.
- This can also be derived from the truth table by finding the sum of all the terms that correspond to those combinations for which 'f' assumes the value 1.

For example:

$f(A,B,C) = \bar{A}B + \bar{B}C$

$= \bar{A}B (C+\bar{C}) + \bar{B}C (A+\bar{A})$

$= \bar{A}\bar{B}C + \bar{A}B\bar{C} + \bar{A}BC + A\bar{B}C$

- The product term which contains all the variables of the functions either in complimented or uncomplemented form is called a minterm.
- The minterm is denoted as m_0, m_1, m_2 ....

- An 'n' variable function can have 2n minterms.
- Another way of representing the function in canonical SOP form is by showing the sum of minterms for which the function equals 1.

For example

$f(A, B, C) = m_1 + m_2 + m_3 + m_5$

or

$f(A, B, C) = \Sigma m(1, 2, 3, 5)$

where Σm represents the sum of all the minterms whose decimal codes are given the parenthesis.

Product- of - Sums Form

- This form is also called Conjunctive Canonical Form (CCF) or Expanded Product - of – Sums Form or Canonical Product Of Sums Form.
- This is by considering the combinations for which f = 0
- Each term is a sum of all the variables.

The function

$(A,B,C) = (\bar{A}+\bar{B}+C\cdot\bar{C}) + (A+B+C\cdot\bar{C})$

$= (\bar{A}+\bar{B}+C) + (A+\bar{B}+\bar{C})(A+B+C)(A+B+\bar{C})$

The sum term which contains each of the 'n' variables in either complemented or uncomplemented form is called a maxterm.

Maxterm is represented as $M_0, M_1, M_2, \ldots$

Thus, CCF of 'f' may be written as:

$f(A, B, C) = M_0 \cdot M_4 \cdot M_6 \cdot M_7$

or

$f(A, B, C) = (0, 4, 6, 7)$

Where represented the product of all maxterms.

Conversion Between Canonical Form

The complement of a function expressed as the sum of minterms equals the sum of minterms missing from the original function.

Example

$f(A, B, C) = \Sigma m(0,2,4,6,7)$

This has a complement that can be expressed as

$f(\overline{A, B, C}) = \Sigma m(1, 3, 5) = m_1 + m_3 + m_5$

If we complement f by De-Morgan's theorem we obtain 'f' in a form.

$f = \overline{(m_1 + m_3 + m_5)} = \overline{m_1} \cdot \overline{m_3} \cdot \overline{m_5}$

$= M1\ M3\ M5 = \prod M(1, 3, 5)$

Example

Expand $A(A+B)(A+B+C)$ to maxterms and minterms.

Solution:

In POS form

$A(A+B)(\bar{A}+B+\bar{C})$

$A = A + B\bar{B} + C\bar{C}$

$= (A+B)(A+\bar{B}) + C\bar{C}$

$= (A+B+C\bar{C})(A+\bar{B}+C\bar{C})$

$= (A+B+C)(A+B+\bar{C})(A+\bar{B}+C)(A+\bar{B}+\bar{C})\ A$

$= A + B + C\bar{C}$

$= (\bar{A} + B + C)(\bar{A} + B + \bar{C})$

Therefore,

$A(\bar{A}+B)(A+B+\bar{C})$

$= (A+B+C)(A+B+\bar{C})(A+\bar{B}+C)(A+\bar{B}+\bar{C})(\bar{A}+\bar{B}+C)(\bar{A}+\bar{B}+\bar{C})$

$= (000)(001)(010)(011)(100)(101)$

$= M_0 \cdot M_1 \cdot M_2 \cdot M_3 \cdot M_4 \cdot M_5$

$= \prod M(0, 1, 2, 3, 4, 5)$

The maxterms M6 and M7 are missing in the POS form.

So, the SOP form will contain the minterms 6 and 7

Karnaugh Map or K-Map

- The K-map is a chart or a graph, composed of an arrangement of adjacent cells, each representing a particular combination of variables in sum or product form.
- The K-map is a systematic method of simplifying the Boolean expression.

Two Variable K-Map

A two variable expression can have $2^2 = 4$ possible combinations of the input variables A and B.

Mapping of SOP Expression

- The 2 variable K-map has 22 = 4 squares. These squares are called cells.
- A '1' placed in any square indicates that the corresponding minterm is included in the output expression, and a 0 or no entry in any square indicates that the corresponding minterm does not appear in the expression for output.

	B=0	B=1
A=0	$\bar{A}\bar{B}$	$\bar{A}B$
A=1	$A\bar{B}$	AB

Example

Map expression $f = \bar{A}B + A\bar{B}$

Solution: -

The expression minterms is

$F = m_1 + m_2 = m(1, 2)$

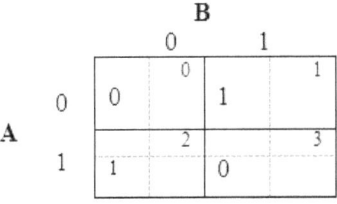

Minimization of SOP Expression

To minimize a Boolean expression given in the SOP form by using K- map, the adjacent squares having 1s, that is minterms adjacent to each other are combined to form larger squares to eliminate some variables.

The possible minterm grouping in a two variable K- map are shown below

- Two minterms, which are adjacent to each other, can be combined to form a bigger square called 2 – square or a pair. This eliminates one variable that is not common to both the minterms.
- Two 2-squares adjacent to each other can be combined to form a 4- square. A 4- square eliminates 2 variables. A 4-square is called a quad.
- Consider only those variables which remain constant throughout the square, and ignore the variables which are varying. The non-complemented variable is the variable remaining constant as 1. The complemented variable

is the variable remaining constant as a 0 and the variables are written as a product term.

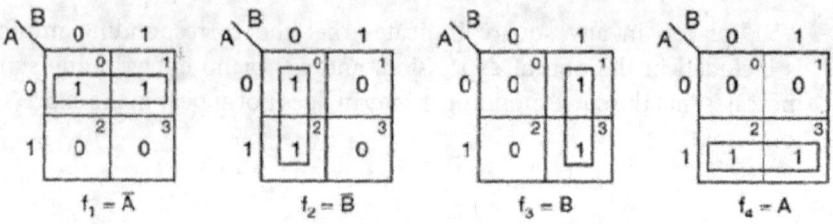

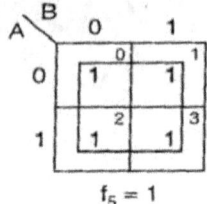

Example

Reduce the expression using mapping.

Solution:

Expressed in terms of minterms, the given expression is

$f = m_0 + m_1 + m_3 = m(0, 1, 3)$

$f = \bar{A} + B$

$F = A + B$

Mapping of POS Expression

Each sum term in the standard POS expression is called a Maxterm. A function in two variables (A, B) has 4 possible maxterms,

A+B, A+B̄, Ā+B and Ā+B̄. They are represented as M0, M1, M2 and M3 respectively.

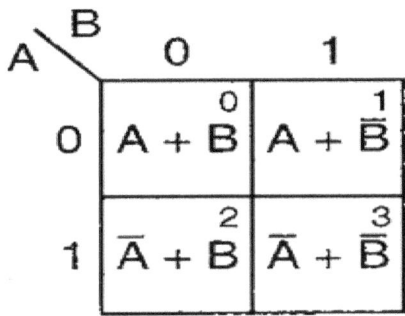

The maxterm of a two variable K-map

Example

Plot the expression f= (A + B)(A + B)(A + B)

Solution:

Expression in terms of maxterms is f = πM (0, 2, 3)

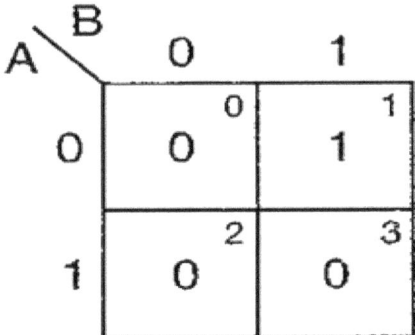

Minimization of POS Expressions

In POS form the adjacent 0s are combined into as large squares as possible. If the squares have a complemented variable then the value remains constant as a 1 and the non-complemented variable if its value remains constant as a 0 along the entire square and then their sum term is written.

The possible maxterms grouping in a two variable K-map are shown below

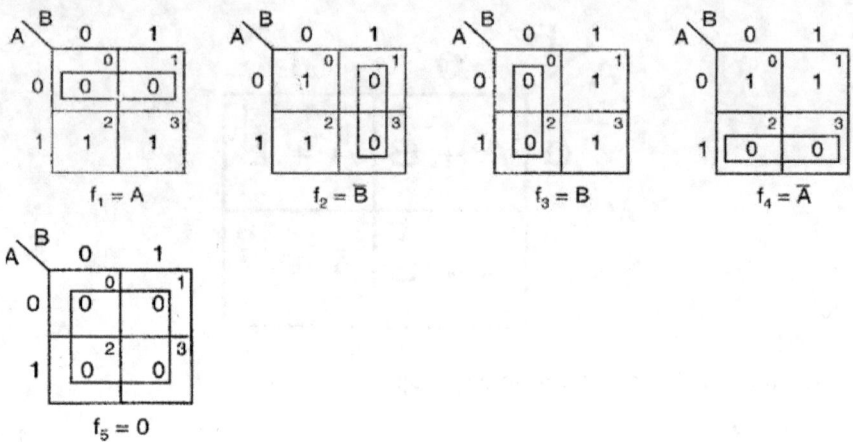

Example
Reduce the expression $f = (A+\bar{B})(\bar{A}+\bar{B})(A+B)$ using mapping

Solution:

The given expression in terms of maxterms is $f = \pi M(0, 1, 3)$

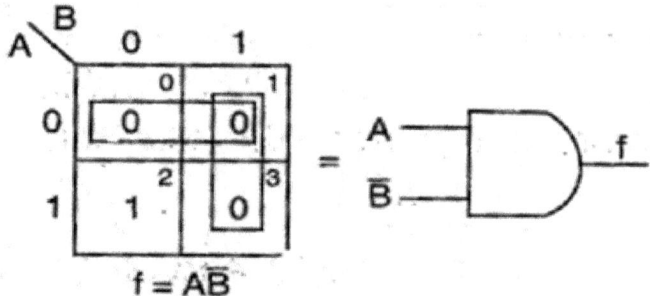

Three Variable K-MAP
A function in three variables (A, B, C) can be expressed in SOP and POS form having eight possible combinations. A three variable K-map has 8 squares or cells and each square minterm or maxterm is shown in the Figure below

Example
Map the expression $f = \bar{A}\bar{B}C + A\overline{BC} + A\bar{B}C + \bar{A}BC + \bar{A}BC$

Solution:

Minimization of SOP and POS Expressions

For reducing the Boolean expressions in SOP (POS) form the following steps are given below

- Draw the K-map and place 1s (0s) corresponding to the minterms (maxterms) of the SOP (POS) expression.
- In the map 1s (0s) which are not adjacent to any other 1(0) are the isolated minterms (maxterms). They are to be read as they are because they cannot be combined even into a 2-square.
- For those 1s (0s) which are adjacent to only one other 1(0) make them pairs (2 squares).
- For quads (4- squares) and octet (8 squares) of adjacent 1s (0s) even if they contain some 1s (0s) which have already been combined. They must geometrically form a square or a rectangle.
- For any 1s (0s) that have not been combined yet then combine them into bigger squares if possible.
- Form the minimal expression by summing (multiplying) the product (sum) terms of all the groups.

Some of the possible combinations of minterms in SOP form

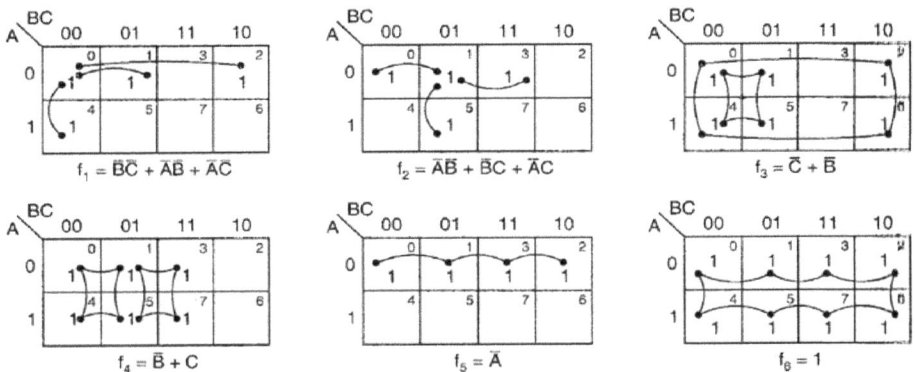

These possible combinations are also for POS but 1s are replaced by 0s.

Four Variable K-Map

A four variable (A, B, C, D) expression can have 24 = 16 possible combinations of input variables. A four variable K-map has 24 = 16 squares or cells and each square on the map represents either a minterm or a maxterm as shown in the figure below. The binary number designations of the rows and columns are in the gray code. The binary numbers along the top of the map indicate the conditions of C and D along any column and binary numbers along the left side indicate the conditions of A and B along any row. The numbers in the top right corners of the squares indicate the minterm or maxterm designations.

Sop Form

AB\CD	00	01	11	10
00	$\bar{A}\bar{B}\bar{C}\bar{D}$ (m_0) [0]	$\bar{A}\bar{B}\bar{C}D$ (m_1) [1]	$\bar{A}\bar{B}CD$ (m_3) [3]	$\bar{A}\bar{B}C\bar{D}$ (m_2) [2]
01	$\bar{A}B\bar{C}\bar{D}$ (m_4) [4]	$\bar{A}B\bar{C}D$ (m_5) [5]	$\bar{A}BCD$ (m_7) [7]	$\bar{A}BC\bar{D}$ (m_6) [6]
11	$AB\bar{C}\bar{D}$ (m_{12}) [12]	$AB\bar{C}D$ (m_{13}) [13]	$ABCD$ (m_{15}) [15]	$ABC\bar{D}$ (m_{14}) [14]
10	$A\bar{B}\bar{C}\bar{D}$ (m_8) [8]	$A\bar{B}\bar{C}D$ (m_9) [9]	$A\bar{B}CD$ (m_{11}) [11]	$A\bar{B}C\bar{D}$ (m_{10}) [10]

SOP form

So, in the SOP form the expression is $f = \Sigma m (1, 5, 2, 6, 7)$

A\BC	00	01	11	10
0	0 [0]	1 [1]	0 [3]	1 [2]
1	0 [4]	1 [5]	1 [7]	1 [6]

Example

Map the expression $f = (A+B+C)(\bar{A}+B+C)(\bar{A}+\bar{B}+\bar{C})(\bar{A}+B+\bar{C})(\bar{A}+\bar{B}+C)$

Solution:

So, in the POS form the expression is $f = \pi M (0, 5, 7, 3, 6)$

BC				
A	00	01	11	10
0	0 (0)	1 (1)	0 (3)	1 (2)
1	1 (4)	0 (5)	0 (7)	0 (6)

POS FORM

AB\CD	00	01	11	10
00	$A+B+C+D$ (M_0)	$A+B+C+\bar{D}$ (M_1)	$A+B+\bar{C}+\bar{D}$ (M_3)	$A+B+\bar{C}+D$ (M_2)
01	$A+\bar{B}+C+D$ (M_4)	$A+\bar{B}+C+\bar{D}$ (M_5)	$A+\bar{B}+\bar{C}+\bar{D}$ (M_7)	$A+\bar{B}+\bar{C}+D$ (M_6)
11	$\bar{A}+\bar{B}+C+D$ (M_{12})	$\bar{A}+\bar{B}+C+\bar{D}$ (M_{13})	$\bar{A}+\bar{B}+\bar{C}+\bar{D}$ (M_{15})	$\bar{A}+\bar{B}+\bar{C}+D$ (M_{14})
10	$\bar{A}+B+C+D$ (M_8)	$\bar{A}+B+C+\bar{D}$ (M_9)	$\bar{A}+B+\bar{C}+\bar{D}$ (M_{11})	$\bar{A}+B+\bar{C}+D$ (M_{10})

Minimization of SOP and POS Expressions

For reducing the Boolean expressions in SOP (POS) form the following steps are given below

- Draw the K-map and place 1s (0s) corresponding to the minterms (maxterms) of the SOP (POS) expression.
- In the map 1s (0s) which are not adjacent to any other 1(0) are the isolated minterms (maxterms). They are to be read as they are because they cannot be combined even into a 2-square.
- For those 1s (0s) which are adjacent to only one other 1(0) make them pairs (2 squares).
- For quads (4- squares) and octet (8 squares) of adjacent 1s (0s) even if they contain some 1s (0s) which have already been combined. They must geometrically form a square or a rectangle.

- For any 1s (0s) that have not been combined yet then combine them into bigger squares if possible.
- Form the minimal expression by summing (multiplying) the product (sum) terms of all the groups.

Example

Reduce using mapping the expression $f = \Sigma\, m\, (0, 1, 2, 3, 5, 7, 8, 9, 10, 12, 13)$

Solution:

The given expression in POS form is $f = \pi\, M\, (4, 6, 11, 14, 15)$ and in SOP form $f = \Sigma\, m\, (0, 1, 2, 3, 5, 7, 8, 9, 10, 12, 13)$

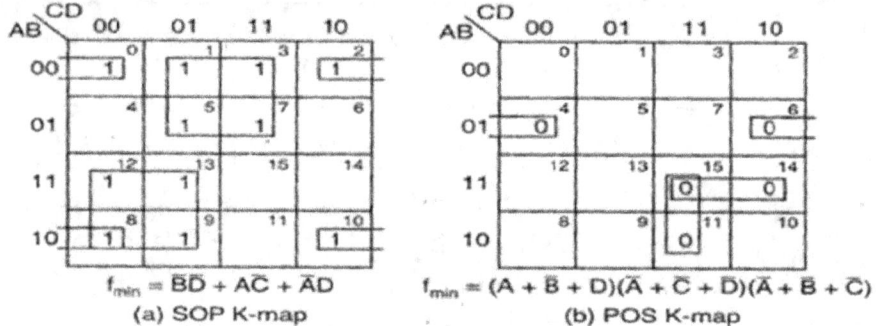

The minimal SOP expression is $f_{min} = BD + AC + AD$

The minimal POS expression is $f_{min} = (\bar{A}+\bar{B}+\bar{D})\,(\bar{A} + C + \bar{D})\,(A + B + C)$

Don't Care Combinations

The combinations for which the values of the expression are not specified are called don't care combinations or optional combinations and such expressions stand incompletely specified. The output is don't care for these invalid combinations. The don't care terms are denoted by d or X. During the process of designing using SOP maps, each don't care is treated as 1 to reduce the map, otherwise it is treated as 0 and left alone. During the process of designing using POS maps, each don't care is treated as 0 to reduce the map, otherwise it is treated as 1 and left alone.

A standard SOP expression with don't cares can be converted into standard POS form by keeping the don't cares as they are, and the missing minterms of the SOP form are written as the maxterms of the POS form. Similarly, to convert a standard POS expression with don't cares can be converted into standard SOP form by keeping the don't cares as they are, and the missing maxterms of the POS form are written as the minterms of the SOP form.

Example

Reduce the expression f = Σ m(1, 5, 6, 12, 13, 14) + d(2, 4) using K- map.
Solution:

The given expression in SOP form is f = Σ m (1, 5, 6, 12, 13, 14) + d(2, 4)

The given expression in POS form is f = π M (0, 3, 7, 8, 9, 10, 11,15) + d(2, 4)

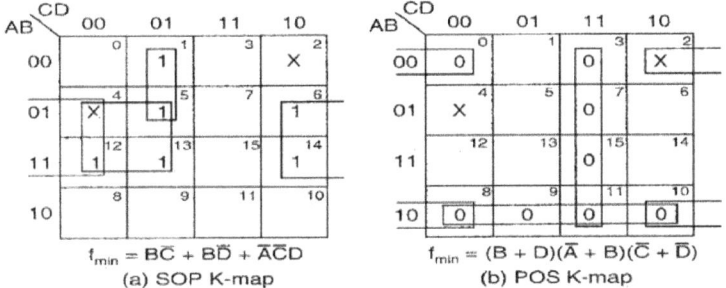

(a) SOP K-map   (b) POS K-map

The minimal of SOP expression is f_{min} = BC + B$\bar{D}$ +$\bar{A}$CD

The minimal of POS expression is f_{min} = (B + D)(A + $\bar{B}$) (C + $\bar{D}$)

Note: *f and F can be used interchangeably*

Chapter 16
Sequential Logic Circuit

Sequential Circuit
- It is a circuit whose output depends upon the present input, previous output and the sequence in which the inputs are applied.

How The Sequential Circuit is Different From Combinational Circuit?
- In combinational circuit output depends upon present input at any instant of time and does not use memory. Hence previous input does not have any effect on the circuit. But a sequential circuit has memory and depends upon present input and previous output.
- Sequential circuits are slower than combinational circuits and these sequential circuits are harder to design.

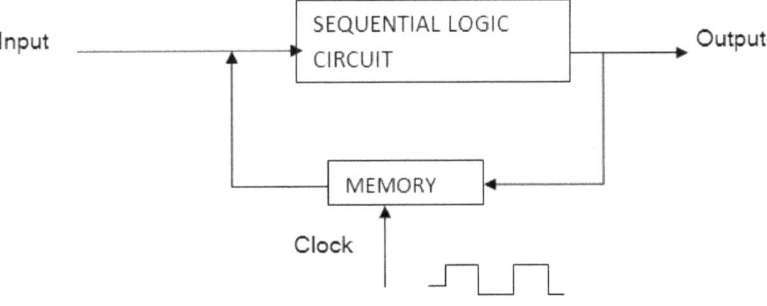

[Block diagram of Sequential Logic Circuit]

- The data stored by the memory element at any given instant of time is called the present state of a sequential circuit.

Types
Sequential Logic Circuits (SLC) are classified as:

a. Synchronous SLC
b. Asynchronous SLC
- The SLC that are controlled by clock are called synchronous SLC and those which are not controlled by a clock are asynchronous SLC.
- Clock: A recurring pulse is called a clock.

Flip-Flop and Latch

- A flip-flop or latch is a circuit that has two stable states and can be used to store information.
- A flip-flop is a binary storage device capable of storing one bit of information. In a stable state, the output of a flip-flop is either 0 or 1.
- Latch is a non-clocked flip-flop and it is the building block for the flip-flop.
- A storage element in a digital circuit can maintain a binary state indefinitely until directed by an input signal to switch state.
- Storage elements that operate with signal level are called latches and those that operate with clock transitions are called flip-flops.
- The circuit can be made to change state by signals applied to one or more control inputs and will have one or two outputs.
- A flip-flop is called so because its output either flips or flops meaning to switch back and forth.
- A flip-flop is also called a bi-stable multi-vibrator as it has two stable states. The input signals which command the flip-flop to change state are called excitations.
- Flip-flops are storage devices and can store 1 or 0.
- Flip-flops using the clock signal are called clocked flip-flops. Control signals are effective only if they are applied in synchronization with the clock signal.
- Clock-signals may be positive-edge triggered or negative-edge triggered.
- Positive-edge triggered flip-flops are those in which state transitions take place only at the positive- going edge of the clock pulse.

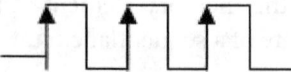

- Negative-edge triggered flip-flops are those in which state transitions take place only at the negative- going edge of the clock pulse.

- Negative-edge triggered flip-flops are those in which state transitions take place only at negative- going edge of the clock pulse.

- Some common type of flip-flops includes
    » SR (set-reset) F-F
    » D (data or delay) F-F
    » T (toggle) F-F and
    » JK F-F

SR latch

- The SR latch is a circuit with two cross-coupled NOR gates or two cross-coupled NAND gates.
- It has two outputs labeled Q and Q'. Two inputs are there labeled S for set and R for reset.
- The latch has two useful states. When Q=0 and Q'=1 the condition is called reset state and when Q=1 and Q'=0 the condition is called set state.
- Normally Q and Q' are complements of each other.
- The figure represents a SR latch with two cross-coupled NOR gates. The circuit has NOR gates and as we know if any one of the inputs for a NOR gate is HIGH then its output will be LOW and if both the inputs are LOW then only the output will be HIGH.

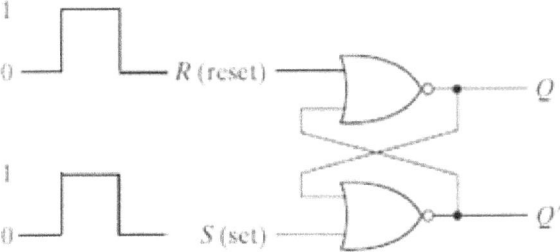

- Under normal conditions, both inputs of the latch remain at 0 unless the state has to be changed. The application of a momentary 1 to the S input causes the latch to go to the set state. The S input must go back to 0 before any other changes take place, in order to avoid the occurrence of an undefined next state that results from the forbidden input condition.

- The first condition (S = 1, R = 0) is the action that must be taken by input S to bring the circuit to the set state. Removing the active input from S leaves the circuit in the same state. After both inputs return to 0, it is then possible to shift to the reset state by momentarily applying a 1 to the R input. The 1 can then be removed from R, whereupon the circuit remains in the reset state. When both inputs S and R are equal to 0, the latch can be in either the set or the reset state, depending on which input was most recently a 1.
- If a 1 is applied to both the S and R inputs of the latch, both outputs go to 0. This action produces an undefined next state, because the state that results from the input transitions depends on the order in which they return to 0. It also violates the requirement that outputs be the complement of each other. In normal operation, this condition is avoided by making sure that 1's are not applied to both inputs simultaneously.
- Truth table for SR latch designed with NOR gates is shown below.

Input		Output				Comment
S	R	Q	Q'	QNext	Q'Next	
0	0	0	1	0	1	No change
0	0	1	0	1	0	
0	1	0	1	0	1	Reset
0	1	1	0	0	1	
1	0	0	1	1	0	Set
1	0	1	0	1	0	
1	1	0	1	X	X	Prohibited state
1	1	1	0	X	X	

Symbol for SR NOR Latch

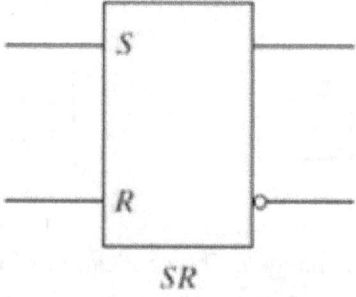

SR

Racing Condition

In case of a SR latch when S=R=1 input is given both the output will try to become 0. This is called Racing condition.

SR latch using NAND gate

- The below figure represents a SR latch with two cross-coupled NAND gates. The circuit has NAND gates and as we know if any one of the inputs for a NAND gate is LOW then its output will be HIGH and if both the inputs are HIGH then only the output will be LOW.
- It operates with both inputs normally at 1, unless the state of the latch has to be changed. The application of 0 to the S input causes output Q to go to 1, putting the latch in the set state. When the S input goes back to 1, the circuit remains in the set state. After both inputs go back to 1, we are allowed to change the state of the latch by placing a 0 in the R input. This action causes the circuit to go to the reset state and stay there even after both inputs return to 1.

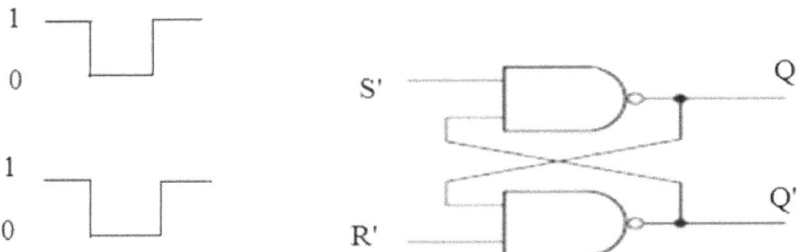

- The condition that is forbidden for the NAND latch is both inputs being equal to 0 at the same time, an input combination that should be avoided.

In comparing the NAND with the NOR latch, note that the input signals for the NAND require the complement of those values used for the NOR latch. Because the NAND latch requires a 0 signal to change its state, it is sometimes referred to as an S'R' latch. The primes (or, sometimes, bars over the letters) designate the fact that the inputs must be in their complement form to activate the circuit.

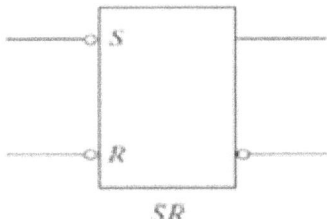

The above represents the symbol for inverted SR latch or SR latch using NAND gate. Truth table for SR latch using NAND gate or Inverted SR latch

S	R	Qnext	Q'next
0	0	Race	Race
0	1	0	1 (Reset)
1	0	1	0 (Set)
1	1	Q (No change)	Q' (No change)

D Latch

- One way to eliminate the undesirable condition of the indeterminate state in the SR latch is to ensure that inputs S and R are never equal to 1 at the same time.

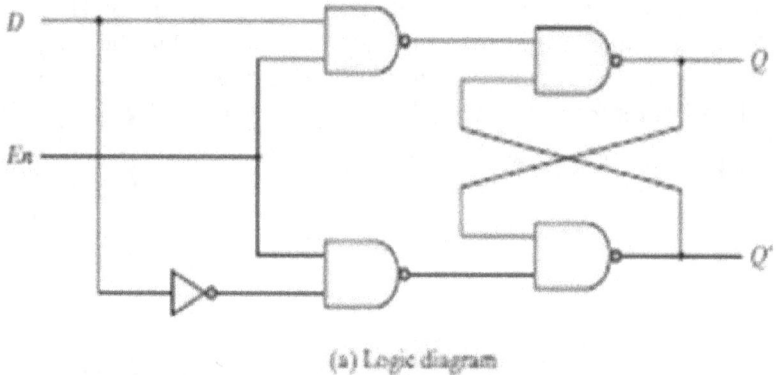

(a) Logic diagram

- This is done in the D latch. This latch has only two inputs: D (data) and En (enable).
- The D input goes directly to the S input, and its complement is applied to the R input.

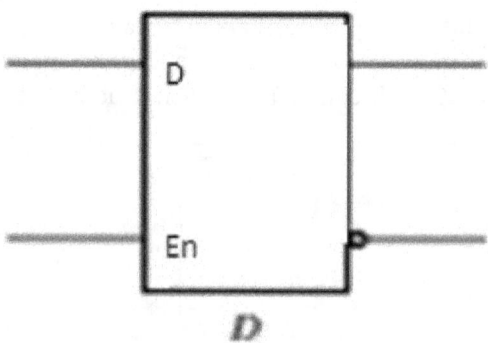

(Symbol for D-Latch)

Sequential Logic Circuit

- As long as the enable input is at 0, the cross-coupled SR latch has both inputs at the 1 level and the circuit can't change state regardless of the value of D.
- The below represents the truth table for the D-latch.

En	D	Next State of Q
0	X	No change
1	0	Q=0;Reset State
1	1	Q=1;Set State

The D input is sampled when En = 1. If D = 1, the Q output goes to 1, placing the circuit in the set state. If D = 0, output Q goes to 0, placing the circuit in the reset state. This situation provides a path from input D to the output, and for this reason, the circuit is often called a TRANSPARENT latch.

Triggering Methods

- The state of a latch or flip-flop is switched by a change in the control input. This momentary change is called a trigger, and the transition it causes is said to trigger the flip-flop.
- Flip-flop circuits are constructed in such a way as to make them operate properly when they are part of a sequential circuit that employs a common clock.
- The problem with the latch is that it responds to a change in the level of a clock pulse. For proper operation of a flip-flop it should be triggered only during a signal transition.

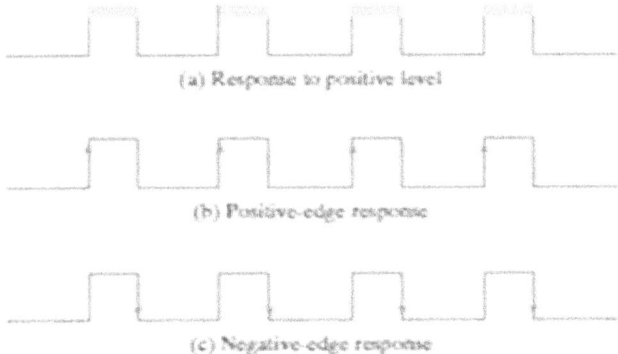

(a) Response to positive level

(b) Positive-edge response

(c) Negative-edge response

- This can be accomplished by eliminating the feedback path that is inherent in the operation of the sequential circuit using latches. A clock pulse goes through two transitions: from 0 to 1 and the return from 1 to 0.

- A way that a latch can be modified to form a flip-flop is to produce a flip-flop that triggers only during a signal transition (from 0 to 1 or from 1 to 0) of the synchronizing signal (clock) and is disabled during the rest of the clock pulse.

JK FLIP-FLOP

- The JK flip-flop can be constructed by using a basic SR latch and a clock. In this case the outputs Q and Q' are returned back and connected to the inputs of NAND gates.
- This simple JK flip Flop is the most widely used of all the flip-flop designs and is considered to be a universal flip-flop circuit.
- The sequential operation of the JK flip flop is exactly the same as for the previous SR flip-flop with the same "Set" and "Reset" inputs.
- The difference this time is that the "JK flip flop" has no invalid or forbidden input states of the SR Latch even when S and R are both at logic "1".

(The below diagram shows the circuit diagram of a JK flip-flop)

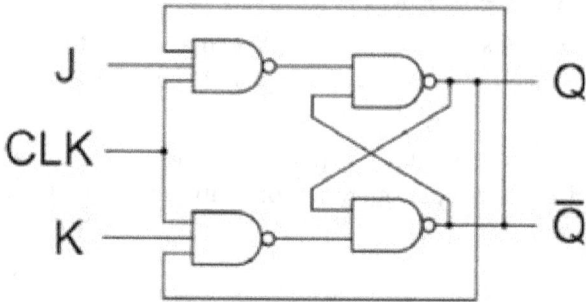

- The JK flip flop is basically a gated SR Flip-flop with the addition of a clock input circuitry that prevents the illegal or invalid output condition that can occur when both inputs S and R are equal to logic level "1".
- Due to this additional clocked input, a JK flip-flop has four possible input combinations, "logic 1", "logic 0", "no change" and "toggle".
- The symbol for a JK flip flop is similar to that of an SR bistable latch except the clock input.

Sequential Logic Circuit

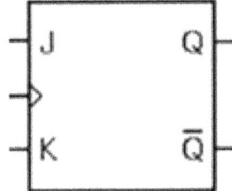

(The above diagram shows the symbol of a JK flip-flop.)

- Both the S and the R inputs of the SR bi-stable have now been replaced by two inputs called the J and K inputs, respectively after its inventor Jack and Kilby. Then this equates to: J = S and K = R.
- This cross coupling of the SR flip-flop allows the previously invalid condition of S = "1" and R = "1" state to be used to produce a "toggle action" as the two inputs are now interlocked.
- If the circuit is now "SET" the J input is inhibited by the "0" status of Q' through the lower NAND gate. If the circuit is "RESET" the K input is inhibited by the "0" status of Q through the upper NAND gate. As Q and Q' are always different we can use them to control the input.

(Truth table for JK flip-flop)

Input		Output		Comment
J	K	Q	Qnext	
0	0	0	0	No change
0	0	1	1	
0	1	0	0	Reset
0	1	1	0	
1	0	0	1	Set
1	0	1	1	
1	1	0	1	Toggle
1	1	1	0	

- When both inputs J and K are equal to logic "1", the JK flip flop toggles.

T Flip-Flop

- Toggle flip-flop or commonly known as T flip-flop.
- This flip-flop has the similar operation as that of the JK flip-flop with both the inputs J and K are shorted i.e. both are given the common input.

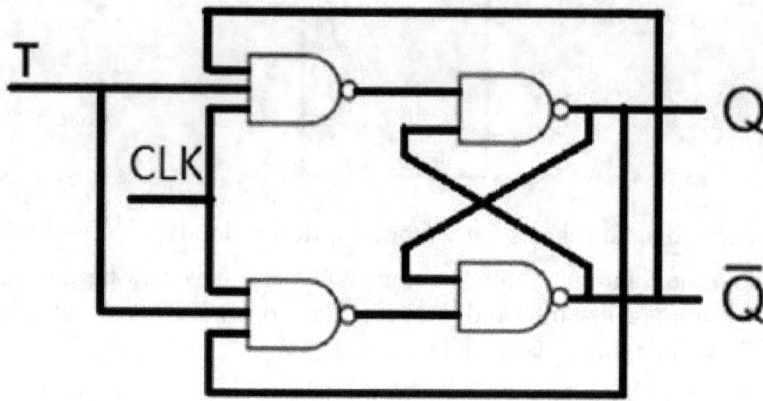

- Hence its truth table is the same as that of JK flip-flop when J=K= 0 and J=K=1. So its truth table is as follows.

T	Q	Qnext	Comment
0	0	0	No change
	1	1	
1	0	1	Toggles
	1	0	

Characteristic Table

- A characteristic table defines the logical properties of a flip-flop by describing its operation in tabular form.
- The next state is defined as a function of the inputs and the present state.
- Q(t) refers to the present state and Q(t + 1) is the next.
- Thus, Q(t) denotes the state of the flip-flop immediately before the clock edge, and Q(t + 1) denotes the state that results from the clock transition.
- The characteristic table for the JK flip-flop shows that the next state is equal to the present state when inputs J and K are both equal to 0. This condition can be expressed as Q(t + 1) = Q(t), indicating that the clock produces no change of state.

Characteristic Table of JK Flip-Flop

J	K	Q(t+1)	
0	0	Q(t)	No change
0	1	0	Reset
1	0	1	Set
1	1	Q'(t)	Complement

- When K = 1 and J = 0, the clock resets the flip-flop and Q(t + 1) = 0. With J = 1 and K = 0, the flip-flop sets and Q(t + 1) = 1. When both J and K are equal to 1, the next state changes to the complement of the present state, a transition that can be expressed as Q(t + 1) = Q'(t).
- The characteristic equation for JK flip-flop is represented as

$$Q(t+1) = JQ' + K'Q$$

Characteristic Table of D Flip-Flop

D	Q(t+1)
0	0
1	1

- The next state of a D flip-flop is dependent only on the D input and is independent of the present state.
- This can be expressed as Q (t + 1) = D. It means that the next-state value is equal to the value of D. Note that the D flip-flop does not have a "no-change" condition and its characteristic equation is written as Q(t+1) = D.

Characteristic Table of T Flip-Flop

T	Q(t+1)	
0	Q(t)	No change
1	Q'(t)	Complement

- The characteristic table of T flip-flop has only two conditions: When T = 0, the clock edge does not change the state; when T = 1, the clock edge complements the state of the flip-flop and the characteristic equation is

$$Q(t+1) = T \oplus Q = T'Q + TQ'$$

Master-Slave JK Flip-Flop

- The Master-Slave Flip-Flop is basically two gated SR flip-flops connected together in a series configuration with the slave having an inverted clock pulse.
- The outputs from Q and Q' from the "Slave" flip-flop are fed back to the inputs of the "Master" with the outputs of the "Master" flip flop being connected to the two inputs of the "Slave" flip flop.
- This feedback configuration from the slave's output to the master's input gives the characteristic toggle of the JK flip flop as shown below.

The Master-Slave JK Flip Flop

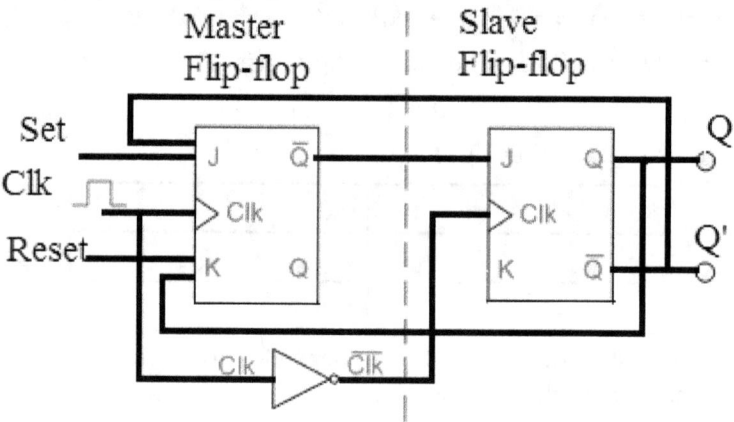

- The input signals J and K are connected to the gated "master" SR flip flop which "locks" the input condition while the clock (Clk) input is "HIGH" at logic level "1".
- As the clock input of the "slave" flip flop is the inverse (complement) of the "master" clock input, the "slave" SR flip flop does not toggle.
- The outputs from the "master" flip flop are only "seen" by the gated "slave" flip flop when the clock input goes "LOW" to logic level "0".
- When the clock is "LOW", the outputs from the "master" flip flop are latched and any additional changes to its inputs are ignored.
- The gated "slave" flip flop now responds to the state of its inputs passed over by the "master" section.
- Then on the "Low-to-High" transition of the clock pulse the inputs of the "master" flip flop are fed through to the gated inputs of the "slave" flip flop and on the "High-to-Low" transition the same inputs are reflected on the output of the "slave" making this type of flip flop edge or pulse-triggered.

- Then, the circuit accepts input data when the clock signal is "HIGH", and passes the data to the output on the falling-edge of the clock signal.
- In other words, the Master-Slave JK Flip flop is a "Synchronous" device as it only passes data with the timing of the clock signal.

Flip-Flop Conversions

SR Flip Flop to JK Flip Flop

For this J and K will be given as external inputs to S and R. As shown in the logic diagram below, S and R will be the outputs of the combinational circuit.

The truth tables for the flip flop conversion are given below. The present state is represented by Q_p and Q_{p+1} is the next state to be obtained when the J and K inputs are applied.

For two inputs J and K, there will be eight possible combinations. For each combination of J, K and Q_p, the corresponding Q_{p+1} states are found. Q_{p+1} simply suggests the future values to be obtained by the JK flip flop after the value of Q_p. The table is then completed by writing the values of S and R required to get each Q_{p+1} from the corresponding Q_p. That is, the values of S and R that are required to change the state of the flip flop from Q_p to Q_{p+1} are written.

S-R Flip Flop to J-K Flip Flop

Conversion Table

J-K Inputs		Outputs		S-R Inputs	
J	K	Q_p	Q_{p+1}	S	R
0	0	0	0	0	X
0	0	1	1	X	0
0	1	0	0	0	X
0	1	1	0	0	1
1	0	0	1	1	0
1	0	1	1	X	0
1	1	0	1	1	0
1	1	1	0	0	1

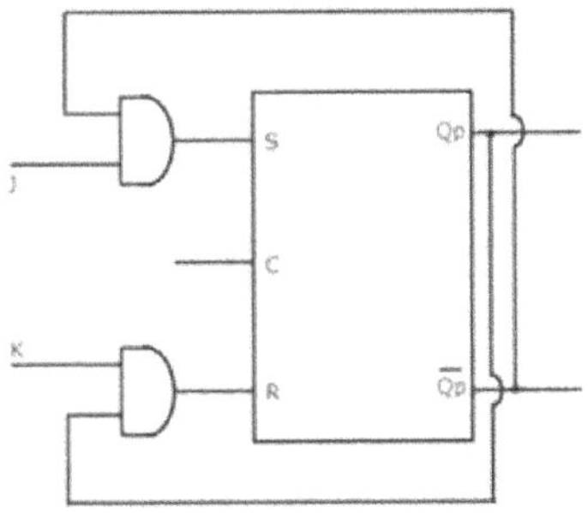

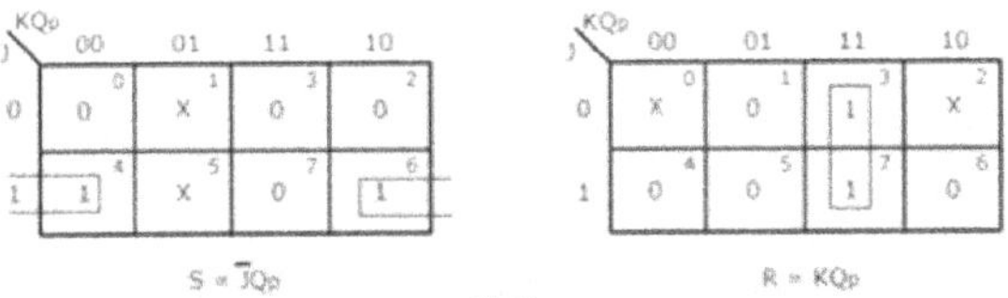

K-Map

$S = J\overline{Q_p}$

$R = KQ_p$

JK Flip Flop to SR Flip Flop

- This will be the reverse process of the above explained conversion. S and R will be the external inputs to J and K. J and K will be the outputs of the combinational circuit. Thus, the values of J and K have to be obtained in terms of S, R and Qp.
- A conversion table is to be written using S, R, Qp, Qp+1, J and K.
- For two inputs, S and R, eight combinations are made. For each combination, the corresponding Qp+1 outputs are found out.
- The outputs for the combinations of S=1 and R=1 are not permitted for an SR flip flop. Thus, the outputs are considered invalid and the J and K values are taken as "don't cares".

J-K Flip Flop to S-R Flip Flop

Conversion Table

S-R Inputs		Outputs		J-K Inputs	
S	R	Qp	Qp+1	J	K
0	0	0	0	0	X
0	0	1	1	X	0
0	1	0	0	0	X
0	1	1	0	X	1
1	0	0	1	1	X
1	0	1	1	X	0
1	1		Invalid	Dont care	
1	1		Invalid	Dont care	

Logic Diagram

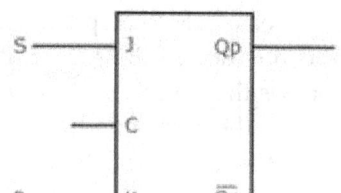

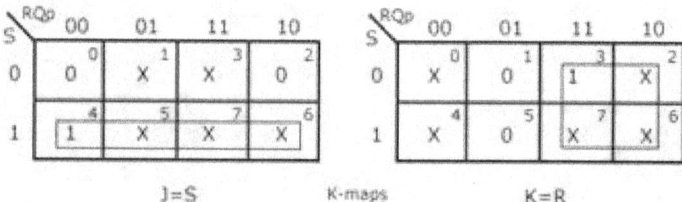

SR Flip Flop to D Flip Flop

- S and R are the actual inputs of the flip flop and D is the external input of the flip flop.

- The four combinations, the logic diagram, conversion table, and the K-map for S and R in terms of D and Qp are shown below.

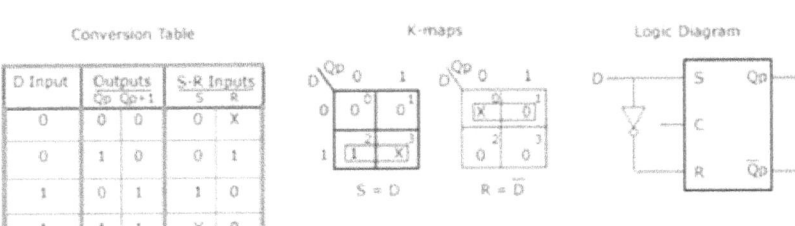

S-R Flip Flop to D Flip Flop

D Flip Flop to SR Flip Flop

- D is the actual input of the flip flop and S and R are the external inputs. Eight possible combinations are achieved from the external inputs S, R and Qp.
- But, since the combination of S=1 and R=1 are invalid, the values of Qp+1 and D are considered as "don't cares".
- The logic diagram showing the conversion from D to SR, and the K-map for D in terms of S, R and Qp are shown below.

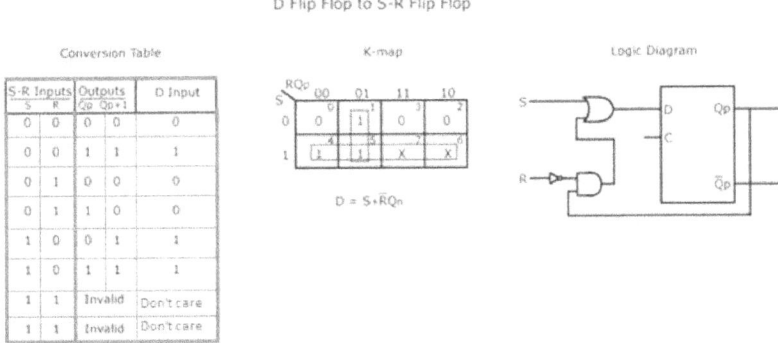

D Flip Flop to S-R Flip Flop

JK Flip Flop to T Flip Flop

- J and K are the actual inputs of the flip flop and T is taken as the external input for conversion
- Four combinations are produced with T and Qp. J and K are expressed in terms of T and Qp.
- The conversion table, K-maps, and the logic diagram are given below.

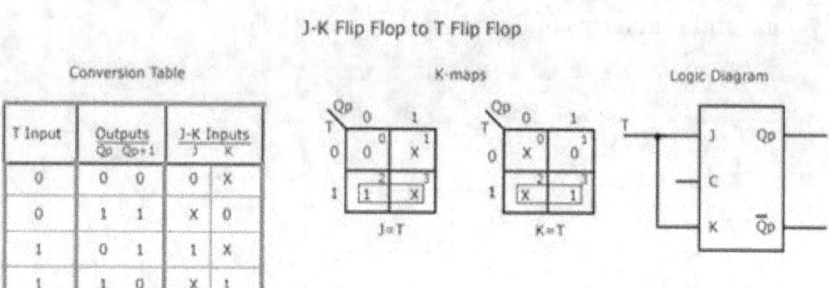

D Flip Flop to JK Flip Flop

- In this conversion, D is the actual input to the flip flop and J and K are the external inputs.
- J, K and Qp make eight possible combinations, as shown in the conversion table below. D is expressed in terms of J, K and Qp.
- The conversion table, the K-map for D in terms of J, K and Qp and the logic diagram showing the conversion from D to JK are given in the figure below.

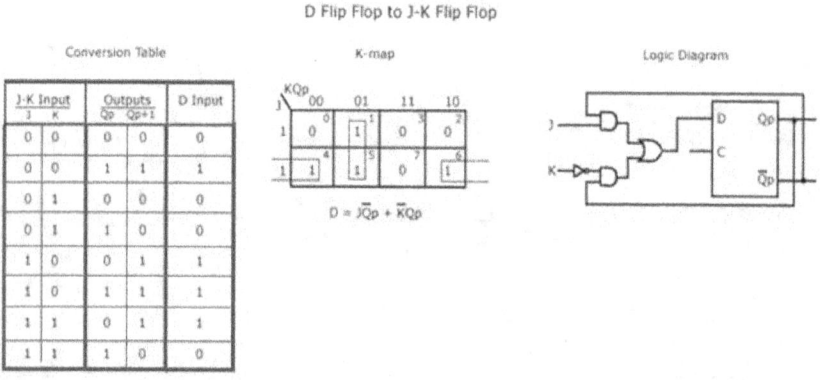

JK Flip Flop to D Flip Flop

- D is the external input and J and K are the actual inputs of the flip flop. D and Qp make four combinations. J and K are expressed in terms of D and Qp.
- The four-combination conversion table, the K-maps for J and K in terms of D and Qp.

Sequential Logic Circuit

J-K Flip Flop to D Flip Flop

Conversion Table

D Input	Outputs		J-K Inputs	
	Q_p	Q_{p+1}	J	K
0	0	0	0	X
0	1	0	X	1
1	0	1	1	X
1	1	0	X	0

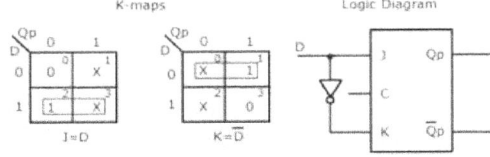

K-maps   Logic Diagram

$J = D$ $K = \overline{D}$

Chapter 17
Combinational Logic Circuit

Introduction

- A combinational circuit consists of logic gates whose outputs at any time are determined from only the present combination of inputs.
- A combinational circuit performs an operation that can be specified logically by a set of Boolean functions.
- It consists of an interconnection of logic gates. Combinational logic gates react to the values of the signals at their inputs and produce the value of the output signal, transforming binary information from the given input data to a required output data.
- A block diagram of a combinational circuit is shown in the below figure.
- The n input binary variables come from an external source; the m output variables are produced by the internal combinational logic circuit and go to an external destination.
- Each input and output variable exists physically as an analog signal whose values are interpreted to be a binary signal that represents logic 1and logic 0.

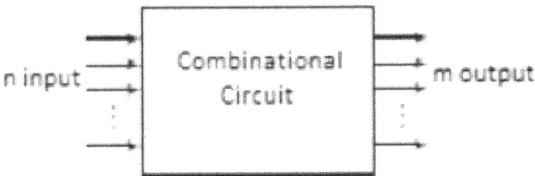

Binary Adder–Subtractor

- Digital computers perform a variety of information-processing tasks. Among the functions encountered are the various arithmetic operations.
- The most basic arithmetic operation is the addition of two binary digits. This simple addition consists of four possible elementary operations: 0 + 0 = 0, 0 + 1 = 1, 1 + 0 = 1, and 1 + 1 = 10.

- The first three operations produce a sum of one digit, but when both augend and addend bits are equal to 1; the binary sum consists of two digits. The higher significant bit of this result is called a carry.
- When the augend and addend numbers contain more significant digits, the carry obtained from the addition of two bits is added to the next higher order pair of significant bits.
- A combinational circuit that performs the addition of two bits is called a half adder.
- One that performs the addition of three bits (two significant bits and a previous carry) is a full adder. The names of the circuits stem from the fact that two half adders can be employed to implement a full adder.

Half Adder

- This circuit needs two binary inputs and two binary outputs.
- The input variables designate the augend and addend bits; the output variables produce the sum and carry. Symbols x and y are assigned to the two inputs and S (for sum) and C (for carry) to the outputs.
- The truth table for the half adder is listed in the below table.
- The C output is 1 only when both inputs are 1. The S output represents the least significant bit of the sum.
- The simplified Boolean functions for the two outputs can be obtained directly from the truth table.

x	y	D	B
0	0	0	0
0	1	1	0
1	0	1	0
1	1	0	1

Truth Table

- The simplified sum-of-products expressions are

$S = x'y + xy'$

$C = xy$

- The logic diagram of the half adder implemented in sum of products is shown in the below figure. It can be also implemented with an exclusive-OR and an AND gate.

Combinational Logic Circuit

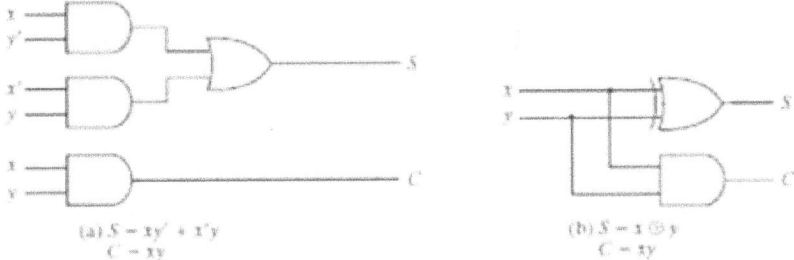

(a) $S = xy' + x'y$
$C = xy$

(b) $S = x \oplus y$
$C = xy$

Full Adder

- A full adder is a combinational circuit that forms the arithmetic sum of three bits.
- It consists of three inputs and two outputs. Two of the input variables, denoted by x and y, represent the two significant bits to be added. The third input, z, represents the carry from the previous lower significant position.

x	y	z	C	S
0	0	0	0	0
0	0	1	0	1
0	1	0	0	1
0	1	1	1	0
1	0	0	0	1
1	0	1	1	0
1	1	0	1	0
1	1	1	1	1

Truth Table

- Two outputs are necessary because the arithmetic sum of three binary digits ranges in value from 0 to 3, and binary representation of 2 or 3 needs two bits. The two outputs are designated by the symbols S for sum and C for carry.
- The binary variable S gives the value of the least significant bit of the sum. The binary variable C gives the output carry formed by adding the input carry and the bits of the words.

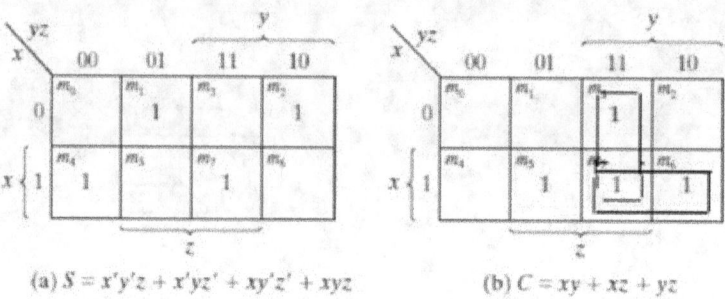

(a) $S = x'y'z + x'yz' + xy'z' + xyz$ (b) $C = xy + xz + yz$

K-Map for full adder

- The eight rows under the input variables designate all possible combinations of the three variables. The output variables are determined from the arithmetic sum of the input bits. When all input bits are 0, the output is 0.
- The S output is equal to 1 when only one input is equal to 1 or when all three inputs are equal to 1. The C output has a carry of 1 if two or three inputs are equal to 1.
- The simplified expressions are

  $S = x'y'z + x'yz' + xy'z' + xyz$

  $C = xy + xz + yz$
- The logic diagram for the full adder implemented in sum-of-products form is shown in figure.

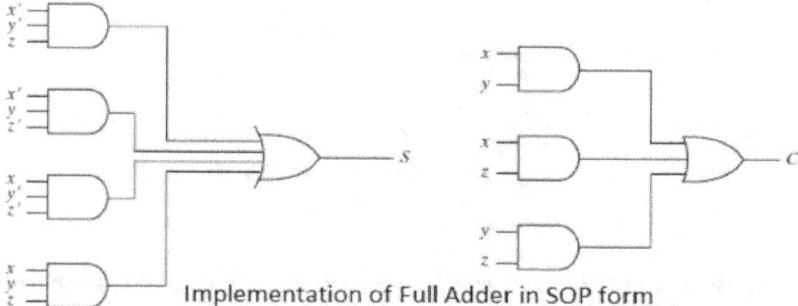

Implementation of Full Adder in SOP form

- It can also be implemented with two half adders and one OR gate as shown in the figure.
- A full adder is a combinational circuit that forms the arithmetic sum of three bits.

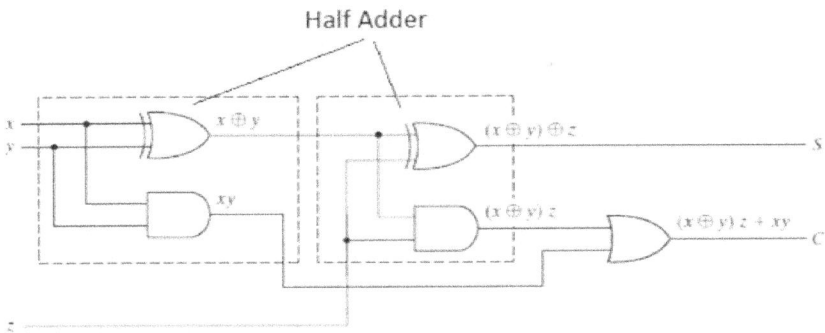

Implementation of Full Adder using Two Half Adders and an OR gate

Binary Adder

- A binary adder is a digital circuit that produces the arithmetic sum of two binary numbers.
- It can be constructed with full adders connected in cascade, with the output carry from each full adder connected to the input carry of the next full adder in the chain.
- Addition of n-bit numbers requires a chain of n full adders or a chain of one-half adder and n-1 full adders. In the former case, the input carry to the least significant position is fixed at 0.
- The interconnection of four full-adder (FA) circuits to provide a four-bit binary ripple carry adder is shown in the figure.
- The augend bits of A and the addend bits of B are designated by subscript numbers from right to left, with subscript 0 denoting the least significant bit.
- The carriers are connected in a chain through the full adders. The input carry to the adder is C_0, and it ripples through the full adders to the output carry C_4. The S outputs generate the required sum bits.
- An n-bit adder requires n full adders, with each output carry connected to the input carry of the next higher order full adder.
- Consider the two binary numbers A = 1011 and B = 0011. Their sum S = 1110 is formed with the four-bit adder as follows:

Subscript i:	3	2	1	0	
Input carry	0	1	1	0	C_i
Augend	1	0	1	1	A_i
Addend	0	0	1	1	B_i
Sum	1	1	1	0	S_i
Output carry	0	0	1	1	C_{i+1}

- The bits are added with full adders, starting from the least significant position (subscript 0), to form the sum bit and carry bit. The input carrying C_0 in the least significant position must be 0.
- The value of C_i+1 in a given significant position is the output carry of the full adder. This value is transferred into the input carry of the full adder that adds the bits one higher significant position to the left.
- The sum bits are thus generated starting from the rightmost position and are available as soon as the corresponding previous carry bit is generated. All the carries must be generated for the correct sum bits to appear at the outputs.

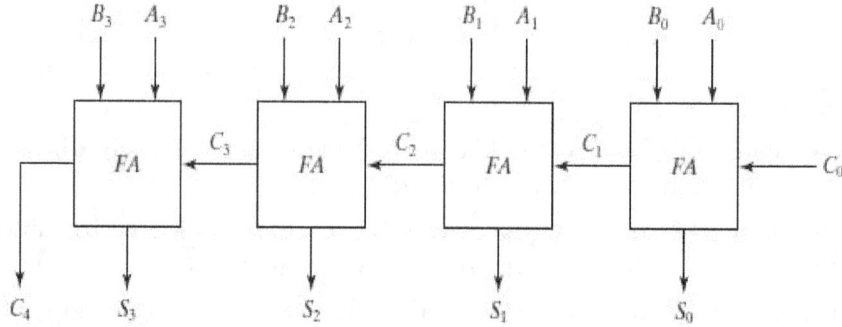

Four Bit Binary Adder

Half Subtractor

- This circuit needs two binary inputs and two binary outputs.
- Symbols x and y are assigned to the two inputs and D (for difference) and B (for borrow) to the outputs.
- The truth table for the half subtractor is listed in the below table.

Combinational Logic Circuit

x	y	D	B
0	0	0	0
0	1	1	1
1	0	1	0
1	1	0	0

Truth Table

- The B output is 1 only when the inputs are 0 and 1. The D output represents the least significant bit of the subtraction.
- The subtraction operation is done by using the following rules as

    0-0=0;

    0-1=1 with borrow 1;

    1-0=1;

    1-1=0.

- The simplified Boolean functions for the two outputs can be obtained directly from the truth table. The simplified sum-of-products expressions are

    $D = x'y + xy'$ and $B = x'y$

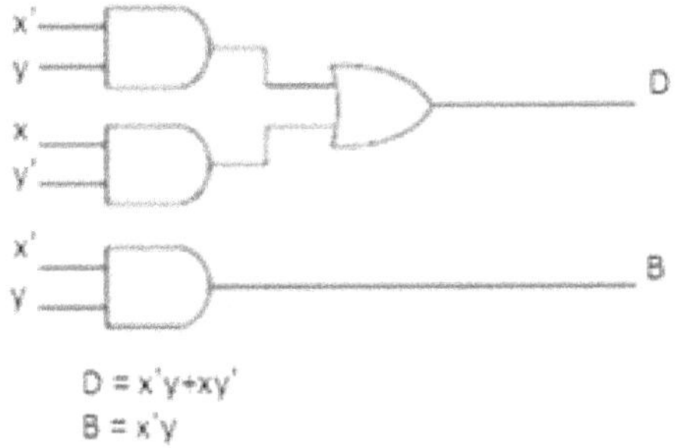

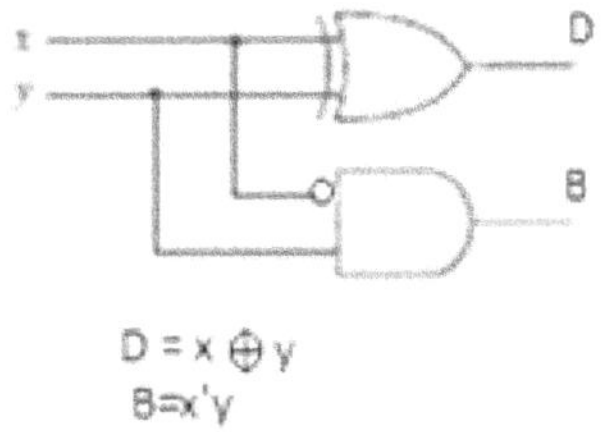

$D = x'y + xy'$
$B = x'y$

$D = x \oplus y$
$B = x'y$

- The logic diagram of the half adder implemented in the sum of products is shown in the figure. It can be also implemented with an exclusive-OR and an AND gate with one inverted input.

Full Subtractor

- A full subtractor is a combinational circuit that forms the arithmetic subtraction operation of three bits.
- It consists of three inputs and two outputs. Two of the input variables, denoted by x and y, represent the two significant bits to be subtracted. The third input, z, is subtracted from the result 0f the first subtraction.

x	y	z	D	B
0	0	0	0	0
0	0	1	1	1
0	1	0	1	1
0	1	1	0	1
1	0	0	1	0
1	0	1	0	0
1	1	0	0	0
1	1	1	1	1

Truth Table

- Two outputs are necessary because the arithmetic subtraction of three binary digits ranges in value from 0 to 3, and binary representation of 2 or 3 needs two bits. The two outputs are designated by the symbols D for difference and B for borrow.

- The binary variable D gives the value of the least significant bit of the difference. The binary variable B gives the output borrow formed during the subtraction process.

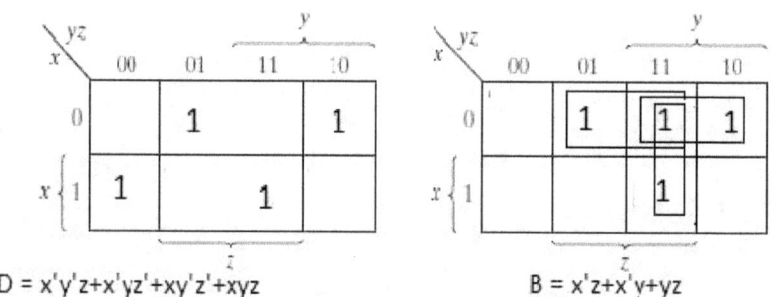

$D = x'y'z + x'yz' + xy'z' + xyz$ $\qquad$ $B = x'z + x'y + yz$

K-Map for full Subtractor

- The eight rows under the input variables designate all possible combinations of the three variables. The output variables are determined from the arithmetic subtraction of the input bits.

- The difference D becomes 1 when any one of the inputs is 1 or all three inputs are equal to 1 and the borrow B is 1 when the input combination is (0 0 1) or (0 1 0) or (0 1 1) or (1 1 1).

- The simplified expressions are

Combinational Logic Circuit

$D = x'y'z + x'yz' + xy'z' + xyz$

$B = x'z + x'y + yz$

- The logic diagram for the full adder implemented in sum-of-products form is shown in figure.

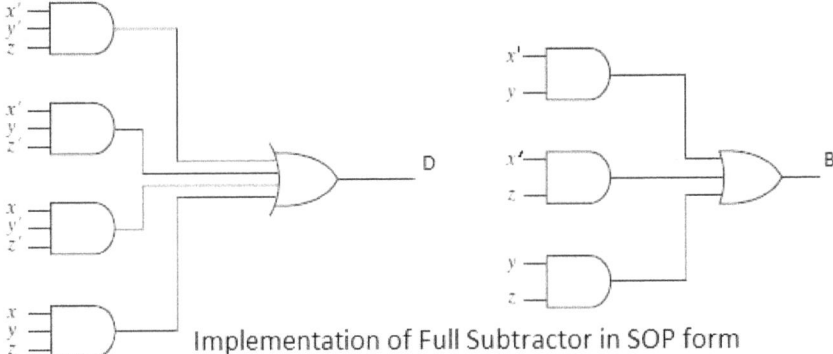

Implementation of Full Subtractor in SOP form

Magnitude Comparator

- A magnitude comparator is a combinational circuit that compares two numbers A and B and determines their relative magnitudes.
- The following description is about a 2-bit magnitude comparator circuit.
- The outcome of the comparison is specified by three binary variables that indicate whether A < B, A = B, or A > B.
- Consider two numbers, A and B, with two digits each. Now writing the coefficients of the numbers in descending order of significance:

$A = A_1 A0$

$B = B_1 B_0$

- The two numbers are equal if all pairs of significant digits are equal i.e. if and only if $A_1 = B_1$, and $A_0 = B_0$.
- When the numbers are binary, the digits are either 1 or 0, and the equality of each pair of bits can be expressed logically with an exclusive-NOR function as

$x_1 = A_1 B_1 + A_1' B_1'$

And $x_0 = A_0 B_0 + A_0' B_0'$

- The equality of the two numbers A and B is displayed in a combinational circuit by an output binary variable that we designate by the symbol (A = B).
- This binary variable is equal to 1 if the input numbers, A and B, are equal, and is equal to 0 otherwise.

- For equality to exist, all xi variables must be equal to 1, a condition that dictates an AND operation of all variables:

  $(A = B) = x\, x_0$

- The binary variable $(A = B)$ is equal to 1 only if all pairs of digits of the two numbers are equal.
- To determine whether A is greater or less than B, we inspect the relative magnitudes of pairs of significant digits, starting from the most significant position. If the two digits of a pair are equal, we compare the next lower significant pair of digits. If the corresponding digit of A is 1 and that of B is 0, we conclude that A > B. If the corresponding digit of A is 0 and that of B is 1, we have A < B. The sequential comparison can be expressed logically by the two Boolean functions

$(A > B) = A_1 B_1' + x_1 A_0 B_0'$

$(A < B) = A_1' B_1 + x_1 A_0' B_0$

A_1	A_0	B_1	B_0	A>B	A<B	A=B
0	0	0	0	0	0	1
0	0	0	1	0	1	0
0	0	1	0	0	1	0
0	0	1	1	0	1	0
0	1	0	0	1	0	0
0	1	0	1	0	0	1
0	1	1	0	0	1	0
0	1	1	1	0	1	0
1	0	0	0	1	0	0
1	0	0	1	1	0	0
1	0	1	0	0	0	1
1	0	1	1	0	1	0
1	1	0	0	1	0	0
1	1	0	1	1	0	0
1	1	1	0	1	0	0
1	1	1	1	0	0	1

Truth Table

Combinational Logic Circuit

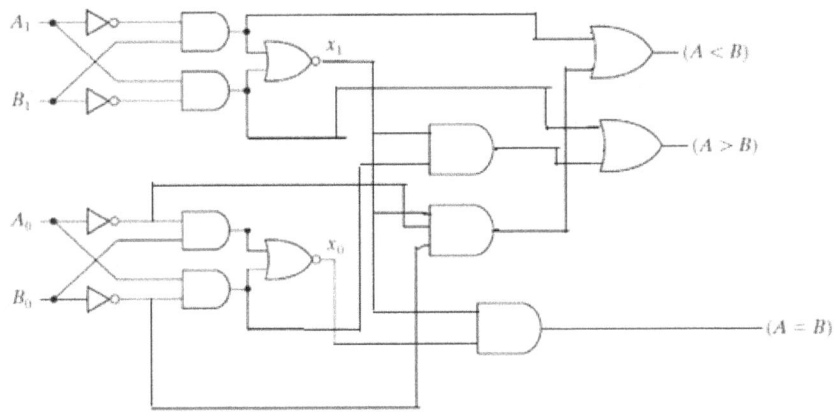

Logic Diagram of 2-bit Magnitude Comparator

Decoder

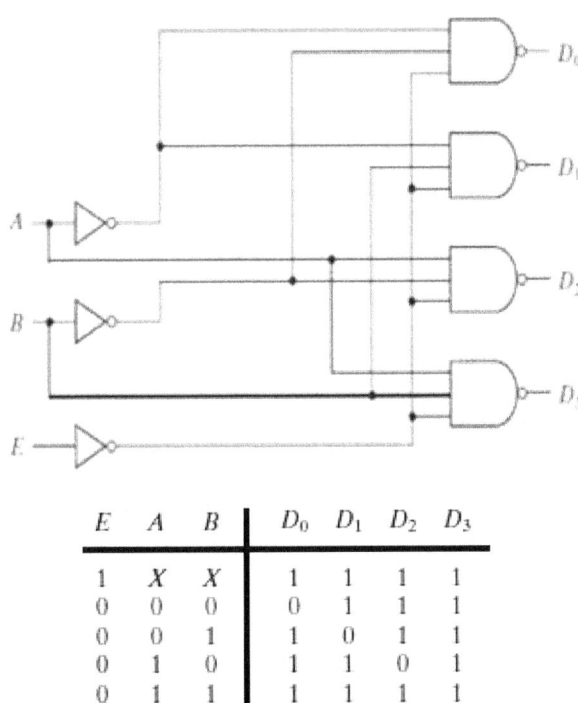

E	A	B	D_0	D_1	D_2	D_3
1	X	X	1	1	1	1
0	0	0	0	1	1	1
0	0	1	1	0	1	1
0	1	0	1	1	0	1
0	1	1	1	1	1	1

- A decoder is a combinational circuit that converts binary information from n input lines to a maximum of 2n unique output lines.
- If the n-bit coded information has unused combinations, the decoder may have fewer than 2n outputs.
- The decoders presented here are called n-to-m-line decoders, where m ... 2n.
- Their purpose is to generate the 2n (or fewer) minterms of n input variables.
- Each combination of inputs will assert a unique output. The name decoder is also used in conjunction with other code converters, such as a BCD-to-seven-segment decoder.
- Consider the three-to-eight-line decoder circuit of three inputs decoded into eight outputs, each representing one of the minterms of the three input variables.
- The three inverters provide the complement of the inputs, and each one of the eight AND gates generate one of the minterms.
- The input variables represent a binary number, and the outputs represent the eight digits of a number in the octal number system.
- However, a three-to-eight-line decoder can be used for decoding any three-bit code to provide eight outputs, one for each element of the code.
- A two-to-four-line decoder with an enable input constructed with NAND gates is shown in Fig.
- The circuit operates with complemented outputs and a complement enable input. The decoder is enabled when E is equal to 0 (i.e., active-low enable). As indicated by the truth table, only one output can be equal to 0 at any given time; all other outputs are equal to 1.
- The output whose value is equal to 0 represents the minterm selected by inputs A and B.
- The circuit is disabled when E is equal to 1, regardless of the values of the other two inputs.
- When the circuit is disabled, none of the outputs are equal to 0 and none of the minterms are selected.
- In general, a decoder may operate with complemented or un-complemented outputs.
- The enable input may be activated with a 0 or with a 1 signal.
- Some decoders have two or more enable inputs that must satisfy a given logic condition in order to enable the circuit.

Combinational Logic Circuit

- A decoder with enable input can function as a demultiplexer— a circuit that receives information from a single line and directs it to one of 2n possible output lines.
- The selection of a specific output is controlled by the bit combination of n selection lines.
- The decoder of Fig. can function as a one-to-four-line demultiplexer when E is taken as a data input line and A and B are taken as the selection inputs.
- The single input variable E has a path to all four outputs, but the input information is directed to only one of the output lines, as specified by the binary combination of the two selection lines A and B.
- This feature can be verified from the truth table of the circuit.
- For example, if the selection lines AB = 10, output D_2 will be the same as the input value E, while all other outputs are maintained at 1.
- Since decoder and demultiplexer operations are obtained from the same circuit, a decoder with an enable input is referred to as a decoder – demultiplexer.
- An application of this decoder is binary-to-octal conversion.

Encoder

- An encoder is a digital circuit that performs the inverse operation of a decoder.
- An encoder has 2n (or fewer) input lines and n output lines.
- The output lines, as an aggregate, generate the binary code corresponding to the input value.

Inputs								Outputs		
D_0	D_1	D_2	D_3	D_4	D_5	D_6	D_7	x	y	z
1	0	0	0	0	0	0	0	0	0	0
0	1	0	0	0	0	0	0	0	0	1
0	0	1	0	0	0	0	0	0	1	0
0	0	0	1	0	0	0	0	0	1	1
0	0	0	0	1	0	0	0	1	0	0
0	0	0	0	0	1	0	0	1	0	1
0	0	0	0	0	0	1	0	1	1	0
0	0	0	0	0	0	0	1	1	1	1

- The above Encoder has eight inputs (one for each of the octal digits) and three outputs that generate the corresponding binary number.
- It is assumed that only one input has a value of 1 at any given time.
- The encoder can be implemented with OR gates whose inputs are determined directly from the truth table.

- Output z is equal to 1 when the input octal digit is 1, 3, 5, or 7.
- Output y is 1 for octal digits 2, 3, 6, or 7, and output x is 1 for digits 4, 5, 6, or 7.
- These conditions can be expressed by the following Boolean output functions:

  $z = D_1 + D_3 + D_5 + D_7$

  $y = D_2 + D_3 + D_6 + D_7$

  $x = D_4 + D_5 + D_6 + D_7$

- The encoder can be implemented with three OR gates.
- The encoder defined above has the limitation that only one input can be active at any given time.
- If two inputs are active simultaneously, the output produces an undefined combination.
- To resolve this ambiguity, encoder circuits must establish an input priority to ensure that only one input is encoded, which is done in the Priority Encoder.

Priority Encoder

- A priority encoder is an encoder circuit that includes the priority function.
- The operation of the priority encoder is such that if two or more inputs are equal to 1 at the same time, the input having the highest priority will take precedence.

Inputs				Outputs		
D_0	D_1	D_2	D_3	x	y	V
0	0	0	0	X	X	0
1	0	0	0	0	0	1
X	1	0	0	0	1	1
X	X	1	0	1	0	1
X	X	X	1	1	1	1

- In addition to the two outputs x and y, the circuit has a third output designated by V; this is a valid bit indicator that is set to 1 when one or more inputs are equal to 1.
- If all inputs are 0, there is no valid input and V is equal to 0.
- The other two outputs are not inspected when V equals 0 and are specified as don't-care conditions.
- Here X's in output columns represent don't-care conditions, the X's in the input columns are useful for representing a truth table in condensed form.

Inputs				Outputs		
D_0	D_1	D_2	D_3	x	y	V
0	0	0	0	X	X	0
1	0	0	0	0	0	1
X	1	0	0	0	1	1
X	X	1	0	1	0	1
X	X	X	1	1	1	1

- Higher the subscript number, the higher the priority of the input.
- Input D_3 has the highest priority, so, regardless of the values of the other inputs, when this input is 1, the output for xy is 11 (binary 3).
- If $D_2 = 1$, provided that $D_3 = 0$, regardless of the values of the other two lower priority inputs the output is 10.
- The output for D_1 is generated only if higher priority inputs are 0, and so on down the priority levels.

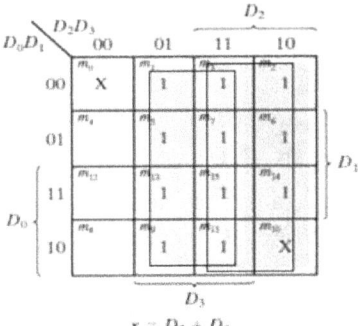

$x = D_2 + D_3$

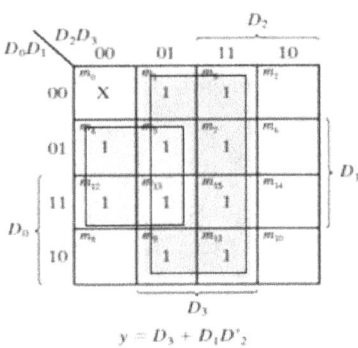

$y = D_3 + D_1 D'_2$

- The maps for simplifying outputs x and y are shown in above Fig.
- The minterms for the two functions are derived from its truth table.
- Although the table has only five rows, when each X in a row is replaced first by 0 and then by 1, we obtain all 16 possible input combinations.
- For example, the fourth row in the table, with inputs XX10, represents the four minterms 0010, 0110, 1010, and 1110. The simplified Boolean expressions for the priority encoder are obtained from the maps.
- The condition for output V is an OR function of all the input variables.
- The priority encoder is implemented according to the following Boolean functions:

$x = D_2 + D_3$
$y = D_3 + D_1 D'_2$
$V = D_0 + D_1 + D_2 + D_3$

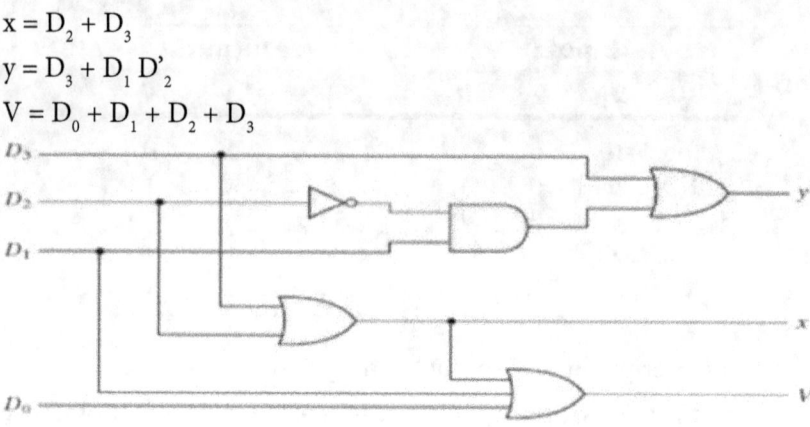

Multiplexer

- A multiplexer is a combinational circuit that selects binary information from one of many input lines and directs it to a single output line.
- The selection of a particular input line is controlled by a set of selection lines.
- Normally, there are 2n input lines and n selection lines whose bit combinations determine which input is selected.
- A four-to-one-line multiplexer is shown in the below figure. Each of the four inputs, I0 through I3, is applied to one input of an AND gate.
- Selection lines S_1 and S_0 are decoded to select a particular AND gate. The outputs of the AND gates are applied to a single OR gate that provides the one-line output.
- The function table lists the input that is passed to the output for each combination of the binary selection values.
- To demonstrate the operation of the circuit, consider the case when
  $S_1 S_0 = 10$.
- The AND gate associated with input I2 has two of its inputs equal to 1 and the third input connected to I2.
- The other three AND gates have at least one input equal to 0, which makes their outputs equal to 0. The output of the OR gate is now equal to the value of I2, providing a path from the selected input to the output.
- A multiplexer is also called a data selector, since it selects one of many inputs and steers the binary information to the output line.

Combinational Logic Circuit

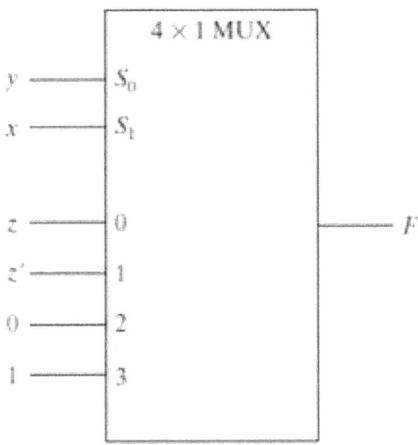

(b) Multiplexer implementation

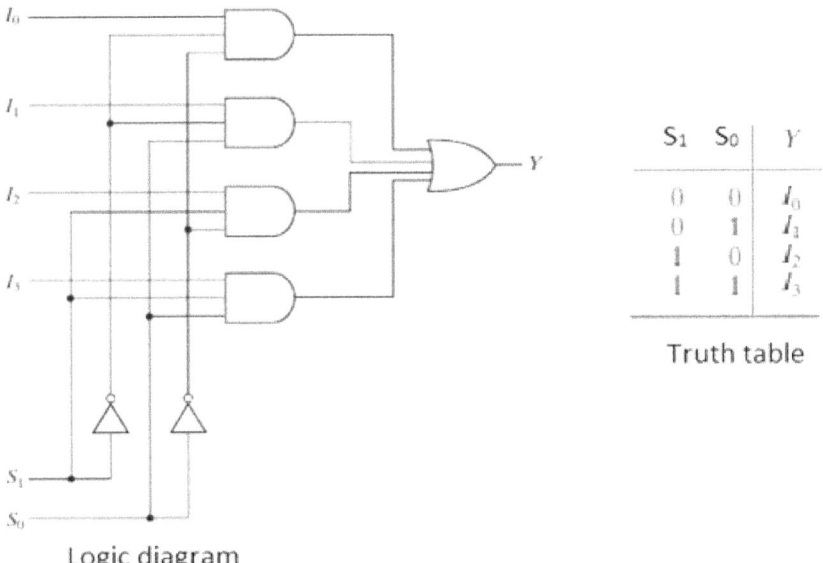

Logic diagram

Truth table

Demultiplexer

- The data distributor, known more commonly as a Demultiplexer or "Demux" for short, is the exact opposite of the Multiplexer.
- The demultiplexer takes one single input data line and then switches it to any

one of a number of individual output lines one at a time. The demultiplexer converts a serial data signal at the input to a parallel data at its output lines as shown below.

- The Boolean expression for this 1-to-4 demultiplexer above with outputs A to D and data select lines a, b is given as:

F = (ab)'A + a'bB + ab'C + abD

- The function of the demultiplexer is to switch one common data input line to any one of the 4 output data lines A to D in our example above. As with the multiplexer the individual solid-state switches are selected by the binary input address code on the output select pins "a" and "b" as shown.

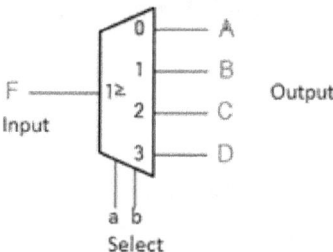

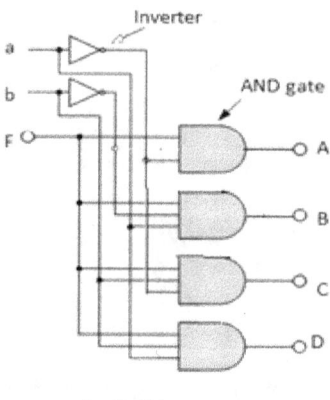

Logic Diagram

- Unlike multiplexers which convert data from a single data line to multiple lines and demultiplexers which convert multiple lines to a single data line, there are devices available which convert data to and from multiple lines and in the next tutorial about combinational logic devices.

Combinational Logic Circuit

- Standard demultiplexer IC packages available are the TTL 74LS138 1 to 8-output demultiplexer, the TTL 74LS139 Dual 1-to-4 output demultiplexer or the CMOS CD4514 1-to-16 output demultiplexer.

Output Select		Data output Selected
b	a	
0	0	A
0	1	B
1	0	C
1	1	D

Truth Table

Chapter 18
Logic Families

A circuit configuration or approach used to produce a type of digital integrated circuit is called Logic Family.

By using logic families, we can generate different logic functions, when fabricated in the form of an IC with the same approach, or in other words belonging to the same logic family, will have identical electrical characteristics.

The set of digital ICs belonging to the same logic family are electrically compatible with each other.

Some common Characteristics of the Same Logic Family include Supply voltage range, speed of response, power dissipation, input and output logic levels, current sourcing and sinking capability, fan- out, noise margin, etc.

Choosing digital ICs from the same logic family guarantees that these ICs are compatible with respect to each other and that the system as a whole performs the intended logic function.

Types of Logic Family

- The entire range of digital ICs is fabricated using either bipolar devices or MOS devices or a combination of the two.
- Bipolar families include

    Diode Logic (DL)

    Resistor-Transistor Logic (RTL)

    Diode-transistor Logic (DTL)

    Transistor- Transistor Logic (TTL)

    Emitter Coupled Logic (ECL)

    (also known as Current Mode Logic (CML))

    Integrated Injection Logic (I2L)
- The Bi-MOS logic family uses both bipolar and MOS devices.

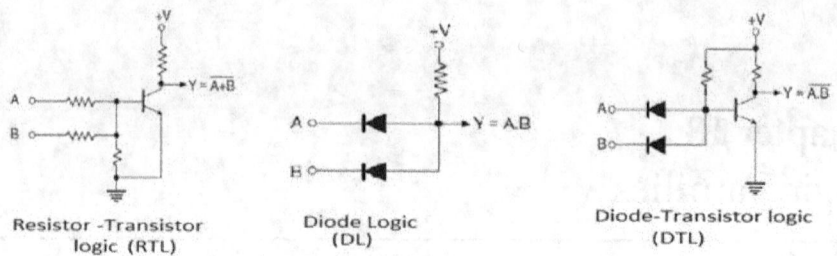

- Above are some examples of DL, RTL and DTL.
- MOS families include: -

  ThePMOS family (using P-channel MOSFETs)

  The NMOS family (using N-channel MOSFETs)

  The CMOS family (using both N- and P-channel devices)

Some Operational Properties of Logic Family

DC Supply Voltage

- The nominal value of the dc supply voltage for TTL (Transistor-Transis-Tor Logic) and CMOS (Complementary Metal-Oxide Semiconductor) devices is +5V. Although omitted from logic diagrams for simplicity, this voltage is connected to the Vcc or VDD pin of an IC package and ground is connected to the GND pin.

TTL Logic Levels

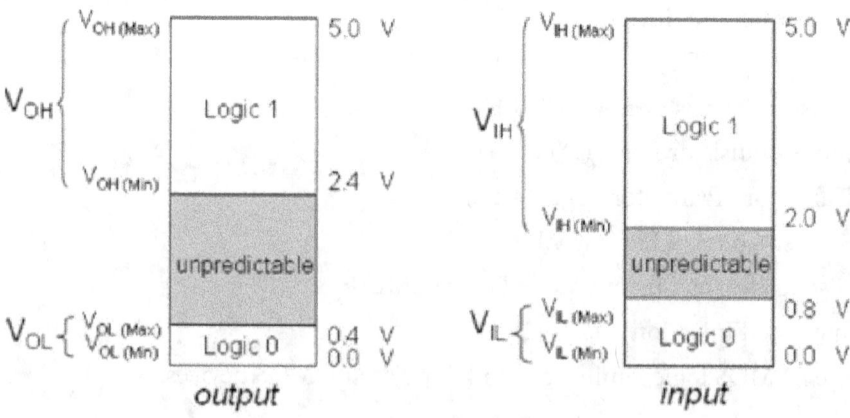

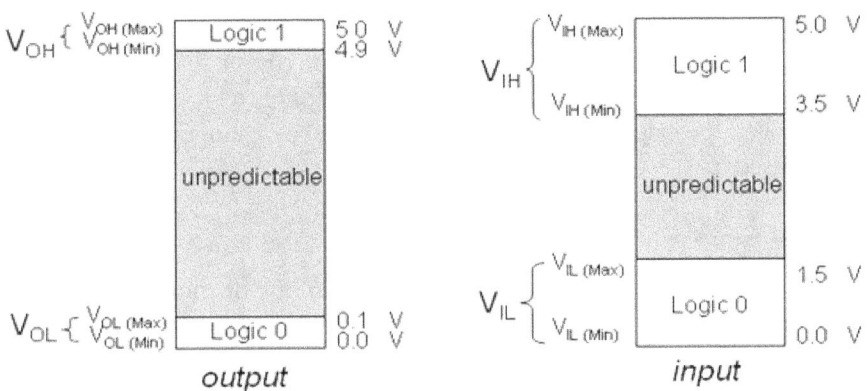

CMOS Logic Levels

Noise Immunity

- Noise is the unwanted voltage that is induced in electrical circuits and can present a threat to the poor operation of the circuit. In order not to be adversely affected by noise, a logic circuit must have a certain amount of 'noise immunity'.
- This ability to tolerate a certain amount of unwanted voltage fluctuation on its inputs without changing its output state is called Noise Immunity.

Noise Margin

- A measure of a circuit's noise immunity is called 'noise margin' which is expressed in volts.
- There are two values of noise margin specified for a given logic circuit: the HIGH (VNH) and LOW (VNL) noise margins.

  These are defined by following equations:

  $V_{NH} = V_{OH} (Min) - V_{IH} (Min)$ $V_{NL} = VIL (Max) - V_{OL} (Max)$

Power Dissipation

- A logic gate draws ICCH current from the supply when the gate is in the HIGH output state, draws ICCL current from the supply in the LOW output state.
- Average power is
  PD = VCC ICC where ICC = (ICCH + ICCL) / 2

Propagation Delay time
- When a signal passes (propagates) through a logic circuit, it always experiences a time delay as shown below. A change in the output level always occurs a short time, called 'propagation delay time', later than the change in the input level that caused it.

Fan Out of Gates
- When the output of a logic gate is connected to one or more inputs of other gates, a load on the driving gate is created. There is a limit to the number of load gates that a given gate can drive. This limit is called the 'Fan-Out' of the gate.

Transistor-Transistor Logic
- In Transistor-Transistor logic or just TTL, logic gates are built only around transistors.
- TTL was developed in 1965. Through the years basic TTL has been improved to meet performance requirements. There are many versions or families of TTL.
- For example
  » Standard TTL
  » High Speed TTL (twice as fast, twice as much power)
  » Low Power TTL (1/10 the speed, 1/10 the power of "standard" TTL)
  » Schottky TTL etc. (for high-frequency uses)
- All TTL logic families have three configurations for outputs
  » Totem pole output
  » Open collector output
  » Tristate output

Totem Pole Output
- Addition of an active pull up circuit in the output of a gate is called totem pole.
- To increase the switching speed of the gate which is limited due to the parasitic capacitance at the output totem pole is used.
- The circuit of a totem-pole NAND gate is shown below, which has got three stages
  » Input Stage
  » Phase Splitter Stage

» Output Stage

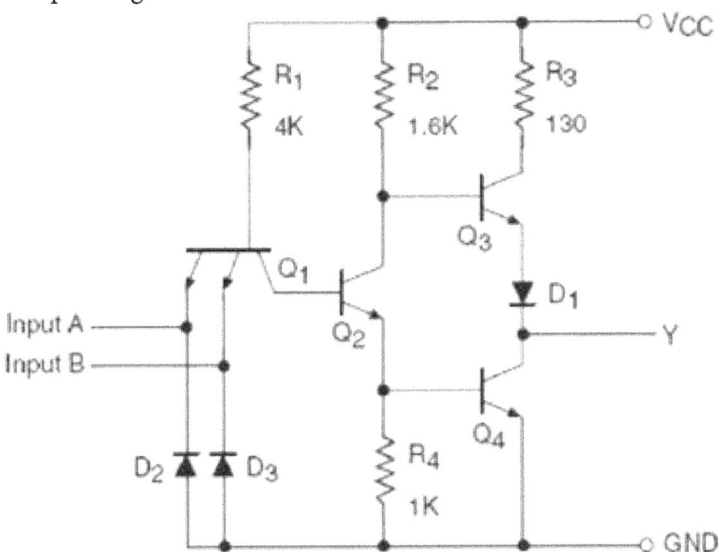

- Transistor Q1 is a two-emitter NPN transistor, which is equivalent to two NPN transistors with their base and emitter terminals tied together.
- The two emitters are the two inputs of the NAND gate
  In TTL technology multiple emitter transistors are used for the input devices Diodes D2 and D3 are protection diodes used to limit negative input voltages.
- When there is large negative voltage at input, the diode conducts and shorting it to the ground Q2 provides complementary voltages for the output transistors Q3 and Q4.
- The combination of Q3 and Q4 forms the output circuit often referred to as a totem pole arrangement
- (Q4 is stacked on top of Q3). In such an arrangement, either Q3 or Q4 conducts at a time depending upon the logic status of the inputs
- Diode D1 ensures that Q4 will turn off when Q2 is on (HIGH input) The output Y is taken from the top of Q3

Advantages of Totem Pole Output

- The features of this arrangement are
  » Low power consumption
  » Fast switching
  » Low output impedance

Open Collector Output

- Figure below shows the circuit of a typical TTL gate with open-collector output Observe here that the circuit elements associated with Q3 in the totem-pole circuit are missing and the collector of Q4 is left open-circuited, hence the name open-collector.

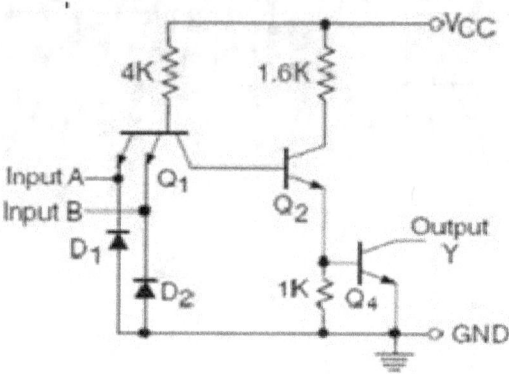

- An open-collector output can present a logic LOW output. Since there is no internal path from the output Y to the supply voltage VCC, the circuit cannot present a logic HIGH on its own.

Advantages of Open Collector Outputs

- Open-collector outputs can be tied directly together which results in the logical ANDing of the outputs.
- Thus the equivalent of an AND gate can be formed by simply connecting the outputs.
- Increased current levels - Standard TTL gates with totem-pole outputs can only provide a HIGH current output of 0.4 mA and a LOW current of 1.6 mA. Many open-collector gates have increased current ratings.
- Different voltage levels - A wide variety of output HIGH voltages can be achieved using open-collector gates. This is useful in interfacing different logic families that have different voltage and current level requirements.

Disadvantage of open-Collector Gates

- They have slow switching speed. This is because the value of pull-up resistor is in kW, which results in a relatively long time Constants

Comparison of Totem Pole and Open Collector Output

- The major advantage of using a totem-pole connection is that it offers low-output impedance in both the HIGH and LOW output states

Totem Pole	Open Collector
Output stage consists of pull-up transistor (Q3), diode resistor and pull-down transistor (Q4)	Output stage consists of only pull-down transistor
External pull-up resistor is not required	External pull-up resistor is required for proper operation of gate
Output of two gates cannot be tied together	Output of two gates can be tied together using wired AND technique
Operating speed is high	Operating speed is low

Tristate (Three-State) Logic Output

- Tristate output combines the advantages of the totem-pole and open collector circuits.
- Three output states are HIGH, LOW, and high impedance (Hi-Z).

EN	IN	OUT
0	X	HI-Z
1	0	0
1	1	1

- For the symbol and truth table, IN is the data input, and EN, the additional enable input for control. For EN = 0, regardless of the value on IN(denoted by X), the output value is Hi-Z. For EN = 1, the output value follows the input value.
- Data input, IN, can be inverted. Control input, EN, can be inverted by addition of "bubbles" to signals IN OUT EN.
- This requires two inputs: input and enable EN is to make output Hi-Z or follow input.

Standard TTL Nand Gate

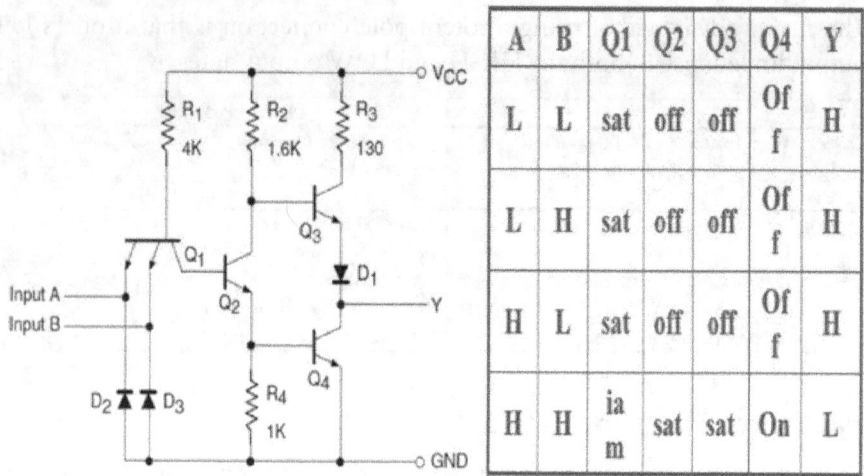

A	B	Q1	Q2	Q3	Q4	Y
L	L	sat	off	off	Off	H
L	H	sat	off	off	Off	H
H	L	sat	off	off	Off	H
H	H	iam	sat	sat	On	L

CMOS Technology

- MOS stands for Metal Oxide Semiconductor and this technology uses FETs.
- MOS can be classified into three subfamilies:

   PMOS (P-channel)

   NMOS (N-channel)

   CMOS (Complementary MOS, most common)

- The following simplified symbols are used to represent MOSFET transistors in most CMOS. The gate of a MOS transistor controls the flow of the current between the drain and the source. The MOS transistor can be viewed as a simple ON/OFF switch.

Advantages of MOS Digital ICs

- They are simple and inexpensive to fabricate.
- Can be used for Higher integration and consume little power.

Disadvantages of MOS Digital ICs

- There is a possibility for Static-electricity damage.
- They are slower than TTL.

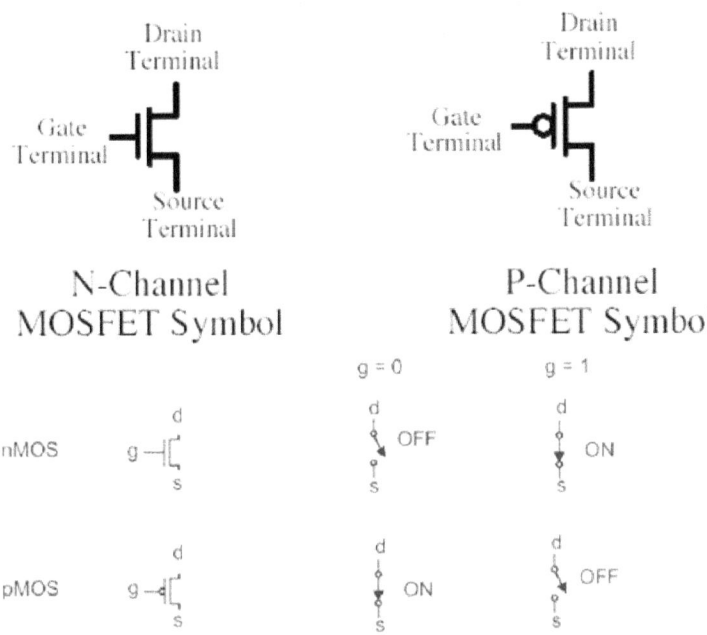

ECL: Emitter-Coupled Logic

- The key to reduce propagation delay in a bipolar logic family is to prevent a gate's transistors from saturating. It is possible to prevent saturation by using a radically different circuit structure, called Current-Mode Logic (CML) or Emitter-Coupled Logic (ECL).
- Unlike the other logic families in this chapter, ECL does not produce a large voltage swing between the LOW and HIGH levels but it has a small voltage swing, less than a volt, and it internally switches current between two possible paths, depending on the output state.

Basic ECL Circuit

- The basic idea of current-mode logic is illustrated by the inverter/buffer circuit in the figure. This circuit has both an inverting output (OUT1) and a non-inverting output (OUT2).
- Two transistors are connected as a differential amplifier with a common emitter resistor.
- The supply voltages for this example are VCC = 5.0, VBB = 4.0, and VEE = 0 V, and the input LOW and HIGH levels are defined to be 3.6 and 4.4 V. This

circuit actually produces output LOW and HIGH levels that are 0.6 V higher (4.2 and 5.0 V). The diagram below shows a basic ECL inverter circuit with input high.

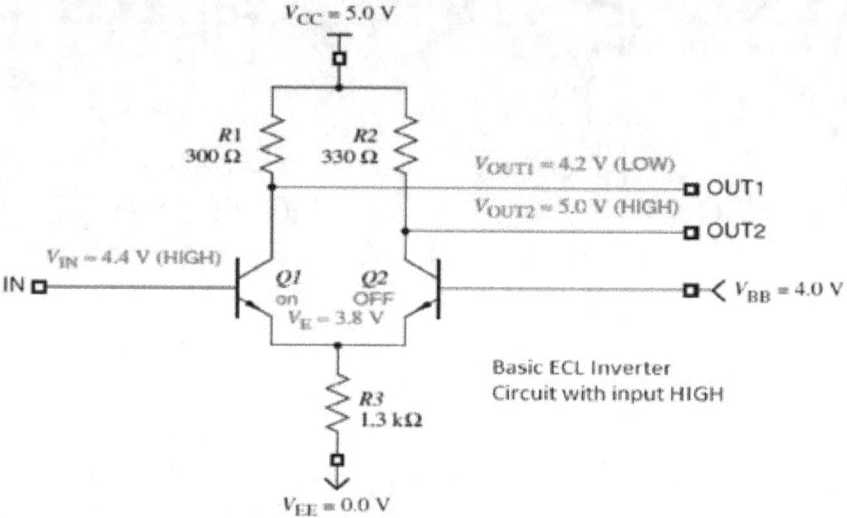

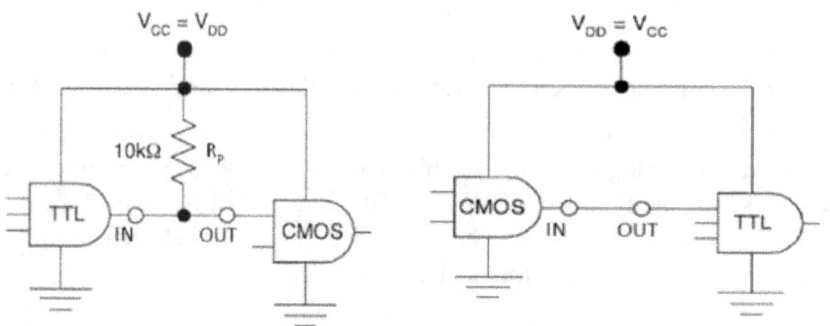

TTL vs. CMOS

- TTL has less propagation delay than CMOS i.e. TTL is good where high speed is needed.
- And CMOS 4000 is good for Battery equipment and where speed is not so important.
- CMOS requires less power than TTL i.e. power dissipation and hence power consumption is less for CMOS.

Chapter 19
Counter

A counter is a device which stores (and sometimes displays) the number of times a particular event or process has occurred. In electronics, counters can be implemented quite easily using register-type circuits.

A counter is a sequential logic circuit consisting of a series of flip-flops arranged in such a way that they count the number of clock pulses. Counters can be used to count events, divide frequencies, or generate specific time delays. The count sequence can be binary or follow another code, such as BCD (Binary-Coded Decimal).

There are different types of counters, viz.

- » Synchronous counter
- » Asynchronous (ripple) counter
- » Binary Counter
- » Modulus counter.
- » Decade counter
- » Up/down counter
- » Johnson counter
- » Ring counter

Synchronous Counter

A synchronous counter is a type of counter in which all the flip-flops are driven by the same clock signal. This means that all flip-flops change their state simultaneously (in synchronization) with the clock pulse. Due to this simultaneous switching, synchronous counters eliminate the delay issues present in asynchronous counters and can operate at higher frequencies.

Characteristics
- All flip-flops receive the clock pulse simultaneously.
- No ripple effect; transitions occur at the same time.

- Faster operation compared to asynchronous counters.
- More complex design due to additional logic required to ensure simultaneous switching.

A 4-bit synchronous counter using JK flip-flops is shown in the following Figure. Some important points about synchronous counter are:

- In synchronous counters, the clock inputs of all the flip-flops are connected together and are triggered by the input pulses. Thus, all the flip-flops change state simultaneously (in parallel).
- The circuit below is a 4-bit synchronous counter.
- The J and K inputs of FF0 are connected to HIGH. FF1 has its J and K inputs connected to the output of FF0, and the J and K inputs of FF2 are connected to the output of an AND gate that is fed by the outputs of FF0 and FF1.
- A simple way of implementing the logic for each bit of an ascending counter (which is what is depicted in the image to the right) is for each bit to toggle when all of the less significant bits are at a logic high state.

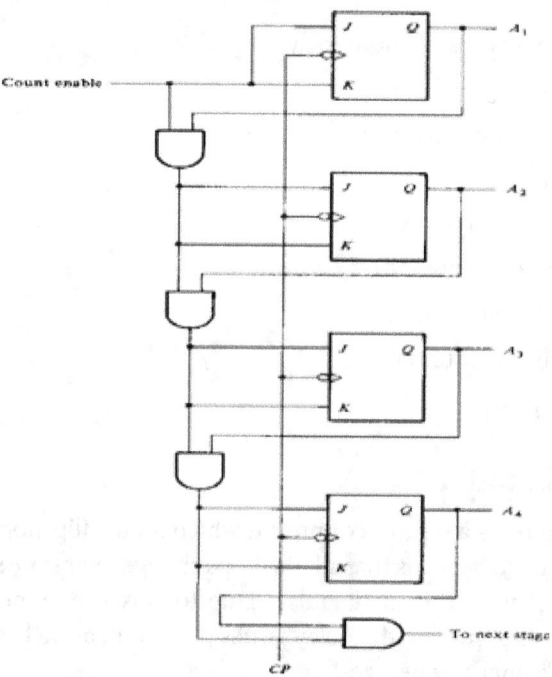

- For example, bit 1 toggles when bit 0 is logic high; bit 2 toggles when both bit 1 and bit 0 are logic high; bit 3 toggles when bit 2, bit 1 and bit 0 are all high; and so on.

- Synchronous counters can also be implemented with hardware finite state machines, which are more complex but allow for smoother, more stable transitions.

Asynchronous Counter

An asynchronous counter, also known as a ripple counter, is a type of counter where the flip-flops are not clocked simultaneously. Instead, the output of one flip-flop serves as the clock input for the next flip-flop in the series. This results in a delay that propagates through the flip-flops, causing a ripple effect.

Characteristics

- Flip-flops are clocked sequentially, one after another.
- The output of one flip-flop triggers the next.
- Ripple effect causes cumulative delay, limiting speed.
- Simpler design and easier to implement than synchronous counters.
- Slower operation due to the cumulative delay.
  Some important points about asynchronous counter are given below:
- An asynchronous (ripple) counter is a single D-type flip-flop, with its J (data) input fed from its own inverted output.
- This circuit can store one bit, and hence can count from zero to one before it overflows (starts over from 0).
- This counter will increment once for every clock cycle and takes two clock cycles to overflow, so every cycle it will alternate between a transition from 0 to 1 and a transition from 1 to 0.
- This creates a new clock with a 50% duty cycle at exactly half the frequency of the input clock.
- If this output is then used as the clock signal for a similarly arranged D flip-flop, remembering to invert the output to the input, one will get another 1-bit counter that counts half as fast. These together yield a two-bit counter.
- Additional flip-flops can be added, by always inverting the output to its own input, and using the output from the previous flip-flop as the clock signal. The result is called a ripple counter, which can count to 2n

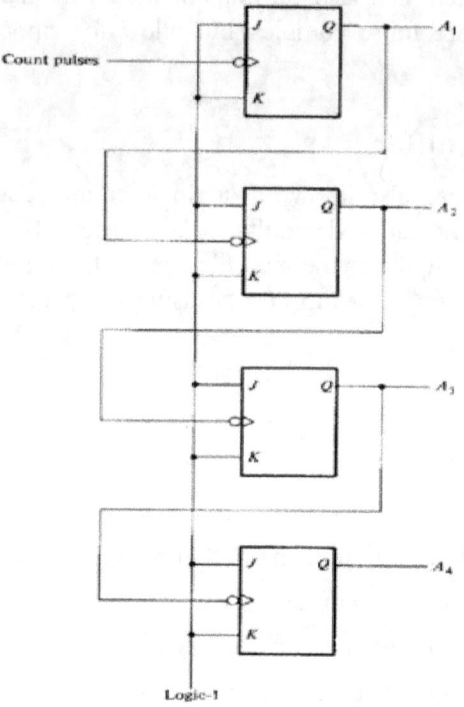

- Where n is the number of bits (flip-flop stages) in the counter.
- Ripple counters suffer from unstable outputs as the overflow's "ripple" from stage to stage, but they find application as dividers for clock signals.

Feature	Synchronous Counter	Asynchronous Counter
Clocking	Simultaneous for all flip-flops	Sequential from one flip-flop to the next
Speed	Faster (higher frequency operation)	Slower due to ripple delays
Complexity	More complex	Simpler
Delay	Minimal to none	Cumulative ripple delay
Example	74LS161 (4-bit synchronous counter)	74LS393 (dual 4-bit asynchronous counter)

Counters, whether synchronous or asynchronous, are fundamental components in digital electronics, used for counting operations, frequency division, and timing applications.

Binary Counter

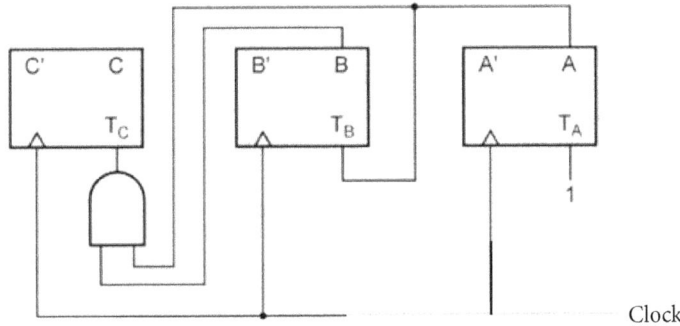

Modulus Counter

- A modulus counter is that which produces an output pulse after a certain number of input pulses is applied.
- In the modulus counter the total count possible is based on the number of stages, i.e., digit positions.
- Modulus counters are used in digital computers.
- A binary modulo-8 counter with three flip-flops, i.e., three stages, will produce an output pulse, i.e., display an output one-digit, after eight input pulses have been counted, i.e., entered or applied. This assumes that the counter started in the zero-condition.

Decade Counter

A decade counter is a binary counter designed to count to 1001 (decimal 9).

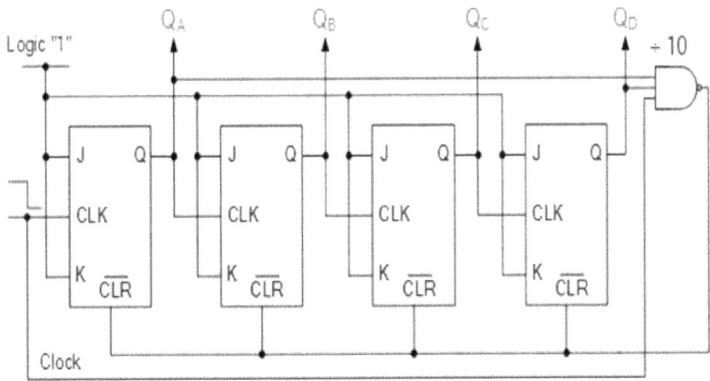

A decade counter can count from BCD "0" to BCD "9".

- A decade counter requires resetting to zero when the output count reaches the decimal value of 10, ie. when DCBA = 1010 and this condition is fed back to the reset input.
- A counter with a count sequence from binary "0000" (BCD = "0") through to "1001" (BCD = "9") is generally referred to as a BCD binary-coded-decimal counter because its ten-state sequence is that of a BCD code but binary decade counters are more common.
- This type of asynchronous counter counts upwards on each leading edge of the input clock signal starting from 0000 until it reaches an output 1001 (decimal 9).
- Both outputs QA and QD are now equal to logic "1" and the output from the NAND gate changes state from logic "1" to a logic "0" level and whose output is also connected to the CLEAR (CLR) inputs of all the J-K Flip-flops.
- This signal causes all of the Q outputs to be reset back to binary 0000 on the count of 10. Once QA and QD are both equal to logic "0" the output of the NAND gate returns back to a logic level "1" and the counter restarts again from 0000. We now have a decade or Modulo-10 counter.

Decade Counter Truth Table

Clock Count	Output bit Pattern				Decimal Value
	QD	QC	QB	QA	
1	0	0	0	0	0
2	0	0	0	1	1
3	0	0	1	0	2
4	0	0	1	1	3
5	0	1	0	0	4
6	0	1	0	1	5
7	0	1	1	0	6
8	0	1	1	1	7
9	1	0	0	0	8
10	1	0	0	1	9
11	Counter Resets its Outputs back to Zero				

Up/Down Counter

- In a synchronous up-down binary counter the flip-flop in the lowest-order position is complemented with every pulse.
- A flip-flop in any other position is complemented with a pulse, provided all the lower-order pulse equal to 0.
- Up/Down counter is used to control the direction of the counter through a certain sequence.

Up	Q_2	Q_1	Q_0	Down
↓	0	0	0	↑
	0	0	1	
	0	1	0	
	0	1	1	
	1	0	0	
	1	0	1	
	1	1	0	
	1	1	1	

- From the sequence table we can observe that
- For both the UP and DOWN sequences, Q_0 toggles on each clock pulse.
  - For the UP sequence, Q_1 changes state on the next clock pulse when $Q_0=1$.
- For the DOWN sequence, Q_1 changes state on the next clock pulse when $Q_0=0$.
- For the UP sequence, Q_2 changes state on the next clock pulse when $Q_0=Q_1=1$.
- For the DOWN sequence, Q_2 changes state on the next clock pulse when $Q_0=Q_1=0$.

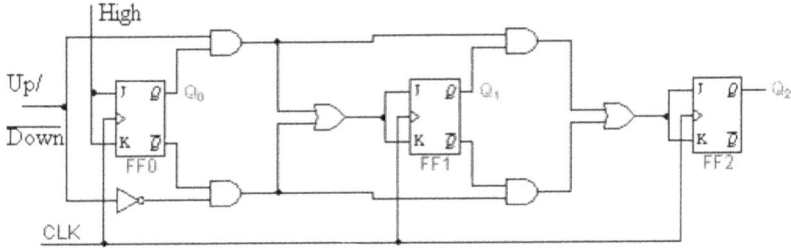

- These characteristics are implemented with the AND, OR & NOT logic connected as shown in the logic diagram above.

Johnson Counter

The Johnson counter is a modification of ring counter. In this the inverted output of the last stage flip flop is connected to the input of first flip flop. If we use n flip flops to design the Johnson counter, it is known as 2n bit Johnson counter or Mod 2n Johnson counter.

This is an advantage of the Johnson counter that it requires only half number of flip flops that of a ring counter uses, to design the same Mod.

The main difference between the 4 bit ring counter and the Johnson counter is that, in ring counter, we connect the output of last flip flop directly to the input of first flip flop. But in Johnson counter, we connect the inverted output of last stage to the first stage input.

The Johnson counter is also known as Twisted Ring Counter, with a feedback. In Johnson counter the input of the first flip flop is connected from the inverted output of the last flip flop.

The Johnson counter or switch trail ring counter is designed in such a way that it overcomes the limitations of ring counter. Mainly it reduces the number of flip flops required for designing the circuit.

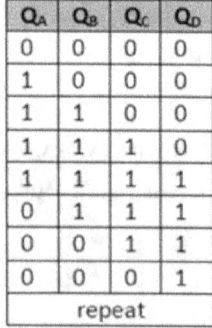
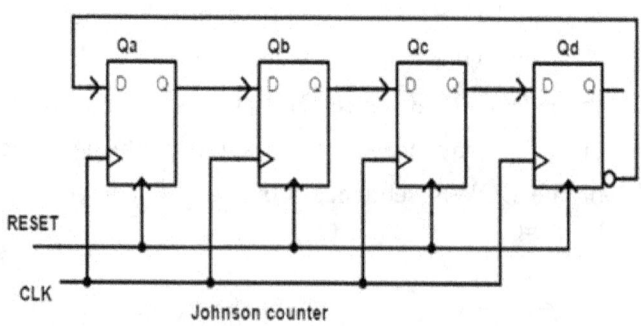

Johnson counter

Similar to the ring counter, the clock signal in Johnson counter is connected to the clock input of each flip flop simultaneously.

Operation of Johnson Counter

The Johnson counter designed with D flip flop is shown below. It has four stages i.e. four flip flops connected in series type or cascaded. Initially zero / Null is fed to the Johnson counter and on applying the clock signal, outputs will change to "1000", "1100", "1110", "1111", "0111", "0011", "0001", "0000" in a sequence and the sequence will repeat for next clock signal.

The Johnson counter produces a special pattern by passing four 0's and then four 1's and thus it produces a special pattern by counting up down.

Truth table of Johnson Counters

The truth table of the 4-bit ring counter is explained below.

Q_A	Q_B	Q_C	Q_D
0	0	0	0
1	0	0	0
1	1	0	0
1	1	1	0
1	1	1	1
0	1	1	1
0	0	1	1
0	0	0	1
repeat			

The state diagram indicates that how the data transfers from one flip flop to another for every clock pulse. The 4 stage Johnson ring counters are used as frequency dividers, by varying their feedback connections. So they can be used as frequency divider circuits also.

Advantage
- It has more outputs than ring counter.

Disadvantage
- Only out of 15 states are only 8 are used.

Ring Counters

Ring counter is a sequential logic circuit that is constructed using shift register. Same data recirculates in the counter depending on the clock pulse.

Ring counters are of two types
1. Ordinary Ring counters
2. Johnson counters

4-bit Ring Counter

The ring counter is a cascaded connection of flip flops, in which the output of last flip flop is connected to input of first flip flop. In ring counter if the output of any stage is 1, then its reminder is 0. The Ring counters transfers the same output throughout the circuit.

That means if the output of the first flip flop is 1, then this is transferred to its next stage i.e. 2nd flip flop. By transferring the output to its next stage, the output of first flip flop becomes 0. And this process continues for all the stages of a ring counter. If we use n flip flops in the ring counter, the '1' is circulated for every n clock cycles.

The circuit diagram of the ring counter is shown below.

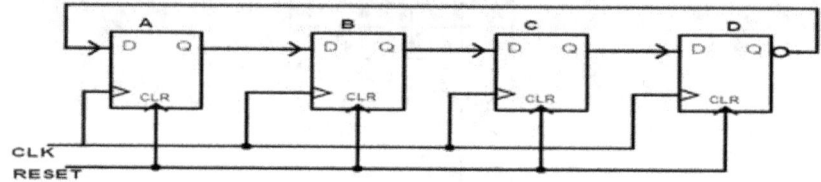

Here we design the ring counter by using D flip flop. This is a Mod 4 ring counter which has 4 D flip flops connected in series. The clock signal is applied to clock input of each flip flop, simultaneously and the RESET pulse is applied to the CLR inputs of all the flip flops.

Truth table of Ring Counter

The truth table of the 4-bit ring counter is explained below.

Q_0	Q_1	Q_2	Q_3
1	0	0	0
0	1	0	0
0	0	1	0
0	0	0	1

When CLEAR input CLR = 0, then all flip flops are set to 1. When CLEAR input CLR = 1, the ring counter starts its operation. For one clock signal, the counter starts its operation. On next clock signal, the counter again resets to 0000. Ring counter has 4 sequences: 0001, 0010, 0100, 1000, 000.

Advantages

- Can be implemented using D and JK flip-flops. It is a self-decoding circuit.

Disadvantages

- Only four of the 15 states are being utilized.

Applications of Ring counters

- Ring counters are used to count the data in a continuous loop.
- They are also used to detect the various numbers values or various patterns within a set of information, by connecting AND & OR logic gates to the ring counter circuits.
- 2 stage, 3 stage and 4 stage ring counters are used in frequency divider circuits as divide by 2 and divide by 3 and divide by 4 circuits, respectively.
- The 3 stage Johnson counter is used as a 3 phase square wave generator which produces 1200 phase shift.
- The 5 stage Johnson counter circuit is generally used as synchronous decade (BCD) counter and also as divider circuit.
- The 2 stage Johnson counters are also known as "Quadrature oscillator" which is used to produce 4 level individual outputs which are out of phase with 900 with each other. This quadrature generator is used to produce 4 phase timing signal.

Chapter 20
Registers

Introduction
- The sequential circuits known as registers are a very important logical block in most of the digital systems.
- Registers are used for storage and transfer of binary information in a digital system.
- A register is mostly used for the purpose of storing and shifting binary data entered into it from an external source and has no characteristic internal sequence of states.
- The storage capacity of a register is defined as the number of bits of digital data it can store or retain.
- These registers are normally used for temporary storage of data.

Buffer Register
- These are the simplest registers and are used for simply storing a binary word.
- These may be controlled by Controlled Buffer Register.
- D flip – flops are used for constructing a buffer register or other flip- flop can be used.
- The figure shown below is a 4- bit buffer register.
- The binary word to be stored is applied to the data terminals.
- When the clock pulse is applied, the output word becomes the same as the word applied at the input terminals, i.e. the input word is loaded into the register by the application of the clock pulse.
- When the positive clock edge arrives, the stored word becomes:
$$Q_4 Q_3 Q_2 Q_1 = X_4 X_3 X_2 X_1$$
or
$$Q = X.$$

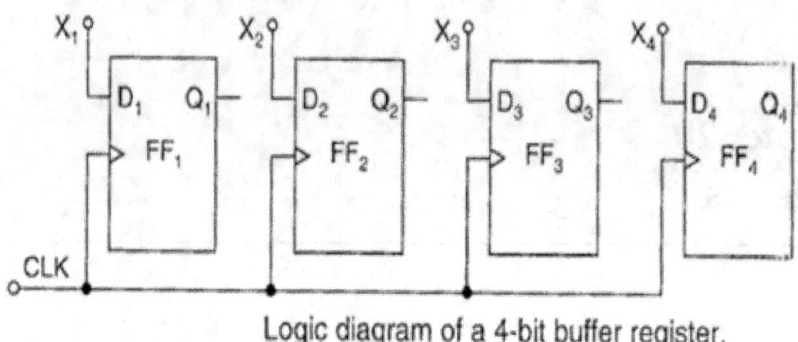

Logic diagram of a 4-bit buffer register.

- This circuit is too primitive to be of any use.

Controlled Buffer Register

- The figure shows a controlled buffer register.

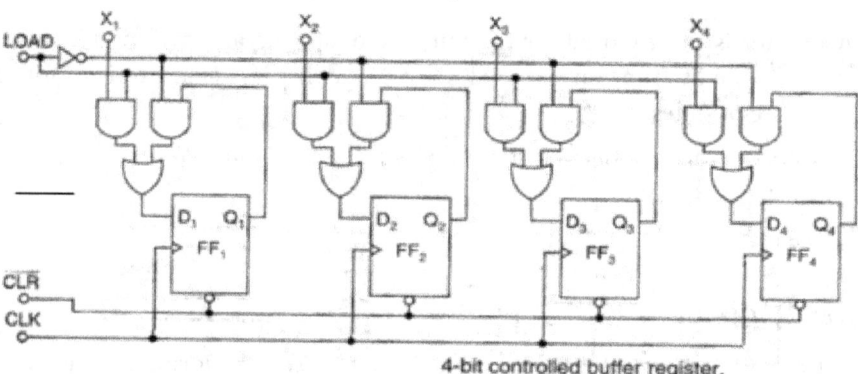

4-bit controlled buffer register.

- If CLR goes LOW, all the flip-flops are RESET and the output becomes, Q = 0000.
- When CLR is HIGH, the register is ready for action
- LOAD is control input.
- When LOAD is HIGH, the data bits X can reach the D inputs of FFs.
- At the positive going edge of the next clock pulse, the register is loaded, i.e.

$$Q_4 Q_3 Q_2 Q_1 = X_4 X_3 X_2 X_1$$

or

$$Q = X.$$

- When LOAD is LOW, the X bits cannot reach the FFs. At the same time the inverted signal LOAD is HIGH. This forces each flip-flop output to feedback to its data input.
- Therefore, data is circulated or retained as each clock pulse arrives.
- In other words, the content register remains unchanged in spite of the clock pulses.
- Longer buffer registers can be built by adding more FFs.

Controlled Buffer Register

- A number of FFs connected together such that data may be shifted into and shifted out of them is called a shift register.
- Data may be shifted into or out of the register either in serial form or in parallel form.
- There are four basic types of shift registers
  » Serial in, serial out
  » Serial in, parallel out
  » Parallel in, serial out
  » Parallel in, parallel out

Serial in, Serial out Shift Register

- This type of shift register accepts data serially, i.e., one bit at a time and also outputs data serially.
- The logic diagram of a four-bit serial in, serial out shift register is shown in below figure:
- In 4 stages i.e. with 4 FFs, the register can store up to 4 bits of data.
- Serial data is applied at the D input of the first FF. The Q output of the first FF is connected to the D input of the second FF, the output of the second FF is connected to the D input of the third FF and the Q output of the third FF is connected to the D input of the fourth FF. The data is outputted from the Q terminal of the last FF.
- When a serial data is transferred to a register, each new bit is clocked into the first FF at the positive.
- Going edge of each clock pulse.
- The bit that is previously stored by the first FF is transferred to the second FF.

- The bit that is stored by the second FF is transferred to the third FF, and so on.
- The bit that was stored by the last FF is shifted out.
- A shift register can also be constructed using J-K FFs or S-R FFs as shown in the figure below.

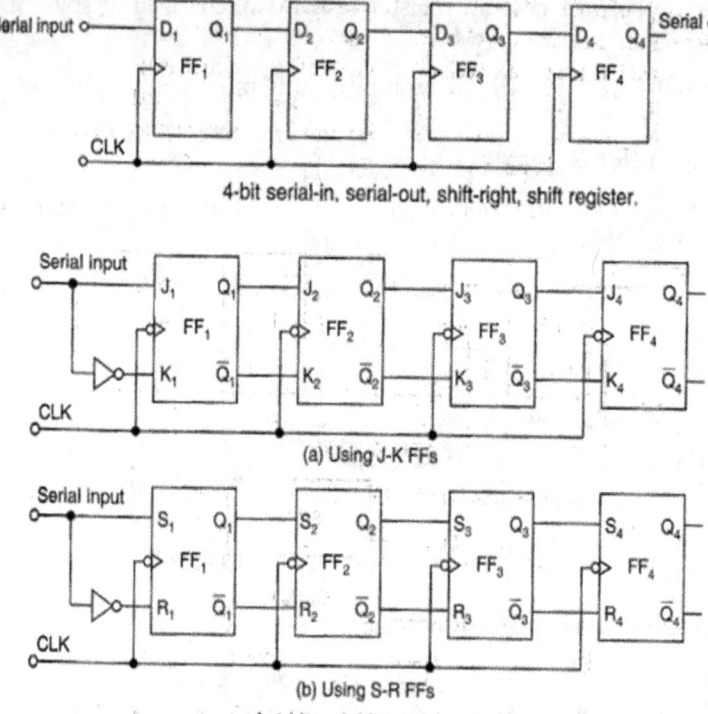

4-bit serial-in, serial-out, shift-right, shift register.

(a) Using J-K FFs

(b) Using S-R FFs

A 4-bit serial-in, serial-out, shift register.

Serial in, Parallel out Shift Register

- In this type of register, the data bits are entered into the register serially, but the data stored in the register serially, but the stored in the register is shifted out in the parallel form.
- When the data bits are stored once, each bit appears on its respective output line and all bits are available simultaneously, rather than bit – by – bit basis as in the serial output.
- The serial in, parallel out shift register can be used as a serial in, serial out shift register if the output is taken from the Q terminal of the last FF.
- The logic diagram and logic symbol of a 4-bit serial in, parallel out shift register is given below.

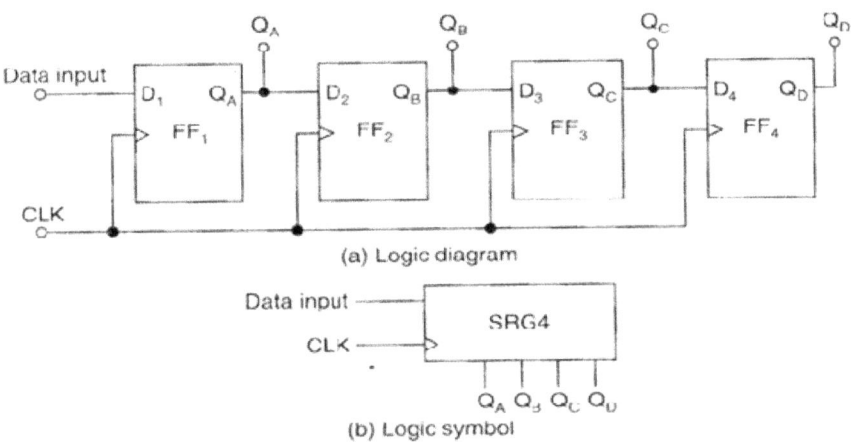

A 4- bit serial in, parallel out shift register

Parallel in, Serial out Shift Register

- For parallel in, serial out shift register the data bits are entered simultaneously into their respective stages on parallel lines, rather than on bit by bit basis on one line as with serial data inputs, but the data bits are transferred out of the register serially, i.e., on a bit by bit basis over a single line.
- The logic diagram and logic symbol of 4 bit parallel in, serial out shift register using D FFs is shown below.
- There are four data lines A, B, C and D through which the data is entered into the register in parallel form.
- The signal Shift /LOAD allows
- The data to be entered in parallel form into the register and
- The data to be shifted out serially from terminal Q_4.
- When the Shift /LOAD line is HIGH, gates G_1, G_2, and G_3 are disabled, but gates G_4, G_5 and G_6 are enabled allowing the data bits to shift right from one stage to next.
- When the Shift /LOAD line is LOW, gates G_4, G_5 and G_6 are disabled, whereas gates G_1, G_2 and G_3 are enabled allowing the data input to appear at the D inputs of the respective FFs.
- When a clock pulse is applied, these data bits are shifted to the Q output terminals of the FFs and therefore the data is inputted in one step.

- The OR gate allows either the normal shifting operation or the parallel data entry depending on which AND gates are enabled by the level on the Shift / LOAD input.

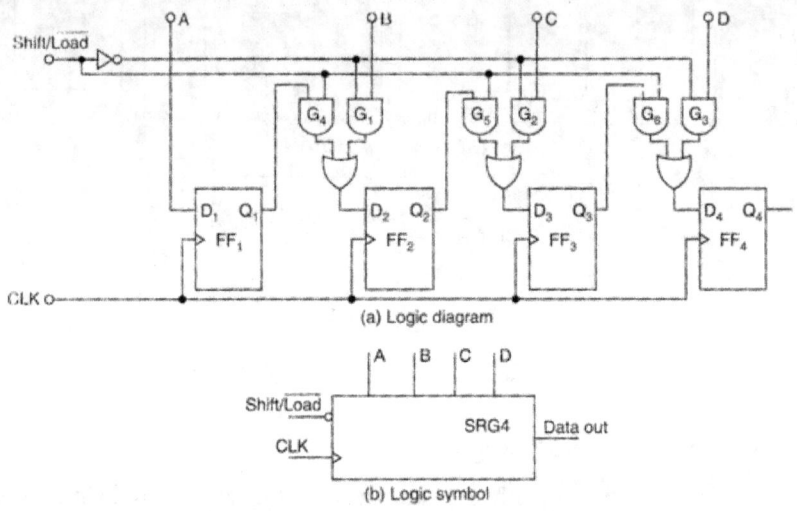

(a) Logic diagram

(b) Logic symbol

A 4- bit parallel in, serial out shift register

Parallel in, Parallel out Shift Register

- In a parallel in, parallel out shift register, the data entered into the register in parallel form and also the data taken out of the register in parallel form. Immediately following the simultaneous entry of all data bits appear on the parallel outputs.
- The figure shown below is a 4 bit parallel in parallel out shift register using D FFs.
- Data applied to the D input terminals of the FFs.
- When a clock pulse is applied at the positive edge of that pulse, the D inputs are shifted into the Q outputs of the FFs.
- The register now stores the data.
- The stored data is available instantaneously for shifting out in parallel form.

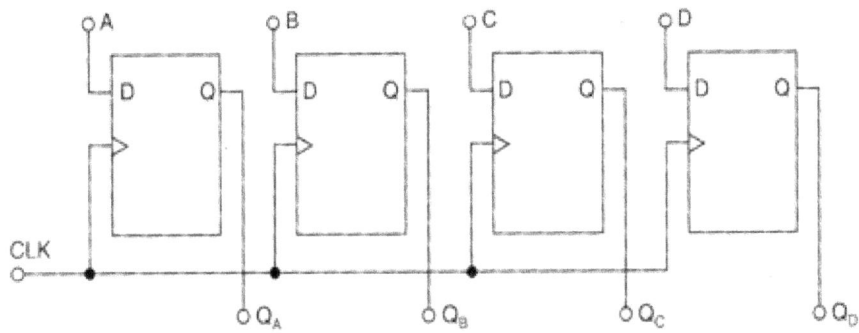

Logic diagram of a 4 – bit parallel in, parallel out shift register

Bidirectional Shift Register

- A bidirectional shift register is one in which the data bits can be shifted from left to right or from right to left.
- The figure shown below the logic diagram of a 4 bit serial in, serial out, bidirectional (shift-left, shift- right) shift register.
- Right /Left is the mode signal. When Right /Left is a 1, the logic circuit works as a shift right shift register. When Right /Left is a 0, the logic circuit works as a shift right shift register.
- The bidirectional is achieved by using the mode signal and two AND gates and one OR gate for each stage.
- A HIGH on the Right/Left control input enables the AND gates G_1, G_2, G_3 and G_4 and disables the AND gates G_5, G_6, G_7 and G_8 and the state of Q output of each FF is passed through the gate to the D input of the following FF. When a clock pulse occurs, the data bits are effectively shifted one place to the right.
- A LOW Right/Left control input enables the AND gates G_5, G_6, G_7 and G_8 and disables the AND gates G_1, G_2, G_3 and G_4 and the Q output of each FF is passed to the D input of the preceding FF. When a clock pulse occurs the data bits are then effectively shifted one place to the left.
- So, the circuit works as a bidirectional shift register.

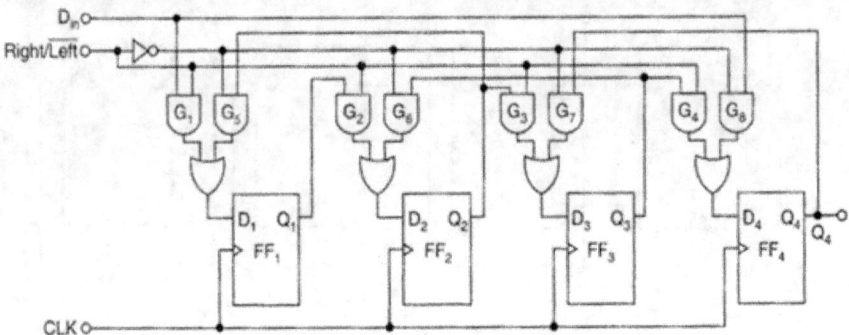

Logic diagram of 4- bit bidirectional shift register

Universal Shift Registers

- The register, which has both shifts and parallel load capabilities, is referred to as a universal shift register. So, the universal shift register is a bidirectional register, whose input can be either in serial form or in parallel form and whose output also can be either in serial form or parallel form.
- The universal shift register can be realized using multiplexers.
- The figure shows the logic diagram of a 4 bit universal shift register that has all the capabilities of a general shift register.

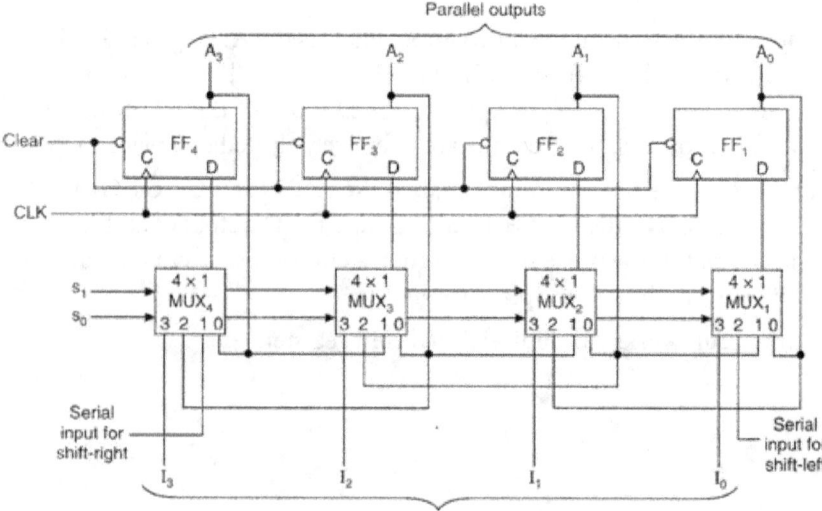

Fig- (a) 4-bit universal shift register

- It consists of four D flip- flops and four multiplexers.
- The four multiplexers have two common selection inputs S1 and S0.
- Input 0 in each multiplexer is selected when $S_1S_0 = 00$, input 1 is selected when $S_1S_0 = 01$, and input 2 is selected when $S_1S_0 = 10$ and input 3 is selected when $S_1S_0 = 11$.
- The selection inputs control the mode of operation of the register according to the function entries shown in the table.
- When $S_1S_0 = 00$ the present value of the register is applied to the D inputs of flip-flops. This condition forms a path from the output of each FF into the input of the same FF.
- The next clock edge transfers into each FF the binary value it held previously, and no change of state occurs.
- When $S_1S_0 = 01$, terminal 1 of the multiplexer inputs have a path of the D inputs of the flip- flops. This causes a shift right operation, with serial input transferred into FF_4.
- When $S_1S_0 = 10$ a shift left operation results with the other serial input going into the FF_1.
- Finally when $S_1S_0 = 11$, the binary information on the parallel input lines is transferred into the register simultaneously during the next clock edge.

Functional table for the register of Fig – a:

Mode control		Register operation
S_1	S_0	
0	0	No change
0	1	Shift right
1	0	Shift left
1	1	Parallel load

Applications of Shift Registers

Time delays

- In digital systems, it is necessary to delay the transfer of data until the operation of the other data has been completed, or to synchronize the arrival of data when processed with other data.
- A shift register can be used to delay the arrival of serial data by a subsystem where it is a specific number of clock pulses, since the number of stages corresponds to the number of clock pulses required to shift each bit completely through the register.

- The total time delay can be controlled by adjusting the clock frequency and by the number of stages in the register.
- In practice, the clock frequency is fixed and the total delay can be adjusted only by controlling the number of stages through which the data is passed.

Serial / Parallel data conversion

- Transfer of data in parallel form is much faster than that in serial form.
- Similarly the processing of data is much faster when all the data bits are available simultaneously. Thus in digital systems in which speed is important so to operate on data parallel form is used.
- When large data is to be transmitted over long distances, transmitting data on parallel lines is costly and impracticable.
- It is convenient and economical to transmit data in serial form, since serial data transmission requires only one line.
- Shift registers are used for converting serial data to parallel form, so that a serial input can be processed by a parallel system and for converting parallel data to serial form, so that parallel data can be transmitted serially.
- A serial in, parallel out shift register can be used to perform serial-to parallel conversion, and a parallel in, serial out shift register can be used to perform parallel- to –serial conversion.
- A universal shift register can be used to perform both the serial- to – parallel and parallel-to- serial data conversion.
- A bidirectional shift register can be used to reverse the order of data.

Ring and Johnson Counter

- Ring counters are constructed by modifying the serial-in, serial-out, shift register.
- There are two types of ring counters
    » Basic ring counter
    » Johnson counter
- The basic ring counter can be obtained from a serial-in serial- out shift register by connecting the Q output of the last FF to the D input of the first FF.
- The Johnson counter can be obtained from serial-in, serial- out, shift register by connecting the Q output of the last FF to the D input of the first FF.

- Ring counter outputs can be used as a sequence of synchronizing pulses.
- The ring counter is a decimal counter.

D/A and A/D Converter

Weighted Resistor Network

The most significant bit (MSB) resistance is one-eighth of the least significant bit (LSB) resistance. RL is much larger than 8R. The voltages V_A, V_B, V_C and V_D can be either equal to V (for logic 1) or 0 (for logical 0). Thus there are 24 = 16 input combinations from 0000 to 1111. The output voltage V_0, given by Millman's theorem is

$V_0 = ?$ (out of scope of this book)

When input is 0001, $V_A = V_B = V_C = 0$ and $V_D = V$ and output is V/15. If input is 0010, $V_A = V_B = V_D = 0$ and $V_C = V$ giving an output of 2V/15. If input is 0011, $V_A = V_B = 0$ and $V_C = V_D = V$ giving an output of 3v/15. Thus, the output voltage varies from 0 to V in steps of V/15.

Binary Ladder Network

The weighted resistor network requires a range of resistor values. The binary ladder network requires only two resistance values. From node 1, the resistance to the digital source is 2R and resistance to ground is also 2R. From node 2, the resistance to digital source is 2R and resistance to ground =

R + (2R) (2R) / (2R+2R) = 2R

Thus, from each of the nodes 1,2,3,4, the resistance to source and ground is 2R each. A digital input 0001 means that D is connected to V and A, B, C are grounded. The output voltage V0 is V/16. Thus, as input varies from 0000 to 1111, the output varies from V/16 to V in steps of V/16.

A complete digital-to-analog converter circuit consists of a number of ladder networks (to deal with more bits of data), operational amplifier, gates etc.

Performance Characteristics of D/A Converters

The performance characteristics of D/A converters are resolution, accuracy, linear errors, monotonicity, setting time and temperature sensitivity.

a. **Resolution:** It is the reciprocal of the number of discrete steps in the D/A output. Evidently resolution depends on the number of bits. The percentage resolution is [1/ (2N-1)] * 100 where N is the number of bits. The percentage resolution for different values of N is given in the table given below.

b. **Accuracy:** It is a measure of the difference between actual output and expected output. It is expressed as a percentage of the maximum output voltage. If the maximum output voltage (or full-scale deflection) is 5 V and 0.1 accuracy is ±0.1%, then the maximum error is 0.1/100 * 5 = 0.005 V or 5 mV. Ideally the accuracy should be better than ±0.5 of LSB. In an 8 bit converter, LSB is 1/256 or 0.39% of full scale. The accuracy should be better than 0.2%.

c. **Setting Time:** When the input signal changes, it is desirable that the analog output signal should immediately show the new output value. However, in actual practice, the D/A converter takes some time to settle at the new position of the output voltage. Setting time is defined as the time taken by the D/A converter to settle within ±1/2 LSB of its final value when a change in input digital signal occurs. The final time taken to settle down to a new value is due to the transients and oscillations in the output voltage. Figure shows the definition of setting time.

Table	
3 bit Binary word	**Analog voltage**
000	0
001	1
010	2
011	3
100	4
101	5
110	6
111	7

Figure 20.1: *The percentage resolution*

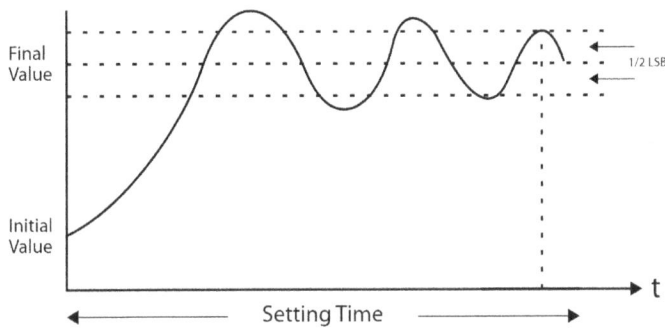

Figure 20.2: *Setting time of D/A converter*

Quantization Error

An analog to digital converter changes analog signal into digital signal. It is important to note that in a D/A converter the number of inputs is fixed. In a 4-bit D/A converter there are 16 possible inputs and in a 6-bit D/A converter there are 64 possible inputs. However, in an A/D converter the analog input voltage can have any value in the specified range but the digital output can have only 2N discrete levels (for N bit converter). This means that there is a certain range of input voltage which corresponds to every discrete output level.

Consider a 4-bit A/D converter having a resolution of 1 count per 100 mV. Fig (b) shows the analog input and digital output. It is seen that for input voltage range of 50 mV to 150 mV, the output is same i.e. 0001, for input voltage range of 150 mV to 250 mV, the output is the same, i.e. 0010. Thus, we have one digital output for each 100-mV input range. If the digital signal of 0010 is fed to a D/A converter, it will show an output of 200 V whereas the original input voltage was between 150 V and 250 v. This error is called quantisation error and in this case this quantisation error can be ±50 mV and is equal to ±1/2 LSB.

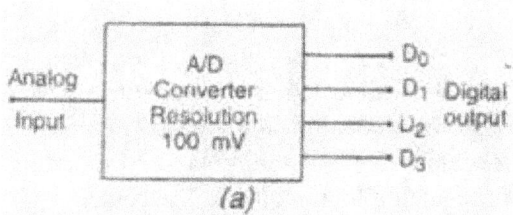

Figure 20.2(a): *A/D Converter*

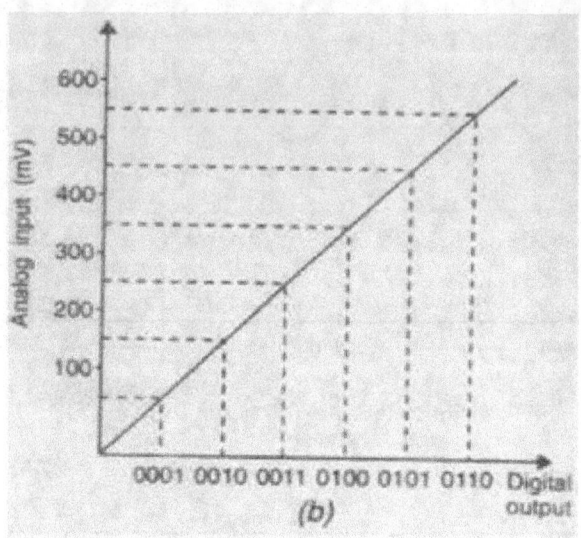

Figure 20.2(b): *Quantisation error*

Stair Step A/D Converter / Ramp A/D Converter

This converter is also called digital ramp or the counter type A/D converter. Figure shows the configuration for the 8 bit converter. As seen in figure it uses a D/A converter and a binary counter to produce the digital number corresponding to analog input. The main components are comparator, AND gate, D/A converter, divided by 256 counters and latches. The analog input is given to the non-inverting terminal of the comparator. The D/A converter provides stair step reference voltage.

Let the counter be in reset state and output of D/A converter be zero. An analog input is given to the non-inverting terminal of the comparator. Since the reference input is 0, the comparator gives High output and enables the AND gate. The clock pulses cause advancing of the counter through its binary states and stair step reference voltage is produced from D/A converter. As the counter keeps advancing, successively higher stair step output voltage is produced. When this stair step voltage reaches the level of analog input voltage, the comparator output goes Low and disables the AND gate. The clock pulses are cut off and counter stops. The state of the counter at this point is equal to the number of steps in reference voltage at which comparison occurs. The binary number corresponding to this number of steps is the value of the analog input voltage. The control logic causes this binary number to be loaded into the latches and the counter is reset.

This converter is rather slow in action because the counter has to pass through the maximum number of states before a conversion takes place. For an 8-bit device this means 256 counter states.

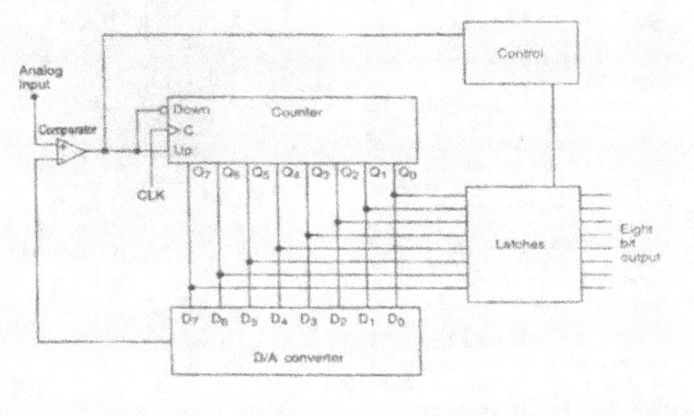

Figure 20.3(a): *8 bit up-down counter type A/D converter*

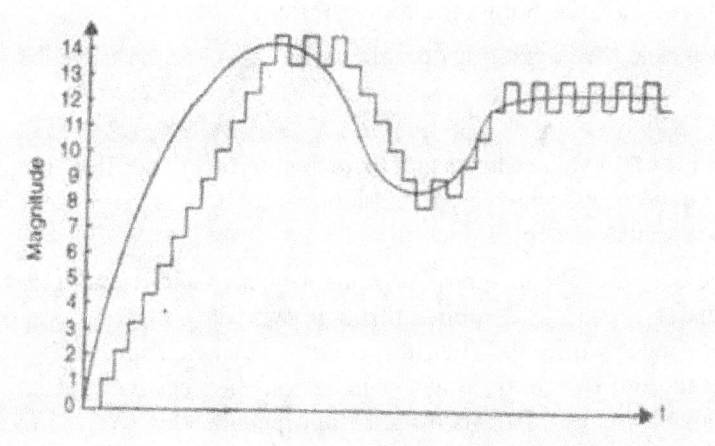

Figure 20.3(b): *Tracking action of updown counter type A/D Converter*

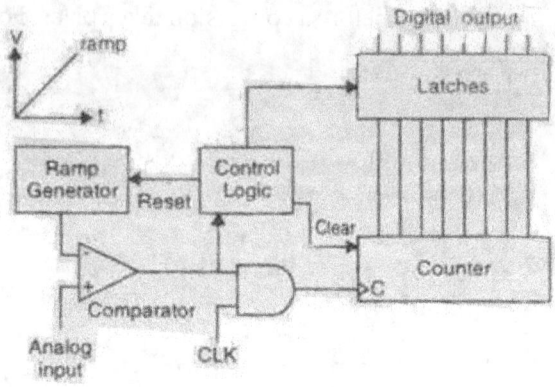

Figure 20.3(c): *Single slope A/D converter*

Dual Slope A/D Converter

The single slope A/D converter is susceptible to noise. The dual slope converter is free from this problem. It uses an op-amp used as an integrating amplifier for ramp generators. It is a dual slope device because it uses a fixed slope ramp as well as variable slope ramp. Fig. Shows the configuration.

It is seen that the integrating op-amp uses a capacitor in the feedback path.

Output voltage of integrating op-amp = $-\frac{1}{C}\int i\, dt = -\frac{1}{RC}\int V_{in}\, dt$ t

Thus the output voltage is integral to analog input voltage. If V_{in} is constant, we get an output - Vin RC which is a fixed slope ramp. If V_{in} is varying, we get a ramp with fixed as well as variable slope.

Let the output of the integrating amplifier be zero and the counter be reset. A positive analog input Vin is applied through switch S, we get a ramp output and the counter starts working. When the counter reaches a specified count, it will be reset again and the control logic switches on the negative reference voltage - Vref (through switch S). At this instant the capacitor C is charged to a negative voltage - V proportional to analog input voltage. When - Vref is connected the capacitor starts discharging linearly due to constant current from - Vref. The output of the integrating amplifier is now a positive fixed slope ramp starting at - V. As capacitor discharges, the counter advances from the reset state. When the output of the integrator becomes zero, the comparator output becomes Low and disables the clock signal to the AND gate. The counter is therefore stopped and the binary counter is latched. This completes one conversion cycle. The binary count is proportional to analog input V_{in}.

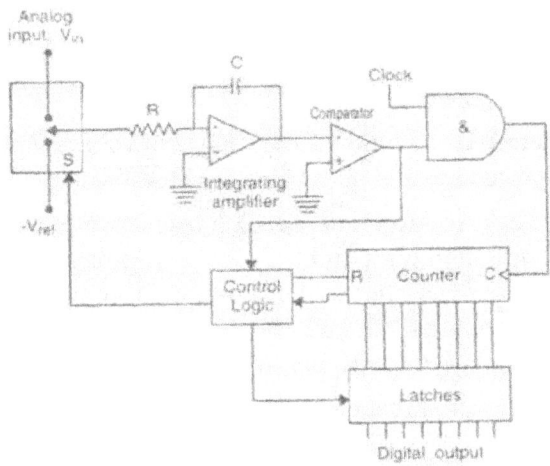

Figure 20.4: *Dual slope A/D Converter*

Successive Approximation A/D Converter

This is the most widely used A/D converter. As the name suggests the digital output tends towards analog input through successive approximations. Fig. Shows the configuration. The main components are op-amp comparator, control logic, SA (successive approximation) register and D/A converter. As shown, it is a six bit device using a maximum reference of 64 V.

Let the analog input be 26.1 v. The SA register is first set to zero. Then 1 is placed in MSB. This is fed to the D/A converter whose output goes to the comparator. Since the analog input (26.1 V) is less than D/A output (i.e. 32 V) the MSB is set to zero. Then 1 is placed a bit next to MSB. Now the output of D/A is 16 V. Since analog input is more than 16 V, this 1 is retained in this bit position. Next 1 is placed in the third bit position. Now the D/A output is 24 V which is less than analog input. Therefore this 1 bit is retained and 1 is placed in the next bit. Now the D/A output is 28 V, which is more than analog input. Therefore this 1 bit is set to zero and 1 is placed in 5th bit position producing a D/A output of 26 V. It is less than analog input. Therefore this 1 bit is retained. Now 1 is placed in LSB producing a D/A output of 27 V which is more than analog input. Therefore, LSB is set to zero and the converter gives an output of 26 V.

The successive approximation method of the A/D converter is very fast and takes only about 250 ns/ bit.

Performance Characteristics of A/D Converters

The performance characteristics of A/D converters are resolution, accuracy, A/D gain and drift and A/D speed.

a. **Resolution:** A/D resolution is the change in voltage input necessary for a one bit change in output. It can also be expressed as percent.

b. **A/D Accuracy:** The accuracy of A/D conversion is limited by the ±1/2 LSB due to quantisation error and the other errors of the system. It is defined as the maximum deviation of digital output from the ideal linear reference line. Ideally it approaches ±1/2 LSB.

c. **A/D gain and Drift:** A/D gain is the voltage output divided by the voltage input at the linearity reference line. It can usually be zeroed out.

d. Drift means change in circuit parameters with time. Drift errors of up to ±1/2 LSB will cause a maximum error of one LSB between the first and the last transition. Very low drift is quite difficult to achieve and increases the cost of the device.

e. **A/D Speed:** It can be defined in two ways, i.e. either the time necessary to do one conversion or the line between successive conversion at the highest rate possible. Speed depends on the settling time of components and the speed of the logic.

Bibliography

1. Vivek M. Patil, "Information Technology in Veterinary Science", New India Publishing Agency, New Delhi. ISBN 978-81-908512-4-4, (2009).

2. Pradeep K. Sinha, Priti Sinha, "computer fundamentals" Published by BPB Publications, ISBN 10: 8176567523 ISBN 13: 9788176567527.

3. Von Neumann, John (1945), "First Draft of a Report on the EDVAC", retrieved August 31, (2020).

4. Goldstine, Herman H., "The computer: from Pascal to von Neumann", Princeton, New Jersey: Princeton University Press. ISBN 0-691-02367-0, (1972).

5. Stern, Nancy, "From ENIAC to UNIVAC, "An appraisal of the Eckert-Mauchly Computers", Bedford, Massachusetts: Digital Press. ISBN 0-932376-14-2., (1981).

6. M.D. Godfrey and D.F. Hendry, "The Computer as von Neumann Planned It," IEEE Annals of the History of Computing, Vol. 15, No. 1, 1993, pp. 11-21, doi:10.1109/85.194088, (1993).

7. Suri, Pradeep and Sushil, Professor, "Introduction to E-Governance ", pp 1-24, ISBN: [978-981-10-2175-6], doi:10.1007/978-981-10-2176-3_1, (2017).

8. Bannister, Frank and Connolly, Regina, "Defining e-Governance", e-Service Journal, VOL 8, 10.2979/eservicej.8.2.3, PP 3-25, (2012).

9. Dawes, S., "The Evolution and Continuing Challenges of E-Governance", Public Administration Review (Special Issue), pp. S86–S101, December, (2009).

10. Arun Kumar," E-commerce". New Delhi, Global India Publications, 2010.

11. Gupta, M. P., Prabhat Kumar and Jaijit Bhattacharya, "Government online: Opportunities and challenges", New Delhi, Tata McGraw-Hill,2004.

12. Ubramanya, S.R. & Lakshmi Narasimhan, Computer viruses. Potentials, IEEE. 20. 16-19. DOI :10.1109/45.969588, (2001).

13. Raghavendra Kulkarni and Sanjay Mainalli, "E-Commerce and E-Governance", https://api.semanticscholar.org/Corpus ID:220703443,(2016).

14. Khan, Imran," An introduction to computer viruses: Problems and solutions", Library Hi Tech News, 29. 8-12, DOI: 10.1108/07419051211280036, (2012).

15. S.R. Subramanya, N. Lakshmi Narasimhan "computer virus", IEEE Potentials 20(4):16 - 19 ·, DOI: 10.1109/45.969588, November (2001)

16. N.N. Basak, "Surveying & Levelling", Mc Graw Hill Education, (1994).

17. Sami H. Ali1, Najat Qader Omar, Sohaib K. M. Abujayyab, "Investigation of The Accuracy of Surveying and Buildings with The Pulse (Non-Prism) Total Station", International Journal of Advanced Research, Volume 4, Issue 3, ISSN: [2320- 5407], (2016)

18. Sanjeev Gill, Aswin Aryan, "To Experimental Study for Comparison Theodolite and Total Station", International Journal of Engineering Research & Science (IJOER), Vol-2, Issue-3, ISSN: [2395-6992], March- (2016).

19. Brian E. Mennecke, Martin D. Crossland "Geographic Information Systems: Applications and Research Opportunities for Information Systems Researchers" 29th Annual Hawaii International Conference on System Sciences (1996), IEEE.

20. Miroslav Rusko, Roman Chovanec, Dana Roskova, "An Overview of Geographic Information System and Its Role and Applicability in Environmental Monitoring and Process Modelling", Faculty of Materials Science and Technology In Trnava, 2011

21. Abha Damani, Manish Vala, "Global Positioning System for Object Tracking", International Journal of Computer Applications (0975 – 8887) Vol-109, No-8, January 2015.

22. Chun Fui Liew, Danielle DeLatte, Naoya Takeishi, "Recent Developments in Arial Robotics: A Survey and Prototype Overview", (2017).

23. Zhiguo Gao, Yang Song, Changhui Li, Fanyang Zeng, Feng Wang, "Research On The Application Of Rapid Surveying And Mapping For Large Scare Topographic Map By UAv Aerial Photography System", International Conference on Unmanned Aerial Vehicles in Geomatics, 4–7 September 2017.

24. Correa-Muñoz, N.A. and Cerón-Calderón, L. A, "Precision and accuracy of static GNSS for surveying networks used in Civil Engineering.Ingeniería e-Investigación", 38(1), 52-59.DOI: 10.15446/ing.investig.v38n1.64543, (2018).

25. MC-NPL Computer, Lab, 1001 Powell St, Norristown, PA 19401, www.mc-npl.org.

26. MS office, Department of Statistics and Information and Communication Technology (ICT) Centre Federal University of Technology, Owerri PMB 1526, Owerri, Imo State, NIGERIA

27. Natarajan, Dhanasekharan, "Fundamentals of Digital Electronics" 1st ed. 2020. Cham: Springer International Publishing, 2020. Web.

28. Jacob Millman and D. Halkias, "Integrated Electronics Analog Digital Circuits", ISBN: [13- 9780071321747], McGraw Hill.

29. S. Salivahanan, N. Sureshkumar, "Electronic Devices and Circuits", 5th Edition ISBN: [9355322062, 9789355322067], McGrawHill.

30. K. Lal Kishore, "Electronic Devices and Circuits". S Publications

31. G.S.N. Raju, Electronic Devices and Circuits, I.K. International Publications, New Delhi, 2006.

32. John F. Wakerly, "Digital Design", Fourth Edition, Pearson/PHI, 2006

33. John Yarbrough, "Digital Logic Applications and Design", Thomson Learning, 2002.

34. Charles H. Roth, "Fundamentals of Logic Design", Thomson Learning, 2003.

35. Ashenden, Peter J. The Designer's Guide to VHDL, 2nd ed. San Francisco: Morgan Kaufmann Publishers, 2002.

36. Bhasker, J. "A Guide to VHDL Syntax", Upper Saddle River, NJ: Prentice-Hall, 1995.

37. Bhasker, J. "VHDL Primer", 3rd ed. Upper Saddle River, NJ: Prentice-Hall, 1999.

38. Brayton, Robert, et al., "Logic Minimization Algorithms for VLSI Synthesis". Secaucus, NJ: Springer, 1984.

39. Givone, Donald D," Digital Principles and Design". New York: McGraw-Hill, 2003.

40. Katz, Randy H. and Gaetano Borriello "Contemporary Logic Design", 2nd ed. Upper Saddle River, NJ: Prentice Hall, 2004.

41. Mano, M. Morris, "Digital Design", 3rd ed. Upper Saddle River, NJ: Prentice Hall, 2001.

42. Mano, M. Morris and Charles R. Kime, "Logic and Computer Design Fundamentals," 4th ed. Old Tappan, NJ: Pearson Prentice Hall, 2008.

43. Marcovitz, Alan B, "Introduction to Logic Design", 2nd ed. New York: McGrawHill, 2002.

44. McCluskey, Edward J, "Logic Design Principles". Upper Saddle River, NJ: Prentice Hall, 1986.

45. Miczo, Alexander, "Digital Logic Testing and Simulation", 2nd ed. New York: John Wiley & Sons, Ltd West Sussex, England, 2003.

46. Patt, Yale N. and Sanjay J. Patel, "Introduction to Computing Systems: From Bits and Gates to C and Beyond", 2nd ed. New York: McGraw-Hill, 2004.

47. Roth, Charles H. Jr. and Lizy Kurian John, "Digital Systems Design Using VHDL", 2nd ed. Toronto, Ontario: Thomson, 2008.

48. Rushton, Andrew, "VHDL for Logic Synthesis", 2nd ed. West Sussex, England: John Wiley & Sons, Ltd, 1998. Wakerly.

49. John F., "Digital Design Principles & Practices", 4th ed. Upper Saddle River, NJ: Prentice Hall, 2006.

50. Weste, Neil and Kaamran Eshraghian. "Principles of CMOS VLSI Design", 2nd ed. Reading, MA: Addison-Wesley, 1993.

Index

1's Complement Representation 346
2's Complement Representation 347
4 449
(also known as Current Mode Logic (CML)) 427
(NASSCOM) 14
(RAM) 2, 11

A

Absorption Laws: 373
Accessibility: 29
Access Mechanism 49
Access Time 47
Accuracy 2, 460, 466, 468
Active Tab 174
A/D Accuracy 466
Adding Visual Interest 204
Address bar 207, 208, 251
Address bus 11
A/D gain and Drift 466
Adjusting Print Settings 217
A/D Speed: 466
Advantages of MOS Digital ICs 434
Advantages of Open Collector Outputs 432
Advantages of Totem Pole Output 431
Align Cell Entries 303
AND 54, 84, 112, 332, 355, 356, 357, 360, 362, 369, 370, 373, 408, 413, 416, 418, 422, 432, 443, 454, 455, 462, 464
And Gate 356
AND Laws 370
Application Layer 116
Application Layer: 116
Application/Other System Software Layer 56
Apply a Chart Layout 323
Applying Formatting to Pictures 243

ARPANET 129, 130
Array 335
Artificial Intelligence xvii, 155, 158, 163, 164
Artistic 248
ASCII CODE 351
Associative Laws: 371
Asynchronous Counter 439
Attrib 77
Auditory Learning 160
Augmented Reality (AR) and Virtual Reality (VR) Integration 101
Autosum 302
Average 313, 329, 429
AVERAGEIF Function 328
Axioms and Laws of Boolean Algebra 369

B

B2C Business-to-Consumer 110
Backbone 124
Background 204, 205, 248
Barcode Readers 27
Basic ECL Circuit 435
Batch Processing System 60
Battery Light Pen 22
BCD Addition 349
BCD Subtraction 350
Bidirectional Shift Register 455
Binary Adder 407, 411
Binary Addition 345
Binary Arithmetic Operation 345
Binary Coded Decimal (BCD) 349
Binary Division 346
Binary Ladder Network 459
Binary Multiplication 345
Binary Number System 338, 339
Binary Subtraction 345
Binary to Decimal Conversion 339
Binary to Hexadecimal Conversion 340

Bins_array 333
BIOS or firmware 67
Blinking cursor/insertion point 179
Bold 198, 203, 204, 252, 315
Boolean Algebra 369
Boot Viruses 119
Boxes 237, 246
Break 78, 125, 165
Broadcasting Model 87
Buffer 78, 449, 450, 451
Buffer Register 449, 450, 451
Business-to-Business 109
Bus Topology 124

C

C2B Consumer-to-Business 110
C2C Consumer-to-Consumer 110
Called monitor 60
Cathode Ray Tube (CRT) monitors 30
Chain/ Belt /Band Printer 36
Change a Cell Entry 297
Change the Size and Position of a Chart 324, 325
Changing Alignment 199
Changing Line Spacing 199
Changing Paragraph Indentation 199
Characteristics of a LAN 128
Characteristics of a WAN 129
Characteristics of MAN 129
Characteristic Table 398, 399
Chip Card Readers 27
CHS (Cylinder Head Sector) or Disk Geometry addressing 46
Click 172, 176, 177, 178, 179, 180, 182, 183, 184, 185, 186, 187, 188, 189, 190, 191, 192, 193, 194, 195, 196, 197, 198, 199, 200, 202, 203, 204, 205, 206, 208, 209, 210, 211, 212, 213, 214, 216, 217, 218, 219, 220, 222, 223, 224, 225, 226, 228, 230, 231, 232, 233, 234, 235, 236, 237, 238, 239, 240, 241, 242, 243, 244, 245, 246, 247, 248, 249, 250, 251, 253, 255, 256, 257, 258, 259, 260, 261, 262, 263, 264, 265, 266, 267, 268, 269, 270, 271, 272, 273, 275, 276, 277, 278, 280, 281, 282, 283, 284, 285, 286, 287, 290, 294, 296, 298, 299, 302, 303, 304, 305, 306, 307, 308, 309, 310, 312, 315, 316, 317, 318, 319, 320, 321, 322, 323, 324, 325, 326, 327
Client Tier 116
Clipboard 197
Close Excel 299
Cloud computing 141, 142
CMOS (Complementary MOS, most common) 434
CMOS Logic Levels 429
CMOS Technology 434
Collapsing a Section 278
Color 198, 204, 236, 248
Columns 203, 233, 234, 235, 236, 283, 305, 306
Combinational Circuit? 389
Command Interpretation 59
Command Line Interface 59
Commutative Laws 370
Comparative Analysis Model 89
Comparison of Totem Pole and Open Collector Output 433
Complementation Laws 369
Components of GIS 147
Computer i, iii, xiii, xv, xvii, 1, 2, 4, 8, 12, 26, 119, 123, 128, 145, 147, 155, 156, 163, 164, 208, 467, 468, 469, 470
Computer History/Evolution/ Computer Generations 4
Computer Network 123, 128
Computer Viruses 119
Config. 78
Conjunctive Canonical Form (CCF) 377
Connection to Computer 26
Consensus Theorem 373
Content pane 207
Contents 270, 272, 273, 274, 275, 276, 277
Contextual Tab 174

Contributes to AI 156
Control Gate: 50
Controlled Buffer Register 449, 450, 451
Conversion Between Canonical Form 377
Conversion from One Number System to Another 339
Copy 72
Copy and Paste 197
Correcting Individual Words 211
Correction and Editing Tools 208
Counter 437, 439, 441, 442, 443, 458
COUNTIF Function 329
Cover 270
Creating 64, 155, 181, 191, 252, 270, 272, 282, 289, 310, 321
Creating a Document 181
Creating Charts 289, 321
Crop Picture Effect 249
CRT monitor 31
Cryptography 58
Current-mode logic (CML) or emitter-coupled logic (ECL). 435
Customization 180
Cut and Paste 197, 304
Cylinder 46, 321

D

D/A and A/D Converter 459
Data_array is an array of or reference to a set of values for which you want to count frequencies 333
Data Communication 123, 136, 137
Data Scanning Devices 23
Data Tier 116
DC Supply Voltage 428
Decade Counter Truth Table 442
Decimal Number System 338, 341
Decimal to Binary Conversion 341
Decimal to Hexadecimal Conversion 342
Decimal to Octal Conversion 342
Delete a Cell Entry 298
Deleting 51, 235
Democratization 86

De Morgan's Theorem 374
Demultiplexer 423
Depth Cameras 29
Designer Light Pen 22
Device 22, 79, 181, 184
D Flip Flop to JK Flip Flop 404
D Flip Flop to SR Flip Flop 403
Different Types of Logic Gates 355
Digital Codes 348
Digital India programme (DIP) 84
Digitizer 17, 25
Diligence 2, 167
Diode logic (DL) 427
Diode-transistor logic (DTL) 427
DIR 69
Direct Access 44
Disadvantage of open-Collector Gates 432
Disadvantages of MOS Digital ICs 434
Disk Operating System: (Internal/External) Commands 67
Disk Pack 45
Distributed Operating Systems 66
Distributive Laws 371
D Latch 394
Don't Care Combinations 386
Dormant Phase 121
Dot Matrix Printers 33
Drum Plotter 39
Duality 375
Dual Slope A/D Converter 464
Dynamic Resizing 177

E

E-Advocacy Model 89
EBCDIC Code 352
Echo 78
ECL: Emitter-Coupled Logic 435
E-Commerce 8, 13, 109, 111, 114, 115, 136, 468
Effect 248, 249
Effective Communication 86
Effects 175, 218, 220, 248, 254
E-Governance 12, 13, 81, 82, 83, 85, 87, 467, 468

E-Governance in India 83
Electromagnetic or Resistive Technology 26
Electronic card-based devices 26
Electronic Mail 131
E-Mail Viruses 120
Emitter Coupled Logic (ECL), 427
Encoder 419, 420
Enter Data 295
Execution Phase 121
External Security Module 58
Eye-Fi 54
Eye-Fi Memory Card 54
Eye-Tracking Systems: 29

F

Facial Recognition Systems 30
Fan Out of Gates 430
FAT viruses 120
Fifth Generation 7, 122
File Explorer 179, 207, 218, 219, 259, 270
File Management Module 58
Files 79, 222
File Tab 178
File Transfer Protocol (FTP) 132
Fill Cells Automatically 315
Fill Numbers 316
Fill Times 316
Find/Replace 209
First Generation 4
Flash Drive: (Pen Drive) 49
Flatbed Plotter 39
Flatbed Scanner 24
Flip-Flop 390, 397, 399, 400, 401
Flip-Flop Conversions 401
Flipped Classroom 96
Floating Gate: 50
Floating height or flying height. 46
Forgetting to Save 190
Format 78, 219, 221, 243, 244, 245, 246, 247, 248, 249, 250, 251, 274, 276, 289, 307, 308, 309, 323
Format Numbers 308

Formatting 198, 199, 236, 243, 289, 299
Formatting a Paragraph 199
Formatting Text 198
Fourth Generation 7, 122
Four Variable K-Map 383
FREQUENCY Function 332
Full Adder 409
Full-Duplex 138
Full Subtractor 413
Functions 56, 58, 118, 289, 310, 311, 336
Functions/Modules of an OS 56

G

G2C2G 90
Geographic 143, 144, 145, 152, 468
Gesture Recognition Systems 29
GIS (Geographic Information System) 143
GIS Maps 150
GIS Model 146, 147
GIS Server 146
Goals of AI 155
Go to Cells Quickly 293
Governance 12, 13, 81, 82, 83, 85, 87, 105, 467, 468
Government 81
Government-2-Business (G2B) 85
Government-2-Citizen (G2C) 85
Government-2-Government (G2G) 86
Government-2-Representative (G2E) 85
Gray Code 353
Gray- To - Binary Conversion 354
Groups and Buttons 174
GUI (Graphical User Interface) 59

H

Half Adder 408
Half-Duplex 138
Half Subtractor 412
Hard Real-Time Operating Systems 67
Hardware Layer 55, 56
Harvard Business Review 164
Head crash 47

Index

Header 202, 203, 204, 206, 272, 274, 276, 277
Headers and Footers 201
Head gap 46
Hexadecimal Number System 339, 344
Hexadecimal to Binary Conversion 344
Hexadecimal to Decimal Conversion 344
Hexadecimal to Octal Conversion 344
Highest Number 313
History of AI 158
History of Information Technology 14
History of Internet 130
Human and Machine Intelligence 161
Hybrid Topology 127
Hyper-Surveillance 86

I

Idempotence Laws: 372
IF Function 331
Image Scanner: 24
Image Screen Projector 40, 41
Inaccessibility 87
Increases Efficiency 86
Increase Throughput 86
Information xvii, 1, 11, 12, 13, 14, 15, 82, 83, 84, 135, 143, 144, 145, 152, 164, 166, 168, 180, 231, 351, 467, 468, 469
Information and Communications Technology (ICT) 12
Information technology 1, 12, 14, 15, 164
Inkjet Printer: 34
Input Devices 17
Input Module 9
Inserting a Picture from a Webpage 251
Inserting Rows and Columns 233
Insertion Point 192
Integrated Injection logic (I2L) 427
Integration with Applications 28
Intelligent Robots 157
Internal commands and external commands 67
Internal Security Module: 58

Internet Services 131
Internetwork or Internet 130
IoT 137, 139, 140, 141
ITAA 12
IT Acts 164

J

JK FLIP-FLOP 396
JK Flip Flop to D Flip Flop 404
JK Flip Flop to SR Flip Flop 402
JK Flip Flop to T Flip Flop 403
Job control language (JCL) 59
Joystick 18, 19, 20

K

Karnaugh Map or K- Map 378
Keyboard Devices 17
Keyboard Keys 192

L

Label 78, 265, 286
Lack of Equality 86
LAN (Local Area Network) 128
Large Scale Integration 6
Laser Printer 37
Latch 390, 392, 394, 396
Latency: 47
LCD monitors 31, 32
LED Light Pen 22
Level Logic 355
Light Pen 21, 22
Linguistic Intelligence 159, 161
Liquid Crystal Display (LCD) 30
List 213, 225, 226, 228, 229, 259, 260, 265, 267, 268, 278, 282
Locate 176, 182, 197
Logic Families 427
Logic Gates 355
Long 270, 306
Loosely coupled: 65

M

Machine Vision Systems 30
Macro Viruses 119
Magnetic Disk 45, 48
Magnetic Stripe Readers 27
Magnetic Tape 44
Magnitude Comparator 415
Mail 120, 131, 259, 260, 261, 262, 263, 264, 265, 266, 267, 268, 269, 270, 279, 280, 281, 282, 285, 286
Mailbox 131, 132
MAN (Metropolitan-Area Network) 129
Manual Loading System 60
Manual loading systems 60, 61
Mapping of POS Expression 380
Mapping of SOP Expression 379
Massive Open Online Course" (MOOCs), SWAYAM, National Programme on Technology Enhanced Learning (NPTEL) 13
Master-Slave JK Flip-Flop 400
Maxterm. 377
M-Commerce 109, 111
Medicine 14
Medium Scale Integration 6
Memory Card (MMC /SD) 51
Memory Management Module 58
Memory Storage Devices 49
Menu 234, 235, 236, 251
Merge 236, 259, 260, 261, 262, 263, 264, 265, 266, 267, 268, 269, 270, 279, 280, 281, 282, 285, 286, 287
Mesh Topology 123
Message Transfer Agent (MTA) 132
Micro SD 53
Micro SDHC 54
Microsoft Excel 289, 290, 291, 292, 299, 301, 306, 308, 310, 311, 315, 318, 321, 336
Microsoft Office? 171
Minimization of SOP and POS Expressions 383, 385
Minterm 376, 379, 382, 383, 384, 418

Moderated Newsgroup 134
Modifying an Existing List 228
Modulus Counter 441
Monitors 30, 33
MOOCs 13, 91, 92, 93, 94, 95, 96, 97, 98, 99, 100, 101, 102, 103, 105, 106, 107
MOSFET 434
Most significant bit (MSB) 459
Motor Learning 160
Move a Chart to a Chart Sheet 325
Move Around a Worksheet 292
Moving Around a Table 231
Moving Around in a Document 191
Moving Text 197
Multilevel Lists 226
Multiplexer 422, 423
Multiprocessing 64, 65
Multiprogramming 58, 59, 62, 63, 65
Multitasking 63
Multithreading 63

N

NAND Flash 50
Nand Gate 357, 360, 434
Natural Language Processing (NLP) 28
Navigating the Document 277
Navigation pane 207, 208, 219, 277
Negative Logic 355
Network Topologies 123
New 57, 62, 74, 166, 172, 179, 191, 255, 256, 257, 264, 282, 326, 329, 334, 467, 469, 470
NMOS (N-channel) 434
Noise Immunity 429
Noise Margin 429
Non-Moderated NewsGroup 134
NOR Flash 50
Nor Gate 358, 362
Not Gate (Inverter) 355
Number System 337, 338, 339, 341, 343, 344

Index

O

Object Detection and Tracking Systems 30
Objectives of OS 56
Observational Learning 160
OCR (Optical Character Recognition) Readers 27
Octal Number System 339, 343
Octal to Binary Conversion 343
Octal to Decimal Conversion 343
Octal to Hexadecimal Conversion 343
Office 365? 171
Open Collector Output 432, 433
Open Educational Resources (OER) and Open Access Initiatives 102
Opening a Practice File 191
Operating System 55, 56, 60, 66, 67, 135
Operating System Layer: 56
Optical Character Recognition (OCR) 25
Optical Disk 48
Organisation for Standards (ISO) 133
OR Gate 356
OR Laws 370
Output Devices 30
Output Module 9

P

Page 200, 201, 203, 204, 205, 206, 248, 270, 293, 317, 318
Page Background 204, 205, 248
Painter 249, 250, 251
Parallel in, Parallel out Shift Register 454
Parallel in, Serial out Shift Register 453
Perceptual Learning: 161
Performance Characteristics of A/D Converters 466
Performance Characteristics of D/A Converters 459
Perform Mathematical Calculations 299
Philosophy of AI 155
Physical Structure: A digitizer typically consists of a flat surface, often with a grid pattern 26
Picture Tools 243, 246, 248, 249
Plotters 30, 39
PMOS (P-channel) 434
Point and Draw Devices 18
Point-of-sale (POS) 13
Positive Logic: 355
POST (Power on Self-Test) 67
Power Dissipation 429
Presentation Layer 116
Pressure Sensitivity 26
Primary Memory 9
Printers 30, 33
Printing a Word Document 216
Print Preview 216, 319
Priority Encoder 420
Process? 57
Process Management Module 57
Process State 57
Product- of - Sums Form 377
Projector 30, 40, 41
Propagation Delay time 430
Protocol 132, 134, 137

Q

Quantization Error 461
Quick Access Toolbar 172, 176, 177, 193, 254, 255, 291

R

Racing Condition 393
Radix or Base 337
Radix Point 337
Raffle Tickets 257
RAM 2, 9, 11, 43, 44
Random Access or Direct Access 44
Range xvii, 30, 47, 91, 92, 103, 105, 106, 107, 146, 165, 217, 310, 319, 320, 328, 329, 332, 333, 334, 335, 427, 459, 461
Ready 57, 62
Real-Time Feedback 28
Real-Time Operating System 66

Redo 194, 255
Redundant Literal Rule (RLR): 372
Registers 449, 456, 457
Reliability: 4, 142
Rem 78
Remove 185, 186, 248, 257, 272
Resistor-Transistor logic (RTL) 427
Resizing Inserted Objects 240
Resizing Rows and Columns 233
Reviewing the Entire Document 211
RFID Readers: 27
Ribbon 172, 173, 176, 177, 234, 235, 291, 311
Ribbon Display Options Button 176
Ribbon Method 234, 235
Right 84, 180, 199, 211, 234, 235, 252, 257, 272, 276, 293, 455
Ring and Johnson Counter 458
Ring Network Topology 123, 126
Rows 233, 234, 235, 305, 306
Running 57, 62

S

Saving a Document under a Different Name 218
Saving the File 182
Scandisk 77
SDHC Memory Card 52
SD (Secure Digital) Cards 52
SDXC Memory Card 53
Secondary Memory 9
Secondary storage memory or Auxiliary memory 43
Second Generation 5
Security Management Module 58
Seek Time: 47
Select a Paragraph 196
Select a Sentence 196
Selecting Parts of a Table 231
Select Table 232, 236, 237, 260, 266, 268
Self-Regulatory Bodies 167
Sequential Access 43

Sequential Circuit 389
Sequential processing machine 11
Serial in, Parallel out Shift Register 452
Serial in, Serial out Shift Register 451
Set Print Options 317
Setting Time 460
Shapes 237, 244, 245, 249
Shell 79
Sigma 335
Signed Number 347
Simplex Mode 137, 138
Small-scale integration 6
Soft Real-Time Operating Systems 67
Spatial Learning 161
Speech Recognition Software 28
Speech Synthesizer 41, 42
Speed: 1, 466
Spelling & Grammar Check 210
SR Flip Flop to D Flip Flop 402
SR Flip Flop to JK Flip Flop 401
SR latch 391, 392, 393, 394, 395, 396
SR latch using NAND gate 393, 394
Stair Step A/D Converter / Ramp A/D Converter 462
Star Network Topology 123, 126
Status Bar 180, 224, 292
Storage 2, 9, 43, 45, 46, 48, 49, 141, 390
Stored-program 10, 11
Style 236, 272, 276, 278, 309, 310, 323, 324, 331
Style of a Chart 323
Styles 236, 241, 243, 244, 245, 247, 273, 276, 323
Stylus or Pen 26
Subtraction Using Complement Method 347
Successive Approximation A/D Converter 465
SUMIF Function 328
Sum - of - Products Form 376
SWAYAM 13, 84, 103, 105
System calls 59

Index   479

T

Table 3, 4, 120, 230, 231, 232, 234, 235, 236, 237, 243, 246, 260, 266, 268, 270, 272, 273, 274, 275, 276, 277, 398, 399, 442
Task Classification of AI 163
Telecommunication 136
Telnet 131, 133
Templates 179, 255
T Flip-Flop 397, 399
TFT Monitors 33
The AND Function 332
The Critical flow Model 88
The Formula Bar 292
The Interactive Service Model 90
The Microsoft Excel Window 290
The Microsoft Office Button 290
The sum range 328
The Threshold Elements 364
The Title Bar 291
The ZTEST Function 335
Third Generation 5, 6
Threading 63
Three Tier Architecture 116
Threshold Logic 363
Tightly coupled 65
Time delays 457
Time Sharing System 65
Time slice or quantum 66
Title Bar 172, 291
Toolbar 172, 176, 177, 193, 254, 255, 291
Totem Pole Output 430, 431
Touch Screen 23
Trackball 20, 21
Training and Adaptation 28
Transfer Rate 47
Transistor-Transistor Logic 430
Transistor- Transistor logic (TTL) 427
Transmission media 136, 137
Transparency and Accountability 86
Transposition Theorem 374
Tree 78
TREND Function 333

Triggering Phase 121
Tristate (Three-State) Logic Output 433
Trojan Viruses 119
TTL Logic Levels 428
TTL vs. CMOS 436
Two Tier Client -Server Architecture 115
Two Variable K- Map 378
Types of E-Governance 85
Types of Intelligence 159
TYPES OF LOGIC FAMILY 427
Types of Operating Systems 59
Types of Scanners 24

U

Ultra large-scale Integration (ULSI 6
Undo 172, 193, 194, 233, 234, 235, 236, 237, 241, 255
Universal Gates 360
Universality of A T-Gate 366
Universal Shift Registers 456
Up/Down Counter 443
USB Device 181, 184
USB flash drive 181
Usenet News 131, 134
User Agent (UA) 132
User Layer 56
Using Reference Operators 310

V

Versatility 2
Very-large-scale Integration (VLSI): 6
Views 180
Virus Generations 121
Vision based devices 17, 29
Voice Reproduction System: 41
Voice Response Systems 41
Von Neumann' architecture 10

W

Wait 37, 182
Waiting 57, 62

WAN (Wide Area Network) 128, 129
Watermark 205
Webcams and RGB Cameras 29
Weighted and Non-Weighted Codes 349
Weighted Resistor Network 459
White Labelling 113
Wholesaling and Warehousing 112
Wired Photosensitive Device 22
Worksheets 291
Workspace 179
World Wide Web (WWW) 134
Worm Viruses 119

Wrapping 241
Wrap Text 297, 298
WWW Browser 135

X

XS-3 Subtraction 351

Z

Zoom Slider 180

www.ingramcontent.com/pod-product-compliance
Lightning Source LLC
LaVergne TN
LVHW020425070526
838199LV00003B/288